We Remain
Race, Racism, and
the Story of the American Indian

KEITH R. BURICH, PH.D.

NFB Publishing
Buffalo, New York

Printed in the United States of America

We Remain: Race, Racism and the Story of the American Indian/
Burich 1st Edition

ISBN: 978-1-953610-40-9

1. Native American History
2. Cultural Anthropology
3. Native American Demographic Studies
4. General Anthropology
5. Sociology- Racism- Native Americans
6. Historical Study
7. History & Philosophy of Science
8. Discrimination & Racism
9. Historical Trauma

NFB
NFB Publishing/Amelia Press
119 Dorchester Road
Buffalo, New York 14213

Table of Contents

INTRODUCTION

I AM A HISTORY professor, now retired from Canisius College in Buffalo, New York, where I specialized in Native American history. Yet, this is not a typical history textbook recounting in chronological detail the battles, broken treaties, and failed government policies of the past. To the contrary, it is an attempt to reinterpret the historical record by examining the role of race and racism in the conquest, degradation, oppression, and near extermination of the Native population of North America from 1500 to the present.

Racism and the violence it engenders course through American history. They're in the nation's DNA. There is perhaps no better example of that than the racially motivated mistreatment of Indians over the past 500 years, which all too often gets swept under the historical rug. Suffering and heartache abound in the long and tragic story of genocidal assaults on the lands, the lives, the freedoms, and the well-being of America's Indians. I share some of them in the pages that follow.

But this is also a story of the unyielding determination of Native Americans to maintain their identities and sovereignty as Indians. It's a story that can't be learned in textbooks, libraries, or archives. Rather, it's the story of what I experienced, what I learned, and what I felt during more than 25 years of visiting reservations across America and Canada. They inspired me to write this book.

During those years, I saw and heard things that disturbed, depressed, and angered me--even brought me to tears. At the same time, I met people who are addicted to laughter and devoted to their families, people who love their children, and people who simply find joy in being Indian. Even more remarkable, they are the most welcoming, generous, and resilient people

I have ever met, despite the trauma White people have inflicted on them. This is the story of survivors of 500 years of racial hatred and the genocidal efforts to eradicate and erase them and their cultures from America and American history—the story of those who struggle from day to day to stay alive, and above all else, to remain Indians.

My travels to reservations in New York, Canada, and across the American West, mostly involved taking college students on cultural immersion trips each summer. Over that time, I visited reservations spanning from the Iroquois in New York and Ontario in the East to the Hopi in the West. I've been on reservations from A to Z, from Acoma to Zuni. I visited the Navajo, the largest; and the Tuscarora and Rocky Boy, a couple of the smallest. I spent time on Pine Ridge and Standing Rock, two of the most famous; and Fort Hall, Fort Peck, and Fort Belknap, some of the most obscure. And in between, I've been to Crow and Northern Cheyenne, Southern and Mountain Ute, Rosebud and Fort Berthold, Santee and Cheyenne River.

My journeys have taken me to sacred and historically significant sites such as Canyon de Chelly, Mesa Verde, and Chaco Canyon in the Southwest; to the Medicine Wheel and Devil's Tower in Wyoming; to Bear Butte and Harney Peak in the Black Hills of South Dakota; and to the Deer Medicine Rocks in Montana, where Sitting Bull had his prophetic vision of the momentous battle that took place along the banks of the Little Bighorn River.

I have been to the ancient mound-building sites in the Ohio and Mississippi valleys, including the Great Serpent Mound in Ohio and Cahokia in Illinois, and I participated in archaeological digs. I even ventured to Belize and Mexico to examine the wondrous ruins of the great Maya civilization of 1,000 years ago. I have also visited the scenes of massacres at Wounded Knee on Pine Ridge, Sand Creek in Colorado, Bear Paws and Marias River in Montana, and Whitestone Hill in North Dakota.

Along the way, my journeys through Indian Country afforded me opportunities few non-Indians, and even many Indians, have experienced. I've participated in sweat lodge and healing ceremonies, and attended Sun Dances, and Navajo and Hopi ceremonies. I have taken a Lakota man up

Bear Butte in the Black Hills for a vision quest, attended the commemoration of the Indian Monument at Little Bighorn Battlefield, and walked with the Iroquois to celebrate the signing of the Canandaigua Treaty between the Iroquois Confederacy and the United States. I have made *piki* bread with the Hopi and horsehair pottery with the Navajo. I've danced at powwows and made a fool of myself doing the Bear Dance on the Southern Ute Reservation. I've put up and slept in many a teepee, helped build sweat lodges and ready them for sweats, and attended giveaways, naming ceremonies, funerals, and memorials. I have worked with members of the Seneca Nation to gather sap from maple trees and turn it into syrup. I've attended Iroquois lacrosse games, snow-snake competitions, and a particularly nasty game on the Tuscarora Reservation called fireball, in which the participants kick, throw, and catch a ball that is, as the name implies, on fire.

I also saw history in the making. I was at Standing Rock on a freezing cold night in November 2016 when all hell broke loose, and the police used water cannons to subdue the Dakota Access Pipeline protestors. Witnessing the disproportionate response by the police to a ragtag bunch of protestors who bore a striking resemblance to hippies of the 1960s had an influence on me that runs through this book.

I tried to capture history in a documentary that my students and I produced about life on the Crow Reservation. I even was portrayed in *Re-Creation Story*, an autobiographical play written by the Onondaga author and artist Eric Gansworth, and attended its augmented staged reading at The Public Theater in New York City. But probably the one thing that surprises people most is that I have participated in buffalo hunts in the Bighorn Mountains on the Crow Reservation, where I helped skin and gut buffalo carcasses.

Although I've seen extreme poverty and desperation on the reservations I've visited, I've had humorous experiences as well. I served as a witness at a bow-and-arrow—aka shotgun—wedding on Rosebud and tried my hand at counseling a lovesick Crow woman. Then there was the sweat lodge ceremony in January on Crow when the temperature was below zero.

I'm not revealing any secret when I say the Crow do their sweats naked. Accordingly, we stripped, crawled into the lodge, and sat shivering as we waited for the red-hot rocks to warm us up. As they were brought in, I remember relaxing in the warmth and dozing off while listening to a coyote yipping in the distance. I was thinking this must have been what it was like 200 years ago, when all of sudden, someone's cellphone went off and ruined my reverie.

And there was the time I camped in Chaco Canyon, hoping to have the spiritual experience others told me about, only to be surrounded by people waiting for UFOs to appear. Later, I decided to give my students the experience of herding sheep at Many Farms on the Navajo Reservation, only to have the sheep immediately scatter across the countryside. Chasing them in the 100-degree heat across fields infested with rattlesnakes is something I wish I could forget.

There were some experiences that were not quite so humorous, like the time I climbed down more than 600 feet of a sandstone cliff into Canyon de Chelly on the Navajo Reservation, on what is appropriately called the Bare Trail for its lack of vegetation and the sheerness of its walls. On the way out of the canyon, when we had nearly reached the top, my feet went out from under me. I went over the cliff and was saved by a lowly sagebrush bush to which I desperately clung while my daughter screamed for help and my Navajo friends came to my rescue.

I'll never forget their faces peering down at me as I dangled there trying not to look at the rocks 600 feet below me. They pulled me out and saved my life. Later, when we could laugh about it, they teased me. I felt like just another clumsy White guy. Today we remain friends, even though separated by 2,000 miles.

It's friendships like that, forged by my experiences in Indian Country, that made this book possible. I have learned so much from them, not only about Indians, but about America, Americans, and myself. For example, I now know a firm handshake and looking a person straight in the eye are considered acts of aggression or intimidation. The more I think about it, I agree they are. I have seen elderly Navajo men standing side by side, gazing straight ahead to avoid looking into each other's eyes as they talked. I learned that White people talk too much and too loudly, and don't listen enough, a trait Indians have complained about for centuries. Incidentally, if it's true that Indian women pierced the ears of the dead soldiers after the Battle at Little Bighorn, perhaps it was so the men would be able to listen when they passed on to the spirit world.

I learned not to talk too loudly to them like they're deaf, or too slowly like they're mentally challenged, to never say goodbye, and never to point. If you ask Indians for directions, they will pucker their lips and motion with their heads rather than point with their fingers. Never ask Indians for directions.

I learned that many Indigenous people do not like being called Native Americans since many do not consider themselves Americans, even though they are citizens and have the highest percentage of any ethnic group serving in the U.S. military. Instead, they prefer to be identified by their tribal and clan names, or simply as Indians. That's why, when people ask about buying products that are labeled "Authentic Native American," I tell them they probably aren't. There is no such thing as a monolithic Native culture, religion, or history.

In that same vein, I have to bite my tongue when someone asks me about Native American religion or culture. Sadly, this way of thinking homogenizes Indigenous people and ignores the wonderful diversity among them, not just in the United States but across North and South America. It also makes it easier to stereotype them—you've seen one, you've seen them all. There are more than 500 recognized tribes in the United States and more than 200 unrecognized ones, and just about as many languages and cultures.

There are seemingly as many jealousies, rivalries, and conflicts between tribes, many of which date back hundreds of years. Today the battles are not fought with guns or arrows, but with jokes, like the Crow story that the fastest animal on the neighboring Northern Cheyenne Reservation is a dog. (The Cheyenne eat dogs at their ceremonies.) And the shot a Crow tribal police officer took at the Lakota people. When I mentioned Pine

Ridge to him, he remarked rather pointedly that he wouldn't go there, despite the fact he carries a gun. In fact, most tribes describe themselves in their own languages as the original or real people, *Ogwe' oweh* in Seneca, to distinguish themselves from others.

I learned not to try to be an Indian or what my students cleverly dubbed "Whindian." Native people resent it, and you can become the butt of jokes, especially when you mangle their languages. Neither do Indians want to be treated, as one Navajo woman selling jewelry on the bottom of Canyon de Chelly told me, "like specimen in zoos," or as I like to put it, artifacts to be studied like an extinct species. I have been reminded any number of times that they are still here and very much alive.

I learned about unconditional friendship; about giving without expecting anything in return. It's a wonderful trait, but government authorities and missionaries always complained about it, since it prevented the accumulation (and subsequent) inheritance of wealth.

Probably the most valuable advice about Indians that I ever received came from a Lakota professor at the Oglala Community College on Pine Ridge, whom I asked for help. The first question he posed was if I wanted my students to do community service on the reservation. When I said no, that I was looking for a cultural-immersion experience for them, he replied, "Good. You people have helped us enough."

At first, I was taken aback, but then I realized it made perfectly good sense. Indians learned long ago not to trust White people bearing gifts. For centuries, missionaries and government agents offered the benefits of civilization to "the poor savages," but they always came with strings attached. At the same time, the Indians knew their rejection of White beneficence would be met with a disproportionate and often lethal response. It was a no-win situation.

The distrust and fear of the "White man's" motives and intentions are not without reason. I have seen the scars and festering wounds left by 500 years of suppression and oppression. I have seen the unrelenting and grinding poverty produced by a malignant contempt and neglect made worse by wrongheaded, destructive government policies and actions that have deprived Native people of adequate housing, health care, education, and food.

I have seen large extended families living together in grandma's trailer without running water, electricity, and heat, and with cardboard-covered windows to shut out the cold. I have seen children going to school simply to get warm and have something to eat. I have seen families shattered and reservations paralyzed by substance use disorders. I have seen lives shortened by epidemic levels of disease, violence, accidents, and self-destructive behaviors. I have seen too many young people end up pregnant or in jail, or worse. Desperate and despairing, powerless and hopeless, they give up and take their own lives, convinced that being Indian and being a failure are one and the same.

I've listened to the stories of boarding school survivors, and have shed tears over what happened to them and how those horrible ordeals continue to hurt them. Finally, my travels around Indian Country brought me face to face with an ugly side of American history in the form of a pernicious and persistent racism.

I always knew it was there. As a teenager, I saw on television the scenes of brutality against civil rights marchers and freedom riders, and I went to graduate school and subsequently taught in the South when segregation was unraveling. I was aware of the darker side of America and Americans.

In fact, when I was a child in the 1950s, my parents took my brother and me on the original *National Lampoon's Vacation* with many of the same mishaps, only they weren't quite so humorous. On our way across South Dakota, we stopped in Kadoka just outside Badlands National Park. Air conditioning wasn't widespread back then, and it was terribly hot, so we went into a saloon to cool off and get something to drink. Having grown up watching television Westerns, I was excited. It was an honest-to-goodness cowboy saloon with sawdust on the floor and spittoons, and real cowboys in cowboy hats and boots. However, my enthusiasm was tempered by a sign posted outside the door that read "No Indians Allowed." Later, we stopped at a diner, where we asked the waiter about the sign. He told us people around there, himself excluded, of course, hated Indians.

At the time I saw that sign, the U.S. Supreme Court had ruled in *Brown v. Board of Education,* Rosa Parks had ridden her bus, and schools had been integrated in Little Rock. Yet, 60 years later, Indians still have not been included in the national debate over racism. The killing of unarmed Black men by police has been forced into the national consciousness by the media and the Black Lives Matter movement, but the unequal treatment of Indians by police and the justice system, and the racism and injustices Indians face on a daily basis have all but been ignored. As I was writing this book, America was rocked by the murder of George Floyd in Minneapolis. Tens of thousands—perhaps hundreds of thousands—of people poured into the streets in cities across America to protest police brutality against African Americans.

I watched hours of television coverage and was buoyed by the numbers and diversity of the protesters. Politicians, business and religious leaders, and media outlets tripped over themselves to express outrage, demand justice and police reform, and declare that changes have to and will be made. It was as if Americans had a national epiphany and suddenly realized that systemic racism exists and that the constant unrelenting stress of discrimination, poverty, and violence has taken a dreadful toll on the mental and physical health of African Americans. It was a collective *mea culpa,* a transformational moment, a reaffirmation of America's moral exceptionalism, except for America's Indians.

"Systemic racism" has become part of the nation's lexicon. It suggests that U.S. institutions are steeped in racism, which seems to absolve individuals of their culpability. I believe instead racism is in America's blood, and it courses through the nation's history from the first European footsteps on the continent. Everybody shares in it.

I am certainly not the first to say this. David E. Stannard, in his aptly titled book *American Holocaust,* declared there can be "little doubt that the colonists were driven by a racist zeal to eliminate the Indians." As Stannard elaborates, the "dominant sixteenth- and seventeenth-century ecclesiastical, literary, and popular opinion in Spain and Britain and Europe's American colonies regarding the native people of North and South America was that they were a racially degraded and inferior lot—borderline humans as far as most whites were concerned."[1] It probably dates back even earlier, as Europeans discovered the "other" during the Age of Exploration.

At any rate, they brought it with them to America, and the result, as the title of Stannard's book implies, was genocide that went beyond the immediate and wholesale slaughtering of Native men, women, and children. According to Raphael Lemkin, who coined the word, genocide "does not necessarily mean the immediate destruction of a people."[2] It need only include actions that lead to the "disintegration of the political and social institutions, of culture, language, national feelings, religion, and the economic existence of national groups, and the destruction of the personal security, liberty, health, dignity, and even the lives of the individuals of such groups." That's exactly what happened to the Indigenous people of the Americas. Behind it was the same brand of racism that brought hundreds of thousands of African slaves to the United States. For Indians, it was no less destructive. Indeed, it was lethal.

As I watched clips of George Floyd gasping for breath and calling out for his mother, I thought of Robert Many Horses in neighboring South Dakota. He died of suffocation after being stuffed into a garbage can by a group of White boys. No protests, no speeches, no promises. His murderers went free.

After Barack Obama was elected president, there was a lot of talk about a post-racial America and even suggestions that reparations were in order; Indians weren't mentioned. They are just as likely, or even more likely, to be killed by police or to die in police custody as are Black people and at a far greater rate than the general population. They are more likely to be incarcerated and receive harsher punishments. Indian women tend more often to be victims of violence and sexual assault, the majority by non-Indians. In fact, thousands of Indian women have disappeared, and have probably been murdered or forced into prostitution.

None of this makes the nightly news. Neither do the forced steriliza-

[1] David E. Stannard, *American Holocaust* (New York: Oxford University Press, 1992), 278.

[2] Raphael Lemkin, *Axis Rule in Occupied Europe* (Washington, DC: Carnegie Endowment for International Peace, 1943), 79.

tion of Native women, the removal of Indian children from their families through forced adoption and foster care, and the disproportionate suspension of Indian children from schools. The mistreatment of Indians in America is a sordid story that dates back 500 years to when Columbus stumbled across an island in the Caribbean. It goes far beyond the genocidal wars and atrocities, and the failed government policies like concentrating Indians on reservations, and interring them in dreadful boarding schools, not to mention the incompetence and heartlessness of government officials.

Behind it all is a racism just as violent and virulent as that directed at African Americans. I have heard it, seen it, felt it, and even experienced it. It's not just responsible for the poverty, unemployment, hunger, shattered families, and indignities and injustices that are part and parcel of discrimination. Racism seeps into its victims' pores. It conditions their behavior and is responsible for their self-loathing and self-destructive conduct, plus the epidemic of suicide that is so prevalent among Native people.

Life is hard and exhausting for Indians on and off reservations. Yet, as I traveled around Indian Country, I've seen signs of hope and revitalization. There is a young medicine man on Rosebud who invited me to his Sun Dance. He uses his spiritual powers to preserve and revitalize Lakota culture, and to heal his fellow Lakota people, both spiritually and physically. I've seen it in the growing number of Sun Dances on Pine Ridge and Rosebud, which were outlawed before 1978, and the increasing participation of young people. I've seen it at countless powwows in the tiny tots, the youngest dancers who enter the dance circle at the Grand Entry, dressed in their regalia and trying hard to emulate their parents and grandparents. I've seen it in the return of educated Indians like Wizipan Little Elk, who came back to Rosebud to lead the Rosebud Economic Development Corporation, and the young Navajo man who returned to the reservation to care for his family land at the bottom of Canyon de Chelly. And I have seen it at the home of Sarah and Wayne Dallas in Moenkopi, Arizona. They left the Hopi Reservation, attended college, and pursued careers off the reservation, only to come back to a life without running water and electricity to regain the spiritual life they sorely missed. I have seen it in tribes fighting to regain their sovereignty and their control over their economic and political destinies. And most of all, I have seen it in Native people's remarkable resilience, probably built into their DNA after hundreds of years of trauma, that has enabled them to survive centuries of assaults on their lands, their persons, their freedoms, and their identities as Indians.

This is the story of those survivors. It is not the story of the traditional heroes of Indian resistance: Tecumseh, Crazy Horse, Sitting Bull, and Geronimo. They are what Thomas King refers to as "dead Indians" and are the ones most Americans, and even Europeans, imagine. Nor is it about the modern warriors of Alcatraz, Mount Rushmore, Wounded Knee, and Standing Rock who make headlines. Instead, it's the story of the Indians who continue to struggle day to day and hand to mouth to stay alive and to stay Indian.

It is the story of Dewey Bull Tail and his sister Carol from the Crow Reservation in Montana, who sell dried deer, elk, and buffalo meat to support a large extended family. It is the story of Martha Moccasin on Rosebud. Suffering from heart disease and diabetes, she couldn't afford propane to fend off the cold Dakota winters. It's the story of Louisa Tsosie on Navajo, who never went to school, speaks no English, and has spent more than 70 years sitting cross-legged before her loom, weaving rugs that she has often been forced to sell to traders for a proverbial song. It's the story of Elliott Tallchief, Ron Kraft, and Katie Wheeler, who grew up in boarding schools. Their stories make up the fabric of Native life across America. And yet, they are stories that are virtually untold.

In recent years, there has been a deluge of books about Indians and things Indian, with most focusing on wars and atrocities, or failed government policies such as removal and especially boarding schools. In fact, I authored a book on the Thomas Indian School, a boarding school on the Cattaraugus Seneca Reservation in New York.[3] In researching that book, I interviewed survivors whose life stories gave me the idea for the theme of

---

[3] Keith R. Burich, *The Thomas Indian School and the "Irredeemable" Indian Children of New York* (Syracuse, NY: Syracuse University Press, 2016).

this book. While I encountered so many sad stories, and shed more than a few tears over them, I was impressed by the resilience of those who managed to endure, albeit not without psychological, emotional, and behavioral scars.

This book is about those survivors, the ones who persist despite the burden of racism, the baggage of their past, the hardships of life as an Indian in America. It is, in short, a testament to those Indians who continue to struggle from day to day just to stay alive, and most of all, to stay Indian. For better or worse, it is the story of America and Americans.

After all, Native American history is American history. As the Comanche Paul Chaat Smith observed, "There is nothing more American about America than American Indians."

A Little Help from My Friends

Like most American children growing up in the 1950s and 1960s, what I knew about Indians came from watching Westerns on television. The scenes of Indians whooping, yipping, and attacking wagon trains and homesteaders until the cavalry came to the rescue were burned into my impressionable mind, leaving me with an image of Native people as irredeemably savage.

I remember going on a family fishing trip to Lake Nippissing in Ontario, Canada. Across the road from our cabins was a settlement of Native people. I was curious, but I was warned by the owner of the fishing camp not to go there because it was dangerous. So, of course, I went.

Imagining myself sneaking into a camp of hostile Indians, just like in the movies, I crept up to one of the houses to peek inside. The window had no glass or screen, something I would later find quite common in reservation housing. I had to stand on something, I can't remember what, to peer through the window. When I did, there staring back at me was a young Indigenous boy or girl who was probably just as surprised as I was. I beat a hasty retreat because I was trespassing on enemy territory.

When I got home, I told my friends about my adventure, with perhaps a little embellishment of the dangers I narrowly escaped and the usual jokes about nearly getting scalped. Little did I know it was the beginning of a long journey that would require me to unlearn everything I knew about Indians. One that would culminate with this book.

I had forgotten about the incident until this writing, and just thinking about it makes me chuckle at how little I knew about Native people beyond games of cowboys and Indians, and Thanksgiving pageants in elementary school. Sadly, I am not alone. Most Americans' knowledge of Native people is woefully inadequate, and what little they have learned is generally wrong. The problem is that teachers are unable to offer more than projects making dream catchers or replicas of villages out of papier-mache, Popsicle sticks and pipe cleaners. College professors are in the same boat.

As I was returning to the classroom after a stint in administration, I began looking for a gimmick to pique the interest of 18-year-olds who thought they knew everything there was to know—that they wanted to know—about American history. I tried immigration history, since Buffalo is a heavily ethnic town, and African American history, since it also has a substantial Black community, but it wasn't until I introduced more about American Indians into my classes that I finally struck a chord. After more than 20 years of teaching in secondary schools and colleges, I realized just how little I knew and how little I had included about Indians in my history courses.

That was the early 1990s, and as luck would have it, controversies were erupting over the building of Indian casinos in New York and the collection of state taxes on reservations. The conflicts even became violent, with the Seneca people on the Cattaraugus Reservation west of Buffalo closing the New York State Thruway, which runs through their territory, with piles of burning tires. The controversies, violence, threats of violence, and endless lawsuits opened old wounds and brought out long-standing prejudices, along with the usual racial stereotypes and epithets, to which a new one was added: "tire burners." Needless to say, they didn't need any new ones.

Many people, including some of my students and close friends, continue to mouth the stereotype of the drunken, lazy Indian who doesn't pay taxes, choosing instead to live off welfare and food stamps, or the proceeds from casinos, and the sale of tax-free cigarettes and gasoline. Even in Buffalo, which is surrounded by four reservations and three Indian casinos, most of my friends have never met a "real, live" Indian. Some have confided in me they are afraid to go onto the reservations, much like people are afraid to go into inner-city neighborhoods, a comparison I found most appropriate and useful in writing this book. I've even been told pizza shops won't deliver to local reservations.

In light of the controversies, it occurred to me that including material on Native people was about more than simply filling a glaring hole in my American history classes; it was necessary to counteract the misconceptions about Indians that most Americans harbor and the bigotry those misconceptions engenders. However, I felt uncomfortable speaking for Indians, and the textbooks available at the time didn't help. They were out of date, and most were written by non-Indians. The only way to combat those misconceptions that had hardened into stereotypes was to let Indians speak for themselves.

I decided to reach out to the Native community in the hope of finding Indians who would be willing to tell their stories to my classes in their own ways and in their own words. I was warned the reservations were closed communities and even hostile to White people. I found the opposite to be true. Everywhere I went, Native people were willing to take me into their homes and into their lives. More importantly, they were open to sharing their stories with me, and more, they were eager and even grateful for the opportunity to talk about their culture and heritage.

I had to do a lot of legwork, but it was worth it. Helping me in my search was Jackie Labonte, a Mohawk from the Six Nations Reserve in Ontario. She became my angel, inviting me to ceremonies and events. She also introduced me to members of the Iroquois and Ojibwe tribes (or more properly *Haudenausaunee* and *Annishnabee*) from New York and Canada, who were happy for the opportunity to share their stories and knowledge with my students. Before long, I opened my classes to the public, attracting large audiences that sometimes numbered in the hundreds and included local Native people who came because they were never taught about their culture, language, or heritage in school. In some cases, they were left in the dark because their parents did not want them to be Indian.

There were far too many speakers to list here, but I'll mention a few nevertheless. One of my favorites was Clayton Logan, a Seneca man who spent 24 years in the Navy, mostly in Spain. As you can imagine, there aren't many people fluent in Seneca in the Navy or in Spain, so he practiced his language by finding quiet spots in which he could talk to himself. He opened the first class of the semester with the *Ganö:nyök* or "thanksgiving address," the words that come before all else and are recited to open all Iroquois gatherings. He performed it in the same call-and-response rhythm you might hear in African American churches.

There also was Basil Johnston, an Ojibway man from Canada who was taken from his family as a child and handed over to Jesuits at a residential school. You could hear a pin drop when he recounted being sexually abused upon arriving at the boarding school. Incidentally, Basil was one of the leaders of the Truth and Reconciliation movement that forced the Canadian government to apologize and pay reparations to the survivors of the residential school system in Canada.

Another special guest was Al Parker, a descendent of Eli Parker, General Grant's aide who wrote the terms of Robert E. Lee's surrender at Appomattox. And there was Chief Ken Patterson of the Tuscarora Nation; a medicine man, Roy Stone from Rosebud; and the storytellers Dovie Thomason and Perry Ground, Kiowa-Apache and Onondaga, respectively.

The ultimate goal of the project was education in the best sense of the word: to overcome the stereotypes, and deep-seated and often unconscious prejudices that Americans have harbored from the very first contact between Europeans and the Indigenous people of the Americas. Not only did the speakers inform and entertain, they gave my students and the others in the audience the chance to see, hear, and talk to real, live Indians who were not ignorant, drunken, wild savages. Indeed, that was the goal.

The surprising interest in my courses and programs inspired me to take groups to reservations, and historical and cultural sites out West for authentic Native experiences. I had considered it for some time, probably because I had a fascination with the West and the frontier from my childhood days, but I had no idea where to start.

Someone at a conference where I presented a paper recommended the Navajo Reservation or Diné College at Tsaile, Arizona, a beautiful and welcoming place. However, the deal I thought I had negotiated fell through. I would eventually return there, but in the meantime, I visited Wind River in Wyoming, Fort Hall in Idaho, and Crow in Montana before I was told about the professor at the Oglala Community College on Pine Ridge, whom I mentioned earlier. I don't remember his name, but he suggested I contact Albert White Hat or Duane Hollow Horn Bear on Rosebud Reservation. I tried, but I couldn't reach them before I set out for a conference on Plains Indians at the Buffalo Bill Cody Museum in Cody, Wyoming.

As luck would have it, the program included a presentation on teepees by Don Moccasin, a Sicangu Lakota man from Rosebud, and his wife, Maggie. I introduced myself to Don and told him I was trying to get in touch with two fellows from Rosebud named Albert White Hat and Duane Hollow Horn Bear. He smiled, extended his hand, and said, "Albert's my uncle, and Duane is my cousin." I shouldn't have been surprised; I soon learned everybody is somehow related to everybody else on reservations. When I told Don I wanted to bring students out for a cultural immersion experience, he didn't hesitate.

The next thing I knew, I was in Mission, South Dakota, in Don's pickup truck, riding across the prairie in a snowstorm as he took me for a tour of the reservation, of which he was clearly very proud. It was the beginning of a friendship that lasted until his untimely death at 61 from a congenital heart condition. Through Don, I learned to appreciate the spiritual and physical beauty of lands most Americans would find bleak, destitute, and foreboding. I also began to unlearn what I knew about Indians and reservation life. It was the first leg of a journey that has taken me to places most people never see. I also met people I would otherwise never have encountered, and had experiences I could never have imagined.

I accepted Don's invitation to bring students to Rosebud. We would stay on his property, a beautiful piece of rolling prairie marked by one of the buttes in the shape of old-fashioned haystacks that dot the area. I have to admit, I was a bit nervous about bringing students out there after Maggie told me, when I asked for directions to their house, that all the street signs had been shot out. Nevertheless, I persisted, and I'm so grateful I did. It was the beginning of a wonderful friendship.

Don taught my students and me how to put up teepees and build a sweat lodge. He included us in powwows, ceremonies, celebrations, and giveaways. He took us to sacred places such as Wounded Knee on Pine Ridge, and Bear Butte and Harney Peak in the Black Hills. He and I took a group of students and Lakota people from Rosebud to the commemoration of the Indian monument at the Little Bighorn Battlefield. It was there I had the honor of escorting Edna Little Elk, Don's grandmother, to view the monument to the warriors who fought and died at the famous battle.

Her name for me was "that bald White guy with glasses," which didn't distinguish me from most other middle-aged White guys, but I gladly answered to it. I admired her for any number of reasons. First and foremost, I respected her for having occupied Mount Rushmore in 1970 with a group of Lakota people to protest the government's taking of the Black Hills in violation of the 1851 and 1868 Fort Laramie treaties. The thought of that diminutive woman scaling the monument makes me chuckle to myself, the same way I laugh at the thought of another member of that group, Lame Deer, supposedly peeing from George Washington's nose.

Don came to Buffalo to speak at my college, bringing with him Medicine Man Roy Stone and five helpers to conduct a *Yuwipi* or "healing ceremony." We held it in the basement of the college chapel, for which I received a lot of criticism. He was a guest in our home as well. In fact, I'll never forget Don's laughable attempt to navigate my canoe on the Erie Canal. He was a horse Indian, and it showed. Over the years, Don taught me just how much he loved horses; almost as much as he loved his family, his tribe, and his reservation.

His Indian name was *Akicita Isnala Najin* or "Warrior Who Stands Alone." But he was never alone. He went around the world, taking his stories about Native life and spirituality with him. As much as he traveled, he always returned to Rosebud. Unfortunately, as mentioned earlier, Don suffered from a congenital heart problem that shortened his life. Before he died, I was present at a ceremony honoring Don's dad, where I had the special job of carrying a picture of his father around the gathering. As I made my way through the room with the picture, Don began to sing a mournful song in Lakota. I didn't understand a word of it; I didn't have to. I knew he was singing his death song. It was palpable; I could feel it in my heart.

I visited him again, and as I was leaving Rosebud, I telephoned my wife to tell her it was probably the last time I would see Don alive. I was right. Within a year he was gone. When he died, I was on the Crow Reservation, high in the Bighorn Mountains at a place called Windy Point, far from cellphone coverage. Suddenly and quite unexpectedly, my phone rang. It was Maggie, telling me the sad news. It was as if Don were reaching out to me from the spirit world. I will never forget it or his death song. It still haunts me.

I miss Don. I miss his beaming smile, his hearty laugh, and his warm, welcoming, and generous spirit. Most of all, I miss his willingness—indeed, eagerness—to share his time, knowledge, and profound spirituality with me and my students. In fact, with anyone who was willing to listen and learn. They were qualities that gave rise to his habitual tardiness, but it was easy to forgive him for what many might consider a character flaw. The truth was, Don's *tiyospaye* or "extended family" was more important than being on time. I can't tell you how often I was left waiting because "Something came up." I always knew the delay was due to family or friends needing help.

I learned from Don to appreciate the beauty of the land and of the people who have all but been forgotten by most Americans. As a result, I found an answer to the question that began nagging at me the first time I visited Rosebud and came face to face with the poverty endemic to so many reservations. I had seen some of it on reservations in New York and Canada, but what I witnessed on Rosebud and on side trips to Pine Ridge eclipsed everything I knew and most of what I could imagine.

Statistics can't begin to measure its scope or depth. Particularly jarring is the contrast between the beauty of the land and the residue of neglect that litters the reservation. At first, I couldn't put my finger on it, or maybe I was just unwilling to face it, but one of my students crystallized it when he asked, "Why don't they just leave?" I can't tell you how many times I have been asked that question. It's not an unreasonable one, considering the poverty and the attendant social problems on one of the poorest, most isolated places in America.

As I pondered this question and tried to come up with an adequate answer, I realized that in one form or another, it's a curiosity that has defined the relationship between Indians and Europeans dating back to first contact. From the beginning, Europeans encouraged, bribed, tricked, and forced Indians to give up their wigwams, teepees, and hogans, take up the so-called White man's plow, send their children to school, adopt Christianity, sell their lands, and move to cities. In other words, assimilate.

Europeans celebrated whenever Indians took the bait, and reacted angrily and forcibly when they resisted. Indeed, Indians' disinterest in becoming like White people justified genocidal policies, including removal from their traditional lands and ways of life. Adding to that were plans and practices that resulted in concentrating them on reservations without adequate housing, food, water, and medical care; and remanding their children to boarding schools or to foster care and adoption by non-Indian families, not to mention conducting warfare that targeted women and children. In the end, it was Don who provided me with the answer to the question regarding why they stay. They just want to be Indians, and there's nothing wrong with that. In fact, they may have a lot to teach non-Indians. His life exemplified that.

Still, the old nostrums die hard. In her book *A New Trail of Tears,* Naomi Schaefer Riley finds young Indians on reservations have embraced American popular culture, or as she puts it, "chosen civilization," as if they weren't civilized before. "The music coming from their cars, the videos on their phones, the clothing they wear—these are largely the same as in any area of the country."[4]

According to Riley, Indians really want to be Americans, but they are held back by failed government policies and bureaucratic incompetence. Everywhere she went on the reservations she visited, she found poor houses, poor schools, poor food, and not surprisingly, poor people and all the problems attendant to poverty. I can't quibble with her complaints about the incompetence and wrongheadedness of government policies and practices, but her solutions are overly simple, if not simplistic. Give up the il-

[4] Naomi Schaefer Riley, *A New Trail of Tears* (New York: Encounter Books, 2016), 176.

lusion of sovereignty, disband tribal governments, abandon collectivism, stop blaming the past, liquidate the land, and let private property work its "almost magical force."[5] Sound familiar? They're the same old remedies government agents, missionaries, and reformers have offered for centuries, and they're just as hard for Indians to swallow today as in the past.

I could add a few things to Riley's list of the modern conveniences and gadgets Indians have appropriated from White people. They like oversized pickup trucks and big-screen televisions on which they watch and root for the Dallas Cowboys, America's team. They use Facebook and Twitter, shop at Walmart, eat at McDonald's, and like to gamble. First-time visitors to reservations find it disconcerting to see Indians walking around in cowboy hats and boots, wearing Wrangler jeans rather than animal skins, and eating pizza instead of buffalo meat. In fact, I found it more than a little amusing when I first saw traditional six-sided hogans on the Navajo Reservation sprouting satellite dishes.

However, none of these things transforms Indians into White Americans or suggests they are eager to assimilate as Riley maintains. Thanks to Don, as I spent more time on Rosebud and other reservations, I came to understand, admire, and respect my Indian friends for their remarkable resilience and fierce resistance to 500 years of efforts to divest them of their "Indianness" and erase them from American history, and America's consciousness and conscience. They stay on their reservations because they want to, and those who leave often return—or at least wish they could.

That's a bit disconcerting to the rest of America, as Indians remain what Thomas King labeled an "inconvenient" and embarrassing reminder of the country's repressive treatment of its Indigenous people. To add insult to so-called injury, they have lately become a loud and persistent aggravation to the government and pipeline companies. Despite Riley's misgivings, they're not going anywhere.

Don taught me a lot that helped me as I moved around Indian Country, and so has a wonderful character named Dewey Bull Tail, whom I met on the Crow Reservation in Montana. Just like Don, he happily took me,

[5] Ibid., xi.

my children, and my students into his family. Our friendship arose from another conference at the Buffalo Bill Cody Museum, where a Northern Cheyenne woman suggested I take my students to Crow Fair, the largest gathering of Indians each summer. It is so large, in fact, it bills itself as the "Teepee Capital of the World."

I had heard of it and understood it took place on the Crow Reservation in Montana, but otherwise, I knew nothing about it. I assumed it was just another powwow. The Cheyenne woman gave me two names of people to contact—Kineta Red Star and Dewey Bull Tail—but no information on how to contact them other than the fact that Kineta worked at the Chief Plenty Coups Museum in Pryor, Montana, a place that barely rated a dot on the map of that vast reservation.

I still can't explain why I took off for Montana with only the vaguest information about two people I knew nothing about on a reservation that is roughly 100 miles across in any direction. Perhaps it was the sense of adventure, not unlike crossing that road in Canada many years earlier. At any rate, I found myself flying to Montana and taking an early-morning drive to locate Kineta's museum, about 35 miles south of Billings.

The museum was closed when I got there. I took a walk around a little park next to the museum, considering my next move. A car pulled up alongside me, and a tall, lanky Indian got out. He was wearing a cowboy hat and boots, and he had a cigarette hanging from his lips. I walked over to him, and we exchanged pleasantries and made small talk. He proudly pointed out Big Pryor Mountain and told me stories about it and other sites, and then he gave me a little history of the museum and the reservation. He finally got around to asking what I was doing there, and I told him I was waiting for Kineta. He said she would be along soon, at which point I added I was also looking for a guy named Dewey Bull Tail. Just as when I met Don, the man smiled, extended his hand, and said, "I'm Dewey Bull Tail."

That I should find him on my first try on such a huge reservation was a shock, but even more surprising was his response when I asked him if I could bring a group of students to his camp at Crow Fair. Without hesitation, in a drawl made raspy by years of smoking, he simply said, "Oh, hell, yes." I soon learned that "Oh, hell, yes" means he has no idea what he has agreed to, but he has never failed to deliver. For my part, I had no clue what I was getting myself into when I showed up with about 15 people— some students and some older groupies—at the Bull Tail camp at Crow Fair, which is held each August in Crow Agency, the tribal headquarters.

Crow Fair started 100 years ago as a typical county fair, where the Crow or *Absaalooke* people brought their agricultural products and horses to display and sell, and gathered to celebrate in their traditional ways, something that was forbidden by the government, except on special occasions. Today, thousands of people from around the world, and Indians from across America and Canada come every year to watch the dancing and listen to the drumming and singing that continue into the early hours of the morning.

In many ways, it would be a typical powwow were it not for thousands of teepees planted along the banks of the Little Bighorn River, just below Last Stand Hill, where the famous battle was fought. There's a dance circle with an arbor covered with cottonwood branches and a slew of vendors selling a gamut of concession items, from Indian tacos to Chinese food, not to mention the best curly fries I've ever tasted. You can also buy everything from cheap souvenirs to expensive jewelry and animal furs. There are carnival rides, and you can even take in an Indian rodeo.

Every morning promptly at 6, you'll be rudely awakened by the camp crier, who wends his way through the camp singing in Crow over loudspeakers. And later each morning, you can watch the Crow, dressed in their finest outfits and with their horses draped in prized Pendleton blankets with the price tags still attached, process through the winding roads of the camp. They love their horses and take great pride in showing them off to the crowds lining the parade route.

The Bull Tail camp is in a prime location, across the road from the dance circle, in a spot that has been passed down through the generations. The accommodations are basic—no running water or electricity, a rug or tarp on the ground in a teepee for a bed with no privacy, and port-a-potties that swelter in the summer heat. But there is plenty to eat. The kitchen is always open, even in the middle of the night, and there are vacant spots in the teepees so people can crash. We took in an array of strays over the years. Anyone looking for a place to stay or something to eat was welcomed.

After the initial introductions when we arrived, the first job was to put up our sleeping quarters. Teepees are a source of pride and envy, and Crow Fair is a place for Indians to display the number and quality of their teepees, and their skill in putting them up. The Bull Tails take great pains in erecting them, every step carefully orchestrated by tradition. The canvas must be perfectly taut with no sags or wrinkles. Suburban homeowners could not be prouder of their homes than the Bull Tails are of their teepees. I've driven around the camp with them and listened to them critique the teepees we passed, while they disparage the teepees of other tribes, which they can identify on sight. My students became quite proficient at putting up teepees, and one group supposedly set a speed record. The Bull Tails taught them well.

Like Don Moccasin, Dewey is clearly proud of his reservation, people and culture. He took us on tours of the reservation as we looked for firewood or cooled off in Lodge Grass Creek or at Yellowtail Dam. He arranged for sweat lodges, included us in family gatherings and ceremonies, and invited us to join the family for an evening at the tribal bingo hall. He and his brother Wales took pains to teach us about Crow customs, traditions, history, and language, including buffalo hunts.

The hunts were always the highlight of our visits to the Bighorn Mountains, which lapse across the Wyoming border into the reservation. The tribe has several buffalo herds that roam freely across some of the most beautiful country I have ever seen. Tribal members can hunt on a limited basis, but non-tribal members are not allowed on the buffalo pasture without permission or accompaniment by tribal members. We secured permits with Dewey's help, and each summer we would travel high up into the mountains with an entourage of family members and anyone else who wanted to tag along for the hunt.

The trip into the mountains began with everybody jumping into the backs of pickup trucks and speeding off, leaving me to plod along in a 15-seat van. I'll never forget my young daughter, who was in the back of one those trucks, running up to me when I finally caught up with the caravan. "Dad, we hit 100!" she shouted. All I could say was, "Don't tell Mom!" Sometimes what happens at Crow Fair needs to stay at Crow Fair.

Our first stop was at the IGA in the town of Lodge Grass, where we would fill up with gas and load up with a healthy amount of unhealthy food, which was not necessarily bad since the fresh foods were often past their expiration dates. As we traveled into the mountains over bone-jarring roads, we would stop along the way to fill water cans from mountain springs and take pictures of places few White people have ever seen or will ever see. As we did, we always kept an eye open for a buffalo herd. Finding a herd is not always easy. Sometimes it takes hours of traveling across the rugged terrain and off-roading in the truest sense, since there are no roads.

Finally a herd would be spotted, and the hunt would begin. Sometimes we would sneak up on it to get within shooting range. Other times we would drive our pickups into the herd to cull out several before they had a chance to take off into the woods. When we did, I imagined what it was like for Indians riding their ponies into a herd of stampeding buffalo in order to get a good shot. A buffalo stampede is a frightening but exciting thing to behold.

Whenever I tell people about the buffalo hunts, they inevitably ask whether buffalo are an endangered species, and do the Indians still use bows and arrows. No, they aren't endangered, and no, we didn't use bows and arrows. The Indians supplied the guns and generally did the shooting. The one time we let a White guy fill the role, he froze, and we almost lost the herd. He explained he couldn't find the safety on the gun. The Indian who owned the gun grabbed it and downed the buffalo, politely pointing out he never has the safety on. I shuddered to think about my students and my children riding in a truck over the bumpy terrain with a loaded gun without its safety on. That's life on the reservation.

The shooters are always careful to make the first shot count, so the buffalo neither escapes nor suffers. They have to hit a spot the size of a silver dollar behind the animal's ears to ensure a quick kill, which they did every time I was with them.

Then the butchering would begin. My students joined in with more gusto than I expected. I'll never forget one girl cutting out the heart and without hesitation, squeezing the blood out of it and all over herself. Some would take their bloody shirts home with them as souvenirs. After the heavy butchering was done, the Indian women would begin cleaning the organs, including the intestines. When the stomachs were slit open, I was amazed at the enormous quantity of grass the animals had consumed. The meat would then be divided up among family and friends, and someone would claim the skin and somebody else the head—nothing was left to waste. Finally it was time to eat.

I laugh when people ask whether we ate authentic Indian food on our trips. I once heard a joke that traditional powwow food is bologna sandwiches, or as they are often named, "wake sandwiches," so called because they're often served at funerals. Think a slice of bologna between two slices of white bread. Sometimes, as at a ceremony I attended in New York, a slice of turkey or ham is substituted for bologna. I have also heard of lard and spaghetti sandwiches, but I've never had them. A Tuscarora woman once told me that Indians rely on what she called "poor people's food"—simple, basic meals of soups and stews made from whatever is available. Dewey prefers canned food like Vienna sausages and would get mad at me if I bought anything remotely healthy, including peanut butter and jelly.

Still, gathering extended family and friends to participate in a hunt and share in its fruits is as traditional as it gets. It's reminiscent of the times when Plains Indians would come together for their summer hunts, as they did that fateful summer of 1876 in the valley of the Little Bighorn. It was through those experiences in the Bighorns that I learned why the loss of the buffalo was so devastating to Plains Indians. The hunts were not just about food; they were a means of connecting families and communities to assure their mutual survival. Once the buffalo were gone, so was an important tie that bound them together.

It might seem that my chance encounters with Dewey and Don, and the deep and fast friendships that followed were just dumb luck, but similar meetings have happened on other reservations with other Indians too many times to be mere coincidences. Eventually I took groups to the Northern Cheyenne, Navajo, Hopi, and Southern Ute reservations, and everywhere we went, we were welcomed and received with the same generosity. The Dallas family on Hopi invited me and my students into their home, and the Navajo rugmaker Louisa Tsosie and her family on Navajo taught us how to weave rugs. Philip White Man, Jr. and his family on the Northern Cheyenne Reservation took us to Deer Medicine Rocks, where, as I mentioned earlier, Sitting Bull had his fateful vision of the momentous battle to come.

I'll never forget the honoring song Philip's father sang at the craggy outcrop that still bears a carving of Sitting Bull's prophetic vision of soldiers falling upside down into the Lakota camp. Neither will I forget lying around the campfire on Rosebud watching for shooting stars with my Mohawk friend Jackie Labonte, or floating down the Niobrara River in Nebraska with Don's family, capped with a meal prepared by his sister Martha. Or making cowboy coffee over an open fire with Dewey as the sun came up. Or meeting one of the last of the World War II Navajo Code Talkers, watching a Navajo sand painter work his magic, and hiking through Canyon de Chelly with our Navajo guides. Neither can I erase the memory of what seemed like thousands of children who reminded us that their culture was not dead or even dying. Most of all, I'll never forget the generosity of the Lakota, Crow, Cheyenne, Hopi, Ute, and Navajo people. They have so little, and yet, they give so much, asking for nothing in return.

As each trip came to an end, tears would be shed and hugs exchanged between people who just a few days earlier were total strangers. A profound sense of sadness would wash over me. On the one hand, I was relieved that nothing serious had happened on the trip beyond maybe a sprained ankle, a case or two of food poisoning, and a broken windshield. Of course, we all wanted to return home to our families and our beds, especially after sleeping on the ground with six or seven people to a teepee. As much as I wanted to leave, I wanted to stay. And when I got back home, I began looking for excuses to return to Indian Country. My students often told me our trips were life changing. I believe them.

I know I have changed over the course of 25 or so years. I no longer see Indians as victims, but rather, as people steadfastly determined to preserve their identities and independence, and remarkably resilient in the face of centuries of efforts to erase them literally and figuratively from American history. It has cost them dearly, but it has allowed them to survive against all odds. It has also stoked my admiration and respect for them, and enabled me to look beyond the poverty and the littered landscapes of reservations to find joy in the laughter that comes so easily to them, even in the face of hardship.

I have come a long way since that first harrowing encounter with Native people on the shores of Lake Nipissing, but not without a little help from my friends.

Race, Racialization, and Racism

RACE IS A TROUBLING question for a nation that likes to consider itself exceptional, especially after the murder of George Floyd and the massive demonstrations that followed. These days, the United States is having to face the fact that racism did not die when slavery ended or when Black people were finally allowed to drink from the same water fountains as White people. It is indelibly imprinted on American society through the process of racialization—the characterization of groups of people on the basis of their race. So much so, medical authorities have declared racism a public health crisis.

Let's stop and remind ourselves there is no scientific basis for race. As Kathryn Paige Harden declares in her book *The Genetic Lottery*, "... Race does not stand up scientifically, period." Therefore, "... Any claims about 'genetic' differences in intelligence or educational attainment or any behavioral traits are scientifically baseless." Instead, race is a social construct that has been used to create a racial hierarchy with White people of European descent planted squarely and firmly at the top, as befitting a culturally, morally, and technologically superior people, with people of color clearly inferior and undeserving of the same rights and privileges as White people.[6]

The hierarchy has been perpetuated by attributing certain stereotypical qualities or behaviors to dark-skinned people in order to demean, degrade, and dehumanize them, and to justify the conquest, colonization, and even genocide of Indigenous people around the world. For Africans, racialization and racist stereotypes means enslavement, slavery, segregation, and discrimination that has lasted more than 400 years, up to and including

[6] Kathryn Paige Harden, *The Genetic Lottery: Why DNA Matters for Social Equality* (Princeton, NJ: Princeton University Press, 2012), 82-5.

the death of George Floyd in 2020. Like too many other young Black men, Floyd was murdered by stereotype.

For Native Americans, racialization spells 500 years of genocidal policies and practices that brought them to near extinction, which was deemed appropriate for people who were seen as never having evolved beyond the most primitive stages of civilization and stood little chance of competing against the moral, intellectual, and technological superiority of White people.

Many are of a mind that stereotypes beget harmless jokes, and anyone who takes offense at them is just being too sensitive or too politically correct. If you can't take a joke, too bad. Remember Polish jokes? Q: How many Pollacks does it take to screw in a light bulb? A: Three. One to hold the bulb and two to turn the ladder.

This is just one of many variations on the theme that Poles are intellectually challenged, or—forgive the pun—not the brightest bulbs. Evidently, Polish jokes started in Europe and reflected the Germans' disdain for their Polish neighbors, a hatred they acted on when they invaded Poland in September 1939. In that case, Polish jokes were neither funny nor harmless.

Stereotypes are intended to establish racial, ethnic, or gender inferiority. This has been especially true for dark-skinned Indigenous people from geographical areas such as Africa, the Amazonian rainforests, and the heavily forested shores of North America. The fear of them is deeply embedded in European and American culture, and it fuels the racial stereotypes that persist today. They are not laughable, and they are anything but benign. Indeed, they have real life-and-death implications for their targets.

While race may be scientifically baseless, it is nevertheless used by scientific or biological racists to racialize or categorize groups by ascribing to them certain genetically inheritable and inherited social, cultural, and/ or behavioral characteristics to establish their inferiority. It is out of this process of racialization that racism arises. It's been used by White people to justify slavery, and in the case of Indians, the genocidal acts of conquest, oppression, and near extermination of the Native people of the Americas.

In Europe, the racialization of dark-skinned people was underway long before Christopher Columbus stumbled on a tiny island in the Bahamas. Coming face to face with people who bore little resemblance to him, he had only to fall back on what he knew. Contrary to what has often been assumed, racism or racial hatred did not develop out of the interaction of Europeans with the dark-skinned people they conquered and colonized; they carried it with them, spreading it throughout the world.

Racism was deeply rooted in European culture. It was the driving force behind colonialism, as Europeans spread out to exploit the human and natural resources of lands just waiting to be discovered. For most Europeans, skin color was enough to justify the enslavement, and the physical and sexual exploitation of the niggers, negroes, negers, nigers, negres, or nigras, as they were called. Even the Old Bard, Shakespeare, thought it pernicious enough in Elizabethan society to address it in *Othello.* The titular character was a Moor, a term that became synonymous with blackness and that was used to describe dark-skinned people as far away as Sri Lanka.

As Winthrop Jordan convincingly demonstrates in his groundbreaking book *White Over Black,* Europeans on the eve of colonization associated black or blackness with evil, sin, death, dirt, disgrace, danger, sinisterness, malignance, and atrocity.[7] Modern dictionaries list all of those and add "repugnant, repulsive, threatening, hideous, foreboding, and unpleasant."

When I asked my students what black meant to them, they responded like Europeans might have 500 years ago: witches, death, dirt, black magic, black market, and evil. They all know bad guys wear black, good guys and brides wear white, and black cats are bad luck. I've never heard anyone complain about the white sheep of the family. The fear, repulsion, and loathing of blackness is ingrained in European, and by extension, American culture. It has been projected onto people of color around the world in the form of racist assumptions about their inferiority, which then evolved into stereotypes.

There is no better example of this than the treatment of African Americans, who have been the objects of vicious, vile stereotypes throughout U.S. history. Black people have been typecast as brutish, apelike creatures

---

[7] Winthrop Jordan, *White Over Black* (Chapel Hill, NC: University of North Carolina Press, 1968).

who are lazy, stupid, dirty, violent, and on welfare or some other form of public assistance. Think of the slurs directed at them that refer to simian-like, subhuman characteristics: "porch monkeys," "spearchuckers," "jungle bunnies," "knuckle draggers," "welfare monkeys," and the less imaginative "gorillas" and "baboons." Just when I thought I had heard them all, I found "branch manager," which has nothing to do with bank branches, but refers to monkeys swinging through trees.

The biological connection between Africans and apes even had the support of Thomas Jefferson, who suggested that "oranootans" lusted after African women. Conversely, he believed Africans lusted after White women.[8] Jefferson didn't need Darwin to justify his evolutionary speculations. He had the Great Chain of Being, dating back to Plato and Aristotle. The hierarchical structure places all species on an evolutionary ladder, with White people at the top, Africans at the bottom, and "American savages" just slightly above the lowest rung.

It was embraced in Nazi Germany and persists in America today in the form of racial profiling. Who can forget the Los Angeles police officer who characterized a disturbance involving Black people as straight out of the movie *Gorillas in the Mist,* a statement that was used as evidence against the police officers involved in the Rodney King beating. Even worse are the images of Barack and Michelle Obama that were edited to make the president and first lady look like apes. All of these racial stereotypes, and unfortunately, too many more, work to dehumanize Black people in a way that allowed their enslavement and led to their continued oppression long after slavery ended.

One of the most common slurs when I was growing up was "coon," a shortened version of raccoon, which is in and of itself dehumanizing. The term evidently grew out of 19th century minstrel shows that depicted Black people as slow-moving, slow-talking, lazy, dimwitted buffoons. The coon caricature carried over into the 20th century and was portrayed in many movies, most notably by the actor Lincoln Theodore Perry—better known by his stage name Stepin Fetchit—whose character and screen name be-

---

[8] Thomas Jefferson, *Notes on the State of Virginia* (Boston: Lilly and Wait, 1785), 145.

came associated in the popular imagination with the actual characteristics of Black men.

Until World War II, most Americans outside the South had little contact with Black people, so what they knew often came from the movies. On the other hand, I grew up in a mixed neighborhood and went to school, rode the bus, and played sports with Black kids. I even had a Black kindergarten teacher, which was a rarity in 1952 Ohio. Yet, I believed and even mouthed the stereotypes about Black people.

I remember when my brother went off to college and found out he had a Black roommate. My mother warned him to watch his money. "Those people steal," she said. Once, when a Black woman knocked on our door and asked to use our bathroom in an emergency, we let her in, but after she left, my mother did everything short of calling out a hazmat team to clean the area. "Those people are dirty," she exclaimed.

Stereotypes such as these demeaned and dehumanized Africans and justified their enslavement. When slavery ended, racialization persisted, and Black people were segregated and trapped in poorer neighborhoods with weaker schools and few opportunities to escape. The image of "welfare queens" fueled the backlash against the social welfare system in the 1970s and 80s, and it persists today. The names, the jokes … they're not funny or harmless.

The overt racism of the past may have been driven underground by political correctness, or perhaps Americans have become more adept at disguising their racism, that is until the White supremacy movements made it popular once again. Either way, at least most people now use the term "N-word" rather than "nigger." However, while Americans have become more circumspect in their choice of words, they do not seem to draw the same conclusions about the negative stereotypes of Native Americans that pervade nearly every aspect of U.S. culture.

In the same way stereotypes of Africans as less than human led to their deportation, enslavement, and exploitation, the mocking and hateful depictions of Indians led to their conquest and continued colonization. To be sure, Indians are now called "Native Americans," and there have been protests against racist caricatures such as Chief Wahoo of Cleveland's baseball franchise, and the team logos of the Washington Redskins, Chicago Blackhawks, and Kansas City Chiefs. In fact, both Chief Wahoo and the Washington football team's emblem have been dropped, and both teams found new names to replace "Indians" and "Redskins." Schools have changed their mascots, cities and states have changed Columbus Day to Indigenous Peoples Day, and the stories about Thanksgiving and Pocahontas have been revised to include the murderous actions of European settlers against Native people.

Still, most Americans do not appreciate just how damaging the stereotypes have been to Indians over the past 500 years. The potency of the racism was the same as that directed at Black people, but what happened to the Indigenous people of America was different. The estimated 600,000 Africans imported to the United States before the slave trade was outlawed in 1810 grew to more than 4 million by 1860, while the number of Indians declined from 15 million to 250,000 during roughly the same period. A similar brand of racism, but for Indians, it was lethal.

Most people have had little if any contact with Indians, unless they live around reservations or were in the military, where Indians are over-represented, or they visit Indian casinos, which are generally run and staffed by non-Indians. By the end of the 19th century, most Indians had been safely tucked away on isolated, remote reservations, mostly west of the Mississippi River on lands that are jokingly referred to as "flyover country," since the only way most Americans see them is through the windows of airplanes as they fly from one coast to another. In fact, the only reason Indians are on those lands is that White people didn't want them; if they had, they likely would have taken them. Even those who have relocated to urban areas, which accounts for most of their numbers, have found themselves largely confined through various discriminatory devices to poorer sections of cities, where they are just as invisible.

Moreover, their numbers were so reduced, James Earle Fraser's famous sculpture *The End of the Line,* with the Native rider slumped over his horse, lance pointing downward, became the accepted icon of the vanishing Indians. Today, their population has rebounded, but they remain invisible. So much so, that in government reports and other studies, they are either excluded or included in the category of "other." In the media coverage of racial injustice, the term "people of color" almost always means Black and Brown people, not Indians. They are overlooked and forgotten, except when they leave the reservation. Then they are profiled, harassed, and abused.

Just visit towns near reservations, such as Hardin, Montana; Rapid City, South Dakota; and Gallup, New Mexico; as I have, and you can feel the tension between White people and Indians. When Indians venture off their reservations, as they must do to shop, go to school, and run errands, they are subjected to racial taunts and epithets as vile and vicious as those directed at Black people, including a surprising number of variations of "nigger." The most common is "prairie nigger," but there's also "bush nigger," "swamp nigger," "timber nigger," "tundra nigger," and "red, cherry, or salmon nigger."

Besides slurs, stereotypes have found their way into common parlance. Children who misbehave are acting like "wild Indians." Someone selling tickets illegally is a "scalper." People go "off the reservation" or engage in an "Indian hunting party." The most insulting one I came across is "Indian underwear," as in "They're always creeping up on me." There's also "squaw," which is an English word loaded with racial and sexual connotations. Squaws, like Indian men, are dirty, stupid, alcoholic, and promiscuous, and like Black women, they have children just to stay on public assistance.

However, the racially motivated attacks against Native people are not limited to words. Indians are all too often victims of physical, and for women, sexual assaults. To add to their humiliation, Indians figured out long ago, just as Black people learned, that retaliation would only make matters worse. Powerless to defend themselves against racial and physical attacks, Indians very often chose to simply isolate themselves on their reservations, many of them taking refuge in self-destructive behavior.

Most Americans are unaware of the racism endured by Native people, or they believe it is a thing of the past. In fact, many believe Indians in general are a thing of the past. Absent any direct contact, they have come to know Indians through the caricatures and characterizations of popular culture.

Thomas King, again in his book *The Inconvenient Indian,* lists numerous examples of the appropriation of Native images and names, from automobiles like the Jeep Cherokee and the now defunct Pontiac, to military weapons like the Tomahawk missile and Apache helicopter, to tobacco and alcohol products like Red Man chewing tobacco and Crazy Horse Malt Liquor. His personal favorite is Land O'Lakes butter, with an Indian maiden on its package, which is ironic since many Indians are lactose intolerant.[9] In fairness, the image of the Indian maiden has been removed from the Land O'Lakes packages, just as Aunt Jemima has been deleted from pancake-mix boxes and syrup bottles.

Still, Americans hit the road in their Winnebago RVs that might be insured by the Mutual of Omaha insurance company and travel across the country from Shinnecock Hills on Long Island to Tacoma, Washington, and lots of other places with distinctive Indian names. Baby boomers like me may remember Princess Summerfall Winterspring, Chief Thunderthud, and Chief Featherman of the Tinka Tonka tribe on the *Howdy Doody Show.* It was Chief Thunderthud who made "cowabunga" popular.

Others may recall Lonesome Polecat, another name for a skunk. He was the stereotypical-looking Indian who was the purveyor of Kickapoo Joy Juice to the residents of Dogpatch in the "Li'l Abner" comic strip. Even *The Three Stooges* has an episode where the boys, dressed like Pilgrims, outsmart the dimwitted and clumsy Indians, or "savages" as they are called, led by Chief Rain in the Puss.

The names are silly, but they are nonetheless offensive. So is the idea that Indians are so ignorant and backward that even Curly, Larry, and Moe can outsmart them. Yet, many Americans continue to think about Native people in stereotypical, almost comical terms that characterize them as primitive relics from the past.

I often get sniggers when I mention my Indian friends' names, like Bull Tail, Birding Ground, Kills Straight, and Gets Down. I remember one

[9] Thomas King, *The Inconvenient Indian* (Toronto: Anchor Canada, 2013), 56-7.

student telling me after listening to a Tuscarora linguist who came to my class, that she was surprised that Indians had a language with a vocabulary, grammar, and syntax. I suppose she thought they all talked in grunts or pidgin English like Tonto on *The Lone Ranger*. Based on what she surely learned as a child, who could blame her?

I can assure you, having been insulted by parents at a local high school for speaking against its Redskins team name, many Americans do not understand or necessarily even care that reducing Native people to comical caricatures with funny-sounding names is hurtful and harmful. Nor do they comprehend how offensive are the hand-over-mouth mocking of the Indian war cry, the mimicking of the *leelee*, the shrill honoring cry of Native women, and nicknames like "chief" and "squaw."

For some, it's simple but sincere ignorance. For others, America has become too politically correct, and the Indians should just get over the past, something I hear all too often. They don't seem to understand that the seemingly harmless stereotypes of the present have been used to justify the conquest and colonization of Indians going back centuries. For still others, it's simple and outright racial hatred.

There is no shortage of Indian stereotypes. There's Pocahontas, the Indian princess of American folklore and the Disney film of the same name, and Minnehaha or "Laughing Water," the "loveliest of Dacotah women" from Henry Wadsworth Longfellow's poem "Hiawatha." There's Jean Jacques Rousseau's "noble savage," uncorrupted by civilization, who has been resurrected in the deeply spiritual Indian, who is, in probably the most clichéd descriptions of Indians, "one with nature." Rousseau's noble savage notwithstanding, the Europeans who invaded North America brought with them the belief that Indians were merciless savages, probably learned from Spanish experiences in Latin America that were popularized throughout Europe at that time.

These beliefs were cemented in the American mind through Indian wars over the course of four centuries, and they became a staple of popular culture dating back to the novels of James Fenimore Cooper, the Wild West shows and dime novels of the 19th century, and sensationalist art like the 1804 painting *The Death of Jane McCrea*. In the 20th century, they became the staple of television and movie Westerns. For generations, Indian barbarity has dominated popular culture. Although they're no longer as popular as when I was growing up, Westerns have almost universally depicted Indians as warlike, half-naked savages yipping and whooping on the warpath.

For example, Cooper included the massacre of British and American soldiers after the surrender of Fort William Henry in 1757 during the French and Indian War in his novel *The Last of the Mohicans*. Cooper's most famous novel was published in 1826, at a time when the removal of Indians across the Mississippi River was well underway, and most Americans east of the river had very little if any contact with real, live Indians. For them, Cooper rekindled the stories of Indian atrocities, including the kidnapping and murder of White women, that their great-grandparents presumably endured, and which became a part of the mythology of the American frontier. *The Last of the Mohicans* became an American classic. It was republished numerous times and made into at least nine movies, a play, an opera, and a made-for-television movie. I became acquainted with it through Classics Illustrated comic books.

Along the way, it was imprinted on the American psyche in the image of the brutally savage Indian that has informed American popular culture down to the present and has even invaded academia. In the debate over whether genocide was committed against Indigenous people in the Americas, genocide deniers, including some of my academic colleagues, are quick to point out that European attacks were often in reprisal for Indian atrocities and therefore justified.

Whenever I talk to people about the violence visited upon Indians, someone will inevitably bring up stories of murder and torture that could have come straight out of *The Last of the Mohicans*. In fact, Naomi Riley, wanting to correct the historical record, noted with apparent disdain that today's students learn about the starvation, disease, and massacres Indians experienced, but "They'll rarely hear about the brutalities that Indians committed against white settlers ...."[10]

One of the first books I read in an undergraduate history class was *Drums Along the Mohawk,* a Revolutionary War historical novel that features the attack of frenzied, bloodthirsty Native people on God-fearing settlers along the Mohawk River in New York. It is replete with the murder, torture, scalping, and worst of all, the kidnapping, torture, and murder of White women.[11]

The movie version is less graphic but nevertheless has Indians ransacking and burning settlers' homes and fields, and attacking women and children who have holed themselves in a blockhouse while the menfolk are away. There is even a pair of drunken Indians assaulting a White woman in her home. In one scene, the local pastor implores God to deliver the settlers from what one of them describes as "murdering painted heathen." I wonder if they would have been more acceptable if they were pious Indians. Of course, if they were good Christians, they wouldn't murder, plunder, torture, and rape.

The threat Indians posed to White women on the frontier is captured in the aforementioned painting depicting the abduction, murder, and scalping of the White woman Jane McCrea. The painting portrays a real event during the Revolutionary War, although the details are not certain. In the painting, the fair-skinned maiden is held captive by two swarthy Native men, one brandishing a tomahawk and the other a knife as he holds her by her hair as if he is about to scalp her.

The incident was performed in a circus and is the subject of a poem turned popular folk song. Although the original painting faded into obscurity, it was copied in many forms and came to represent Indian brutality, especially directed toward White women. If you want proof that the image of the savage Indian as portrayed in that painting became a staple of popular culture, just look at movie posters, mostly from B-grade Westerns like *Tomahawk Trail, Yellow Tomahawk, War Drums, War Paint,* and *Massacre,* which feature Indians attacking settlers and/or wagon trains.

---

[10] Riley, xi.

[11] Walter D. Edmonds, *Drums Along the Mohawk* (Boston: Little Brown, 1936).

There are more than I ever imagined or could track down, and they have some things in common. They usually have "Fort" in their titles, like *Fort Bowie, Fort Defiance,* and *Fort Apache,* often in combination with "Massacre," like *Fort Massacre,* with the cavalry shielding the settlers from the bloodthirsty Indians. They also feature images of Indians assaulting White women, usually holding them by their hair with a tomahawk or a knife at the ready to kill and scalp them. The scenes on the posters are simply updated versions of *The Death of Jane McCrea.*

Like television Westerns, these movies are fictional, but their characters often express racist sentiments that have historically typified the vast majority of relations between White people and Indians. In one, *Valley of the Sun,* settlers proclaim the best way to deal with marauding Indians is to "shoot them damn redskins when they got the chance." After all, "The sooner they get rid of them, the safer the country will be for us Americans."

Perhaps the most famous and arguably the most racist movie is *The Searchers,* starring John Wayne as Ethan Edwards, a Confederate veteran of the Civil War. He pursues, like Ahab in *Moby Dick,* his niece, a young White girl kidnapped by Comanche who have killed her mother and younger brother. Edwards is brutal, but his vengeful and sadistic acts are justified by the savagery of the Indians, especially the kidnapping and rape of White women. He eventually finds the girl. She is dead and presumably raped.

The word "rape" is never used in the movie, probably because of censorship rules in the 1950s, but make no mistake, the insinuation is unmistakable. When Edwards has to inform the girl's fiancé of her fate, he omits that grizzly detail. When the young man continues to ask, "Was she?" Wayne responds in his signature angry growl, "What do you want me to do, draw you a picture? Spell it out? Don't ever ask me. Long as you live, don't ever ask me more."[12]

Of course the Indians committed the unspeakable; that's what they did. Like White Southerners who obsessed over preserving the honor of White women from the sexual predations of their slaves, Americans in general

[12] *The Searchers,* John Ford, director. 1956. Warner Bros. Pictures.

fixated on the abduction and rape of White women by Indians. The stereotype of Indians as dark-skinned, violent, libidinous heathens has had real-life implications.

In 1823, in the famous case *Johnson v. McIntosh,* U.S. Supreme Court Chief Justice John Marshall opined that the original inhabitants of America were nothing more than "fierce savages, whose occupation was war, and whose subsistence was drawn chiefly from the forest." White settlers lived under the "perpetual hazard of being massacred," leaving them no choice but to enforce their claims to the land with "the sword."[13]

Similarly, in the 1876 case *Standing Bear v. George Crook,* the district judge grudgingly admitted Standing Bear was indeed a person, but he proceeded to declare that Indians were a "wasted race" that was "once numerous and powerful, but now weak, insignificant, unlettered, and generally despised ...."[14]

These opinions affirmed in law the popular stereotypes that have allowed government authorities to concentrate Indians on reservations under the watchful eye of the cavalry, and later, local, state, and federal law enforcement agencies. They have allowed the government to renege on its treaty obligations to Indians, neglect their welfare, and strip them of their sovereignty. The have allowed White people to rob Indians of their land, water, oil, and timber. They have allowed the injustices of the past to be continued right up to the present. Life may often imitate art, but in Ethan Edwards' case—and perhaps even in Waynes'—art imitates life.

In a 1971 interview, when asked if he empathized with Indians, who were often central to his movies, Wayne replied, "I don't feel we did wrong in taking this great land from [them]. Our so called stealing of this country from them was just a matter of survival. There were great numbers of people who needed new land, and the Indians were selfishly trying to keep it for themselves."[15]

---

[13] *Johnson & Graham's Lessee v. McIntosh,* 21 U.S. 543 (1923).

[14] *U.S. ex Rel. Standing Bear v. Crook,* 25 F. Cas. 695 (D. Neb. 1879).

[15] Eli, Rosenberg. "'I believe in white supremacy': John Wayne's notorious 1971 Playboy interview goes viral on Twitter." *The Washington Post* (Feb. 20, 2019).

The Searchers influenced a number of other movies, including *Two Rode Together,* starring Jimmy Stewart, who, like the Edwards protagonist, searches for two children kidnapped five years earlier, once again, by Comanches. He eventually finds them, but they are too far gone to be reintroduced to White society, especially the boy, who is described as a "mad dog" who bears the scars of the Sun Dance and has already learned to kill and scalp White people.

Both movies are loosely based on a real incident in Texas involving the kidnapping of White people by members of the Comanche tribe, which also inspired the book *Empire of the Summer Moon* by Sam C. Gwynne from Texas. The book chronicles the battle between White settlers and the Comanche for Texas, and in fairness, it doesn't discriminate when it comes to attributing atrocities. However, in the end, the (White) Texans are on the side of righteousness, as evidenced by the fact that the famed Comanche leader Quanah, himself the child of a Comanche man and a kidnapped White woman, was reclaimed from his Indian ways. He adopts the surname Parker, becomes a rancher, invests wisely, and purportedly becomes the richest Indian in America.[16] Evidently his better half saved him from his baser instincts.

Quanah Parker notwithstanding, the stereotype persists of the violent Indian who poses a threat to White America. And that brings us back to the dilemma Indigenous people in the Americas have faced from the moment of contact: assimilation or annihilation. Parker's conversion seems to vindicate the Texans' brutality, since the Comanche and others who were victims of ethnic cleansing were offered the opportunity to lay down their arms and assimilate, as Parker does.

As political leaders, missionaries, land speculators, and farmers all agreed, there was more than enough land for everybody. The reduction in Indian lands was beneficial because it forced them to give up the hunt and their other extraction economies, settle down on individual plots of land, become farmers, get an English and Christian education, and pay taxes that would qualify them for citizenship. The problem was—and is—that

---

[16] S.C. Gwynne, *Empire of the Summer Moon* (New York: Charles Scribner's Sons, 2011).

unlike Quanah Parker, most Indians have chosen not to give up their lives and identities as Indians.

In the eyes of the government and most White people, they remain uncivilized and unredeemable. Using Thomas King's word, they are inconvenient reminders of the injustices of the past, giving lie to Americans' belief in their exceptionalism. Despite efforts to eradicate them, and when that failed, erase them from history, the Indians are still here. In fact, they are more defiant than ever.

In the meantime, Americans wonder why Indians don't want to assimilate. Why don't they want to leave the dismal conditions on their reservations?

That is the question for the rest of this book.

POPSICLES

PERHAPS THE MOST ENDURING and certainly one of the most denigrating stereotypes of Native people is that of the drunken Indian. One question I am frequently asked is why Indians drink so much. The stereotype dates back to colonial times, when the settlers introduced alcohol to the Native people, and the Indians engaged in what today would be called binge drinking, consuming all of the liquor at one time whenever they could get their hands on it.

It has become self-fulfilling and a way to define Indians in the American imagination. Even Indians have bought into the stereotype. As one told me, Indians drink because they are Indians; that's what Indians do. Stereotype or not, alcohol abuse is a serious problem among Native people on and off reservations, particularly in towns bordering reservations, which often exist solely to supply alcohol to them. However, there are those who defiantly insist that the firewater myth, which claims that Indians can't hold their liquor, is just that—a myth. They argue that Indians are no more predisposed to substance use disorder than White people. There is some truth to that belief. White people are in fact more likely to drink than Indians. Still, the damage alcohol has done to Native families and communities over the past 500 years is definitely not a myth.

The relationship between Indians and alcohol is an issue I'm quite sensitive about. Although I'm not an Indian, I'm an alcoholic, and I came from a family with alcoholics on both sides. As I was writing this, I was reminded of my Uncle Tony, my father's younger brother. He was one of the unlucky ones drafted before World War II started; consequently, he was one of the first to be thrown into the fight. He was at Guadalcanal in 1942, where he was wounded and lay in the rain and mud for 24 hours before he was rescued. I never saw it, but I was told he had a hole in his side as big as a fist.

When he came back from the war, he was never the same. He couldn't hold a steady job, lived off my grandmother, bummed money and drinks, and finally, drank himself to death. There are lots of funny stories about my uncle, like the time a local bar owner called and asked me to come and get Tony's dentures; he had left them in the tavern. But I remember him more for the time he came into a neighborhood bar where I was working.

He stopped in early one morning, just after I opened. He was already drunk and out of money, and he asked me for a free drink. I told him no; he had had enough. I hated to turn him down. He was my uncle, after all, so I finally relented. I'll never forget the drink; it was a cheap whiskey by the name of Old Thompson, washed down with warm water. He left, and as he was walking out, I stood there looking at him and shaking my head. A longtime family friend was in the bar, taking it all in. He must have seen the look of disapproval (or worse) on my face. He looked me squarely in the eyes and said something I'll never forget: "Remember what he went through."

Uncle Tony eventually died of a heart attack while crossing the street on his way back from a liquor store, clutching a quart of beer to his chest. I like to think he died happy. If nothing else, he was finally at peace.

The incident in the bar that morning taught me a lesson I remember more than 50 years later. There was a story behind Uncle Tony's drinking, a painful one, but it was easier to poke fun at him, shake my head, shrug my shoulders, and blame him for his drinking rather than take into account what happened to him in the jungles of Guadalcanal. In the same way, the stereotype of the drunken Indian has made it easier to shift the blame for their problems onto their alcoholism, and their moral and character weaknesses than to look at them as individuals who have suffered and are suffering … as human beings with stories to tell.

Indeed, if one is assigning blame, we need to at least consider the part White people played. Indians acquired their taste for liquor from European coasters plying their wares along the shores and rivers of North America. Rum was the stock in trade of colonialism around the world, and settlers quickly learned its value as currency for furs, land, and slaves. In fact, one of the causes of the American Revolution was the Sugar Act of 1764 that taxed imported sugar, from which the colonists made rum for sale and trade.

Indians were some of their best customers, and the detrimental effects of alcohol on Native communities was no secret. Benjamin Franklin suggested in 1753 that rum would be the most efficient way of ridding the country of Indians, as "It has already annihilated all the tribes that formerly inhabited the sea coast."[17]

Indians and missionaries protested the trade in liquor, and colonial governments passed laws against it, which did little to restrict it, especially after the American Revolution. As settlers moved farther and farther west, so did alcohol. The government was powerless to stop it, and settlers became very adept at turning their excess corn into liquor. To make matters worse, purveyors of alcohol along the frontier added strychnine to their watered-down alcohol to give it an extra kick. If consumed in large enough quantities, it proved fatal.

So serious was the problem, that in 1802, President Thomas Jefferson asked Congress to prohibit the sale of "spirituous liquors" to Indians. That same year, Jefferson wrote a letter to the Seneca prophet Handsome Lake, applauding him for preaching abstinence to his people in light of "the ruinous effects which the abuse of spirituous spirits have produced upon them. It has weakened their bodies, enervated their minds, exposed them to hunger, cold, nakedness, & poverty, kept them in perpetual broils, & reduced their population."[18] Jefferson wasn't far off, as the story of Mary Jemison, the White Woman of the Genesee, and her sons, John, Thomas, and Jesse, suggests.

Mary Jemison was born at sea in 1743 to a Scots Irish family on its way to Pennsylvania to begin a new life in the colonies. Taken captive at the age of 12 by a Shawnee raiding party during the French and Indian War, she

---

[17] Benjamin Franklin, *The Autobiography of Benjamin Franklin* (New Haven, CT: Yale University Press, 1964), 198-9.

[18] Thomas Jefferson, "Letter to Handsome Lake, November 3, 1802" in *Thomas Jefferson: Writings* (New York: Library of America, 1984), 555-7.

was given to the Seneca people at Fort Duquesne, adopted into a Seneca family, and given a Seneca name. She eventually married a Lenape (Delaware) man in New York, and when he died, she married a Seneca man. Mary Jemison's home still stands in New York's Letchworth State Park, where she lived to the ripe old age of 89 or 90, refusing to leave the Seneca people and return to live among White people when given the chance.

She was a remarkable woman whose life was marred by alcohol. Three of her sons were killed, two by their own brother in drunken brawls. Thomas, her oldest, killed John over charges of witchcraft, which led to another drunken brawl in which Thomas killed Jesse. Thomas was finally murdered in another drunken fight.[19] Alcohol killed all three, in this case proving it was the scourge Franklin and Jefferson said it was. It didn't go unnoticed; Congress finally responded in 1832 with a law that prohibited the introduction of liquor into Indian Country.

That law stood until 1953, but it did little to curb the use of alcohol among Indians or its use by White people to prey upon Indians, particularly in the making of treaties. The combination of alcohol and White hunger for land led to the alienation of millions of acres through treaties like the Quashquamme Treaty of 1804, in which four Sauk Indians under the influence of alcohol gave away 50 million acres of their land along the Mississippi River in Illinois and Iowa. When Black Hawk, leader of the Sauk and Fox, tried to reclaim the land in 1832, the Black Hawk War broke out, a fight for which Abraham Lincoln volunteered. It was all for naught. Black Hawk surrendered before Lincoln could fire a shot, and the lands were lost.[20]

The Buffalo Creek Treaty of 1836 has a similar story. Through the liberal use of alcohol, as well as bribery and deceit, the Seneca of Western New York almost lost their land and would have been removed to Kansas. The treaty was one of the most fraudulent in the long history of fraudulent treaties. Even the U.S. Senate, which never saw an Indian treaty it didn't like, found the courage to reject it. However, it wasn't a case of all's well that

[19] James E. Seaver, *A Narrative of the Life of Mary Jemison Who Was Taken By the Indians in 1755* (Syracuse, NY: Syracuse Univ. Press, 1990).

[20] Christina Rose, "Native History: Alcohol and Murder Result in Theft of Fifty Million Acres," *Indian Country Today* (April 6, 2014).

ends well. The treaty of 1836 was replaced in 1842 with a second treaty of the same name. It permitted the Seneca to remain in New York, but on a tiny fraction of the 4 million acres of land recognized as their territory in the Canandaigua Treaty of 1794.[21]

There are many depictions of drunken Indians in popular culture, but the one I found most curious and intriguing was in a little-known short story by Ernest Hemingway entitled "Ten Indians." It's named after the 19th century counting rhyme "Ten Little Indians," which, incidentally, has also been called "Ten Little Niggers." Agatha Christie borrowed "Ten Little Indians" for the title of one of her murder mysteries, and it has since come to be associated with murder or death. For Indians, it signifies death on a grand scale. Indeed, it signifies genocide.

Hemingway's short story begins with one of the characters dragging a drunken Indian out of the roadway and proclaiming in disgust, "That makes nine of them just between here and the edge of town." The 10th Indian is a young girl whom the main character, Nick Adams, secretly loves. He can't admit it because she is a squaw and therefore, not a good girl.

The Indians are so detestable, they are impersonally and consistently referred to as "them Indians." Over the course of that story and the next, "The Indians Moved Away," not only are the Indians described as drunks, they all look alike, dress alike, and smell alike. In fact, they smell like skunks, and their odor is so strong and offensive, one can smell them coming from a distance. In addition, their homes are uninhabitable by White people, and their drinking and other character flaws invariably lead them to failure. "There are no successful Indians," per the story's dialogue. But it is the infidelity and presumed promiscuity of Nick's secret girlfriend, who is seen having a tryst or "quite a time" in the woods with another man, that completes the stereotype of the drunken, wanton Indian. The statement "And then there were none" concludes the story.[22]

Written in 1927, just a few decades after the Native population had

[21] Laurence M. Hauptman, *Conspiracy of Interests: Iroquois Dispossession and the Rise of New York State* (Syracuse, NY: Syracuse University Press, 1999), 175-90.

[22] Ernest Hemingway, "Ten Indians" in *The Complete Short Stories of Ernest Hemingway* (New York: Charles Scribner's Sons, 1987), 253-57.

reached its nadir and the Indian wars were long over, Hemingway was expressing the common belief that Indians were a race vanishing by their own hands, or as Franklin predicted, by alcohol. The image of drunken, shiftless, promiscuous Indians was so fixed and pervasive in the American consciousness, it could be used as a literary device with which Hemingway's readers were familiar and comfortable. As stereotypes tend to do, it homogenized the group—in this case Indians—and degraded and dehumanized them by denying their individuality and reducing them to a simple and self-evident common denominator. They all look alike, they all dress alike, they're all promiscuous, they all smell alike, and they're all drunks.

The staying power of this image cannot be overestimated. When one of the characters in the movie *Kit Carson* says you can smell Indians a mile away, his companion dryly replies, "Two miles."[23] It's become convenient to blame Indians for their troubles and shunt them off to reservations, where they can be more easily forgotten and neglected. Even the social pathologies that plague reservations can be attributed to the Indians' own character weaknesses. If they're poor, unemployed, homeless, victims of crime or violence, and dying untimely deaths, it's because they drink too much (although meth and opioids have eclipsed alcohol).

A Lakota elder on Rosebud, Albert White Hat, told me that when the laws prohibiting the sale of liquor were lifted in 1953, alcohol abuse affected 100% of the reservation population. While that is likely an exaggeration, alcohol use and misuse are nevertheless prolific. I have seen the consequences myself.

On my first visit to Rosebud, I passed through the town of Norris, one of those towns railroad companies built every 10 miles or so along rail lines. The lines are mostly defunct now, but the towns remain. These days, Norris consists of several uninhabited ramshackle buildings and a pool parlor that serves alcohol to Indians from neighboring Rosebud and Pine Ridge. The wreckage was visible everywhere I looked. Intoxicated Indians were

---

[23] *Kit Carson*, George B. Seitz, director. 1950. United Artists Corp.

lying on sidewalks and in the doorways of abandoned buildings. As I left, I passed more Indians trudging their way from the rez.

Every reservation I've visited has towns like Norris bordering them. For example, along U.S. Route 20, which runs south of Rosebud and Pine Ridge in Nebraska, there are: Valentine, Crookston, Kilgore, Nenzel, Cody, Merriman, Gordon, and so on, all strung out some 10 miles apart along another abandoned rail line. The railroad companies created these towns to attract settlers; now they exist largely to sell liquor to Indians.

In Wyoming, it's Riverton next to the Wind River Reservation. In Montana, Hardin is surrounded by the Crow Reservation. In New Mexico and Arizona, the huge Navajo and Hopi territories are surrounded by towns such as Flagstaff in Arizona, and Gallup and Farmington in New Mexico, all of which cater to Indians and supply them with alcohol. That said, you don't always have to drive to town to get alcohol. On the Northern Cheyenne Reservation in Montana, you can walk a few yards across the reservation boundary to the Jimtown Bar and Casino.

I've picked up hitchhikers on reservations and have marveled how far some are willing to go to get a drink. I once picked up a Crow man on his way to Hardin. He used a walker for mobility. I have seen Indians lying in a ditch on the road from Pine Ridge to Whiteclay, Nebraska, another nearly abandoned town infamous for selling 4 million cans of beer a year to Indians from the reservation just across the South Dakota border. I have seen them sleeping in underpasses in Albuquerque, and I've been panhandled by them in Rapid City, South Dakota. Even sadder, I've seen the all-too-numerous skull-and-crossbones roadside signs marking the places where Indians have died in alcohol-related accidents.

I bore witness one night as I drove along a gravel road on one of my first trips to Rosebud. It was pitch dark when a car came roaring past our van, throwing up clouds of dust and spraying us with gravel. I saw the vehicle turn onto the road behind us, coming from the direction of Kilgore, Nebraska. As it passed, I worried that my rental van would be nicked by the gravel, and that I would have to pay for the damage. Then, suddenly, I saw the taillights of the car, now far ahead, flip into the air. When we pulled up to the accident, the car was upside down, completely flattened. There were beer cans strewn everywhere. I got out to see if we could help, but it was too late. I don't remember the number of fatalities, but I was told they were young people.

Some tribes allow alcohol to be sold on their reservations in order to control its sale and use by members. They hope to curtail trips to towns like Kilgore that result in binge drinking that can and does end in tragic accidents like the one I witnessed on Rosebud. Or they have worked to close down towns like Norris and Whiteclay, both of which are now out of the liquor business. But the fact remains: If Indians want alcohol, they can get it—even if they have to turn to bootleggers.

Although two-thirds of reservations are technically free from alcohol—aka dry—the Indian Health Service states that more than half the populations on some reservations have significant drinking problems, and that reservations have mortality rates higher than the national average, with alcohol involved in 75% of Indian deaths and 80% of Indian suicides. Neither is the problem endemic to reservations; Indians in cities such as Tucson, Billings, Albuquerque, and Portland suffer from some of the highest alcohol-related mortality rates in the United States.

Binge drinking is partially to blame. Often associated with White college students, binge drinking starts earlier and continues longer among Indians than it does in the general population. Consequently, it contributes significantly to lower life expectancies among Indians through higher rates of homicides, suicides, and accidents. In one study, 68% of young Indians—a demographic with 10 times the suicide rate of young people in general—reported they started drinking before the age of 13. I have even heard about children starting to drink as young as 5 or 6. The problem is not limited to males either, as is usually depicted in popular culture. Females represent a growing proportion of alcohol abusers among Indians, and they suffer disproportionately from cirrhosis and other alcohol-related morbidities. Altogether, alcohol contributes to four of the 10 leading causes of Indian deaths: cirrhosis, homicide, suicide, and accidents.[24]

[24] Roger Clawson, "Death by Drink: The Sad Battle of America's Indians," *APF Reporter* (1989).

Alcohol abuse also leads to higher rates of incarceration for the Native populations on reservations and in border towns. The rate of Indian incarceration is about 38% higher than the national average, and as many as 90% of those arrests are alcohol related, with crimes ranging from public intoxication to DWIs to homicides. For many Native people battling alcohol and/or drug addiction, jail is the only treatment they get. It's also very often a refuge from life on the street or on the reservation.

In Gallup, New Mexico, (aka "Drunk Town") right off the Navajo Reservation, it's common for police on "ditch patrol" to find drunken Indians lying along the road leading back to the reservation. Those who are frozen to death are cruelly referred to as "Popsicles."[25] In border towns like Gallup and in cities with large Native populations, it's practically a sport for townies to roll or beat drunken Indians, sometimes to death, as in the case of Allison Gorman and Kee Thompson. The two Navajo men were murdered by three teenagers in Albuquerque, evidently for sport.[26]

It was just for the hell of it that Raymond Yellow Thunder was beaten and stripped of his clothes on a cold wintry night in February 1972 in Gordon, Nebraska, a town that borders Pine Ridge. Four townies thought it would be fun to beat up a drunken Indian and humiliate him by tossing him naked into a dance hall. He eventually died from his wounds and exposure inside a junk car, where he had taken refuge.[27]

In 2015 in Lander, Wyoming, near the Wind River Reservation, Roy Clyde, tired of cleaning up after drunken, homeless Indians, went looking for "park rangers," a pejorative term for Indians living in the town's parks. He found two Arapaho men, James "Sonny" Goggles and Stallone Trosper, sleeping in a detox center. He shot them in the head with a .40-caliber

[25] Alysa Landry, "Drunk Town, U.S.A.: The Ditch Patrol Trying to Save Drunks in Gallup, New Mexico," *Indian Country Today* (March 14, 1916).

[26] Ryan Boetel, "Teenage attacker to Homeless victim: 'Eat Mud,'" *Albuquerque Journal* (July 25, 2014).

[27] Stew Magnuson, *The Death of Raymond Yellow Thunder* (Lubbock, TX: Texas Tech University Press, 1998).

semiautomatic pistol. Border towns are dangerous places for Indians.[28]

The toll has been particularly high for Native women. Alcohol, drugs, and poverty make them vulnerable to kidnapping, rape, brutalization, and murder. Many just disappear into the murky world of sex trafficking, especially younger girls, who are thought to be 31% of the Native women who never return. Altogether, an estimated 60% of the thousands of Native women who have vanished are thought to have been murdered. This problem is especially true in cities such as Minneapolis that have large Native populations.

The Native women who have gone missing number in the thousands, but their remains are usually not recovered, nor are the perpetrators, an estimated 80% of whom are non-Native, caught. Sadly, but not shockingly, reports of missing Indian women are usually met with a shrug from authorities. Or they don't bother to identify their ethnicity and simply list them as "other." As a result, many are undercounted in databases, and the cases go unsolved. Why? Why not. After all, they're only Indians, and drunken ones at that. The stereotype of the drunken Indian has deprived Native people of their basic humanity and subjected them to just about every injustice one can name.

It's nothing new. The drunken Indian stereotype has always had tragic consequences for Native people. In 1897, on a farm in Winona, North Dakota, just north of Standing Rock, six members of the Thomas Spicer family, including twin infants, were brutally murdered and their bodies horribly mutilated—allegedly by five Indians. The whole sad affair supposedly began over alcohol. It was illegal to sell it to Indians, and authorities were evidently determined to wipe out the traffic. So, when two of the accused Indians approached a saloonkeeper in Winona for some liquor, he refused, but he told them there was liquor stashed at the Spicer farm. Whether it was to get the alcohol or to get money to buy liquor, the five supposedly went to the farm, where the murders took place.

Memories of Indian wars were still fresh in the minds of settlers west of

---

[28] Sarah Tory, "Fatal shooting in Wyoming raises questions about racism," *High Country Times* (August 11, 2015).

the Missouri River. After all, it had been only seven years since the Ghost Dance had terrified the Dakotas and ended with the massacre at Wounded Knee. It had been only a year since General "Black Jack" Pershing rounded up wandering Cree in neighboring Montana and deported them to Canada.[29] Once again, the countryside was alarmed, anti-Indian fervor was aroused, and the supposed perpetrators were arrested posthaste.

For its part, the press didn't waste any time making the connection between the viciousness of the murders and drunken Indians. *The New York Times* picked up the story and published it with a subheading that blared "Drunken Indians Supposed to Have Committed the Crime." As the story explained, "The murder was most brutal and it is believed that it was the work of drunken Indians several of whom have been skulking about."[30]

The *Jamestown (North Dakota) Weekly Alert* went even further. It pointed out that the "Standing Rock Indian reservation is not far away and when Indians get away and manage to get hold of some whiskey there is going to be trouble."[31] Obviously, Indians were not supposed to "get away." In fact, one man reported having seen a drunken Indian in the area. *The Bismarck Daily Tribune* confidently predicted that the murders were the "work of men crazed or brutalized by liquor," and then repeated the claim that a drunken Indian was seen in the vicinity of the crime.[32] In a letter to the Bismarck paper, H.M. Smee left no doubt that "whiskey was at the bottom of these awful crimes." White people were of course complicit since they sold the liquor to the "poor ignorant Indian" that resulted in an "occasional murder and again a pitiful massacre like that of the present." It was inevitable. "A drunken white man was bad enough, but a drunken Indian or a mixed-blood, with rare exception, was dangerous."[33]

[29] Larry Burt, "Nowhere Left to Go: Montana's Crees, Metis, and Chippewas and the Creation of Rocky Boy's Reservation," *Great Plains Quarterly* 7 (Summer, 1987), 202-3.

[30] "Family of Six Murdered: Drunken Indians Supposed to Have Committed the Crime," *The New York Times* (February 19, 1897).

[31] "Horrible Details," *Jamestown Weekly Alert* (February 25, 1897).

[32] "Horrible Details," *Bismarck Daily Tribune* (February 21, 1897).

[33] H.M. Smee, "Not one of our people," *Bismarck Daily Tribune* (February 21, 1897).

It wasn't just alcohol; White people assumed Indians were brutal by nature. *The Chicago Tribune* concluded the murders could only be the work of "insanity or savage ferocity," and the perpetrators "should be strung up immediately."[34] The Bismarck paper declared, "It is impossible to believe that such cruel and inhuman butchery of women and children could have been perpetrated by other than Indians."[35]

Again, the paper charged the mutilation of the victims at least "partially corroborated the suspicion of Indian murderers." The rumors that two of the women were raped also pointed to Indians—obviously White men would never commit such atrocities.[36] Innate Indian savagery, always lurking beneath the surface and unleashed by alcohol, was responsible for the brutality of the murders. Indians with "hideously painted faces" and "decked out in war paint," were seen "skulking" or "loitering" and just waiting to kill, rape, and mutilate.

Fortunately, as H.M. Smee continued in his letter to the Bismarck newspaper, "The Indian is getting off this earth as quickly as he can, cigarettes, pneumonia, and air-tight log houses are fast decreasing their ranks." Add whiskey to that list, which Smee warned should never have been sold to Indians, and you have the formula for the vanishing Indian. As far as the residents of the Dakotas were concerned, and probably most Americans at that time, it was none too soon.

The Indians suspected in the murders were presumed guilty before their trials began. Two of the younger Indians, one only 13 years old, confessed and fingered the others, although it's not clear they understood enough English to comprehend the charges. The two supposed ringleaders were tried immediately. Remarkably, the trial of one of the men ended in a hung jury, while the conviction of a second was overturned by a higher court. All five remained in jail. The two younger ones, who had confessed, were in the Williamsport town jail as they awaited trial, along with the one whose verdict had been overturned.

---

[34] "Indians Murder Family of Six," *The Chicago Daily Tribune* (February 19, 1897).

[35] "Foully Murdered," *Bismarck Daily Tribune* (February 19, 1897).

[36] "Horrible Murder," *Bismarck Daily Tribune* (February 20, 1897).

The other two were being held in Bismarck. They were the lucky ones. Locals in Williamsport were afraid the trials would end in acquittals, and besides, what more evidence was needed? The citizens decided to take matters into their own hands. A mob of 30 or 40 overpowered the jailer, dragged out the three Indian inmates, tortured them, and then hanged them. The other two were finally released, since the only evidence against them was the confession of two of the three who were hanged. Their stories died with them at the end of a rope, which leaves the question: Who killed the Spicers?

Other than the confessions, the evidence against the five was circumstantial. The doctors who examined the bodies concluded the murders were committed by one person. Today there would be an army of lawyers armed with DNA evidence, claiming the confessions were coerced, searches were unconstitutional, interpreters were incompetent, and the defendants were not informed of their rights. But it 1897, the Indians were guilty by stereotype.[37]

The Spicer murders, sensationalized across the country in lurid newspaper accounts, confirmed the popular image of the drunken, savage Indian who had no place in the modern world. As our friend Smee put it, "Poor lo is no saint. Neither is he useful or particularly ornamental, his one redeeming point—picturesqueness—departed with the buffalo." Smee was writing the Indians' obituary, which was not unreasonable in the 1890s, as the Native population was plummeting toward extinction. Like the buffalo, which were also facing extinction at that time, there was no room for Indians in an America that was hurtling headlong into the 20th century. Homesteaders, railroads, and miners were seeing to that.

There was a widely held belief that the Indian was hopeless; he was beyond redemption and could not be civilized or assimilated. The picturesque image of the noble savage, racing across the plains with headdresses flowing, died with the buffalo. Indians then descended into a world of poverty, disease, and alcohol misuse. Smee was not completely heartless. As the Indian exited the American stage, he believed Americans were obli-

[37] For a more through account of the Spicer family murders, see Peter G. Beidler, *Murdering Indians* (Jefferson, NC: McFarland and Co., 2013).

gated to "keep and treat him half way right anyhow," as long as they did not sneak off the reservation. I'm not sure most Americans would have agreed.

The belief that Indians were unfit for the modern world dates back to the previous century and was ingrained in European as well as American consciousness. Smee's use of "poor lo," commonly used by journalists at that time in reference to Indians, was borrowed from Alexander Pope's "An Essay on Man," written in 1732, which included, among other things, a stanza devoted to Native Americans. It begins, "Lo, the poor Indian! Whose untutored mind Sees God in clouds, or hears him in the wind His soul proud Science never taught to stray Far as the solar walk or milky way."[38]

The "poor Indian's" untutored mind and primitive, superstitious paganism had no place in the world of Newton, Galileo, or Copernicus, let alone America at the end of the 19th century. The well-known editor of the *New York Tribune,* Horace Greeley, invoked Pope's poem in a letter penned during a trip out West in the summer of 1859. He borrowed, "Lo! The Poor Indian!" directly from Pope and went on to describe the conditions he found among the Indians he encountered during his journey:

> But the Indians are children. Their arts, wars, treaties, alliances, habitations, crafts, properties, commerce, comforts, all belong to the very lowest and rudest ages of human existence. Some few of the chiefs have a narrow and short-sighted shrewdness, and very rarely in their history, a really great man, like Pontiac or Tecumseh has arisen among them, but that does not shake the general truth that they are utterly incompetent to cope with the European or Caucasian race. Any band of school boys, from ten to fifteen years of age, are quite as capable of ruling their appetites, devising and upholding a public policy, constituting and conducting a state or community as an average Indian tribe. And, unless they shall be treated as a truly Christian community would treat a band of orphan children providentially thrown on its hands, the aborigines of this country will be practically extinct within fifty years. [39]

[38] John Butt, ed., *The Poems of Alexander Pope* vol. 2 (New Haven, CT: Yale University Press, 1963), 508.

[39] Horace Greeley, "Lo! The Poor Indian" in *An Overland Journey from New York to San Francisco in the Summer of 1859* (New York: C.M. Saxton, Baker and Co., 1860).

The message is clear: Indians were doomed without the paternalism of White America. Perhaps it wouldn't have rescued them anyway, given the fact they were not "capable of ruling their appetites." Journalists and other writers turned Pope's phrase around and used "poor lo" as code for the Indians' innate inferiority and inability to adapt. The belief that Indians were "utterly incompetent to cope with the European or Caucasian race" provided a convenient excuse for their extinction and relieved White America of any responsibility for their demise. Likewise, it provided a logical explanation for the social pathologies still plaguing Native communities, including and especially their appetite for alcohol.

Paraphrasing an Indian saying, they drink because they are neither wolf nor dog, trapped between two worlds, one vanishing and the other out of reach. Their inability or unwillingness to adjust or adapt to the modern world is a tragic flaw that doomed them to lives of poverty, despair, and desperation. At the same time, it gave rise to a culture of drinking characterized by binge drinking that begins at an early age and has deadly consequences, like the accident I witnessed on Rosebud. Miraculously, many Native people have survived, but the image of the drunken, savage, and wanton Indian remains, coloring the way they are profiled by government agencies, law enforcement, and the judicial system.

Alcoholism and alcohol abuse among Native people have often been attributed to the firewater myth, which purports that Indians are more sensitive to the effects of alcohol than White people, more commonly phrased as, "They can't hold their liquor." That's supposedly because they metabolize alcohol more slowly than White people, and therefore, the effects are stronger and last longer. Others have theorized that Indians' drinking is not some pathological defect, but rather, a rational or understandable response to the historical trauma they have experienced. Indian drinking habits, like so much of Native behavior, only seem pathological when measured against some arbitrary, usually White middle-class norm. Today, in this age of blaming everything on DNA, the firewater myth has been displaced by the supposition that they are genetically predisposed to alcohol abuse and alcoholism, although no genetic link has been found. Whether it's their moral or character weaknesses, a physiological condition, or an inherited predisposition to addiction, all these theories tend to pathologize Indian alcoholism and reinforce the historical belief in their innate and unalterable inferiority. It's no different than characterizing them as irredeemable savages. It's in their genes.[40]

And yet, geneticists have now discovered that the genetic code with which all of us are born is not static or unalterable, but can be modified by environmental factors through the process of epigenesis, which literally means "above or added onto one's genetic inheritance." The idea stems from the Hunger Winter in Holland in 1944 to 1945, when the Germans deliberately starved the Dutch in the section of the country they still controlled. Thousands died. Years later, it was discovered that babies in utero during that grim winter suffered higher rates of physical and mental illnesses than babies born before or after.

The epigenetic changes to our genes can be caused by environmental factors ranging from exposure to toxic chemicals to how much or what one eats to traumatic experiences like war, famine, genocide, and epidemics. Those experiences can leave marks or scars in the form of molecular attachments grafted onto genes without changing the underlying DNA. As a result, the genes begin to function differently. The modifications can then be transferred to the next generation and to subsequent generations as well, producing psychological and behavioral tendencies or predispositions often associated with trauma victims. As one writer put it, "You might have inherited not only your grandmother's knobby knees, but also her predisposition toward depression caused by the neglect she suffered as a new born."[41]

Epigenesis offers an explanation for how environmental factors can permanently change the way genes affect behavior and provides a mechanism for the transmission of historical trauma across generations. For ex-

[40] Roxanne Dunbar-Ortiz, Dina Gilio-Whitaker, "What's Behind the Myth of Native American Alcoholism," *Pacific Standard* (October 10, 2016); Maia Szalavitz, "No, Native Americans Aren't Genetically More Susceptible to Alcoholism," *The Verge* (October 2, 2015); Tanya Lee, "Study Says the 'Drunken Indian' Is A Myth," *Indian Country Today* (February 24, 2016).

[41] Dan Hurley, "Grandma's Experiences Leave a Mark on Your Genes," *Discover* (June 24, 2015).

ample, the children of Holocaust survivors are more likely to suffer from post-traumatic stress disorder. These experiences need not be as severe as war, famine, the Holocaust, or other instances of genocide like the Cultural Revolution in China or massacres in Africa. Neglect, physical or sexual abuse, alcohol or drug abuse by parents, and even violence or malnutrition from gestation to adulthood can leave scars or residue that can be passed to future generations.

In other words, your genetic inheritance can determine your physical characteristics and can be modified to affect your psychological and behavioral tendencies also. For Native people, these epigenetic changes can be inherited and switched on simply by the trauma of reservation life or the toxic stress of being an Indian in America. Once triggered or turned on, they can produce affective disorders such as schizophrenia, antisocial disorders such as risky, disruptive, or violent behavior, and even physical disorders such as obesity and hypertension.

For our purposes, it means self-destructive behaviors such as alcohol and drug abuse among Native populations can be viewed and treated as echoes of the traumatic events Indians have suffered over the past 500 years. Their effects can be "turned off" with proper treatment, but treatment is generally not forthcoming for Indians.

Even the most well-intended theories of Indians' alcohol consumption overlook the context in which their drinking occurs. They homogenize Indians and boil them down to statistics, robbing them of their individual identities and even their humanity. I've been to hundreds of Alcoholics Anonymous meetings and have heard heartbreaking stories of average Americans from all backgrounds and walks of life who have lost jobs, houses, relationships, and families. I've listened to accounts of the broken homes, physical and sexual abuse, mental illness, and PTSD at the root of their alcoholism. Many speak of being jailed for DWIs, vehicular manslaughter, and murder.

Each and every person who makes it to AA has a story of pain and suffering, and Indians are no different. They have individual and collective stories or histories that, in the context of epigenesis, help to explain the psychological and behavioral wreckage found among the Native population. Memories of the darkest moments of our past are not forgotten; they are imprinted on our genes and can reverberate across generations.

Uncle Tony's story began in the jungle of Guadalcanal. Perhaps even before that. Today he would have been diagnosed with PTSD like Ira Hayes, the Pima Indian who helped raise the flag on Iwo Jima and may have been the first diagnosed case of the disorder. One Indian, one White man; both became alcoholics, with Hayes dying of exposure and alcohol poisoning in 1955, and Uncle Tony passing away in the middle of the street clutching a beer bottle.

PTSD-related substance use disorder is common on reservations, whether from military service or more generally what are called adverse childhood experiences, such as violence, discrimination, homelessness, dysfunctional families broken by poverty, or the loss of parents though death or incarceration. Or it could be the cumulative effects of intergenerational or historical trauma brought on by centuries of suppression and oppression.

Whatever the causes of alcohol and drug abuse among Indians, there are individual and collective stories behind the so-called Popsicles found in ditches in Gallup, the kids who died in the accident on Rosebud, the incarcerated Indians, and the Native women raped, brutalized, and murdered. Unfortunately, their stories have been shrouded by the stereotype of the drunken Indian unable to control his appetite for liquor, a misconception that still dominates the popular imagination.

As I watched George Floyd dying and pleading for his "Mama," I remembered something Kweisi Mfume, a member of the House of Representatives and the former president of the NAACP, said during a speech at my college. He was talking about the inordinate number of young Black men languishing in jails during the crack cocaine epidemic. Whatever you think of them, he offered, they all have names, stories, histories, and most importantly, mothers; it's their common humanity.

Contrast the stereotype of the drunken Indian with the call to arms raised by the opioid epidemic. Although the scourge has affected Indians and other minorities, 80% of those who have become addicted and over-dosed have been Whites. The epidemic has been fueled by unscrupulous doctors and pharmacists, not to mention drug companies that have preyed on undereducated White people from isolated rural counties hollowed out by globalization, and with high levels of poverty and few job opportunities.

The news was full of stories about "White ghettoes," towns like Beat-tyville, Kentucky, dubbed the poorest White town in America. In the 1960s, it was the centerpiece of President Lyndon Johnson's War on Poverty. In fact, Johnson traveled there in 1964. Since then, tucked away in the hills of eastern Kentucky, it was all but forgotten and abandoned until it became a poster child for the war on opioids, its dwindling population suffering "deaths of despair" from "hillbilly heroin."[42]

The opioid epidemic shed light on the plight of Beattyville and oth-er towns of Appalachia and rural America. As the epidemic spread and threatened White middle-class America, it became a public health emer-gency, and the government threw money at it for treatment and prevention programs. Drug companies were sued and had to pay billions of dollars in settlements. However, that did little for the residents of Blackwater, Arizo-na, on the Pima Reservation, which is the poorest town in America with a population over 1,000, and Allen, South Dakota, on Pine Ridge, which is hands down the nation's poorest town of any size.

It would have been to fun watch White Americans trip over themselves to expose the suffering of rural White America if it weren't for the fact they continue to ignore the demise of rural Native Americans, whose death rate from opioid overdoses is greater than that of rural White people. Except for race, the demographics of the opioid epidemic would fit any reservation. Indians are largely poor, isolated, undereducated, and underemployed. Yet, there has never been any empathy for Indians, whose only access to treat-ment is jail. Indians do not have recourse to rehabs or to the psychotropic drugs that at least one out of every six Americans—mostly White people—use, often on a long-term basis.

---

[42] Chris McGreal, "America's poorest white town: abandoned by coal, swallowed by drugs," *The Guardian* (November 12, 2015).

Benzodiazepines or benzos like Valium and Xanax are the most commonly prescribed drugs in America. They are used to combat various psychiatric disorders, including alcohol addiction and withdrawal, even though they also are addictive and can lead to overdoses and death. This is especially true if they are used in combination with opioids, another class of commonly prescribed drugs. Without treatment, Indians are left to medicate themselves with a 40-ounce bottle of malt liquor, itself a powerful drug. As an Indian once told me, White privilege allows for a broader range of acceptable behavior.

The saddest part of this is many Indians have come to believe their addiction to alcohol and drugs is their own fault; they all too often succumb to self-hatred, and simply give up and live down to expectations. The damage alcohol and drugs have done to the Native community has been compounded by the fact that White people have used that stereotype to blame them for their suffering.

A White woman on Rosebud once told me the Indians protesting the sale of liquor in Whiteclay, Nebraska, have only themselves to blame. If they're poor, unemployed, or homeless, or they are victims of crime or violence, or dying untimely deaths, it's their own damn fault. In turn, it has given White people an excuse to ridicule, cheat, rob, beat, and as we shall see, even murder Indians. It has allowed government authorities to arrest and incarcerate Indians in disproportionate numbers, take children away from their families, renege on treaty obligations, and neglect their welfare.

Stereotypes like those of Hemingway's drunken Indians are not harmless fiction; they have real-life consequences. And yet, there is another side to the question of epigenetic inheritance. The same genetic changes that may have forced Native people to relive historical trauma may have endowed them with the resilience they have shown in the face of centuries of efforts to eradicate them. Perhaps the lessons of the past have been imprinted on their DNA, allowing them to survive and come back from the brink of extinction. They may also have equipped them with the strength to resist the enticements of assimilation and remain Indians despite the costs.

Poor lo indeed.

Killing Members of the Group

By all accounts, there should be no Indians left in America, and that very nearly happened. The lethal cocktail of warfare, slavery, famine, and disease that was unleashed on the Indigenous people of North America reduced the United States' Indian population from an estimated 15 million at contact to 237,000 in 1900. Those who managed to survive were warehoused on reservations or on what the Lakota holy man Black Elk called "islands."

They were concentrated on largely unproductive lands in isolated rural areas west of the Mississippi River, where discrimination, neglect, and destructive government policies continued to take their toll long after the Indian wars concluded. Certainly most 19th century Americans shared H.M. Smee's belief that Indians were on the verge of vanishing, although some Americans were probably willing to concede along with Smee that Native people deserved some sort of palliative care, not unlike hospice patients. That any survived at all is a testament to their unyielding and fierce resistance to the nearly 500 years of slavery, epidemics, removal, allotment, boarding schools, relocation, termination, and outright genocide.

They fooled them all by surviving. To add insult to injury, they remain a troubling and embarrassing reminder of the treatment of Indians at the hands of America and Americans. Perhaps that's why Americans remain unwilling to admit that a crime inextricably tied to the horrors of the Holocaust ever took place in the United States.

Few question that the Indigenous people of the Western Hemisphere were treated horribly by European colonial powers and then by Americans. They might also agree with estimates that 90 to 95% of the Native population was lost after the European invasion. However, they disagree

70

on whether that population loss amounted to genocide, a term that is controversial and hotly contested by those who insist Americans could never have committed anything close to the monstrous acts associated with the Third Reich and other totalitarian regimes.

The word itself is a combination of "genos," meaning species, and "cide," meaning murder. It was coined by Raphael Lemkin, a Polish Jew who escaped to Stockholm after the invasion of Poland by Germany and Russia in 1939. While he escaped the horrors that followed, his family didn't; all except a brother perished in Nazi concentration camps. As a result, Lemkin devoted his life to writing about and campaigning against genocide. Some people were willing to listen. His work was recognized and rewarded in 1948 by the United Nations with the Convention on the Prevention and Punishment of the Crime of Genocide.

Genocide is perhaps the most hideous of crimes. Genocidal acts have been committed throughout history, from Rome's razing of Carthage in 149 B.C. to the Armenian genocide in 1915 to the more recent genocides in Bosnia, Rwanda, and Syria. Nevertheless, genocide almost always calls to mind first the shocking atrocities of Nazi Germany that were accomplished systematically and with staggering savagery and scope. In the popular mind, the word genocide tends to be equated with mass murder and the Holocaust. As a result, that historic event is the yardstick against which all alleged genocides are measured. Anything short of the Nazis' extermination of millions of European Jews, Roma, homosexuals, Jehovah's Witnesses, and other civilians cannot be genocide.

For some, it is the only genocide; all others pale by comparison. That's why the term "Holocaust" is used only in connection with the atrocities of the Third Reich and not any other genocides. And because the Holocaust was orchestrated and carried out with lightning speed and efficiency, it is also assumed any genocide would need to be coordinated by some centralized authority with the expressed intent to exterminate a population. However, a closer examination of the United Nations statute suggests a much broader definition of genocide than murder on an industrial scale.

Article 2 of the United Nations Convention defines genocide as "acts committed with intent to destroy, in whole or in part, a national, ethnical, racial or religious group ...." As might be expected, the first crime listed under that definition is "killing members of the group." However, the next four crimes substantially expand the definition to include "causing serious bodily or mental harm to members of the group, deliberately inflicting on the group conditions of life calculated to bring about its physical destruction in whole or in part, imposing measures to prevent births within the group, and forcibly transferring children of the group to another group."

In other words, murder is not a necessary condition of genocide. Genocidal acts can include anything that contributes to the extermination or extinguishing of a group. Consequently, it need not be immediate; it can be carried out over time. For example, kidnapping and enslaving members of groups would necessarily inflict physical and mental hardships on them, while depriving them of food, shelter, clothing, and health care would create conditions such as leaving them susceptible to diseases that could bring about their physical destruction "in whole or in part."

This was certainly true in the Nazi concentration camps. Many of them predated the extermination camps of Hitler's Final Solution, which was not set in motion until January 1942. Prior to that, and as early as 1933, Hitler sent millions of "undesirables"—Jews, Poles, Communists, Roma, Serbs, POWs—to thousands of concentration camps around Germany and throughout occupied Europe. Once there, they died by the millions from disease, starvation, exposure, and mistreatment. In effect, the Holocaust began before extermination camps such as Sobribor, Treblinka, Belzec, Auschwitz-Birkenau and Majdenak—with their notorious gas chambers and ovens—were put into operation.

Often overlooked are the last two crimes listed in Article 2: preventing births and transferring children from one group to another. Neither directly involves mass murder, but forced sterilizations, abortions, and adoptions can eventually extinguish a people. In fact, Lemkin offered a much broader and less legalistic and literal interpretation of genocide that did not require immediate or mass killings. According to him, genocide occurs when there is a "coordinated plan of different actions aimed at the destruction of the essential foundation of the life of national groups, with the aim of annihilating the groups themselves. The objectives of such a plan would be the disintegration of the political and social institutions of culture, language, national feelings, religion, and the economic existence of national groups, and the personal security, liberty, health, dignity, and even the lives of the individuals belonging to the group."[43]

Following Lemkin's definition, "annihilating a group" involves the "destruction of the essential foundation of life" necessary for its survival. In other words, you don't have to murder group members outright; simply attack the cultural, social, political, economic, and religious constructs that bind them together and allow them to do collectively what they can't accomplish as individuals. These constructs express themselves as customs, traditions, values, morals, norms, and beliefs that are passed down from generation to generation, provide groups with their distinctive identities, and determine their collective behavior in the face of a changing or threatening environment.

Take away any of those basic constructs, and the ties that bind groups together begin to unravel. They are left, in Lemkin's words, "permanently crippled" and unable to provide food, shelter or protection to their members. In turn, it leaves them vulnerable to violence, starvation and disease, and the consequent loss of population and eventual extinction. According to Lemkin, such acts would be genocidal, even though they would necessarily occur in different places and over extended periods of time. As he wrote in 1951, "From the point of view of genocide or the destruction of a human group, there is little difference between direct killings and such techniques which, like a time bomb, destroy by delayed action."[44]

There is another point about the U.N. resolution that gets lost in the fixation with genocide as mass murder. Article 3 states that besides genocide itself, the conspiracy to commit genocide, direct and public incitements to commit genocide, the attempt to commit genocide, and complicity in

---

[43] Raphael Lemkin, *Axis Rule in Occupied Europe,* 79.

[44] David B. MacDonald, "Genocide in the Indian Residential Schools," in *Colonial Genocide in Indigenous North America,* Andrew Woolford, Jeff Benvenuto, and Alexander Laban Hinton, eds. (Durham, NC: Duke University Press, 2014), 309.

genocide are punishable crimes. Simply put, one need not commit geno-cide to be guilty of it. Contributing to it directly or indirectly is enough.

The convention further specifies that "persons committing genocide or any of the other acts enumerated in Article 3 shall be punished, whether they are constitutionally responsible rulers, public officials or private indi-viduals." That private individuals could be charged with genocide means that even those supposedly innocent bystanders who were aware of the genocide, accepted it as the natural course of things, did nothing to stop it, or supported, advocated, or incited actions against groups that resulted in genocide are guilty of the crime of complicity in genocide.

To that point, consider the lesson that if nine Germans are seated at a ta-ble with one Nazi, and none of the nine says anything, there are 10 Nazis at the table. In other words, turning a blind eye to genocide makes one guilty of genocide. To my mind, complicity in genocide requires one merely to lack empathy and compassion for its victims.

Lemkin made one more point that is especially relevant for our purpos-es. As he wrote in *Axis Rule in Occupied Europe,* genocide has two phases: "one, the destruction of the national pattern of the oppressed group, the other, the imposition of the pattern of the oppressor. The imposition, in turn, may be made upon the oppressed population which is allowed to remain, or upon the territory alone after the removal of the population and the colonization of the area by the oppressors' own nationals."[45]

First, Lemkin assumed genocide can involve "colonization" through acts such as the removal of a population from its territory. Second, it doesn't require the physical destruction of the "oppressed" people, only the de-struction of their "national pattern" or the culture of the group, and its replacement with the culture of the colonizer. From the vantage point of 1944, Lemkin knew what he was talking about. The Nazis removed one way or another Poles, Czechs, Russians, Ukrainians, and other Indigenous people in Eastern Europe in order to acquire *Lebensraum*—living space for German colonists. In Poland, they even destroyed cemeteries, as if to erase any evidence that Polish people ever existed. Under this definition, geno-

[45] Lemkin, *Axis Rule in Occupied Europe,* 79.

cide surely has accompanied the conquest and colonization of Indigenous people around the world and for all time.

Based on the provisions of the U.N. resolution and Lemkin's expansive interpretation of the atrocities he identified and named, one can make a compelling argument that what happened to the Indigenous people of the Americas was indeed genocide. Moreover, it took place over the course of 500 years, and much like Lemkin's "time bomb," by "delayed action." However, there is one sticking point.

As mentioned earlier, Lemkin argued that whatever form genocide takes, it requires a "coordinated plan" of annihilation. That, in turn, would suggest the need for a centralized agency to organize and direct any plan of extermination. Surely there is no better example of this than the German SS under Heinrich Himmler.

In America, there never was an explicitly stated and organized plan of extermination coordinated by a centralized authority, a reality that has played into the hands of genocide deniers. They argue there was no plan or order given, and therefore, no intent to exterminate the Native population. Instead, virgin-soil epidemics—diseases for which a community has had no exposure and thus, no immunity—decimated the Indigenous population.

The question of genocide in the United States is an open wound. To admit that a campaign of genocide was carried out against the Native population cuts to the heart of the popular belief that America and Americans are not merely unique or different, but truly exceptional and better than everyone else. Add 400 years of African slavery to the mix, and the United States is suddenly hard-pressed to make a case for being the shining city on a hill.

American exceptionalism is firmly rooted in the nation's identity, flowing from its emergence after the Revolution as the first new nation, separate, distinct, and morally superior to the countries of the Old World. The new nation was destined to spread its values of freedom, equality, and democracy around the world. In fact, Manifest Destiny, a belief popularized in the 1840s, stated Americans were ordained by God to occupy and populate the entire continent and shine the light of White Anglo-Saxon and Protestant values and virtues into the darkest corners of the world.

That America might have violated its sacred principles and done so in its own backyard would taint the righteousness of its anointed mission, poking holes in a narrative too big to fail. The belief in American exceptionalism is built on either the outright denial of genocide or a myriad of excuses to limit the nation's liability for the atrocities visited upon the Indians. In light of talk about paying reparations to African Americans for slavery, admitting the possibility that genocide was waged against Indians might force the government to compensate them as well, as it has Japanese Americans interned during World War II.

Whether what happened to the Native people of the Americas rises to the level of genocide, crimes against humanity, war crimes, or just plain murder, it is important to note that it took 40 years for the United States to finally ratify the United Nations Convention. As Lawrence J. LeBlanc has shown in his book *The United States and the Genocide Convention,* much of the opposition grew out of fears that it would be used by Indians to charge the American government with genocide and all that would imply.[46]

It's no coincidence, therefore, that when crimes against humanity were codified in the Rome Statute of the International Crime Court in 2002, the United States refused to become a party to it. In both cases, the country didn't want to surrender its sovereignty to foreign bodies, which is more than a tad ironic, since for centuries it has been trying to get Indians to give up their sovereignty. However, beneath those rationalizations was the fear that having to admit to genocide or crimes against humanity would undermine the moral authority the United States derived from its exceptional and largely romanticized history, not to mention the values that have been honored largely in the breach. In other words, it would reveal something deeper and darker in the American soul; an underbelly precious few want to see.

Genocide deniers have offered alternative theories about the near exter-

---

[46] Laurence LeBlanc, *The United States and the Genocide Convention* (Durham, NC: Duke University Press, 1991).

mination of the Indians. Probably the most ludicrous argument was one promoted by radio-talk-show host Rush Limbaugh, who argued that Indians killed more White people than the other way around by introducing them to tobacco. By his accounting, the millions of Americans who have died from lung cancer, COPD, and other tobacco-related diseases far outnumber what he considered to be the relative handful of Indians killed by people of European descent.

Add to that the supposed infection of Europeans with syphilis and smallpox, and the annihilation of Indians seems like chump change by comparison. By these lights, the fact that the number of Indians in the United States dwindled to less than 250,000 by the end of the 19th century doesn't look so bad. And since there are more Indians alive today than at the time of Columbus, as Limbaugh alleged, Indigenous people should be grateful. Already out on a limb, he went even further and insisted that Indians owe Americans reparations since "they all have casinos," and the government protected the Indians and provided them with their own land, housing, food, education, and health care. The Indians shouldn't complain; after all, some of them survived.[47]

Limbaugh and other deniers likely would have agreed with John Wayne that Indians had no greater claim to the land than European settlers. The land was an empty wilderness that, along with its inhabitants, needed to be tamed. Would that the Indians had cooperated; so many unpleasantries could have been avoided.

Limbaugh hardly broke new ground with his argument; he was merely mouthing what Americans have long believed. We have never recognized the rights of Native Americans to the land that was empty, virgin, and wild until White people discovered, tamed, peopled, and improved the New World, as is so often mistakenly assumed. Besides, there weren't many Indians in the first place, and they were relatively recent arrivals at that. It was all part of the natural and inexorable process by which inferior people are replaced by superior ones.

---

[47] "Limbaugh on 'holocaust' of 'Indians': 'They have all the casinos—what's to complain about?,'" *The Rush Limbaugh Show,* on Premier Radio Networks, September 25, 2009.

The popular belief that Indians didn't own or deserve the land they inhabited for millennia was first confirmed by the Doctrine of Discovery. Enunciated by Pope Nicholas V in 1453 and affirmed in 1494, it granted possession of the lands and the people on them to the discovering nation. It was adopted by European nations, including England, and it was embraced by U.S. government officials, from Chief Justice Marshall, who ruled that discovery "gave exclusive rights to those who made it," to President Donald Trump, who proclaimed, "Our ancestors tamed a continent," and "We are not going to apologize for it." Or Speaker of the House of Representatives Nancy Pelosi, who said that the land was "God's gift to us," not unlike our Pilgrim and Puritan forefathers, who believed that the land was God's providence.

The assumption that the Americas, and especially North America, were populated by a handful of nomadic interlopers who had no real claim to the land has also received scientific support. At the beginning of the 20th century, the scientific establishment steadfastly held that the first migrations to North America could not possibly have occurred before the end of the last Ice Age, around 10,000 years ago. Before that, their way was blocked by the two massive glaciers that covered the northern half of the continent.

However, the discovery in 1932 of projectile points buried with mammoth bones near Clovis, New Mexico, were estimated to be about 11,500 years old. This upset the prevailing orthodoxy and required a new theory. As the glaciers ebbed, an ice-free corridor running from Alaska though western Canada opened up, creating a pathway south for migrations from Asia across the land bridge, better known as Beringia, that linked the two continents. It was then, and only then, that the migrations from Asia could have occurred. Eventually, the melting glaciers would raise the sea levels, which had dropped nearly 300 feet during the glacial epoch, covering the land bridge and cutting off further migrations.

The happy coincidence of archeological, anthropological, and geological evidence gave rise by the 1960s to a new orthodoxy known as Clovis First, which held that the makers of those stone points found in New Mexico were absolutely the first humans in the Americas. As Clovis points were uncovered throughout North America, Clovis First became a new orthodoxy. But by shattering the older belief, it encouraged its own undoing, as researchers sought evidence of older human habitation in the New World.

Field work by James Adovasio at the Meadowcroft Rockshelter near Pittsburgh, Pennsylvania; Tom Dillehay at Monte Verde in Chile; and many others throughout North and South America has pegged the date of human habitation as far back as 23,000 years ago. Based on archaeological evidence, these early dates have been pushed back even further by studies of Indigenous DNA that suggest the migrations from Asia took place anywhere from 29,000 to 43,000 years ago.

If true, the belief raises other questions. If the last glacial epoch reached its maximum around 26,000 years ago, blocking any route south from Berengia until 12,000 years before present, how did the migrants move south? The answer is both obvious and contentious, like so many other theories about the peopling of the Americas. Either they walked along the narrow strip of land along the coast that was exposed by falling sea levels, or they used boats of some kind.

The first possibility has been supported by discoveries of inhabited sites at Cooper's Ferry in western Idaho, dating to 16,000 years before present, and along the coast of British Columbia, dating to at least 14,000 years ago. The second possibility is supported by the example of the Aboriginal people of Australia, who arrived on that continent as early as 50,000 years ago, presumably by island-hopping along the coasts of modern-day Malaysia, Indonesia, and New Guinea.

The Clovis Firsters did not give up without a struggle. Professional meetings, where the new findings were presented, purportedly broke into fist fights. I'd have paid to see that. As James Adovasio explained to one of my classes, Clovis First had such a stranglehold on archaeologists that they simply stopped digging when they reached the earliest limits of the Clovis culture, which were estimated to be about 11,000 years old. He didn't, and the work at Meadowcroft has found evidence of humans living at the site as early as 19,000 years ago. The moral of the story is you can't find something if you don't look for it. Researchers today are searching for the earliest evidence of human habitation all over North and South America.

All of this may seem academic, but it had two significant consequences. First, it means Indians were not recent arrivals; mere interlopers, as it were. Their ancestors were in the Americas long before the predecessors of modern Europeans arrived in those countries. Northern Europe was uninhabited 12,000 years ago, and the immediate ancestors of today's English population did not arrive there until 4,000 B.C. The Indians had a better claim to their lands than most Europeans had to theirs. Second, the longer the Indigenous people have been in the Americas, the longer they had to do what humans do best: reproduce—well, besides killing each other. If so, then their numbers, and by extension their losses, may have been far greater than previously assumed.

As recently as the 1950s, the total precolonial population of the two continents was estimated at 8 million, including those in the Arctic all the way down to the southern tip of South America, with only 1 million above the Rio Grande. Although earlier estimates were as high as 40 million, the lower numbers held sway from the 1930s until it became clear that Native people had arrived much earlier than 10,000 years ago. Today, the estimates range from 60 million to 140 million overall, with 8 million to 18 million north of Mexico. I usually split the difference and suggest there were around 100 million in the Americas, with about 12 million to 15 million in North America. The numbers, along with the assumptions, methods and evidence used to support them, are controversial, if not a bit shaky. Nevertheless, they clearly demonstrate the Indians were in the Americas longer than assumed, there were very many of them, and they had a long history that included the rise and fall of civilizations and empires that rivaled any of the pre-Columbian world.

Unfortunately, much of that history has either been lost to the unrelenting forces of colonization, rewritten by the colonizers, or ploughed under, paved over, or simply reclaimed by nature. Limbaugh was not alone in downplaying the effects of colonization on the Native population. When the Colorado state legislature introduced a resolution recognizing and condemning the genocide of Native Americans, following a similar resolution condemning the genocide of Jewish, Armenian, and Sudanese people, the legislators changed "genocide" to "atrocities," since, as one legislator argued, some Indians weren't exterminated. Another senator, while admitting "many wrongs" were inflicted on Indians, noted there were also "many blessings."[48] After all, the government introduced them to the benefits of modern civilization.

On the other hand, there have been more thoughtful arguments against American genocide, such as the one presented by Guenter Lewey, an Austrian-born political scientist who escaped the horrors of the Holocaust by moving to Palestine and then emigrating from there to the United States. To Lewey, as to others, the term genocide can only be applied to atrocities of the same magnitude as the Holocaust; all others, including what happened in North America, don't measure up. Lewey's argument rests on the premise that the first colonists were peaceful settlers who looked at the Indians as friends and converts. After all, the Pilgrims invited the Native people to Thanksgiving dinner.

According to Lewey, hostilities began shortly thereafter when offers to Christianize and assimilate the Native people were rebuffed. The colonists found it necessary to defend themselves against the stereotypical behavior of Indian treachery and ruthlessness that included killing, kidnapping, torturing, raping, scalping and even cannibalizing innocent, peaceful colonists. Therefore, whatever atrocities the Pilgrims and their Puritan brothers committed, like burning a Pequot village and watching the Indians melt into human tallow in 1637, were done out of self-defense and were accepted weapons of war at a time when there was "little concern for humane standards of warfare."

While deniers admit settlers and the military committed atrocities over the course of three centuries of warfare, it was almost always out of self-defense, or revenge or retaliation for the brutality of the savages. Lewey dismissed out of hand the allegation that Americans practiced biological warfare by giving Indians blankets infected with smallpox. If the colo-

---

[48] Carol Berry, "When Genocide Lost a Debate," in *Indian Country Today* (April 22, 2012).

nists practiced torture, scalping, and burning of villages, their actions were learned from the Native people and justified by Indian cruelties. After all, the Indigenous people started it.

Lewey used the same argument to explain away some of the most infamous massacres of Indians, the very ones that are often cited as evidence of genocide, from the earliest conflicts in New England and Virginia to Wounded Knee on the Pine Ridge Reservation in South Dakota in 1890. In every case, the supposed massacres could be justified as retaliation for Indian attacks against colonial settlements and the atrocities perpetrated against the settlers. Whenever settlers, local militia, and the U.S. Army retaliated in kind, killing, scalping, and enslaving Indians—including women and children—and destroying their villages and food supplies, their actions were just and necessary. They were merely acting out of self-defense and an understandable desire for revenge.

In addition, he maintained these actions have to be understood in the context of the normal course of warfare at the time. According to Lewey, Indians on the warpath who refused to surrender were legitimate military targets, and the killing of noncombatants—a euphemism for women, children, and elderly—was unfortunate, regrettable, and even tragic, but understandable under the circumstances. Even the destruction of Indian villages and supplies that left Native people exposed to the elements was in keeping with the standards of warfare at the time.

Witness General William T. Sherman's March to the Sea during the Civil War. The deaths of noncombatants were incidental, accidental, and neither intentional nor purposeful. And they certainly did not amount to genocide, since, as Lewey insisted, no order was ever given to exterminate Indians beyond the populist rhetoric of politicians and newspaper editors, and the loose talk of military leaders like General Philip Sheridan. In charge of Indian wars west of the Missouri River, he infamously said, "The only good Indian is a dead Indian." Lewey contended that neither Sheridan nor any other officer issued orders to exterminate the Indians, which meant that there was not a "coordinated plan of annihilation" as Lemkin required, and therefore, no intent to exterminate the Indians. No intent; no genocide.

And yet, there were protests against the mistreatment of the Indians. Probably the most notable was that of Helen Hunt Jackson, who exposed the horrors inflicted on Native people in the nation's first century in her 1881 book, *A Century of Dishonor*. Lewey summarily dismissed her claims. He considered Jackson and other friends of the Indians softhearted Eastern sentimentalists far removed from the realities of frontier life.

To Western homesteaders, ranchers, and miners, the memories of Indian brutalities were fresh, and the threats of new attacks seemed real and immediate. They called for action, and they were willing to take matters into their own hands, as they did in retaliation for the Spicer murders in North Dakota. Lewey argued the Indians brought the tragedy of their near demise on themselves, by their actions and their refusal to assimilate.

To put it more bluntly, "The Indians were not prepared to give up the nomadic life of the hunter for the sedentary life of the farmer. The new Americans, convinced of their cultural and racial superiority, were unwilling to grant the original inhabitants of the continent the vast preserve of land required by the Indians' way of life." The Indians were an obstacle or impediment to progress that had to be removed either by force or assimilation, the latter of which would have required them to adopt White peoples' language, religion, values, and ways of life.[49]

As mentioned earlier, Lewey and other genocide deniers insist the label genocide should only be applied to the most egregious examples of mass murder, as in the cases of the Jews and other groups in Nazi Germany, the Armenians in Turkey, and the Tutsi, Hutu, and Twa in Rwanda. What happened in America was simply a collision between a superior and more advanced culture, and an inferior and primitive one that was unable or unwilling to evolve, and with quite predictable results. To most 19th century Americans, it was the natural course of things, a belief supported by the popularization of Social Darwinism and captured in James Earle Fraser's sculpture *End of the Trail*, which has come to symbolize the demise and disappearance of the Indians.

Moreover, as I've heard so many times, the government offered Indig-

---

[49] Guenter Lewey, "Were American Indians the Victims of Genocide?," *Commentary* (2004).

enous people so-called humane alternatives to extermination, such as removal to reservations to protect them against almost certain annihilation by settlers. Besides land, the government provided them with farm supplies, schools, health care, housing, clothing, and food. The Fort Laramie Treaty of 1868 even offered them small cash annuities if they behaved; $20 a head to those who took up the plow but only $10 dollars to those who continued to hunt. The government also dispatched missionaries to convert them to Christianity.

It's all there in the terms of 370 or so treaties, which admittedly appear generous on the surface. The resulting reservations were to serve as sanctuaries from the predations of land-hungry settlers, and they were designed to save the Indians from themselves as well. Too much land would allow them to continue to follow their nomadic ways rather than settling down and becoming farmers and American citizens. Not only were Americans merciful, they were magnanimous. Had it not been for them, the Indians would never have escaped extinction. If only the Native people had been willing to abandon their primitive ways, the outcome would have been better still. It was sad and tragic, but without an official national policy of extermination, it was not genocide.

However, if it wasn't genocide that reduced the Native population to near extinction levels by 1900, what caused it? The quick and simple answer, and the one that absolves Americans of any guilt in the matter, is that virgin-field epidemics tore through Indigenous populations across the Americas. Lacking immunity to European diseases, 90 to 95% of the Indians were wiped out. The main culprit was smallpox, but there were a number of other diseases, including measles, influenza, bubonic plague, diphtheria, typhus, typhoid, malaria, and more.

The idea that disease killed off most of the Native population was repeated so often, it became accepted as fact. Statistics, like the ones cited above, found their way into textbooks. They've also been mustered to counter accusations of genocide and justify the taking of lands emptied by epidemics. The theory of disease—not Europeans—being the bane of Indians' existence has even been used to defend Columbus Day as a national holiday.

I can't tell you how many times I've been told no matter how heinous the acts of Columbus and his men, microbes—not bullets—killed off *los indios*.

Recent studies show that diseases alone were not and could not have been responsible for that many deaths. To be sure, European diseases undoubtedly took a terrible toll on the Native population of North America. The same is true for Latin America and the White population in North America during the continentwide smallpox epidemic of the 1770s. That said, contact with European diseases did not necessarily lead to an immediate and near total collapse of the Indigenous population.

The bubonic plague—aka the Black Death—spread from Asia to the Middle East and North Africa, to Europe and back to Asia, killing millions from 1347 to 1351. The Spanish flu pandemic of 1918 swept around the world and killed millions in a little more than two years. Nothing as swift and geographically extensive happened in North America. For one thing, microbes don't kill all or even most of their victims. The plague killed about 30% of those infected with the disease, while about 5% of Spanish flu victims died. Smallpox, for all the blame it has received for the decline of the Indigenous population of the Americas, had a historical fatality rate of 30%, similar to that of the Black Death.

Moreover, smallpox did not appear until 1518, long after the Tainos had disappeared from the Caribbean islands. It was also decades after the killing, as recorded by the Spaniards themselves, had started and much of the Native population of the Caribbean had been wiped out. In North America, smallpox didn't hit until almost two centuries after Ponce de Leon's incursions into Florida and the Southeast in 1513, and nearly a century after Jamestown was founded. It took 200 years for it to reach the interior of North America.[50] Indeed, a recent study suggests that diseases did not spread to the Jemez of New Mexico for nearly 100 years after their contact with Spanish conquistadors in the 16th century.[51]

---

[50] Jeff Ostler, "Genocide and American Indian History," in *Oxford Research Encyclopedia of American History* (2015): 3-4.

[51] Lizzie Wade, "New Mexico's American Indian population crushed 100 years after Europeans arrived," *Sciencemag.org* (January 25, 2016).

There were other factors that delayed and mitigated the impact of diseases on America's Indians. For instance, the Native population was widely dispersed in small seminomadic groups, meaning they had fewer, less frequent contacts with infected individuals, which slowed the spread of diseases. Conversely, in the more densely populated regions of the Caribbean and Central America, infected individuals were in closer contact, facilitating the transmission of diseases to larger numbers of people. Hence, the devastating effects of smallpox on the heavily populated Aztec capital of Tenochtitlan during the Spanish siege of 1521.

Regardless of the speed of transmission, Indians survived epidemics, and in between, some of their populations even increased. Had it not been the case, the Spaniards would not have been able to find millions of slaves to work their gold and silver mines in Mexico and South America for more than 250 years, and there would not have been enough left for Californians to enslave during the Gold Rush.[52]

As Robbie Etheridge explains, rather than a dramatic population collapse that wiped out 90 to 95% of the Indigenous population, it was "a gradual, not steep, demographic decline and only after sustained European contact. In addition, scholars agree that disease was but one factor in the demographic decline, and they now point to contributing factors such as incorporation into the modern world economy, slaving, internecine warfare, dropping fertility rates, violent colonial strategies, and general social and cultural malaise from colonial oppression."[53]

All told, enslavement probably had the most disruptive and destructive impact on Native societies and populations. The Indian slave trade was a simple but extremely violent activity. Tribes were often lured into it with the prospect of exchanging captives taken in warfare for European goods, including guns and alcohol, which in turn became agents of disruption and destruction. The demand for Indian slaves set off wars between slave traders and Indians, between Indians and Indians, and between colonial

[52] Peter Nabokov, "Indians, Slaves, and Mass Murder: The Hidden History," *The New York Review of Books* (January 24, 2016).

[53] Robbie Etheridge, "Global Capital, Violence, and the Making of a Colonial Shatter Zone," in *Colonial Genocide in Indigenous North America*, 51.

powers, all of whom vied for control of the trade.

The warfare shattered existing social, cultural, and political structures of Indians. At the same time, it decimated Native populations east of the Mississippi River from 1550 into the early 18th century, when the supply of Indian slaves dwindled along with their populations, and settlers turned to African slaves. The warfare engendered by the slave trade was another example of the violence that accompanied Europeans' imperialism and colonization as they pursued their commercial interests by exploiting Indigenous populations around the world.

The slave trade in North America was conducted in the 16th and 17th centuries, beginning with Spanish slave raids out of Florida into the Southeast. When Hernando de Soto set out in 1539 on his rampage through the American Southeast as far as Texas, he took with him a supply of chains and neck collars for the slaves he hoped to capture, plus tools for making new ones in case he ran out.

The English, Dutch, and French learned from the Spanish experience in Latin America and believed, like Columbus, there was a market for Indian slaves. Trade was conducted through outposts or factories in Charleston, Quebec, Boston, Albany, and Jamestown, similar to those established along the coast of Africa. Eventually, Indian slavery existed in all the European colonies in North America, and colonists shipped Indians they stole or captured in battle, mostly women and children, to the slave markets in the Caribbean. In the early years of the North American colonies, more Indian slaves were exported than African slaves were imported.[54]

Even before there were any extensive settlements in North America, slaving destabilized Indian communities, disrupted their economies, forced their removal from their traditional territories, spread pathogens into the interior and generally disrupted the Native population. It also introduced them to two other lethal agents: alcohol and firearms. How many Indians were taken as slaves, or died from warfare or disease is difficult to determine, but the number is likely staggering. In the Southeast, where

---

[54] Andres Resendez, *The Other Slavery* (Boston: Mariner Books, 2017), 172.

the slave trade was most prevalent, it has been estimated that the Native population was cut in half.[55]

The Indian slave trade petered out east of the Mississippi River in the early 18th century. The Native population had declined, especially in areas closest to colonial settlements, and the appetite for labor switched to African slaves. Tribes devastated by the slaving managed to recover and restructure, only to face an even greater threat from an exploding colonial population that was doubling every 20 years.

England's population likewise had doubled between 1450 and 1620, with the excess spilling over into the expanding British empire. Those settlers brought with them the racist assumptions common to their culture and their times, which they shared with the Spaniards. Despite the Disney fantasies about Pocahontas and the happy talk surrounding Thanksgiving, when schoolkids dress up like Pilgrims and Indians, English colonists approached the Native people with a sense of racial, cultural, and technological superiority. These beliefs had staying power; they continue to shape American attitudes, policies, and actions toward Indians into the 21st century.

The effects of the Indian slave trade were felt long after it ended. According to Linda A. Newsom, enslavement was ultimately the most destructive agent of change inflicted on Indians. It "brought more immediate and profound cultural changes to native settlements, subsistence patterns, social relations and beliefs, the demographic consequences of which rendered the chances of survival more problematic."[56]

Slave raids that reached far into the interior from Spanish Florida to French Canada not only killed and enslaved Indians, they destroyed food supplies and dispersed villages, causing widespread deaths from starvation and exposure. More importantly, most of the slaves taken were women and children, which lowered fertility rates among affected tribes and severely limited their ability to recover. Women also suffered from malnutrition,

---

[55] Etheridge, *Shatter Zone,* 51.

[56] Linda A. Newsom, "The Demographic Collapse of Native Peoples of the Americas, 1492-1650," *Proceedings of the British Academy* 81 (1994): 276.

as food production was often disrupted by warfare and population losses. This, too, affected their fertility.

Especially damaging was the enslavement of Native children. It not only removed them from their tribes, it prevented them from one day reproducing within their group or reproducing at all. There is no better example of just how badly slavery decimated Native populations than the case of California under Spanish and American rule, even though Mexico outlawed slavery in its dominions, and California entered the Union as a free state.

It all began in 1769. Spanish Franciscan priests established a string of outposts along the coast of California, running from San Diego up to San Francisco. The Indians were enslaved under the pretext of Christianizing and civilizing a people whom the Franciscans officially labeled *gente sin razon* or "people without reason." It was probably the nicest thing they said about them. The priest in charge of the missions in 1800, Father Fermin Francisco de Lasuen, described Indians in terms Horace Greeley would have appreciated.

He said they were a "people of vicious and ferocious habits who know no law but force …. They are a people without education, without government, without religion or respect for authority, and they shamelessly pursue without restraint whatever their brutal appetites suggest to them. Their inclination to lewdness and theft is on a par with their love for the mountains. Such is the character of the men we are required to correct, and whose crimes we must punish."[57]

Indians were herded onto the missions via bribes, and when that failed, by military force. Once there, they were baptized, abused, and forbidden to leave. They were subjected to stringent rules and regulations, and stripped of their cultures and languages. They died from overwork, starvation, and mistreatment that included severe punishments for running away, rebelling, or misbehaving. As might be expected, diseases took their toll. So did the drop in fertility rates, which could only be balanced by enslaving more Indians until Mexico gained its independence in 1821 and finally ended slavery in 1829.

---

[57] Robert Archibald, "Indian Labor at the California Missions: Slavery or Salvation," *The Journal of San Diego History* 24, no. 2 (Spring, 1978).

Unfortunately, the damage had already been done. Slaving and slavery reduced Indigenous populations throughout the Spanish empire, and Alta California was no different. The Native population fell from around 300,000 at the time the first missions were established to about 150,000 in 1845. Despite the ban on slavery, both Mexican and American *Californios* continued to rely upon coerced Indian labor that amounted to slavery by any other name.

When Americans seized the territory in 1846 at the start of the Mexican War, the military recognized the shortage of labor. It allowed Indian slavery to continue and even reinforced it by outlawing Indian vagrancy. Indian freedom was essentially criminalized; unemployed Indians found wandering about in California communities were arrested and put to work. In the end, California's hand was forced by the demand for labor in the gold fields after 1848, the seemingly unlimited supply of Indian labor, and the unyielding belief in the inherent inferiority of Indigenous people.

The state codified Indian slavery in 1850 with the euphemistically titled "Act for the Government and Protection of Indians." Although California entered the Union as a free state and many Californians opposed slavery, the act gave coerced Indian labor the force of law. *De facto* Indian servitude became *de jure*.

The law allowed Indian minors to be held and worked until the age of 15 for females and 18 for males, with the consent of parents or "friends." It further authorized White people to arrest Indians "found loitering, strolling about, or frequenting public places where liquors are sold, begging, or leading an immoral or profligate course of life."[58] Those Indians could then be leased to the highest bidder for four months.

Once ensnared in the system of involuntary servitude, Indians found it difficult to escape. If they were not released from their apprenticeships or indentureships, or they were starved, beaten, or raped, they had little, if any, legal recourse. White people could not be convicted of any crimes on the basis of Indian testimony alone. If Indians were released, they ran

---

[58] Benjamin Madley, "'Unholy Traffic in Human Blood and Souls:' Systems of California Indian Servitude Under U.S. Rule," *Pacific Historical Review* 83, no. 4 (November, 2014): 643.

the risk of being arrested again. It was not uncommon for Native people to be set free and plied with alcohol, only to end up back in jail and the convict lease system. Or they could simply be cast adrift without any means of support and left to die. They were considered disposable and easily replaced as White people scoured the hinterlands for new supplies of cheap labor. Raiding parties terrorized Indians, hunting them down, often killing the men, and capturing the women and children, and selling them at slave marts.

Children were the prized possessions. In fact, in 1860, on the eve of the Civil War, the legislature extended the indentureships of young Indian girls to 21 and young boys to 25 to meet the demand for labor. Californians may have opposed African slavery, but killing Indians in slaving raids was different, and the government in its failure to do anything to stop it, seemed to concur.

Slave trading was a profitable business. It continued despite Lincoln's Emancipation Proclamation in 1863 and the 13th Amendment in 1865 that ended slavery throughout the nation. It was disguised as convict leasing, in which Indians were arrested and rented to the highest bidder, or debt peonage, where Indians would work off their financial obligations. For all intents and purposes, Indian slavery continued into the 20th century.

California didn't end convict leasing until 1937. In the meantime, the state's Indian population declined to 30,000 in 1870, and 15,000 by 1900, a loss of 95%, but not immediately and not from virgin-field epidemics. Along with the Indigenous population, the cultures and languages of many of the pre-contact tribes in California were also lost. Of course, there were other factors involved besides slavery. Diseases and almost incessant warfare also contributed, but it was the slaving and slavery that set off the wars, spread diseases, reduced fertility rates, destroyed cultures, and made recovery almost impossible.

While other populations have historically been able to recover from epidemics and wars, including in Latin America, the Native population in North America steadily declined for nearly 500 years. For one thing, the violence over the control of the slave trade shifted to the control of the land as the bourgeoning colonial population set off wars between settlers and Indians, and embroiled both in European wars that spilled over into the colonies. Mortality rates among Indian populations continued to be high as the same destructive tactics employed in the slave trade carried across the continent and continued into the 20th century.

One of the more devastating tactics against Western tribes was deliberately attacking villages in the dead of winter when they were less mobile, and survivors were most vulnerable to exposure and starvation. And don't forget the destruction of the buffalo herds, the main source of protein for the Plains Indians. Both tactics amounted to total warfare, which, by definition, does not distinguish between combatants and noncombatants.

However, more devastating over the long run was the decline in fertility rates caused by the continuing murder, capture, and enslavement of children and Native women of child-bearing age. This made it nearly impossible for Native populations to recover. Newsom offers the striking observation that "... Only a 1% decline in population would result in its reduction in half in 70 years."[59]

If so, and given the fact that Indian wars in North America lasted for nearly 400 years, a dramatic population collapse brought on by virgin-field epidemics was not necessary to reduce the Indigenous population from approximately 15 million to 237,000 by the end of the 19th century. In fact, according to a quick back-of-the-envelope calculation, reducing a population of 15 million by 1% a year for 400 years yields a population of 269,258.

The demographic decline among America's Indians was a gradual but nonetheless tragic consequence of diseases that found fertile ground among populations weakened by warfare, slaving, slavery, malnutrition, starvation, and removal to unfamiliar and harsher environments. In addition, concentrating smaller, seminomadic groups on reservations in government housing exposed them to diseases from which they might otherwise have been isolated, and it provided a larger number of potential hosts that allowed epidemics to last longer and infect more victims. Reservations were, and still are, hothouses for diseases like tuberculosis, and more re-

[59] Newsom, "Demographic Collapse," 255.

cently, COVID-19, which thrive in populations living in overcrowded and unsanitary conditions.

While the focus tends to be on smallpox, tuberculosis became the scourge of Native populations in the 19th and 20th centuries. This was especially true as Indians were forced into government housing that our friend H.M. Smee described as "air-tight log houses" that he predicted would be the cause of their demise. Removal to reservations also substituted government rules and regulations for the traditional social, cultural, and religious systems that had allowed tribes to adjust to changes in their environments, leaving them without the tools they needed to navigate and survive the social, economic, and psychological upheavals they experienced as a result of conquest and colonization.

Continuing population losses and declining fertility rates made it difficult for Native populations to recover. In fact, the losses for some smaller tribes were so great, those communities were no longer genetically viable. That is, there was not enough genetic diversity to produce new generations of tribal members, leading to their extinction or absorption into other tribes. Add to this the introduction of alcohol, and the survival of any Indians at all is a testament to their resilience, not to American benevolence.

The near extinction of the Indigenous population of North America was neither precipitous nor caused by virgin-field epidemics alone. Nor was it the result of a handful of massacres like Sand Creek or Wounded Knee. Rather, it was the culmination of unrelenting warfare. Although it began with the arrival of the first Europeans to the shores of North America about 500 years ago, it intensified after the Revolution. Donald Fixico estimates the clashes along the frontier "led the U.S. government to authorize 1500 wars, attacks and raids on Indians, the most of any country in the world against its indigenous people."[60]

From the Revolution to the War of 1812, hundreds of Native towns were destroyed and looted, with their inhabitants killed or left without food

---

[60] Donald L. Fixico, "When Native Americans Were Slaughtered in the Name of 'Civilization,'" *History, history.com* (March 2, 2018).

or shelter.[61] The cumulative effects of what Lemkin described as the "destruction of the essential foundations of life" though continuous assaults on Native social, cultural, economic, and religious institutions lasted into the 20th century and left Native communities "crippled." In addition, the decline in fertility caused by the killing, kidnapping, and enslaving of Native women and children made population recovery and even survival, as Newsom puts it, "problematic," especially for smaller tribes or bands that lacked the genetic diversity to produce future generations.

All of this would seem to meet Lemkin's broader definition of genocide, and it would also seem to meet the Genocide Convention's strictures against "causing serious bodily or mental harm to members of the group, [or] deliberately inflicting on the group conditions of life calculated to bring about its physical destruction in whole or in part, imposing measures to prevent births within the group, and forcibly transferring children of the group to another group." It didn't happen overnight, but according to Lemkin, genocidal acts do not have to take place at one time or place, and can be as much sociocultural as physical. That explains why the population declines continued after warfare ended and Indians were concentrated on reservations.

Once safely ensconced and their movements restricted by the cavalry stationed around reservations, they were deprived of their traditional ways of life as well as adequate food, housing, and medical care. Even the reforms offered by groups like the Indian Rights Association and carried forth by missionaries to force Indians to give up the hunt, take up farming, convert to Christianity, and attend boarding schools only worked to make matters worse.

Granted, there may not have been an official policy of extermination; there didn't have to be. What happened to America's Indians was an extension of the racial imperative that brought death and destruction to Indigenous people around the world through the twin forces of conquest and colonization. According to Lemkin, they could amount to genocide as colonizers destroyed and replaced the national pattern of the oppressed

---

[61] Ostler, "Genocide and American Indian History," 7.

population, and removed and replaced them with the oppressor's own nationals. With this in mind, Lemkin's metaphorical time bomb began ticking in 1492.

Simply put, Indians were killed because they were Indians and chose to remain Indians, and their resistance was met with a ferocious almost feral response. Whether it was out of fear, revenge, lust for Indian lands, faith in God's providence, or simply racism, American settlers willingly, knowingly, actively, and even gleefully joined in the killing. They supported the assault on Native lands with their votes, clamored for Indian removal in newspaper editorials, and joined in legal and extralegal actions against Native villages, where women, children, and elderly people were killed, enslaved, or left to die of starvation and exposure. Along the way they were aided and abetted by colonial, federal, state, and local officials, including U.S. presidents who unabashedly called for the removal and extermination of the Native population. It was the will of the people, the protests of a handful of bleeding-heart reformers notwithstanding.

Given the body of compelling evidence, Americans cannot deny that genocide occurred, nor can they hide from their complicity in genocide, especially since they benefitted from divesting Indians of their lands and resources. The U.N. Genocide Convention specifies that "persons committing genocide or any of the other acts enumerated in Article 3 shall be punished, whether they are constitutionally responsible rulers, public officials or private individuals."

At the very least, an apology is in order.

The Land Before Time

WHEN THE FIRST EUROPEANS landed along the Atlantic Coast of North America, they brought with them certain preconceptions about what they would find there. They had already explored along the coast of sub-Saharan Africa with its deep, dark equatorial forests with ebony-skinned inhabitants who seemed to resemble a different species. Columbus himself believed the ancient texts that the netherworld was inhabited by monsters or monstrosities—some sort of misshapen, deformed beings.

The Indigenous people of the Americas, whom Columbus dubbed "*los indios*," were not monsters, but they were dark-skinned and—in the minds of the explorers—had strange, shocking, and even repulsive habits that marked them as morally, intellectually, and technologically inferior. Their supposed inferiority was underscored by the way the Spaniards swept across Latin America, including the vast empires of the Aztec and Inka, with apparent ease. In North America, the English, French, and Dutch didn't find the vast populations and wealth that their neighbors from Spain stumbled upon, but neither did they find a land that was barren of people or resources. There were slaves, furs, deerskins, and timber, but the land itself on which millions of Native people had lived and thrived for thousands of years, would prove of greater and lasting value. Transformed into a commodity, it became the greatest source of wealth in American history.

Regardless of when the Indians arrived in the Western Hemisphere, the population densities in some areas had reached the level necessary to support the shift from hunting and gathering to farming by about 10,000 years ago. This is known as the Neolithic Revolution. It first appeared in the Middle East and was marked by the cultivation of wheat, barley, chickpeas, and lentils that gave rise to Sumeria and other early Middle Eastern civilizations.

In the Americas, particularly Meso or Central America, the Agricultural Revolution as it is sometimes called, produced beans, squash, chili peppers, tomatoes, avocados, cacao, and most importantly, maize. The latter took some doing; there is no wild form of corn in nature. Maize was domesticated in southern Mexico about 9,000 years ago, either by interbreeding it with a native plant known as teosinte or by centuries of artificial selection.[62] It eventually spread throughout both continents, and after Columbus' arrival, throughout much of the world.

The impact of the Neolithic Revolution can be seen in ways that are relatable even today. For example, the farming revolution in the Andes produced potatoes. The lumpen potato, the most common variety, spread across Europe as food for the poor. Everyone knows Russians relied on potatoes to make vodka. Meanwhile, Ireland became so dependent on potatoes for food, when the crop failed, it led to the great famine of the 1840s.

Despite the ripple effect felt throughout the world, the impact in Central and South America was most striking. It spawned vast civilizations like the Olmec, Maya, Aztec, Inka, and others that have all but been lost to colonization and the jungles. Their populations totaled in the millions and provided the labor and the talent to build huge pyramids that rivaled those of Egypt, create beautiful works of art, develop writing and accurate calendars, make precise astronomical observations, and record their histories.

The Olmec in southern Mexico were among the earliest civilizations, emerging nearly 4,500 years ago. They are probably best known for the huge stone heads carved out of blocks of volcanic basalt that weighed thousands of pounds and had to be transported as much as 50 miles from the coastal Tuxtla Mountains. It was no mean feat, given the fact the Olmec people didn't have wheels or draft animals to pull or carry loads.

The Olmec developed a form of writing, perfected a 365-day calendar, and figured out how to extract latex from rubber trees and turn it into balls that could be used to play a game popular throughout Mesoamerica. They also built the first pyramids, which became the architectural motif for the

---

[62] Charles Mann, *1491* (New York: Charles A. Knopf, 2005): 17-8.

civilizations that followed, including some in North America.[63] The Olmec civilization began to fall apart around 400 B.C., but it certainly influenced future cultures, most notably the Mayan civilization that arose about the same time in the Yucatan Peninsula, Belize, Guatemala, and El Salvador and lasted until around 800 A.D. Their achievements were even more re-markable.

In the last 50 or so years, researchers have uncovered in the jungles a vast network of cities with populations that numbered in the hundreds of thousands. I visited Belize and southern Mexico to see for myself what I had learned about the Mayas from National Geographic and Smithsonian documentaries. I decided to visit some of the smaller, out-of-the-way sites like one that is accessible only by ferry. I imagined something like the Stat-en Island Ferry pulling up, but instead I found myself floating across a slug-gish stream, using a rope to pull a raft loaded with my car. It was worth it.

On the other side, I found a site hidden beneath the jungle canopy. I soon realized the Mayan culture was not just centered in major urban areas like Chichen Itza and Tikal, to which tourists are directed. I discovered a complex of dozens of urban areas large and small spread across Central America, and judging by the similarities of the architectural motifs to the sites I visited in Mexico, Belize, and Guatemala, they shared a common culture.

Even the smaller urban centers were built around ritual pyramids, pla-zas, and ball courts. The faces of the pyramids were adorned with elaborate carvings that also covered the obelisks or stellae where the Maya record-ed their history. In fact, the Maya developed a form of writing and even had books made from bark paper, almost all of which were destroyed by the Spanish colonists. The Mayan people tracked the motions of the sun, moon, stars, and planets to create three calendars, which, when synchro-nized, were extremely accurate.

However, their most impressive achievement may well have been the use of zero in their mathematical calculations as early as 4 A.D. Zero wasn't used in Europe until the 12th century A.D. As I stood in the plazas at Chichen Itza and any of the smaller cities I visited, I realized ancient

[63] Stannard, *American Holocaust*, 33-5.

Rome, Greece, and Egypt had nothing on the achievements of the Maya. History has just treated them better, fostering a culture of global respect.

In the end, like their Old World counterparts, the Maya succumbed to internal and external forces. By 900 A.D., the vast Mayan civilization had disintegrated. What the Spaniards didn't destroy when they arrived in the 1500s, the jungles reclaimed and kept hidden for nearly 500 years, along with the more than 5 million Mayan descendants who still inhabit the interior of their former homelands.[64]

While there were other Indigenous civilizations that rose and fell before Columbus' arrival, the Aztecs in Mexico and the Inka in Peru are best known because they were still around when the Spanish arrived and chronicled what they found, even as they destroyed them. When Hernando Cortes entered Tenochtitlan, the capital of the Aztec empire in what is now Mexico City, he could hardly believe his eyes at the size of the city and the complexity of Aztec society.

The city was built on Lake Texcoco and was linked to the mainland by four causeways with bridges that allowed passage from one part of the lake to the others. The population numbered around 200,000, which made it larger than London or Rome at that time. It received its supplies from surrounding communities via the causeways or boat, and fresh water was supplied via an aqueduct that was itself an engineering marvel.

Cortes claimed the city was as large as the Spanish cities of Seville and Cordova, and the principal temple or pyramid was larger than the Seville Cathedral. He marveled at the markets, one of which he compared to the one in Salamanca, where thousands gathered each day to trade a wondrous variety of goods and foods. After describing the offerings in great detail, he finally gave up and simply said, "Besides those things I have already mentioned, they sell in the markets everything else to be found in this land, but they are so varied that because of their great number and because I cannot remember many of them nor do I know what they are called I shall not mention them."[65] Unfortunately, the wonders he beheld and compared to

[64] Ibid., 36-9; Mann, *1491*, 19.

[65] Stannard, *American Holocaust*, 7.

the greatest cities of Europe didn't stop him from leveling the city. Nor did they prevent the Spanish from erasing almost all remnants of Aztec civilization, and enslaving or killing its people.

The Aztecs, either through alliances or conquest, created an empire that ruled over as many as 25 million people in central and southern Mexico. They developed a highly stratified and organized society that allowed them to conquer and hold sway over a vast empire and build massive structures like the main temple in Tenochtitlan. They had writing, numbers, and a calendar. They also practiced human sacrifice, the one thing most people tend to know about them. Nevertheless, a little more than two years after Cortes entered Tenochtitlan in 1519, the Aztecs succumbed to Spanish arms, diseases, treachery, and sheer brutality.[66]

The same was true for the Inka people in Peru, who ruled over the largest empire in the world. It stretched over 2,000 miles along the west coast of South America and reached high into the Andes Mountains. They had a system of writing and recordkeeping, practiced metalsmithing, and wove fine cotton fabrics, which they dyed with indigo thousands of years before the plant-based dye was used in either Egypt or China. They built terraces to farm potatoes and other crops on the near-vertical slopes of the Andes.[67]

Both the Aztec and the Inkan empires were made possible by the Neolithic Revolution that produced the foodstuffs to support populations numbering in the millions. But like the Aztec, the Inka were no match for Francisco Pizarro and Hernando de Soto, who arrived in 1532 and brought down their vast empire in one year through superior weaponry and brutality. Despite their remarkable achievements, the Aztec and Inka are most often remembered for their failures.

The collapse of the Aztec and Inka was spectacular, but history is littered with the wreckage of empires large and small that have come and gone. Think of the ancient empires of Babylon, Rome, Egypt, Alexander the Great, Attila the Hun, and the colonial empires of England, France,

[66] Ibid., 4-8.

[67] Mann, *1491*, 64; Aaron Sidder, "Earliest Evidence of Indigo Dye Found at Ancient Peruvian Burial Site," *Smithsonianmag.com* (September 15, 2016).

Spain, and Portugal. But it makes one wonder what might have happened had the Europeans arrived a century or two later. Most Americans are familiar with the stories of the Aztec and Inka, if not necessarily the other civilizations of Latin America; they learned about them from their social studies textbooks.

I discovered them in the Classics Illustrated editions of "The Conquest of Mexico" and "The Glory of the Incas." I had a whole collection of Classics comic books. The moral of their stories was that the Indigenous civilizations, no matter how sophisticated, gave way before European germs, steel, and genes. What gets overlooked in all this interest in the civilizations of Central and South America is that there was a second Neolithic or Agricultural Revolution to the north that produced civilizations that rose and fell, and like the Mayan empire, were almost lost to the forces of nature and colonization.

The transition in North America from hunting and gathering to agriculture began around 3,800 years ago. Corn and squash had been raised by the Puebloan people of New Mexico and Arizona as early as 3,200 years ago, and are still raised in traditional ways in the pueblos of the Southwest. Roughly 2,000 years ago, the early Puebloans began to settle into a sedentary, agricultural life, living in pit houses dug into the ground and covered with domes made from saplings that were then layered with brush, grasses or reeds, and coated with mud. Some of the pits are still visible in places like Mesa Verde National Park in southern Colorado.

Gradually, the Pueblo people moved out of their pit houses into aboveground structures fashioned from local stones that are plentiful in the region. They depended increasingly on agriculture, growing beans and cotton, as well as maize, irrigating their gardens, and making pottery and weaving cloth from the cotton they grew. By about 750 A.D., they began to move into large houses with many rooms until about 1100 A.D., when they began to move into the structures for which they are most famous: the cliff dwellings at Mesa Verde and at other sites in the Southwest.

If you haven't visited Mesa Verde, you should. The cliff dwellings cling to the sheer canyon walls and seem to defy gravity. As I climbed down into

Cliff Palace, Balcony House, and Square Tower House, I was thinking the ironworkers who build our modern urban monuments have nothing on the ancient people who erected and lived in the dwellings along the steep canyon walls at this national monument. I also was surprised by the sharp, square corners of the buildings, the perfectly round kivas or ceremonial pits, and the smooth surfaces of the walls, all of which required sophisticated engineering and masonry skills, and untold hours of labor.

At one time, there were more than 600 dwellings in Mesa Verde, some small and hardly distinguishable from the natural rock formations. Others were massive complexes of houses and kivas like Cliff Palace and Long House, each with more than 100 rooms and many kivas. The houses, some of them several stories high, are tucked into alcoves carved out of the cliffs by the elements. They were constructed of hand-hewn sandstone blocks cemented together with a mixture of mud and water. I often wonder how much labor went into shaping the thousands of blocks used in each dwelling.

The Puebloans farmed the top of the mesa and clambered in and out of the dwellings using ladders, as well as hand and toe holds carved into the canyon walls. About 5,000 people lived atop the mesa at its peak. Although that sounds like a lot, the mesa is a massive hulk brooding over the countryside between Cortez and Mancos, Colorado, with enough arable land to sustain a population of that size. Having driven up the winding road to the top, I don't know how anybody got up there in the first place, but it was nevertheless inhabited for thousands of years before it was suddenly abandoned by 1300 A.D., along with other early Puebloan sites in the area, including Chaco Canyon.

Often referred to as the center of Puebloan culture, Chaco Canyon boasts various ancient Puebloan structures, with Pueblo Bonito being the largest, most impressive, and most famous. The remains are there for all to see. It once was a multistory structure made from the aforementioned sandstone blocks, with approximately 800 rooms housing perhaps 1,000 people and featuring kivas, again perfectly round, 3 to 4 feet deep and as much as 70 feet in diameter. It has been estimated that as many as 240,000 trees were used to provide strength and stability for the walls and floors of the numerous "great houses" at Chaco.[68]

If you go there, be sure to climb the mesa behind Pueblo Bonito to get a sense of its size and the scope of the settlements in the canyon. From that perspective, the kivas look like cupholders. You may also realize why people think it was a landing spot for aliens. While Chaco, Mesa Verde, Bandelier, Aztec, and other ruins in the Four Corners region are impressive, even more amazing are the sites hidden in places like the Canyons of the Ancients in southeastern Utah and even in the backyards of homes in Mancos, Colorado.

Walk across the countryside. You will find them everywhere, spouting evidence of the size and scope of the Puebloan civilization in that area. As many as 40,000 Native people inhabited the region until climatic and other factors forced them to abandon their dwellings. Many of them moved east, presumably driven by an extended drought. You can find some of their ancestors residing in the pueblos along the Rio Grande River, and in the Acoma and Zuni pueblos along Interstate 40 to the south. Only the Hopi people remained safely settled on their three mesas, where they continue to live much like they did thousands of years ago.

The Agricultural Revolution that was responsible for the rise of the Puebloan culture eventually reached the interior of the continent, but not until 900 A.D. Instead, the early farmers in what has become known as the Eastern Agricultural Complex, an area drained by the tributaries of the Ohio, Mississippi, and Missouri rivers, domesticated and harvested plants native to the region as early as 2,500 years ago (perhaps even 2,000 years earlier). The list of plants eventually brought under cultivation runs to at least 25 and includes goosefoot, sunflowers, erect knotweed, marshelder, little barley, maygrass, amaranths, cattails, and bottle gourds. Most are considered weeds today, but 2,500 years ago, they made up as much as two-thirds of Native diets in that region.

I have enjoyed *timsila* (prairie turnips) picked fresh out of the ground,

---

[68] Mari N. Jensen, "Unexpected wood source for Chaco Canyon Great Houses," *news.arizona.edu* (December 7, 2015).

washed off of course, or cooked in stews seasoned with wild onion. Wild plums are equally delicious, although I have been admonished not to refer to them as "wild." Indeed, the nutritional value of many of these plants is finally appreciated and is attracting the attention of seed companies that patent indigenous seeds, something many Native people consider another example of cultural appropriation. Once corn, beans, and squash from Mesoamerica were introduced into the eastern half of the continent, native plants were abandoned as food sources. They still occur naturally throughout the region and are being brought back to life by Native farmers and ethnobotanists interested in finding nutritional alternatives for American diets, plus food to feed a growing world population.

Maize, beans, and squash eventually found their way north by about 900 A.D., but long before that, the crops of the Eastern Agricultural Complex supported the construction of large earthen mounds of various shapes, sizes, and functions throughout the eastern half of the continent. The earliest known mounds are part of the Watson Brake complex in Louisiana. They were built approximately 5,400 years ago, before the pyramids in Egypt and Stonehenge in England. Most of the mounds were built in the drainage areas of the Mississippi and Ohio rivers, and their tributaries in the same area as the Eastern Agricultural Complex. They likewise can be found throughout the eastern half of the continent, where they may have numbered in the tens of thousands. Nobody knows for sure, since many, if not most, have been plowed under or paved over.

In fact, the city of St. Louis is built on a complex of Indian mounds. You can drive right across them on Interstate 70 going west from the Mississippi River. Therein lies a problem. Most of them blend in naturally and are often discovered by accident. At least that's the case of the Poverty Point complex near the Mississippi River in northeastern Louisiana, not far from Watson Brake.

Poverty Point dates back to about 1700 B.C. It consists of six semicircular concentric earthen rings on which shelters were built in case of flooding. The opening of the largest ring measures nearly 4,000 feet across. There is also an effigy mound, 70 feet high, in the shape of a bird in flight, as well as several other smaller mounds. Apparently, none of this fazed the farmer who plowed them up and planted cotton on the planation that gave the site its name. As I walked across the rings, they were so degraded by erosion and farming, they appeared to be natural undulations in the ground. Even the effigy mound covered by trees and brush looks like just another hill. The bird's beak was destroyed by the construction of a road across the site.

Only when I climbed the mound and looked back toward the Mississippi River could I appreciate the size of the site, how much labor went into constructing it, and how many people must have lived there. I also realized why it was built there. Situated on the flood plain of the Mississippi on some of the most fertile land in the world, it was connected to much of the continent by the river and its tributaries, and its backwaters offered a rich diversity of aquatic foods to supplement local foodstuffs. Its residents were definitely not nomads.[69]

There are other sites that have escaped the plow and the bulldozer, and settlers ransacking them out of curiosity, or simply in hopes of finding hidden treasures. The earliest known mound is in Illinois; it dates back to 4000 B.C. and was used for burial. However, most were built after 1000 B.C. by successive cultures that lived in the Ohio, Mississippi, and Missouri valleys, and along the Gulf Coast from Florida to Texas. Indigenous people left behind as many as 10,000 conical mounds in the Ohio Valley alone, most small and almost invisible, but others as high as 60 to 80 feet. They built expansive complexes of mounds in the shapes of circles, octagons, squares, and ellipses linked together with walled walkways or roads. The sites rivaled in area some wonders of the ancient world, including the Egyptian pyramids and the Roman Colosseum.

The geometric earthworks in Newark, Chillicothe, and Marietta, Ohio, are well preserved, even though they are as much as 2,000 years old. There are effigy mounds in the shapes of bears, birds, turtles, and snakes, especially in the upper Mississippi Valley and western Great Lakes region. Further south, around 900 A.D., Native people began to build temple mounds,

[69] Jon L. Gibson, *Ancient Mounds of Poverty Point* (Gainesville, FL: University of Florida Press, 2001).

similar in style to those in Mesoamerica. Square or rectangular in shape, they were flat on top, and often terraced and crowned with wooden structures. You can find them today at the Ocmulgee and Etowah Mounds in Georgia, Moundville in Tuscaloosa, the Spiro Mound complex in Oklahoma, and just about everywhere in between. It's worth visiting some of these thousands of mound sites, which stretch from New England and New York to the Great American Bottom in the middle of the United States. Finding them is easy; many are state or national historical monuments.

Among them—and perhaps the grandest one of all—is the collection of mounds at Cahokia, Illinois, just across the Mississippi from St. Louis. The domestication and cultivation of native plants paved the way for the rise of the mound-building communities in the American Bottom. However, it was the introduction of corn, beans, and squash around 900 A.D. that fueled the rise of the largest and arguably the most impressive one we have.

As I drove toward the site from the east along Collinsville Road just past the dog track, I was struck by the 100-foot-high mound rising out of the flat Illinois prairie. Known as Monk's Mound, it is four-sided, with its southern face terraced in the style of Mesoamerican pyramids. Larger than the pyramid at Giza in Egypt, it required millions of baskets of soil and clay hauled by thousands of workers over hundreds of years to complete.

Nourished by corn, beans, and squash that supplemented the domesticated native crops of the Eastern Agricultural Complex, the estimated population of Cahokia reached 40,000 at its peak in 1250 A.D., making it larger than London, England, at the time. Although Monk's Mound was built out of soil and clay, like all the mounds in North America, the Cahokians engineered it in such a way that it has remained relatively intact after nearly 1,000 years. Its sheer size may have saved it from destruction by farmers and construction crews seeking dirt as fill for roads and other projects.

Cahokia contained at least 20 other mounds and countless other sites of archeological interest, but by 1350 A.D., it was abandoned.[70] Some of the other mound-building communities—like the ones at Tuscaloosa and Etowah—survived until Spanish explorers and slave hunters arrived, but

[70] Stannard, *American Holocaust,* 32; Mann, *1491,* 252-69.

by the end of the 18th century, they dissolved, dispersed, or regrouped, and traces of their presence largely vanished.

Archaeological and anthropological evidence suggests North America had large Indigenous populations with advanced agricultural societies thousands of years before the Europeans arrived. However, when the settlers came across these mounds, they couldn't believe the poor, pathetic, savage Native people they encountered could have designed and constructed anything like the Great Serpent Mound in southern Ohio, a structure more than 1,300 feet long and fashioned in the shape of a snake swallowing an egg.

The Indians were considered too primitive, too few, too nomadic, and lacking the necessary division of labor moving so much soil would have required. So, the European settlers looked for other explanations. For example, the mounds must have been made by an ancient civilization or visitors from faraway places. Maybe it was the lost tribes of Israel, survivors of the lost continent of Atlantis, the Vikings, or the Hindoos of India. Or maybe it was a lost race of giants, a myth that still has adherents in the 21st century. Even Jefferson speculated about it, although he recognized the mounds he examined in Virginia were the work of local Native people. Whoever the mysterious builders were and wherever they came from, it was widely believed they were wiped out by the bloodthirsty ancestors of today's Indians.

However farcical these theories seem today, they reflected and reinforced the popular image of Indians as an intellectually, technologically, and morally inferior species. Furthermore, they established them as recent immigrants themselves who made their claim to the land through force. In other words, they had no more claim to it than the Europeans.

The Moundbuilder Myth found its way into popular culture. There were novels and poems such as "The Prairies" by William Cullen Bryant, which proclaims, "The red man came/ The roaming hunter tribes/ Warlike and fierce/ And the moundbuilders vanished from the earth."[71]

The myth even found its way into the Book of Mormon, which attributes

---

[71] William Cullen Bryant, "The Prairies" in *The Poetical Works of William Cullen Bryant*, Parke Goodwin, ed., vol. 1 (New York: Russell & Russell, 1967), 230.

the mounds to the lost tribes of Israel. After they arrived in America, they split into two warring factions that engaged in an epic struggle. The ungodly Lammenites, who were cursed with red skin, eventually conquered, and eliminated the Nephites, who buried in the Hill Cumorah the gold plates Joseph Smith transcribed into the Book of Mormon. The Moundbuilder Myth was eventually debunked by archaeologists and anthropologists, but its underlying tenets about the inferiority of the Indians continued to define the relationship between Native and White people.

Conquest and Colonization

WHEN THE ENGLISH SETTLERS clambered out of their boats onto the shores of North America, they knew nothing about *los indios,* including their numbers, diversity, cultures, and histories. They likewise knew nothing about mound builders, the Puebloan people, or the hundreds of Indigenous nations spread across the vast interior of the continent. What they did know was there was money to be made in the Indian slave trade, something they may very well have learned from the Spanish explorers.

A veteran slave trader, Columbus quickly realized there was a market for Indian slaves in Europe. He even brought a boatload of slaves back with him on his first trip. While African slaves were exported to the Caribbean islands as early as 1501 to replace the dwindling number of Native slaves there, in Mexico and the Andes, Indian slaves were put to work mining gold and especially silver. From the 16th to the early 19th centuries, millions of Indians were forced to labor in the mines under dreadful conditions.

During that time, 12 times more silver was mined in Mexico than the amount of gold taken out of California during the Gold Rush. Hundreds of thousands, perhaps millions of others throughout Spain's American empire were relocated onto *encomiendas*—large grants of land where they were forced to live and work in villages and become good Christians under the watchful eyes of priests backed by the military. Millions died from overwork, dangerous conditions, malnutrition, disease, and abuse at the hands of the Spanish.[72] When Puebloan people in New Mexico resisted Coronado in the 1540s, the ill-fated conquistador burned 200 of them alive.[73] Perhaps to his credit, the cleric Bartolomeo de Las Casas was so shocked by the

---

[72] Nabokov, "Indians, Slaves, and Mass Murder."

[73] Carrie Gibson, El Norte (New York: Atlantic Monthly Press, 2019), 63.

treatment of Indian slaves, he protested to the Crown. However, he fell short of redeeming himself. His solution to the problem was to use African slaves instead.

The Indigenous people of the Americas were given to enslavement for the same reasons as Africans. Although they were not Black, they were dark enough for the Spanish to brand them with nearly identical repugnant and frightening racial characteristics. Based on their idolatrous religious ceremonies, Indians were seen as heathens and devil worshippers, and therefore, the conflicts set off by their refusal to accept Christianity were so-called just wars that automatically condemned the Indians to slavery or worse. Their marriages were not only impermanent but sacrilegious. They also were accused of being cannibals, a new word derived at the time from *canibales,* the Spanish name for the Carib people, who were suspected of eating human flesh.

Not only were Native people enslaveable, Native women were "rapeable,"[74] and that's no coincidence. Rape has always been a tactic of warfare, conquest, and oppression, including during World War II, when millions of women were sexually assaulted. During the Bosnian War of the 1990s, rape was used as a tactic of terror and ethnic cleansing. We also know slave traders and slave owners used rape to degrade and control their slaves— otherwise known as their property.

The Spanish colonists raped Native women not because they were comely, naked, or available, but because of their presumed promiscuity and perverse sexual habits. They were, in a word, "fornicators," a favorite term of priests of the day. White people assumed the Indians' sexual appetites made them sexually exploitable. In modern terms, they wanted it. Besides, they belonged to the conquerors. Is it any wonder damaging, even lethal, stereotypes germinated?

The racist assumptions about the sexuality of Native women made them natural targets for sexual abuse, and it was a part of the process of conquest, oppression, and colonization. Like slavery, rape debases and dehumanizes its victims, allowing them to be sexually exploited. And yet, the sexual

[74] Andrea Smith, *Conquest* (Cambridge, MA: South End Press, 2005), 1-34.

colonization of Native women did not end with the Colonial Period. The Meriam Report of 1928 notes that White people in communities bordering reservations sexually exploited Native women, something that continues today at an alarming rate, as we have seen.[75]

At least the Spanish suffered pangs of conscience over the enslavement and slaughter of the Indians, thanks to clerics like Las Casas, who argued that Indians were humans with souls, and thus, could be saved and redeemed from their heathenism. Arrayed against them were slave traders and those who employed slave labor in mines and on the *encomiendas.* They countered that Indians were little better than animals. The Spaniards even staged a public debate over the issue in 1550 at Valladolid, which was followed throughout Europe, but it ended in a draw. Even if Las Casas had been triumphant, it would not have stopped the exploitation of Indian slaves, which as noted above, continued for centuries.[76] Racism ruled the day, but at least the Spanish debated the issue, albeit thousands of miles away. In North America, there was no debate.

There was another powerful force at work in the conquest of the Americas as both the Spanish and Portuguese and later other Europeans operated under the authority of the aforementioned Doctrine of Discovery. It gave explorers the right and the obligation to seize non-Christian lands, exploit their natural and human resources, and convert the inhabitants to Christianity. Those lands were declared *terra nullis,* literally "land belonging to nobody" or "no man's lands," which meant either the inhabitants had no right to the land, or they were inhuman. Natives of these lands were legally non-persons, who, along with their resources, belonged body and soul to the conquerors, who could do with them as they wished. And indeed, they did.

The Spanish communicated this to the Indians through the *requerimiento,* which needs no translation. It was read to the Native people, and it threatened to visit all kinds of atrocities upon those who resisted. The

---

[75] Institute for Government Research, *The Problem of Indian Administration* (Baltimore, MD: Johns Hopkins University Press, 1928), 571-2. Hereinafter cited as the Meriam Report.

[76] Stannard, *American Holocaust,* 210-11.

Indigenous people could submit to the authority of Spain and the Catholic Church, or they could face extermination. Any fighting resulting from their resistance was considered a just war, which meant Native people could be killed or enslaved, and their lands and property taken from them. Indigenous people across the Americas were offered the same dismal choice but with different terms. In North America, it was civilization or extermination.

The Indians probably didn't understand Spanish demands, and if they did, many simply refused to submit. When the Spanish proved they meant what they said, the Indians resisted ferociously, which only proved they were indeed savages or beasts. Their resistance must have been the work of the devil; after all, they were devil worshippers.

The atrocities performed by the Spanish under the banners of church and state are well documented. By their own accounts, they plundered and raped, and perpetrated hideous methods of torture and murder. Las Casas accompanied the conquistadors and witnessed the atrocities. He accused his own people:

> ... of odd cruelties, the more cruel the better, with which to spill human blood. They built a long gibbet, low enough for their toes to touch the ground and prevent strangling and hanged thirteen [Natives] at a time in honor of Christ Our Savior and the twelve Apostles. When the Indians were still alive and hanging, the Spaniards tested their strength and their blades against them, ripping chests open with one blow and exposing entrails .... Then, straw was wrapped around their torn bodies and they were burned alive. One man caught two children about two years old, pierced their throats with a dagger, and then hurled them down a precipice.[77]

Again, as we have seen, they enslaved millions under the authority of the Doctrine of Discovery. Although it was issued by the Catholic Church for Catholic countries, Queen Elizabeth I of Protestant England adopted it, and the United States inherited it from England, as confirmed by the U.S. Supreme Court in *Johnson v. McIntosh* in 1823. In that decision, Chief

[77] Stannard, *American Holocaust,* 72.

Justice John Marshall invoked the Doctrine of Discovery to declare that "discovery gave title to the government by whose subjects, or by whose authority, it was made." In turn, that principle, as adopted by all European nations, necessarily "overlooks all proprietary rights of the natives."[78]

Even though many other countries have repudiated the doctrine, the United States continues to recognize its validity to justify its claim to Native lands. In effect, it became the American doctrine of manifest destiny. That right to Indian lands was reaffirmed in 2005 by U.S. Supreme Court Justice Ruth Bader Ginsburg in *City of Sherrill v. Oneida Indian Nation of New York*. Ginsburg wrote, in words Marshall would have approved, that under the Doctrine of Discovery, "fee title to the lands occupied by Indians when the colonists arrived became vested in the sovereign—first the discovering European nation and later the original States and the United States."[79]

The problem with Ginsburg's opinion is that the doctrine was not just about land. It also granted the "discovering" nations the right to the people on those lands, and therefore, opened the door for colonists to commit genocide by outright murdering or reducing the inhabitants of those lands to chattel property, especially if they resisted. The Doctrine of Discovery gave legal sanction to the Indian slave trade, and the racist assumptions about the Indigenous people of the Americas made it morally acceptable.

England's population growth in the 15th and 16th centuries spilled over into the expanding British Empire. English colonials brought with them the racist ideas common to their culture and their times; beliefs they shared with the Spanish and other Europeans. English colonists approached the Indians with a sense of racial, cultural, and technological superiority. These attitudes had staying power, continuing to shape American attitudes, policies, and actions toward Indians into the 21st century.

The English believed the stories about dark, dangerous forests in America inhabited by dark, dangerous creatures with shocking habits such as cannibalism. The Puritans in New England used the Old English word

[78] *Johnson v. McIntosh*, 573, 567.

[79] *City of Sherrill v. Oneida Indian Nation* 544 U.S. 197 (2005).

wildeornes ("land inhabited only by wild animals") to describe the forests of New England, and by extension, their inhabitants. The English came to North America convinced they were the most civilized people on earth. By their standards, the Indians failed on all measures.

The settlers found them to be much the same as the Spanish had. In their eyes, the Native people were dirty, spoke in a babel of unintelligible languages, had unpronounceable names, lived in crude huts, were naked or dressed in animal skins, and had no metal tools or utensils. They tattooed and painted their bodies, as might be expected of savages, and worshipped idols, as might be expected of heathens. They had loose marriage and sexual customs, and no governments or laws. If they were humans, they were humans without "breeches." In fact, as one Pilgrim related, they were more like "foxes and wild beasts ...."[80] The settlers' judgments were more than ignorant first impressions; they continued to inform relations between Indians and White people for the next 400 years.

Although their impressions of Indians were similar, there was an important difference between Spanish and British colonialism in America. The Spanish sent only enough colonists to its American possessions to control the population and resources. They used priests to convert the Native people, conquistadors to terrorize them into submission, and slavery to work the land and mine the gold and silver that enriched Spanish coffers. The relatively few Spaniards who ventured over to New Spain along with *creoles* or *criollos*—those who were born in the colonies—were given expansive grants of lands or *encomiendas,* where they lorded over large numbers of Native laborers. In the process, they imposed Spanish culture, religion, laws, and language on the Indigenous people of Latin America, which derived its name from the Latin Mass that was practiced there.

In North America, colonialism worked much the same way except that thousands upon thousands of colonists poured into the English colonies in North America. The number of immigrants to the English colonies in the 17th century doubled the number of Spaniards who immigrated to New

[80] Stannard, *American Holocaust,* 229, 235.

Spain during the previous century.[81] More importantly, English settlers brought their families and came to stay. They claimed the land and turned it into a commodity that could be bought and sold. Consequently, they came to view the Indians more as obstacles to be removed instead of available labor. As in the Caribbean, they eventually resorted to African slaves, of whom there was a steady and more reliable supply.

Oddly enough, despite the Doctrine of Discovery, New Englanders felt compelled to justify their taking of Indian lands on the grounds that the Indians were too few and too primitive to properly use the land. In English eyes, the fact that the Indians did not improve the land by building houses and fences, and raising livestock meant the Indians did not have a legal right to it. As John Winthrop, the first governor of the Massachusetts Bay Colony, explained,

> That which lies in common, and has never beene replenished or subdued is free to any that possesse and improve it; For God hath given to the sonnes of man a double right to the earth; there is a natural right, and a Civill Right. The first right was natural when men held the earth in common where every man sowing and feeding where he pleased: then as men and their cattell increased they appropriated certaine parcells of Grownde by inclosing and peculiar manurence, and this in time gave them a Civill right .... As for the Natives of New England, they inclose noe land, neither have they any settled habytation, nor any tame Cattell to improve the land by, and soe have noe other but a Naturall Right to those Countries, soe as if we leave them sufficient for their use, we may lawfully take the rest, there being more than enough for them and us.[82]

Except there would never be enough for the settlers. Not only did the Indians fail to use the bounty nature afforded them, they were incapable of doing so since they were "not industrious, and neither have art, science, skill, or faculty to use either the land or the commodities of it...." With-

[81] Ibid., 236.

[82] Ibid., 235-6.

out a legal claim to the land, Indian resistance to settler demands became an excuse for war. In the long run, as the continent filled up, it required Americans to erase the Native people. Along with that, White people went about nullifying Indians' claims to the land, either through assimilation, removal, or, as most Americans preferred, extermination. These choices would define the relationship between Indians and White people for the next 400 years.

The influx of people, particularly in New England between 1630 and 1641, when more than 20,000 colonists arrived, immediately set off conflicts between Indians and settlers. The rapid growth of the colonial population in the 18th century, the expansion of the tobacco culture in the Chesapeake region, and the European practice of planting one crop per field instead of the Indian custom of planting three main crops—corn, beans, and squash—together, placed increasing pressure on Indian lands.

Furthermore, cattle, sheep, and hogs imported by the colonists required grazing lands, and the animals trampled and destroyed Indian crops. Colonial villages and fences cut off Indians' seasonal migration routes and access to fishing grounds and shellfish beds. The settlers' voracious appetite for wood and the need to clear land for crops began the greatest deforestation in the history of the world, as land between the Atlantic Ocean and the Mississippi River was almost completely denuded. With the forests went the wildlife, as the tribal ecologies on which the Indians depended for clothes, shelter, and food were destroyed.

The increasing demand for land, a direct result of the swiftly growing colonial population, reflected conflicting views of how land should be used. Although the early settlers admired and even marveled at the productivity of Indian gardens, they condemned the Indians for not fully utilizing the land. They could not understand why, in the midst of such God-given abundance, the Indians chose to eke out meager existences, living from hand to mouth and often suffering through "starving times" rather than working harder and "salting" something away for the future.

The settlers were puzzled and troubled by the fact that Native people were content to starve themselves during winter months, surviving on little more than "fifteen or twenty lumps of meat, or of fish dried or cured in the smoke ..." rather than working harder during summer months to gather more provisions.[83]

On the other hand, Indians seemed to survive starving times better than the settlers. Centuries of being without during lean times may have genetically conditioned them to store fat more readily during times of plenty. Starving may also have had the practical effect of keeping population densities lower, which put less pressure on their ecologies, and ironically, opened more land for the taking by Europeans.

There seemed to be so much land that early settlers sent back accounts of the abundant but underutilized resources awaiting those hardy and brave enough to tackle a wilderness just begging to be claimed and tamed. That's where the myth began, still common in textbooks and popular culture today, of North America being a virgin land devoid of inhabitants, save for a relative handful of savages who roamed around, without permanent habitations and without any of the trappings of civilization.

As William Bradford, the governor of the Plymouth Colony, put it, the woods were inhabited by "wild animals" and "wild men." New England was literally a *terra nullis,* a "no man's land," or a *vacuum domicilium.*[84] Therefore, it belonged to those who discovered, conquered, and tamed it. But the Indians did utilize the land. They just used it differently, and in some ways, more efficiently.

The image of Native people as nomadic hunter-gatherers persisted largely because the Native people along the Atlantic seaboard seemed to move around a lot. However, their migrations were not the aimless wanderings of nomads. Rather, their movements were orchestrated by the seasons and driven by necessity. That is, they moved to habitats where food and other resources were most abundant at different times of the year and could be obtained with the least amount of work.

For example, they might move to coastal areas in the summer when fish were running, and to lands that had been cleared for planting in the spring,

[83] William Cronon, *Changes in the Land* (New York: Hill and Wang, 2003), 40-1.

[84] Stannard, *American Holocaust,* 234-5.

and to hunting camps in the fall, and to areas where wood was abundant in the winter. Still, the settlers could not understand why the Indians seemed to have so little in the midst of such abundance. The differences came down to what William Cronon, in his book *Changes in the Land*, termed "English fixity versus Indian mobility."[85]

For instance, the English arrived, especially in New England, hoping to re-create the country they left behind, with permanent villages surrounded by fenced-in fields and pastures. This was in stark contrast to the Indian way. Native peoples' penchant for mobility required them to travel lightly with little baggage, since they had no draft animals to haul their belongings. So, they lived in small family units or villages consisting of domed wigwams or *wetu* made from saplings and covered with bark, brush, or animal hides. Of course, these patterns varied according to climate and geography, and some tribes, like the Iroquois, built expansive longhouses that could be 70 to 100 feet in length and accommodate multiple families. They were, after all, the *Haudenausaunee* ("the people of the longhouse").

In general, Native people in the eastern half of what is now the United States followed the seasons to where food and other resources could be found in greatest abundance with a minimum amount of work. Can you honestly blame them for wanting to satisfy their needs in the least taxing way? Their mobility also ensured they would not overuse the resources of the ecologies on which they depended. It all made great sense to the Natives, but to the settlers, it signaled the lands they coveted were sparsely populated by nomadic bands, who were wasteful and lazy, and consequently, had no need for or right to the land. In John Winthrop's words, they had no "Civill Right" to the land; they just had to be convinced, which inevitably led to war.

Europeans were no strangers to conflict. Europe was in an almost constant state of war before the Reformation began in the 16th century. From the 14th through the 15th centuries, rarely a year went by without a war or battle going on somewhere in Europe. The effects were devastating. During the Thirty Years War, from 1618 to 1648, population losses amounted to

---

[85] Cronon, *Changes in the Land*, 53.

50% in some areas. Their savagery toward one another was sickening. They beheaded, castrated, disemboweled, quartered, blinded with hot tongs, sawed the limbs off, or crushed their enemies. Women were treated a little better than men; they were generally just burned at the stake.

In England, the frequent executions drew crowds of people willing to pay for the best viewing spots, much like modern-day sporting events. While Europeans on the continent were slaughtering each other, the English were busying themselves subduing the "wild Irish," whom they characterized much like Indians. They were murderous beasts, brutish barbarians, satanic pagans for whom no punishment was too severe. The English destroyed villages and crops, plundered, and murdered. They cut off the heads of men, women, and children, impaling them on stakes as a warning to others. They exported this grisly practice to America, where they used it as a warning to Indians and rebellious slaves.[86]

The English and other Europeans brought the sadistic tactics they honed and polished against one another to the Americas and applied them to the Indians. The Spanish experimented with unspeakable cruelties on Jews, Muslims, and so-called infidels during the Inquisition, which they then used to terrorize Native people into submission. It wasn't just the Indians who were singled out by the Spaniards; they exercised the same tactics against other Europeans in the American colonies. For example, when the French tried to establish outposts in Spanish Florida in the 16th century, the Spaniards hunted them down, killed the men, and took the women and children captive.[87]

The idea that Europeans learned those tactics from the Indians or were only responding in kind is just another rationalization for the barbarity Europeans practiced against Indigenous people around the world. In the 1820s, the British conducted the aptly named "Black War" that essentially wiped out the dark-skinned Native people of Tasmania, who were probably the closest relatives of the African clan from which all humans are descended. Incidentally, in 1818, the English created the Order of St. Mi-

---

[86] Bernard Bailyn, *The Barbarous Years* (New York: Alfred A. Knopf, 2012), 39-42.

[87] Gibson, *El Norte*, 45-6.

chael and St. George to recognize service in the colonies. Honorees were rewarded with a medallion that depicted the archangel with his foot on the head of a black-skinned devil.[88]

During the infamous Pequot War of 1636, New Englanders surrounded and set fire to a Pequot village along the Mystic River and burned men, women, and children alive for having killed some White slavers. About 700 died in the inferno and its immediate aftermath, with survivors sold into slavery in Bermuda and the West Indies. Others were taken as slaves into settlers' homes in Massachusetts and Connecticut. Those who escaped were hunted to near extinction, and the Pequot name was erased from New England maps.

Even before that, our sainted Pilgrim ancestors, led by Miles Standish of the poem "The Courtship of Miles Standish" by Henry Wadsworth Longfellow, lured leaders of the Massachusetts tribe to a meeting in a stockade at Wessagusset, where they stabbed the Indians to death and put the head of one them on a pole. That was in 1623, only two years after the first Thanksgiving celebration.[89]

Likewise, the settlers in Virginia repaid the Powhatans for gifts that saved the colony by plundering their villages and demanding even more from them as tribute to a superior culture, demands backed by superior weaponry. Relations quickly devolved into almost continuous warfare into the 1640s, marked by the disgraceful episode when Pamunkey were invited to peace talks in 1623, and the Virginians poisoned some 200 of them and killed the rest, beheading many of them along the way.[90] It was a tactic that repeated itself more than two centuries later in California.

The English were not alone in their sadism. The Dutch, who settled on Manhattan and throughout the Hudson River Valley before the Pilgrims arrived, were equally vicious. They set about wiping out the Indians along the lower Hudson River, which resulted in one of the least-known wars of

---

[88] Simon de Bruxelles, "Calls for the redesign of royal honour over 'offensive' image," *The Guardian* (June 22, 2020).

[89] Bailyn, *Barbarous Years,* 339-40.

[90] Ibid., 107-8,

the period—Kieft's War—and one of the most hideous atrocities against Indians.

The Dutch attacked a peaceful group of Lenape refugees on what is now New York City's Bowling Green. They tore infants from their mothers' breasts, hacked them to pieces, and burned their dismembered bodies in front of their parents. Or they simply drowned the babies. In addition to being relentless, the Dutch were quite successful in wiping out the tribes up and down the Hudson River.[91] The end result of these wars in the 17th century was the decimation of the Indian population from the Chesapeake to New England though murder, starvation, and disease. To that point, the Powhatan Confederacy was reduced by more than 90% long before smallpox was introduced into the colony toward the end of the 17th century.

In New England, attacks on colonial towns by Wampanoags in 1675 erupted into King Philip's War, the colonial name given to Metacom, the leader of the offending Indians. The war was spawned by colonial incursions on Natives' lands and other tensions between settlers and Indians as New England's population swelled to 80,000. The Wampanoags, joined by the Narragansetts, ravaged colonial towns up and down New England, destroying 12, damaging many more, and killing approximately 1,000 settlers. The colonists responded in kind, destroying Indian villages, crops, and food supplies, creating conditions ripe for epidemics.

The war crushed the Native population of New England. Hard figures are difficult to come by, but of the 10,000 or so Indians before the war, 5,000 died in battle or from starvation and disease in the aftermath; another 1,000 were sold into slavery, including Metacom's wife and children. Metacom himself was killed, and his head was impaled on a pike in the Plymouth colony, his hands were put on display in Boston, and his body parts were hung from trees. Those who survived or escaped the hostilities succumbed to starvation, disease, or exposure.[92]

The slaughter continued even after formal warfare ended, as bands of

---

[91] Theresa Braine, "The Real Bowling Green Massacre," *Indian Country Today* (February 4, 2017); Bailyn, *Barbarous Years*, 191-241.

[92] Eric B. Schultz and Michael J. Tougias, *King Philip's War* (Woodstock, VT: Countryman Press, 2017).

settlers roamed the forests, attacking, killing, and enslaving Indians who escaped. As a matter of fact, they did the same thing to those who had nothing to do with the hostilities. The men were executed and often beheaded as trophies, while the women and children were sold into slavery, making it impossible for Native populations in New England to recover. As Increase Mather, one of the religious leaders of the colony, reported, thus it was that "not above an hundred men left of them who last year were the greatest body of Indians in New England."[93]

As far as the colonists were concerned, even that was too many. In the future, New Englanders would leave nothing to chance. In 1689, at the start of King William's War with the French and their Indian allies, Massachusetts offered a bounty to soldiers for each Indian scalp, an effort aimed at ensuring that the job of eliminating the Indians was done right. As an aside, paying for Indian scalps was a practice that continued late into the 19th century. King Philip's War has been called America's most devastating war, but for the colonists, it was worth it.

They saw the victory and the destruction of the Indians as God's providence, plus vindication of their right to eliminate the heathens and seize their lands. Whether it was divine providence or the Doctrine of Discovery, New Englanders were carrying out the racial imperative that brought them to the shores of North America to conquer, colonize, and prepare the world for the millennium, otherwise known as the second coming of Christ. The racial animus they bore toward the Indians from the very first contact was inflamed by ferocious fighting along the frontier.

Victory convinced the colonists of their moral, cultural, and racial righteousness and superiority. In their opinion, the Indians deserved their fate. They were nothing more than vermin, wolves, beasts, savages, heathens, and devil worshippers, epithets that would be repeated again and again to demonize Native people. Not that there weren't atrocities on both sides; there were. In fact, it took decades for the New England economy to recover, but it did recover. As for the Indians, their population continued to decline, as women and children were killed or sold into slavery, and they were forced to accept the loss of their lands. By the end of the 17th

[93] Stannard, *American Holocaust*, 117.

century, Indians from Virginia to New England had learned the hard way that White people couldn't be trusted, and that resistance was futile against greater numbers and better technology. Moreover, it would be met with a disproportionate response that would show them no mercy.

Unfortunately, these lessons had to be learned and relearned as the frontier receded, pushing tribes farther and farther west and onto reservations. Indians also realized they could not escape becoming embroiled in conflicts between European powers that spilled over to the colonies. From the early 1600s to the American Revolution, the North American colonies were in an almost constant state of war, beginning in 1629 with the Beaver Wars between the English, Dutch, and French and their various Indian allies for control of the fur and slave trade, and lasting until 1701.

There were the larger European conflicts like King William's War in the 1690s and Queen Anne's War in the early 18th century, followed by King George's War. Then there was the granddaddy of them all: the French and Indian War or Seven Year's War, from 1754 to 1763. For all intents and purposes, it was the first world war.

These larger conflicts were interspersed with local battles like Father Rale's War and Father LeLoutre's War, named for two Jesuit priests who led Indians allied with the French in Canada against British and New England forces. Most people have never heard of those wars, or the Tuscarora and the Yamassee wars that devastated the Native population of the Carolinas in the early 18th century. Obscure as they've become, they nevertheless involved more than 100 battles each, which does not include the actions of settlers lashing out on their own against Indians along the frontier.

The colonial powers recruited their Indian allies by providing them with trade goods, especially guns and liquor, upon which the tribes soon became dependent. The big winners were the Six Nations of the Iroquois Confederacy of New York—the Seneca, Cayuga, Onondaga, Oneida, Mohawk, and Tuscarora. Their size and unity under their Great Law of Peace, and their access to guns allowed them to maintain control over their hunting grounds, stretching from southern Ontario southward to Pennsylvania and westward to the Ohio country.

The Great Law of Peace was the message of harmony brought to the five and later six Iroquois nations of New York by Deganawidah, the Peacemaker, and his spokesman, Hiawatha. It established a council of 50 chiefs or sachems selected by clan mothers to settle disputes and end blood feuds. It also had a set of principles—a constitution of sorts that so impressed Benjamin Franklin, he presented it in 1754 as a model for the Albany Plan of Union.

Franklin wasn't the only one to sit up and take notice. Cadwallader Colden, one of the early governors of New York, was so enamored with the Iroquois Confederacy, he declared it to be "the oldest living participatory democracy on earth." Not only was it participatory, it was egalitarian, for they "have such absolute Notions of Liberty that they allow no kind of Superiority of one over another, and banish all Servitude from their Territories."[94]

Although the Iroquois people suffered from the epidemics and warfare of the 17th century, their relative isolation from the colonies to the east and their strategic position along trade routes into the interior for slaves and furs enabled them to enjoy stability and prosperity into the 18th century. However, it came at a price. Their growing dependence on European trade goods such as trade cloth, guns, knives, tobacco, kettles, and even food entangled them in the colonial market economy. Although many continued to pursue their traditional economies of farming, hunting, and gathering, others gravitated to British forts at Niagara in the west, Oswego in central New York, and colonial settlements in the east, where they worked for wages as laborers, scouts, and porters. In this way, they could afford to buy European goods.

Indians' involvement in the colonial market economy left them vulnerable to economic and political forces beyond their control, but it was alcohol that had the most corrosive effect on Iroquois society.[95] As we have seen in

[94] Cadwallader Colden, *The History of the Five Indian Nations of Canada* (London: T. Osborne, 1747).

[95] Gail D. MacLeitch, *Imperial Entanglements: Iroquois Change and Resistance on the Frontiers of Empire* (Philadelphia: University of Pennsylvania Press, 2011); Daniel K. Richter, *The Ordeal of the Longhouse* (Chapel Hill, NC: University of North Carolina Press, 1992).

the case of Mary Jemison, alcohol was responsible for violence, poverty, and loss of life among the Iroquois. It also contributed to the breakdown of families, traditional living patterns, and tribal discipline and order, the latter of which had allowed the Iroquois to maintain their independence and their sway over tribes far into the interior. Whatever the cause, the Iroquois found themselves increasingly vulnerable to the power struggles between the British and French over control of the interior of the continent.

This became abundantly clear after the French and Indian War or Seven Years War that ended in 1763. The Iroquois contributed mightily to the British victory, but in the subsequent Treaty of Fort Stanwix in New York in 1768, the British forced them to relinquish their claim to lands south of the Ohio River. Things only got worse during the American Revolution, when four of the six nations— the Seneca, Mohawk, Onondaga, and Cayuga—bet on the wrong horse, so to speak, and sided with the British. They paid dearly.

Washington ordered General John Sullivan to attack and punish them in 1779. In a letter dated May 31, 1779, he gave Sullivan detailed instructions to reject any overtures of peace, and instead, proceed with the "total destruction and devastation of their settlements and the capture of as many prisoners of every age and sex as possible. It will be essential to ruin their crops now in the ground and prevent their planting more."

Washington's endorsement of total warfare that targeted noncombatants was nothing new; it was standard operating procedure against the Indians from the very beginning, and it continued through the Indian wars of the 19th century. The Seneca in western portion of New York bore the brunt of the assault, after which Sullivan happily reported to George Washington, "The number of towns destroyed by this army amounted to forty besides scattering houses. The amount of corn destroyed, at a moderate computation, must amount to 160,000 bushels, with a vast quantity of vegetables of every kind. Every creek and river has been traced and the whole country explored in search of Indian settlements, and I am well persuaded that, except for one town situated near the Allegana [Allegany]...there is not a single town left in the country of the five nations."[96]

The soldiers not only destroyed villages, crops, orchards, and food stores, and scalped a few Indians along the way, they left behind smallpox. The Seneca needed only one word to describe what had happened to them: "whirlwind." They also had only one word for Washington. They referred to him as *Conotocaurius,* which translates into two words in English: "town destroyer."

The Seneca were left reeling, and along with their Iroquois and other Indian allies, they retreated to the protection of British forts along the Niagara frontier. In the aftermath of the war, the Americans made it clear they would not honor British treaties. In 1786, a second Fort Stanwix Treaty was imposed on the Iroquois, stripping them of their lands south and west of New York.

Eight years later, Iroquois sovereignty was recognized by the American government in the Canandaigua Treaty, which also granted the Seneca 4 million acres in western New York. Their security was short-lived. Three years later, the Big Tree Treaty reduced Seneca holdings to 200,000 acres. I have been told by some Seneca people that because that winter was particularly hard, the tribe was forced to give up its lands in order to survive. The remaining Seneca and Iroquois land was whittled down over the next 40 years, and the tribes were almost forced out of New York. Some would in fact leave for the Indian Territory in what is now Kansas.

The Tonawanda band of Seneca had to buy its lands back to remain in New York. The Cayuga and Oneida were not so lucky. They lost all their lands, with the Oneida ending up in Wisconsin, while the Cayuga were taken in by the Seneca. Multiply the Iroquois experience hundreds of times over, and you have the story of Indians in America.

Their brethren to the south and west learned the same lessons as the colonial population grew and spread into the interior. They agreed to negotiate treaties, surrendering land bit by bit, but that tactic did little more than delay the inevitable. Take the Cherokee, for example. Most people as-

[96] Frederick Cooke, *Journals of the Military Expedition of Major General John Sullivan Against the Six Nations of Indians in 1779* (New York: Knopf, Peck & Thomson, 1887), 307.

sume they lost their land with the Treaty of New Echota in 1835, which led to the Trail of Tears. However, there were 20 treaties dating back to 1721 through which the tribe ceded millions of acres to Virginia, the Carolinas, Tennessee, Kentucky, and the federal government.

Even with the federal government, the treaties weren't worth the paper they were written on. Just ask the Iroquois. Whether it was through dishonesty, bribery, alcohol, starvation, or force, Indians lost most of their lands over the next 100 years via treaties with the new nation. The agreements defrauded the Indians, as documented by Helen Hunt Jackson, and did little to protect them from the states and private individuals. What was most galling about these pacts was that the government magnanimously gave the Indians their own land. And that was the crux of the problem; negotiations were always on the terms and conditions of White men, largely because they had guns.

The seizure of Indian lands received legal sanction by Chief Justice Marshall in his defense of the Doctrine of Discovery in *Johnson v. McIntosh*, but he went further than simply affirming the principle that "Discovery is the foundation of title, in European nations" that gave the discoverers "an exclusive right to extinguish Indian title of occupancy." While the title to all Indian lands had indeed been extinguished by virtue of discovery, conquest, or treaties, Marshall admitted the normal rules that govern the relationship between conqueror and conquered did not apply in the case of the Indians. While he warned that the Indians should not be "wantonly oppressed," he also recognized that "the character and religion of the inhabitants afforded an apology for considering them a people over whom the superior genius of Europe might claim an ascendancy."

Marshall's opinion states that under other circumstances, the conquered were "incorporated" and "blended" into the "victorious nation and become subjects or citizens of the government with which they are connected." In such a case, the rights of the conquered to their land and property were protected, but that was not possible with the Indians. They "were fierce savages, whose occupation was war, and whose subsistence was drawn chiefly from the forest. To leave them in possession of their country, was to leave the country a wilderness; to govern them as a distinct people was impossible, because they were as brave and as high spirited as they were fierce, and were ready to repel by arms every attempt on their independence." Not only was it impossible to govern them, it was "impossible to mix" with them.

In Marshall's narrative of American history, which he traced back to colonial times, the Doctrine of Discovery gave cover to the racial imperative to dispossess Indians of their land, remove and replace them, and if necessary, take up the sword against them. Otherwise, if they were allowed to remain in the "neighbourhood," the "agriculturalists" risked "exposing themselves, and their families to the perpetual hazard of being massacred." The inevitable result was "frequent and bloody wars, in which the whites were not always the aggressors .... European policy, numbers and skills, prevailed. As the white population advanced, that of the Indians necessarily receded. The country in the immediate neighborhood of agriculturalists became unfit for them. The game fled into thicker and more unbroken forests, and the Indians followed." Marshall's narrative not only validated the Doctrine of Discovery, in doing so, he cemented every stereotypical assumption about Native people that Europeans brought with them. The same ones that were hardened by centuries of conflict.

They were a "warlike" and "inferior race" made up of "fierce savages" who lurked in the forests and routinely "massacred" settler families. They were not "agriculturalists" or "cultivators." Instead, they "hunted" and "wandered" without any "idea of individual property in lands." Consequently, they didn't improve their land but left it a "wilderness." Their "character and religion" were such that they could not be "incorporated" or "blended" into the "victorious nation." Nor were they worthy of citizenship, something they would be denied until 1924. Instead, they had to remain under the "protection" and "pupilage" of the government.

As the forest and game receded, so did the Indians, leaving their land to the "superior genius" of the European race. If they refused to give up their land or surrender their "independence," they were met by the sword in "bloody wars." Marshall took pains to point out that "whites were not always the aggressors," but in the end, "European policy, numbers and skills" won out against a people that were simply too few and too primitive. The Doctrine of Discovery granted Europeans an "exclusive right to extinguish Indian title of occupancy," which the Europeans were ready and willing to enforce. As Marshall reassured fellow Americans who may have been squeamish about Indian removal in the 1820s, "The title by conquest is acquired and maintained by force."[97]

Marshall's narrative was nothing more than the Moundbuilder Myth written into law. It captured the story of the European occupation of North America, and it revealed the hateful racial stereotypes behind it. It gave legal sanction to the dispossession of Indian land and the almost incessant warfare that drove Native people west and decimated their population to near extinction levels. In the process, it relieved Americans of any culpability by blaming it all on the Indians, thereby giving Americans license to continue their depredations for the next 200 years. It informed Marshall's decision in *Johnson v. McIntosh, Worcester v. Georgia,* and *Cherokee Nation v. Georgia,* and it consequently informed relations with Indian nations over the next two centuries.

Indeed, it was a playbook employed by all European nations against Indigenous people around the world, most if not all of whom just happened to be dark-skinned.

[97] *Johnson v. McIntosh,* 589-91.

Kill and Scalp All, Little and Big

The American Revolution brought little relief to the Indians east of the Mississippi River as the new nation plowed literally and figuratively into the 19th century. The war that changed the nation's government did not transform its people. In other words, the assaults on Indian lands were more relentless than ever, and total warfare took its toll on Native people's ability to survive. Resistance proved costly and futile, and yet, some were willing to try.

In 1791, the Shawnee and their allies in the Ohio country defeated the far-superior force of General Arthur St. Clair, killing 623 soldiers. At three times the number killed at Battle of the Little Bighorn, it was the largest loss of American lives in any battle during the Indian wars. However, their victory was temporary. Three years later, they were defeated by General Anthony Wayne at Fallen Timbers, and under the terms of the Treaty of Greenville, they were forced to surrender most of what is now the state of Ohio.

The same fate awaited Tecumseh, who organized an alliance along the frontier that stretched from the Great Lakes to the Gulf of Mexico during the War of 1812. It fell apart after the Creek were decimated by Andrew Jackson at the Battle of Horseshoe Bend in 1814, losing 800 men, women, and children, and most of their land. Tecumseh died in battle that same year, and with him, so did Indian resistance east of the Mississippi.

The Indian Removal Act of 1830 and Marshall's decision in *Johnson v. McIntosh* codified what had been happening for 200 years and justified what would happen for another 200. The treaties Indians signed at gunpoint to fend off starvation, or because of bribery or alcohol only staved off hostilities and did not guarantee their rights to their lands—or any land, for that matter. One by one, the Winnebago, Kickapoo, Natchez, Shawnee, Miami, Odawa, and so many others followed the Cherokee on their own trails of tears to unknown and often hostile lands. Once the East was swept clean, Americans set their eyes on the land west of the Mississippi.

The 17th century conflicts established a template for responding to Indian resistance for the next 200 years, setting the stage for more than three centuries of warfare and for America's so-called manifest destiny to spread civilization throughout the new world and even the old world. Warfare finally ended in 1923 with the little-known Posey War in Utah and New Mexico.

Along the way, there were plenty of atrocities on both sides, but it was always the Indians who took the blame. Take scalping, for example. The gruesome practice has always symbolized Indian barbarity even though White people scalped Indians, and colonial and state governments paid bounties for Indian scalps. Indeed, White people who took Indian scalps were celebrated with statues. Such is the case of Hannah Duston from Haverhill, Massachusetts, who was captured and taken in by an Indian family during King William's War in 1697. She managed to escape by killing and scalping 10 of her captives and returned to Massachusetts with her scalps, for which she received a reward of 50 pounds. Her story seems a bit apocryphal, but it was told over and over again. In the 19th century in the midst of the Indian wars, it became a symbol of American bravery in the face of Indian depravity. Ultimately, a 25-foot-high statue of Duston holding the prized scalps was erected and still stands in Dedham, New Hampshire. What was omitted from the story was the fact that six of those scalps were from children.[98]

Indian-led massacres were sometimes fabricated. In February 1867, reports of the sacking of Fort Buford on the Missouri River reached St. Louis and were picked up by newspapers across the East. Supposedly, Lakota Indians attacked the fort and killed everyone except the company commander, Colonel William Rankin, and his wife. Rankin was reportedly burned

---

[98] Barbara Cutter, "The Gruesome Story of Hannah Duston Whose Slaying of Indians Made Her an American Folk Hero," *Smithsonianmag.com* (April 9, 2018).

alive in front of her. She was raped and set free wrapped in a buffalo robe in the freezing Dakota winter. The problem was, no such attack ever happened.[99]

It is a similar story with the Almo Massacre of 300 White people in Idaho in 1861. A plaque was erected and still exists memorializing a bloody slaughter that is nothing more than an urban legend. Then there were all those attacks on the poor wagon trains on television and in the movies. Of the more than 400,000 people who crossed the United States on the Oregon trail, perhaps 400 died from Indian attacks in 25 years. On the other hand, an estimated 65,000 died from diseases, accidents, childbirth, and other hardships on what has been called "America's longest graveyard." So much for wild Indians whooping around intrepid pioneers who were forced to "circle the wagons."[100]

The ferocious fighting that ensued inflamed the fear of and repulsion for Indians and dark-skinned people that settlers brought with them. The accounts of atrocities by Indians fueled the racial hatred, especially on the frontier, that justified genocidal policies and actions by the American government and the extralegal acts of settlers that in some ways continue to this day in Indian Country.

Indians were offered an alternative to warfare. As we have seen, missionaries, government agents, and even presidents tried to persuade the Native people to give up the chase. The Indians listened politely, and many adopted some of what the White man offered, including Christianity, but most remained stubbornly unrepentant and continued to cling to traditional ways. For example, the Cherokee people, who were considered models of assimilation, adopted a constitution in 1827 to assert their cultural and political independence and sovereignty. They were Cherokee; they did not want to become White men.[101] Likewise, Handsome Lake, the Seneca

[99] Robert G. Athearn, "The Fort Buford 'Massacre,'" *The Mississippi Valley Historical Review,* 41, no. 4 (March, 1955), 675-84.

[100] Evan Andrews, "9 Things You May Not Know About the Oregon Trail," *history.com* (October 28, 2018).

[101] "Constitution of the Cherokee Nation," *Cherokee Phoenix* (February 21, 1928).

prophet, preached that the Iroquois people could adopt the White man's plow and log homes, and even send some of their children to school, but his teachings also revitalized Seneca and Iroquois culture in the form of the Longhouse Religion that saved the Iroquois languages and continues to inform Iroquois culture today.[102]

Whether they were Cherokee, Iroquois, Catawba, or Shawnee, they jealously guarded their sovereignty and their identities as Indians. Besides, like treaties, assimilation was offered on the terms and conditions of the White man. That alone was condescending and insulting, for it was offered on the assumption that Indians and their culture were inferior. The resistance and rejection the emissaries of civilization experienced must have been extremely frustrating. After all, they offered the Indians the benefits of civilization and the opportunity to escape sure extermination.

The signs were already obvious. Warfare, diseases, starvation, alcohol, and the breakdown of family and tribal cohesiveness were devastating Indian populations east of the Mississippi. Meanwhile on the frontier, the land-hungry settlers were lusting for the chance to kill Indians and take their lands, not to mention a scalp or two. Yet, the Indians tenaciously defended their sovereign independence and distinctive cultural identities.

I can only imagine the frustration and exasperation of missionaries and government agents as they tried repeatedly to convince Native people that the White road was better than the Red road. Indians no longer resort to arms to protect their independence—although I wouldn't bet on it if push came to shove. But they are just as adamant as their ancestors were about maintaining their sovereignty and all that goes with it. For Americans today, it means headaches for the Bureau of Indian Affairs (BIA), state governments, and pipeline companies. For Americans in the past, especially in the 19th century, it meant securing their conquest "by the sword" rather than risking massacre by "fierce savages, whose chief occupation was war," to quote Justice Marshall.

Despite the best efforts of missionaries and government agents to di-

---

[102] Arthur C. Parker, *The Code of Handsome Lake* (Albany, NY: Univ. of New York, 1913); Burich, *Thomas Indian School*, 27-13.

lute Indians in the great American melting pot, the centuries of warfare that continued throughout the 19th century hardened racial barriers, even though most Americans living east of the Mississippi were little affected by those conflicts, and most probably had never even seen an Indian. The heroic stories of their ancestors, such as Hannah Duston, braving Indian attacks were passed down from generation to generation, and embellished along the way, with no mention of White atrocities.

As the frontier receded and the battles moved farther west, along with the Indians, Americans learned about them through newspaper accounts that, as we have seen, sensationalized and even fabricated stories of Indian viciousness and cruelty to sell papers. It wasn't just the newspapers that whipped up public sentiment against Indians. American presidents, from George Washington to Teddy Roosevelt, took up Justice Marshall's narrative and reinforced public opinion about Indian inferiority and their likely demise.

For example, Washington borrowed the metaphor of the earliest settlers who compared Indians to wolves and declared, "Both were beasts of prey, tho they differ in shape." It was this mentality that justified Washington's orders to General John Sullivan in 1779 to "lay waste" to Iroquois settlements, an order Sullivan dutifully followed.[103] Similarly, Andrew Jackson told his officers to follow the Creek Indians into their "dens" and kill them all, including their "whelps." He told his soldiers at the Battle of Horseshoe Bend in 1814 to cut off the noses of the dead so they could get an accurate count, suggesting they also take strips of skin from the dead bodies to be made into razor strops and other leather goods.[104]

Jefferson, who frequently threatened Indians with extermination, felt it necessary to write Indian savagery into the Declaration of Independence, where he complained about the British bringing "on the inhabitants of our frontiers, the merciless Indian Savages, whose known rule of warfare, is the undistinguished destruction of all ages, sexes, and conditions." Evidently,

[103] Stannard, *American Holocaust,* 119.

[104] Ibid., 240; Smith, *Conquest,* 11.

soldiers who committed atrocities were patriots, while Indians were "merciless" savages.

These examples are well known and frequently referenced, but they're hardly the only cases of anti-Indian statements. Presidents Millard Fillmore and Franklin Pierce characterized Indians as "predatory bands," who, according to Fillmore, raided White settlements, plundering, murdering, and kidnapping, and threatening wagon trains on their way to the West Coast. After the Civil War, James Garfield considered it a "mockery" to "sit down in a wigwam with a lot of painted and half naked Indians" and negotiate. Besides, their names were, in Garfield's word, "unpronounceable." He hoped they would just "slip into extinction as quietly and humanely as possible." Benjamin Harrison labeled Indians an "ignorant and helpless people," and he blamed the massacre at Wounded Knee, which occurred under his administration, on the "naturally warlike and turbulent" Lakota.[105]

Of all the U.S. presidents, Teddy Roosevelt perhaps articulated best the prejudices that dated back to the first contact between Europeans and Indians. For instance, there was his infamous quote that he did not "go so far as to think that the only good Indians are the dead Indians, but I believe nine out of every ten are. And I shouldn't like to inquire too closely into the case of the tenth." Then there was his declaration that "the most vicious cowboy has more principle than the average Indian," not to mention his endorsement of the bloody Sand Creek Massacre of 1864.

But even more instructive was his 1902 order to Indian agencies to deny rations to men who refused to cut their hair. "Short hair by the males will be a great step in advance and will certainly hasten their progress towards civilization." It wasn't just their hair that was retarding their progress. They also painted their faces and refused to discard their "costumes and blankets," while their "dances and feasts are simply subterfuges to cover degrading acts and to disguise immoral purposes." After 300 years, Americans were still obsessing about Indians' hair, clothing, dances, ceremonies, and sexuality, just like their Puritan forefathers.

---

[105] *Indian Country Today* published a series of articles on presidential attitudes toward Indians, which it reprinted in the September 13, 2018, issue under the byline of Alysa Landry. All presidential quotes presented here are from that issue.

Granted, there were presidents who were sympathetic to the Indians' plight, but most doubted Indians could ever be assimilated or even coexist with White people. From James Monroe, who worried that the "degradation and extermination" of the Indians were inevitable "in their present state," to Martin Van Buren, who admitted Indians' population decline was "most rapid," to Garfield, who predicted Indians would soon "be remembered as a strange, weird, dreamlike specter," Indians were a vanishing race. The only hope to stave off extinction, which looked more and more likely by the end of the 19th century, was removal to reservations to protect them from White people and from themselves.

According to Grover Cleveland, Indians needed to be "defended against the cupidity of designing men and sheltered from every influence or temptations that retard their advancement." Of course, they also needed, in Cleveland's terms, heavy doses of "secular education and moral and religious teaching," and "the relinquishment of tribal relations and the holding of land in severalty." That is, the individual ownership of tribal lands, the White man's magic elixir for the "Indian problem."

But it was Ulysses Grant who best summarized during his presidency the dilemma White Americans faced when it came to Indians. He admitted the management of Indian affairs was "embarrassing," and he was concerned that Indians and White people did "not harmonize well, and one or the other has to give way in the end." However, he cautioned his fellow Americans that adopting a "system which looks to the extinction of a race is too horrible for a nation to adopt without entailing upon itself the wrath of all Christiandom and engendering in the citizen a disregard for human life and the rights of others, dangerous to society. I see no substitute for such a system, except in placing all the Indians on large reservations, as rapidly as it can be done, and giving them absolute protections there."

Grant's humanitarian appeals not only fell on deaf ears, they came way too late. Popular antipathy toward Indians, especially in the West, encouraged states and settlers to take matters into their own hands. That's what happened at Sand Creek in Colorado in 1864, when Governor John Evans sent out a call for all citizens to "Go in pursuit of all hostile Indians on the plains ... [and] kill and destroy, as enemies of the country, wherever the Indians may be found." Evans' call to arms was supported by William Byers, editor of the *Rocky Mountain News*, who declared that Indians were "a dissolute, vagabondish, brutal, and ungrateful race, and ought to be wiped from the face of the earth," demanding their "immediate extinction." Evans, with the approval of the secretary of war, mustered a militia of private citizens who were promised the property of any Indians they captured. He placed them under the command of John Chivington, a Methodist minister who had earlier announced his policy to "kill and scalp all, little and big."

The good citizens of Colorado took him at his word. They attacked a defenseless Northern Cheyenne and Arapaho camp. It mattered not that Black Kettle, a leader of the camp, flew a prized American flag given to him by President Lincoln and that he approached the militia waving a white flag. They killed several hundred Indians, including women and children, scalped and mutilated the genitalia of the dead, and plundered and burned teepees and food supplies, making sure any survivors would die of starvation or exposure. They later displayed their trophies to a cheering crowd in a Denver theater.

When asked about killing children, Chivington replied, "Nits make lice."[106] As far as he was concerned, the country needed a good delousing, a term Heinrich Himmler, Hitler's architect of the Final Solution, applied to Jews and other undesirables. As Himmler put it, "Anti-semitism is exactly the same as delousing. Getting rid of lice is not a question of ideology. It is a matter of cleanliness." Massacres like the one at Sand Creek amounted to ritualized cleansings.[107]

The slaughters set off decades of warfare along the frontier, which only confirmed settler belief in the savage nature of the "red devils." Teddy Roosevelt went so far as to declare that the "battle" of Sand Creek was "in spite of certain most objectionable details ... on the whole as righteous and beneficial a deed as ever took place on the frontier."[108]

[106] Stannard, *American Holocaust,* 129-34.

[107] Hugh Raffles, "Jews, Lice, and History," *Public Culture,* 19, no. 3 (September 1, 2007), 521.

[108] Stannard, *American Holocaust,* 134.

Although a Congressional committee considered it a massacre, a statue to honor the brave citizens who carried it out was erected and still stands in Denver. On it was a plaque dedicating the statue to those who fought in the "Battle of Sand Creek." The plaque has recently been removed but not so the name of John Evans from the 14,000-foot mountain in Mount Evans National Forest, while William Byers' name still graces Mount Byers. To add insult to injury, a town in eastern Colorado, not far from the scene of the massacre, is named Chivington. It's now just a wide spot in the road, but its name conjures up those "certain objectionable details" of that horrible day in November 1864.

There was no shortage of so-called battles that were really massacres. Both sides killed women and children, but it has generally been the Indians who were accused of kidnapping, torturing, raping, and murdering. Indian attacks were always considered massacres, while White people fought battles or wars. Thus, the destruction of hundreds of Lakota men, women, and children at Wounded Knee in 1890 was initially termed a battle, for which 20 soldiers were awarded the Congressional Medal of Honor. The same was true for the lesser-known Battle of Whitestone Hill in North Dakota.

In September 1863, driven by calls for revenge, General Alfred Sully set out in pursuit of Dakota Indians who escaped punishment in Minnesota after the bloody Dakota Wars the previous year. There had been several other skirmishes before Sully came across a large encampment of Dakota and Lakota people at Whitestone Hill. The Indians had gathered for a buffalo hunt to put away meat for the coming winter and to celebrate, as was their custom.

As at Sand Creek, the Indians approached the soldiers with a white flag but rejected the Americans' demand that they surrender. In the meantime, the Indians began to pack up their belongings, choosing to flee rather than fight. Sully, worried they would escape, attacked the camp, killing 300 to 400 men, women, and children, and capturing 150 more. The next morning, patrols were sent out to find those who may have escaped, while others killed the wounded who had been left behind. While many did escape, the troopers destroyed teepees, buffalo robes, blankets, and virtually everything the Native people possessed, including their horses and dogs. They also burned an estimated 500,000 pounds of buffalo meat, thereby ensuring many would succumb to the bitterly cold Dakota winter.[109]

Today, there is a monument to mark the site of the Battle of Whitestone Hill. The same doesn't hold true for the site of another bloody but largely unknown massacre that occurred in 1870 along the banks of the Marias River in northwestern Montana. Once again, responding to calls for revenge in the murder of a local rancher, the Army dispatched troops to find Owl Child, a Blackfeet Indian, who had killed the man and was supposed to be hiding in nearby Blackfeet encampments.

In January 1870, following the orders of General Sheridan to "strike them hard," an allegedly drunken Major Eugene Baker led 200 soldiers against a Piegan Blackfeet camp along the Marias River, even though he was warned he had the wrong village; Owl Child was not there. Instead, it was the camp of Heavy Runner, who approached the soldiers and handed the commanding officer his name paper to prove his identity. The officer tore it up, Heavy Runner was shot on the spot, and the destruction began. For three hours, the soldiers fired into teepees, and used butcher knives and axes to hack to death peaceful, largely unarmed Blackfeet Indians, many of whom were suffering from smallpox. By one account, the soldiers smashed infants' heads against rocks. About 50 older children were shot or bayonetted. By another account, the blood ran atop the frozen Marias River for half a mile.

Baker's report said only 33 males were killed as opposed to 90 women and 55 children, although others place the death counts much higher. Since the soldiers destroyed all the Indians' belongings, the survivors were left without shelter, blankets, food, and horses. They had to make their way on foot in the depth of winter to Fort Benton about 90 miles away. We'll never know how many perished on yet another trail of tears.

Baker and his men were celebrated, even though one of his own company commanders, Lieutenant Gus Doane, called it unequivocally "the greatest slaughter of Indians ever made by U.S. troops." Nevertheless, the Boze-

---

[109] Jerry Keenan, "The Battle of Whitestone Hill," *Wild West,* 21, no. 1 (June, 2008): 44-9.

man, Montana, *Pick and Plough* congratulated the soldiers for inflicting on the Indians the punishment they "deserved." As the newspaper explained, "The Indian of poetry and romance is not the Indian of fact; the former is said to be noble, magnanimous, faithful, brave; the latter we know to be possessed of every attribute of beastly depravity and ferocity." The *Helena Daily Herald* simply resorted to an analogy that dated back to colonial times, comparing the battle to hunting wolves. All of this to revenge the death of one White man.[110]

As I stood on the banks of the Marias River, across from the scene of the massacre, I was struck by how quiet and peaceful the valley is. It's silent, serene, and beautiful in its emptiness, seemingly untouched save for a few overgrown and rusting relics. Nature has reclaimed it. I was there at the same time of year as the massacre; the river was beginning to freeze. I tried to imagine the blood flowing across the ice as it did that wintry morning 150 years ago. I tried to imagine the explosion of drunken bloodlust that erupted that morning, and the terror of the men, women, and little children as the soldiers descended on the sleeping village. I tried to imagine the screams of the children as they watched in horror while their parents, relatives, and friends were shot, hacked to death, or burned alive. I tried to imagine the suffering of the survivors as they marched 90 miles in the freezing cold to Fort Benton, some dying along the way. I tried to imagine how the residue of the trauma they experienced would continue to influence their lives and the lives of future generations of Blackfeet people and future generations of other tribes that suffered the same fate. I tried, but it was hard to imagine that it happened at all.

There's no marker, no cemetery, no signs of a battle or massacre. It's almost surreal. Until recently, it had all but been forgotten except by the Blackfeet people, who were just the necessary and unavoidable debris left behind by the unrestrained transcontinental march of White Anglo-Saxon Protestant civilization. But it wasn't only the Blackfeet people who died that day. A way of life was extinguished. The empty valley is emblematic of

---

[110] Paul R. Wylie, *Blood on the Marias: The Baker Massacre* (Norman, OK: University of Oklahoma Press, 2017).

what happened to the Indigenous people of North America after 500 years of efforts to eradicate them and erase any memory of their existence.

What happened at the Marias River is just one of many such incidents during the Indian wars west of the Mississippi. There were several skirmishes that were caused by Mormons moving into Shoshone territory, along with thousands of immigrants and miners passing along the Oregon and California trails. In one case, troops were dispatched in the early morning hours of January 29, 1863, at the request of Mormons in Salt Lake City. The soldiers attacked a sleeping Shoshone camp in the Bear River Valley, indiscriminately killing men, women, and children, and destroying teepees and other property. They left the survivors exposed to frigid winter weather without food or shelter. The river there also ran red after troopers shot Indians who tried to flee by jumping into the water.

The White people's trespassing on Shoshone lands depleted the Indians' traditional food supplies, causing them to attack wagon trains and steal cattle from settlers in order to survive. As usual, newspapers demanded reprisals. The Salt Lake City *Deseret News* hoped the soldiers would wipe out the "bastard class of humans" responsible for the attacks against White settlers. Numbers differ, with one settler counting as many as 493 bodies. If true, it would make the Battle of Bear River Valley one of the bloodiest if least-known massacres of the Indian wars. It was certainly one of the cruelest. The militia tortured and murdered Shoshone people indiscriminately, raping the women, dashing babies' heads against rocks or throwing them in the river to drown, destroying lodges and food supplies, and killing or stealing the horses.[111]

Today, the old plaque marking the site of the Battle of Bear River has been replaced with a new one correctly designating it as a massacre. But even if the Bear River Massacre has been memorialized and included in the National Register of Historic Places, there are a lot of others that have been erased from the national memory.

To wit: Thirteen years before Bear River, Brigham Young ordered a

---

[111] Darren Parry, "Voice from the Dust: A Shoshone Perspective on the Bear River Massacre." Lecture, Brigham Young University, Charles Redd Center for Western Studies, Provo, UT (November 8, 2018).

campaign of extermination against the Timpanogos, a tribe related to the Ute. The sin of the Timpanogos was inhabiting the central portion of Utah, and thus, standing in the way of Mormons settlers who were pouring into the territory along the Mormon Trail in the 1840s and '50s. The Nauvoo Legion—or state militia—was dispatched against the Timpanogos on the pretext that they had stolen cattle.

Members of the militia approached the Indians, promising their mission was peaceful, and then proceeded to hunt down and execute the Indians in front of their families. Approximately 100 were murdered, 50 of whom were decapitated, their heads taken back to Fort Utah and gruesomely displayed as a warning to other Indians. The women and children who survived the slaughter were taken captive to serve as slaves for Mormon families and to be Christianized and civilized. Most of the survivors died or escaped and have essentially been forgotten, like the Fort Utah massacre.

The battles between the Texas Rangers and Comanche people are legendary, but not so the conflicts between the Rangers and the Karankawa, a group of now-extinct tribes along the Texas coast. The Texans came in contact with the Karankawa when the first American settlers began arriving in the territory in 1821. They described the people as half-naked, tattooed cannibals who were barely human. They confidently predicted they would soon be exterminated by the White population, and they were right. By 1824, the Karankawa people were already under attack, and by 1828, it was estimated that there were only 100 still alive. The last of the Karankawa was rumored to have been killed in 1858. There are no plaques or monuments to mark the passing.

In the Arizona territory in 1864, an unknown number of Yuvapai were attacked by Arizona militia at Skull Valley in response to raids on White settlements. The place was supposedly named for the skulls of beheaded Indians whom the soldiers left behind. Although the town built on the site proudly bears that grisly name, there is no memorial to explain what happened there. Nor are there any memorials to mark the spots on or near Pine Ridge Reservation, where the South Dakota Home Guard, responding to the frenzy over the Ghost Dance, massacred and scalped Sun Dancers on Pine Ridge. They also ambushed several wagons of Lakota in the weeks leading up to the well-known massacre at Wounded Knee. There is a monument at Wounded Knee, but even that is a sham, for it only recognizes the 47 "warriors" killed and not the hundreds of women and children buried in the mass grave it rests on.

If the Army and various militias and vigilantes needed excuses to enslave and kill Indians, it came naturally in California and began before the Gold Rush brought more than 200,000 immigrants to the territory. As we have seen, the killing and enslaving of Indians dated back to the Spanish occupation of California in the early 1600s, but even before the United States took possession of the territory in 1848, Americans were continuing Spanish policies and practices toward the Indians. At the start of the Mexican War in 1846, the American Army officer and future presidential candidate John C. Fremont, who had been exploring the area for several years, was ordered to assist American settlers in their revolt against Mexican authorities. Eventually Fremont would accept the Mexican surrender of California to the United States in 1847, but before that, he led a group of volunteers against an Indian camp along the Sacramento River, killing upward of 200 people.

After that, the massacres were routine and frequent occurrences, or better, rituals intended to exorcise the land of murderous savages. They were encouraged by federal and state government officials like Governor Peter Burnett, who in 1851, declared a "war of extermination … until the Indian race becomes extinct …." Burnett believed that an inferior race could not survive in the presence of a superior people, but his racism was not reserved for Indians alone. He believed "people of color," that is, free Black people, should be barred from entering the state on the grounds that their innate inferiority made it impossible for them to live peacefully alongside members of the White race.

The federal, state, and local governments armed citizens with the expressed purpose of killing Indians, and to sweeten the deal, they paid bounties for Indian heads. The federal government shelled out $1.7 million to rid California of Indians at a time when $1 million was a tidy sum.

Their plans almost worked, too. In the years between the Gold Rush and 1873, which marked the end of the Modoc War, there were 370 massacres, roughly defined as the deliberate killing of unnamed combatants or the killing of noncombatants, including women, children, and the elderly.

The number of Indians killed in these deadly sprees ranged from single digits to hundreds to the 1,000 or more who perished during the Round Valley Massacre from 1856 to 1859. These slaughters were often given cover by the term "war" or "battle." That said, there was the Mariposa War, the Owens Valley War, the Mendocina War, the Tula River War, the El Dorado Indian War, the Bald Hills War, Jaboe's War, and the Pease River Battle. Yet, regardless of whether they were called battles, wars, or massacres, the destructive effects of these conflicts cannot be measured via a simple body count. They destroyed homes, crops, food supplies, blankets, and clothing, and they left the survivors vulnerable to starvation, disease, and exposure. In the end, these losses may have killed more Indians than bullets.

The massacres were carried out by the U.S. Army, state militia, and, more often than not, gangs of settlers and miners such as the Blades and the Eel River Rangers. As thousands of miners poured into the state, followed by thousands more hoping to profit from them, conflicts with the tribes throughout California were inevitable. Encouraged by authorities, whipped up by exaggerated accounts of Indian atrocities, and driven by the racial hatred of Indians, White people were determined to take matters into their own hands. This was especially true because authorities seemed unwilling or unable to stop or punish the Indians.

Consequently, the aggressors used any pretext they could find to kill and enslave Indians, including women and children, to seize their lands and property, and to drive some of them into extinction. The notorious Indian killer Ben Wright indiscriminately killed and scalped Indians without provocation and maybe just for the fun of it. Wright even borrowed a tactic from the Pilgrims and the Jamestown settlers when he invited some Modoc people to a peace parley and feast, and supposedly tried to poison them. When that failed, he began shooting. His men joined in, murdering as many as 90 Indians. When the killing was done, Wright and his men were proclaimed heroes as they rode into Yreka, flourishing the scalps they took. Even more sickening, the state paid them for their killing spree.[112]

California has been called the "clearest case of genocide." Slavery in one form or another, the killing of Indians for sport or money, and life on the reservations or on the run decimated the Native population in the so-called Golden State. Many of the more than 40 tribes originally in California vanished either because they were wiped out or because their numbers had been reduced to the point where they were too small and/or lacked the genetic diversity to reproduce. Whatever the cause, what happened to the Indigenous people in California was nothing more than an extension of what had been taking place throughout America since their first contact with Europeans.

The formula never varied: Hunt the Indians down, kill men, women, children, and elderly alike, burn their shelters, destroy their food supplies, loot their possessions, kill their horses and dogs, and enslave or execute captives. They were the same tactics the Pilgrims and Puritans used against Native people in New England, General Sullivan used against the Seneca, and Jackson used against the Creek. In the same vein, when General Phillip Sheridan ordered his troops to attack Indians along the Washita River, he told them to "destroy villages and ponies, to kill or hang all warriors, and bring back all woman and children …."

Indeed, Custer was carrying out Sheridan's orders in November 1868 when he destroyed the Cheyenne village of Black Kettle, who had survived the massacre at Sand Creek. Black Kettle's village was destroyed, and he was killed along with unknown and perhaps unknowable "warriors." Custer also took a number of women and children captive. Leaving nothing to chance, he killed approximately 600 ponies, making the surviving Indians vulnerable to starvation and the frigid winter weather of the Plains.

The killing of ponies was standard operating procedure and an example of the total warfare practiced against the Plains Indians. It not only limited their ability to fight and prevented them from fleeing approaching soldiers,

---

[112] Benjamin Madley, *American Genocide* (New Haven, CT: Yale University Press, 2017); Brendan C. Lindsay, *Murder State* (Lincoln, NE: University of Nebraska Press, 2012).

it kept them from their seasonal migrations in search of food and other resources they needed to survive. Most importantly, it limited their ability to hunt buffalo, their traditional and principal source of protein.

Even more than that, it was a direct attack on their culture and identity. Joe Medicine Crow, the World War II hero who went on to become a leader among the Crow people, told a story many times over about the slaughter of horses on his reservation in Montana when he was a young boy. Ranchers and farmers had evidently complained to the BIA that the horses, numbering in the thousands, were eating the grass and trampling crops on the lands they leased from the Crow. The superintendent of the reservation, Calvin Asbury, decided to eliminate the problem, and with it, other elements of Crow culture by offering ranchers and farmers $4 a head to kill off the horse herds.

I've heard different figures for the number of horses killed, ranging from 25,000 to over 40,000. The carcasses were left to rot until bone collectors came to cart them away and turn them into fertilizer, just as when the buffalo herds were destroyed. When I heard Joe Medicine Crow tell the story at the Buffalo Bill Cody Museum, he was already an old man. The story was based on the memories of a young boy, but he never forgot the smell of the dead horses as they moldered in the sun.

The roundup and slaughter of horse herds was repeated on the Northern Cheyenne and Wind River Reservations, and in each case, it cut to the heart of Plains Indian culture and identity. As Joe Medicine Crow explained at another presentation, "The horse is our brother. We ride them; we parade them; we use them in ceremonies; we give them away to our brothers-in-law. The horse is completely involved in our culture." If you don't believe it, go to Crow Fair some August.[113]

The killing of their ponies, along with the slaughter of the buffalo herds, forced Indians onto reservations, where their numbers continued to decline. It amounted to cultural and economic genocide as tribes everywhere were cut off from their traditional economies. Whether it was the buffalo

[113] Carrie McCleary, "Of Horses and Men: Superintendent Asbury's Deadly Assault on the Crow," *Tribal College,* 14, no. 3 (February 15, 2003).

hunters on the Plains, the sheepherders among the Navajo, or the "Diggers" in California, they all stood in the way of the homesteaders, railroads, miners, and timber companies. They not only had to be removed, they needed to be exterminated.

Once again, what happened in California was consistent with the patterns established more than two centuries earlier: Extinguish Natives' land claims, and if necessary, extinguish the Natives as well, a sentiment shared by most Americans, from pioneers to presidents. What made the massacres in California so shocking was that they took place in such a short period of time. In a mere 25 years, 370 massacres occurred, which means that for every Round Valley or Indian Island massacre, there were dozens more that were too small or too isolated to be recorded. Or they were swept under the historical rug, or were plowed under or paved over and lost forever.

If that same ratio applied to massacres dating back to the Colonial Period, there may have been thousands of smaller unknown and unknowable massacres scattered across the historical landscape. They may not have been the result of some "coordinated plan," but neither were they random outbreaks of violence spurred by local and unrelated events. They were driven by a constant drumbeat of calls to kill, scalp, and enslave the vermin, and destroy the social, economic, and religious institutions upon which their survival depended.

Behind it all was the racial hatred Europeans brought with them and that continued to kill Indians long after the wars ended, albeit in more insidious but nonetheless lethal ways. If the Native people were to survive and be redeemed, they were in need of a good personal, cultural, and moral scrubbing, something Mark Twain even proposed. As he once quipped with his inimitable wit, although a massacre would be a quicker solution to the Indian problem, "Soap and education are not as sudden as a massacre, but they are more deadly in the long run."

Perhaps the best example of this popular sentiment was an 1880s Procter & Gamble advertisement for Ivory Soap:

We were once factious, fierce and wild,
In peaceful arts unreconciled
Our blankets smeared with grease and stains
From buffalo meat and settlers' veins
Through summer's dust and heat content
From moon to moon unwashed we went,
But IVORY SOAP came like a ray
Of light across our darkened way
And now we're civil, kind and good
And keep the laws as people should,
We wear our linen, lawn and lace
As well as people with paler face
And now I take, where'er we go
This cake of IVORY SOAP to show
What civilized my squaw and me
And made us clear and fair to see.[114]

The ad relayed public sentiments about Indians that dated back to the first contact. They were dirty, greasy "blanket Indians" who were without the "peaceful arts" of civilization. They were "fierce and wild" and stained with the blood of "settlers' veins." Most of all, their skin was darker that those with a "paler face," and it was only through the blessings of civilization, and of course, Ivory Soap, that their "darkened" way was lighted, their skin became "fair to see," and they became good little Indians.

The racism in this ad is painfully obvious, but not necessarily fanciful. Take for example, the famous before-and-after photos of Indian children at the Carlisle Indian Industrial School, the first and most famous of the federal Indian boarding schools. They were photographed upon arrival as "blanket Indians" and again after they had been scrubbed clean and civilized. The photos were an advertising ploy to demonstrate the school's therapeutic value and to generate support for its mission. Indeed, the transformations were amazing; the color of the students' skin was remarkably lighter. Perhaps they used Ivory Soap.

[114] Smith, *Conquest*, 9-10.

There were private citizens like Helen Hunt Jackson and the Indian Rights Association that worked to end the bloodshed and reform conditions on the reservations. Unfortunately, sympathy for the Indians was largely limited to the East Coast, where most people probably had never seen a live Indian except in Wild West shows. Out West, where Indians were a real, even if no longer a threatening presence, the racial hatred continued unabated.

For example, in 1881, *The New York Times* reported that the Colorado legislature was considering a bill that would offer bounties of $25 each for skunks or Indian scalps "with ears entire." *The Times* opined that "to class Indians and skunks together is the habit of the free and boundless West." The bill reflected the difference between what the Times called "Boston philanthropy," which assumes that the "Indian is a human being" on one hand, and on the other is the frontier, "where the people are not fettered by traditions, nor swayed by considerations of sickly sentimentality, [and] it is the custom to class Indians with vermin, both of which are to be exterminated."[115]

In short, to those in closest contact with Indians and not affected with "sickly sentimentality," Indians were not humans, and therefore, they were fair game to be hunted to extermination like wolves. L. Frank Baum from South Dakota, an author of children's books, including *The Wonderful Wizard of Oz,* subscribed to this notion. In the wake of Sitting Bull's murder in December 1890 and the consequent massacre at Wounded Knee, Baum proclaimed that Sitting Bull's death symbolized the end of the Indian and the triumph of civilization.

Sounding much like Chief Justice Marshall, Baum declared, "The Whites by law of conquest, by justice of civilization, are masters of the American continent, and the best safety of the frontier settlements will be secured by the total annihilation of the few remaining Indians. Why annihilation? Their glory has fled, their spirit broken, their manhood effaced; better they die than live the miserable wretches that they are."

A few weeks later, after the massacre at Wounded Knee, Baum acknowl-

---

[115] "Indians and Skunks," *The New York Times* (February 18, 1881).

edged it was an unnecessary massacre caused by incompetent and weak military leadership that did not act sooner to put down the "uneasy Indians." The humane thing to do for both the settlers and the Indians was to exterminate the latter, not unlike the action one would take with a sick dog. "The Pioneer has before declared that our only safety depends upon the total extermination of the Indians. Having wronged them for centuries we had better, in order to protect our civilization, follow it up by one more wrong and wipe these untamed and untamable creatures from the face of the earth."[116] Fortunately, Baum's views didn't carry the day, but most Americans still hoped or expected Indians would, in Garfield's terms, quietly "slip into extinction" and "be remembered as a strange, weird dreamlike specter."

Americans were not alone. The European powers used their superior weaponry and moral certitude to replace and exterminate physically, morally, and intellectually inferior species in Africa, South America, Asia, and the South Seas. They no longer needed God's providence to justify their actions; they had Charles Darwin.

He had witnessed the degradation and extermination of the Tasmanians and the Argentinian Indians during his voyage on the *Beagle,* and he certainly knew what was going on in the British Empire and in North America. Evolution was not a process but a civilizing force. Those who could adapt would survive; those who couldn't would perish. As he wrote in the *Descent of Man* in 1871, "At some future period not very distant as measured in centuries, the civilized races of man will almost certainly exterminate and replace throughout the world the savage races."[117]

To the European nations racing to extend their empires, the conquest and extermination of racially inferior people merely sped up the inevitable and inexorable results of evolution. Not only was it inevitable and inexorable, it was merciful; evolution unaided by human agency would only have prolonged their suffering.

---

[116] Mary Pierpont, "Was Frank Baum a racist or just the creator of Oz," *Indian Country Today* (October 25, 2000).

[117] Sven Lindqvist, *Exterminate All the Brutes* (London: Granta Publications, 1990), 100.

Americans such as Teddy Roosevelt couldn't have agreed more. In his book *The Winning of the West,* he wrote, "The most ultimately righteous of all wars is a war with savages … Americans with Indians, Boer and Zulus, Cossack and Tartar, New Zealander and Maori,—in each case the victor, however horrible though many of deeds are, has laid deep the foundations for the future greatness of a mighty people."[118]

Here was a U.S. president admitting Americans had committed "horrible" acts against the Indians in the name of laying the "foundation" of a great nation, just as the European powers were doing to Indigenous people in the darkest corners of the world. Indeed, in the last half of the 19th century, Americans turned their superior and more deadly weaponry developed during the Civil War on warriors and noncombatants alike, hastening the inevitable. When the shooting stopped, they let nature work its course on the reservations, where deprivation and disease would finish the job.

Not only was it righteous, it was a biological imperative. The inferiority of the "savage" species fascinated Americans and Europeans alike, an interest that led to the rise of the comparative study of racial differences. From the Great Chain of Being in the Middle Ages to Darwin's *On the Origin of Species,* Europeans—and Americans by extension—believed human beings could be ranked along an evolutionary scale according to criteria such as the size and shape of their skulls and especially the capacity of their brain cavities. Colonialism had introduced Europeans to Indigenous people from around the world. Not only did they have diverse complexions and physical traits, but varied and even shocking habits that could only be explained by their inherited characteristics, or what today would be called their DNA. These "specimens" were often brought back to be studied or put on display for popular audiences.

Whereas the bodies of a Beothuk couple were dug up and shipped to Edinburgh for examination, the United States was fortunate enough to have a ready supply on its doorstep. The best-known case is that of Ishi, the last of the Yurok tribe in California. Ishi wandered out of the mountains

---

[118] Theodore Roosevelt, *The Winning of the West,* vol. 4 (New York: The Current Literature Publishing Co., 1905), 56.

in 1911 and became something of a celebrity in and around San Francisco. He was examined and observed by anthropologists as one of the last Indians uncontaminated by civilization. When he died in 1916, his brain was removed, despite the tradition of his people that his body should remain intact. It was nevertheless shipped to the Smithsonian, where it was stored until it could be examined along with thousands of other Indian remains. Eventually Ishi's brain became a cause *celebre*. It was finally—and rightfully—returned to California in 2000 to be buried with his other remains.[119]

Ishi's case is sad but not unusual in the 19th and early 20th centuries. There was a fierce competition for Indian remains among anthropologists associated with museums and universities, and collectors looking for souvenirs. The U.S. Army, most of which was stationed in the trans-Mississippi West, was in the best position to take advantage of Indian remains.

Skulls were the prized possessions. In 1868, George A. Otis, a medical doctor and director of the Army Medical Museum, issued a macabre order to Army physicians to collect crania of Native people for the museum "to aid in the progress of anthropological science by obtaining measurements of a larger number of skulls of aboriginal races of North America."[120]

The physicians were in close proximity to battles and reservations, where mortality rates were high, plus they had the experience and tools necessary for amputations. Today's international humanitarian laws prohibit the mutilation of bodies killed in battle, but in the 19th century, the Army medical staff proceeded with abandon. The physicians took the Indian skulls, skinned them, boiled or steeped them in quick lime to remove the flesh, and then shipped them to the museum. They took the skulls from Indians killed in battle and those who died from epidemics. Some even took bodies from freshly dug graves. Yet another source was Indians executed for crimes. Such was the case with the four Modoc in California, who were hanged in 1873 for their role in the Modoc War.[121]

[119] Orin Starn, *Ishi's Brain* (New York: W.W. Norton & Co., 2004).

[120] Ibid.

[121] Robert Aquinas McNally, "Four More Heads for the Indian Trophy Room," *Indian Country Today* (June 15, 2016).

The surgeons were not alone in these mutilations. As mentioned earlier, at the Sand Creek Massacre in Colorado in 1864, members of the militia took souvenirs from dead Indians, including genitalia and other body parts. Indians so feared this practice, they tried to bury their dead in secret. Crazy Horse's family buried him surreptitiously on what is now Rosebud out of fear his body would be treated as a trophy. To this day, the whereabouts of his grave remains a secret. Similarly, we don't know how many died at Wounded Knee because family members spirited their bodies away at night, presumably to prevent them from being stolen and mutilated. The rest were dumped into a mass grave designated by the aforementioned marker that only recognized the 47 "warriors" who were killed in the "battle." There is no mention of the hundreds of women, children, and elderly who died that cold December day.

By 1898, the Army Medical Museum received 2,208 skulls. After examining them, Otis concluded Indians "must be assigned a lower position in the human scale than has been believed heretofore."[122] That was really saying something, given that Americans barely considered Native people to be human at all. Otis' conclusions were hardly necessary. The mutilation of Indian bodies and their preservation as laboratory specimens or as curiosities to be displayed in museums says it all: Indians were not human beings. In other words, they were not just lower than Europeans on an evolutionary scale, they were an entirely different species. In Darwinian terms, they were an inferior species being displaced by a superior one. In the starker terms of Social Darwinism then becoming popular, they were simply not "fit" to compete and survive.

The collection of Indian remains was not limited to the Army Medical Museum. The Smithsonian eventually acquired 18,500 Indian remains, while the Peabody Museum at Harvard had 10,500 in its collections, and the American Museum of Natural History in New York City had 8,000. There were thousands more in smaller museums around the country. Altogether, under the Native American Graves Protection and Repatria-

---

[122] Ibid.; Samuel Redman, "When Museums Rushed to Fill Their Rooms With Bones," *smithsonianmag.com* (March 15, 2016).

tion Act, museums have repatriated 1.7 million goods stolen from Indian graves, 57,00 skeletal remains, and 15,000 sacred goods to their respective tribes.[123] Some Indian remains and belongings even found their way to Finland, of all places. The Finnish government has finally agreed to return the 20 remains and 28 funerary objects taken from Mesa Verde in 1891 by a Swedish researcher.[124]

There were also private collections. Acting on a tip in 2014, the FBI raided the Indiana home of Don Miller, a Christian missionary who amassed a vast collection of archaeological artifacts, including thousands of Indigenous bones, which most believed came from Indians. What is most amazing about this story is that he displayed them in cases in his home and invited Boy Scouts and neighbors to view them. Reporters did stories on them, and nobody thought anything about it. The good news is that efforts have been undertaken to identify the remains in Miller's home and in other collections and return them to their tribes for proper burial under the aforementioned act.[125] The bad news is visitors to Miller's makeshift museum apparently did not find anything wrong with looting Indian graves for souvenirs. Even today, many Americans look upon Indians as an exotic species that should be studied. As one Navajo woman described to me, "We are like specimens in a zoo or museum." That explains why many Native people have asked me whether I am an anthropologist or an archaeologist. I didn't understand why at the time, but now I know.

By the end of the 19th century, the Indians had nearly been exterminated. The few that were left had been exiled to isolated and ever-shrinking reservations with every aspect of their lives—from their religion, to their food, to their education, to the length of their hair—controlled by government agents and missionaries backed by the cavalry. They were considered a racially, morally, and technologically inferior species that had never

---

[123] Chip Colville, "'As Native Americans, We Are in a Constant State of Mourning,'" *The New York Times* (April 4, 2019).

[124] Susan Montoya Bryan and Felicia Fonseca, "Finland agrees to return Native American remains to tribes," *Denver Post* (October 3, 2019).

[125] Sheena Goodyear, "FBI finds thousands of Indigenous bones in raid on elderly missionary's home," *As It Happens,* on Canadian Broadcasting Corporation, February 27, 2019.

evolved and was doomed to extinction and destined to be fodder for museum exhibits.

Never mind that no executive order was issued, and no law was passed. After three centuries of clamoring for their extermination by everybody from settlers to residents of the White House, compounded by lurid stories of Indian brutality, neither was necessary. True, there were a few dissenters like Helen Hunt Jackson, but most Americans tended to agree with Oliver Wendell Holmes, Sr., the 19th-century poet and physician who declared in an oration on the Pilgrims that it was only natural for Americans to "hate" Indians and to hunt them down like "wild beasts." They were, after all, only a sketch in "red crayon" that would soon be erased to make room for a "manhood a little more like God's own image," and for whom there was "only one solution: extermination."[126]

The few survivors were nuisances who were to be sequestered in end-of-life warehouses, aka reservations, "to keep and treat him half way right" until they gradually disappeared, just as our old friend H.M. Smee suggested. The problem was that they stubbornly refused to go away. Neither did they want to assimilate, even though the costs of their resistance were and would continue to be staggering. As a Seneca friend of mine declared regarding his rejection of U.S. citizenship, "I choose to remain an *Ongwe Onwe*—or original real people."

Life would be so much easier if only the Native people could leave their past behind and embrace the American Dream. Instead, they remain a nagging and inconvenient reminder of a nation's ugly past.

And that's a monumental stumbling block for a nation that clings desperately to the idea of its exceptionalism.

---

[126] Oliver Wendell Holmes, Sr., "The Pilgrims of Plymouth," (Oration, December 22, 1855) in Cephas Brainer and Eveline Brainerd, eds., *The New England Society Orations,* vol. 2 (New York: The Century Co., 1901), 298.

Missionization

Missionization is one aspect of the European conquest, colonization, and genocide of Indigenous people that is often overlooked or misconstrued. All colonial enterprises were expected to propagate Christianity among the heathens, pagans, infidels, and just plain savages who inhabited the nether parts of the world.

In Latin America, the Spanish and Portuguese employed Jesuit, Franciscan, and Dominican priests to extend the frontiers of their empires by converting and civilizing Indians. In North America, Spanish religious orders established missions in Florida and the American Southeast in the 16th century and California in the 18th century. The French dispatched Jesuits to spread their influence and Christianity among the Native populations along the St. Lawrence River and the Great Lakes, and all the way down to the mouth of the Mississippi by the end of the 17th century.

Missionization was not as systematic in the Protestant English colonies. This was largely due to the fragmented nature of Protestantism and the paucity of missionaries until the First Great Awakening in the 1730s and 1740s. In addition, there was warfare that decimated the Native populations and fueled colonial contempt for the Indians. However, English sovereigns included the mandate to Christianize the Indians in colonial charters. Although different, all three efforts to convert the Indians had serious demographic consequences for the Indigenous people they contacted. As Linda A. Newson concluded, aside from slavery, "Missionization brought more immediate and profound cultural changes to native settlements, subsistence patterns, social relations and beliefs, the demographic consequences of which rendered the chance of survival more problematic."[127]

[127] Newsom, "Demographic Collapse," 272-6.

For example, missionaries were often responsible for spreading European diseases in the interior of the continent. Beginning in 1615, the French in Canada sent Recollet missionaries to the Wendat or Huron people of what is now Ontario. They were followed by Jesuits in 1626. Although neither had much success converting the Native people, the epidemics both groups brought with them cut the population in half by the 1640s. What the diseases didn't do, the Iroquois from across Lake Ontario finished, as the depleted and sickened Wendants were unable to defend themselves against their foes from the south who were bent upon controlling the fur trade into the interior.

We have already seen the dreadful demographic effects the Spanish missions had on California Indians. The English never put much effort into missionizing the Indians. Although colonial charters contained instructions to convert and civilize the tribes within their boundaries, their efforts generally failed. For example, Virginia's charter in 1606 required the colony to spread "Christian Religion to such people, as yet live in Darkness and miserable Ignorance of the true Knowledge and Worship of God."[128] The colony attempted to start a college for Indians in 1618, and the following year encouraged colonists to take Indian children into their homes, but all that ended with the Indian wars that started in 1622 and lasted for more than two decades. It would take another 70 years before efforts would resume with the founding of William and Mary College in 1693.

Similarly, the charter of the Massachusetts Bay Company in 1629 exhorted the colonists to "wynn and incite the natives … to the knowledge and obedience of the onlie true God and Savior of mankind."[129] Accordingly, Harvard College was established in 1650 to educate colonial and Indian children, although only six Native scholars attended the school before the program ended in 1693.

Meanwhile, John Eliot established 14 Praying Towns beginning in 1646 to convert and civilize Indians, and to protect them from the baleful in-

[128] Bobby Wright, "The Broken Covenant: American Indian Missions in the Colonial Colleges," *Tribal College,* 7, no. 1 (Summer, 1995).

[129] Ibid.

fluences of their unrepentant brethren and the colonists. The experiment had moderate success until King Philip's War in 1676, after which 10 of the towns were dismantled by the colonial government.

It was not the only ill-fated movement. The Society for the Propagation of the Gospel in Foreign Parts, established in England in 1701, tried its hand at converting the Indians in the southern colonies with little if any success, plus its work ended with the Revolution. At William and Mary College, Native students failed to adapt and either died from disease and change of diets, or they simply ran away. In Pennsylvania, Moravian missionaries established a mission to the Lenni Lenape or Delaware at Gnadenhutten, Pennsylvania, but the mission Natives rebelled and killed the missionaries in 1755. The Moravians tried again, this time in Gnaddenhutten, Ohio, but that mission was destroyed by American militiamen, who killed and scalped almost 100 Indian men, women, and children.

Faced with Indian indifference and resistance, and beset with money problems, most missionaries abandoned the mandates of their colonial charters to go forth and Christianize, civilize, and educate the Native people. Of all these efforts, the only one to survive the Revolution was Moor's Charity School. Founded by Eleazar Wheelock in 1754 in Lebanon, Connecticut, it eventually became a preparatory school for Dartmouth College in New Hampshire. The objective of the school, according to Wheelock, was to "cure the natives … of their savage temper, deliver them from their low sordid and brutish manner, and make them good wholesome members of society, and obedient subjects of the King of Zion."[130]

Wheelock was reasonably successful with Moor's, enrolling more than 60 Native girls and boys in the school's first 15 years, along with a number of English students. The girls received a modest classroom education. Given that they were being groomed to be missionary wives someday, they spent most of their time learning "housewifery," something the students and their parents protested. The boys received a classical education of English, Latin, Greek, and Hebrew, and ministerial training, since they were

[130] Eleazar Wheelock to Governor John Wentworth, September 12, 1762, MSS, Dartmouth College History.

expected to become missionaries. In addition, they worked half of each day on the farm to help feed the school and learn the "mysteries" of farming.

The students complained they did not go to the school to become common fieldhands, and their parents that Indians already knew how to farm. Parents also objected to the school's strict regimen. It included corporal punishment that conflicted with the more lenient Native child-rearing practices that spared the rod, and according to missionaries, spoiled the child. There were other problems as well, as the Native students engaged in behavior that Wheelock's own sister, Sarah Bingham, described as "ignorant" and "savage," especially when it came to the consumption of alcohol.[131]

Some parents withdrew their children, and other students left on their own or were expelled. In 1769, on the eve of moving the school to New Hampshire, it had only three Indian students and 16 White pupils. Wheelock maintained Moor's Charity School as a prep school for Dartmouth College, which he founded in 1770.

The schools in general enjoyed some success, with an almost immediate enrollment of 40 Indian and 120 White students, but they were plagued with money problems. At one point, the students complained to the trustees that they were going hungry. More importantly, Wheelock despaired about educating Indians, since most did not go on to become missionaries and missionary wives as he had hoped. But his complaints about the difficulty of educating Native youth were most revealing. Not only did Indian students have trouble with English, let alone Latin, Greek, and Hebrew, they struggled to use furniture.

As he confessed in 1761, They would soon kill themselves with Eating and Sloth, if constant care were not exercised for them at least the first year. They are used to set upon the Ground, and it is as natural for them as a seat to our Children. They are not wont to have to have Cloaths but what they wear, nor will without much Pains be brot to take care of any. They are used to a Sordid Manner of Dress, and love it as well as our Children to be clean. They are not used to any Regular Government, the sad consequences of

---

[131] Sarah Bingham to David McClure, August 1, 1787, MSS, Dartmouth College History.

which you may a little guess at. They are used to live from Hand to Mouth and have no care for Futurity. They have never been used to the Furniture of an English House .... Our Language when they seem to have got it is not their Mother Tongue and they cannot receive nor communicate in that as in their own .... And they are as unpolished and uncultivated without as within.[132]

The contempt for Indians and their culture in Wheelock's confession was palpable and even visceral. He eventually lost interest in Indian education. After he died in 1779, Moor's Charity School closed, and Dartmouth never lived up to its reputation as a school for Indians.

Indian missions in the 18th century generally failed and were eventually abandoned, but they set the stage for future efforts to redeem the so-called savages. For example, the half-day system employed at Moor's Charity School became the staple at Indian boarding schools into the 20th century, as well-intended missionaries and reformers tried to convince Native students to learn the skills of husbandry. In addition, the failures of the 1700s did not stop the new government from trying its hand at missionizing after the Revolution. Rather than relying solely upon threats and outright acts of extermination, General-turned-President George Washington decided to take a softer approach, looking to missionaries to persuade the Indians to give up their savage ways, and of course, their land. For their part, churches jumped at the chance to missionize the Indians and the largely unchurched White settlers on the frontier.

For instance, the Presbyterians and Congregationalists formed a Plan of Union in 1801 to evangelize the trans-Appalachian west, later creating the American Board of Commissioners of Foreign Missions to coordinate missions to such "foreign" places as Indian reservations. The government went so far as to pass the Civilization Fund Act in 1819, which provided $10,000 per year for "civilizing missions" to teach Indians the "arts of civilization" and prevent "the further decline and final extinction of the Indian tribes."

Five years later, the Bureau of Indian Affairs was created to administer the fund and the programs to civilize the Indians. But since the BIA was

---

[132] Wheelock to George Whitefield, July 4, 1761, MSS, Dartmouth College History.

under the Department of War, there was little doubt that the military was the ultimate civilizing force. With missionaries and government agents playing good cop/bad cop, the government tried to persuade rather than coerce Indians to give up their old habits, take up the White man's plow, move into log houses, and send their children to school.

In the new state of New York, it was the Quakers who first took up the challenge. When Quaker missionaries arrived in Iroquois territory in western New York in the 1790s, they brought with them the idea of dividing Indian lands into individual homesteads to encourage Native people to give up the chase. Quakers were some of the first to venture into the hinterlands, while their interest in the Indians dated back to William Penn himself and his first visit to Pennsylvania in 1682. However, troubles with the Delaware and other tribes in the colony, including the infamous Walking Treaty of 1737 and the Gnadenhutten massacre, convinced them to create in 1755 The Friendly Association for Regaining and Preserving Peace with the Indians by Pacific Measures.

Having ministered to tribes in Pennsylvania and New Jersey, the Quakers were invited, upon the advice of none other than George Washington, to advise the Iroquois at the negotiation of the Canandaigua Treaty in 1794, which recognized Iroquois sovereignty and land claims in New York. The Quakers later intervened on behalf of the Iroquois to prevent them from being removed from New York under the fraudulent Buffalo Creek Treaty of 1836. Their determination to convince the Seneca to adopt private property, live in single-family dwellings, and take up the White man's plow became the playbook for missionary activities and government policies. Sadly, it was a strategy that had disruptive effects on Native communities and resulted in serious demographic consequences for tribes across the country.

The Quakers began their work among the Iroquois with the Seneca, the western-most tribe of the Six Nations of the Iroquois, otherwise known as the *Haudenausaunee* Confederacy. The Seneca people were still reeling from General John Sullivan's campaign against them in 1779 during the Revolution. Their population was declining, dropping from 4,000 at the time of the Revolution to about 2,000 in the 1820s. Plus, they had already lost most of the land guaranteed them in the Canandaigua Treaty. The remaining land was spread out over 11 reservations. These ranged in size from Oil Springs, a 640-acre parcel, to Buffalo Creek, now the city of Buffalo, New York, with more than 100,000 acres.

By the 1840s, Seneca lands were whittled down to 87,327 acres. For the first time in their history, after controlling lands in New York, across the Great Lakes, and down the Ohio Valley, the Seneca were confined to reservations and isolated on islands amid a rising tide of land-hungry and often hostile settlers. With the loss of lands and lives, the Seneca and other Iroquois tribes lost confidence in their ability to survive as Seneca, as Iroquois, and even as Indians. As a result, they succumbed to social pathologies marked by violence, accusations, persecutions of witchcraft, and as we have seen, alcohol abuse. Altogether, these pathologies worked to undermine the values and institutions that maintained social order, or conversely, restrained social disorder.

From their first contact with the Native people of North America, Europeans, such as the Jesuit missionaries in Canada, admiringly noted their generosity. "On returning from their hunting, their fishing, and their trading, they exchange many gifts; if they have thus obtained something unusually good ... they make a feast to the whole village with it. Their hospitality towards all sorts of strangers is remarkable; they present to them in feast, the best of what they have prepared ... I do not know if anything similar is to be found anywhere."[133]

According to the Quaker missionary Jabez Hyde, who labored among the Seneca in the early 19th century, sharing the fruits of their labor, whether hunting, gathering, or farming, bound the Iroquois together in an alliance of "mutual dependence" that ensured their survival:

> Those who retain their original habits are a hardy athletic race, glorying in their strength, activity and hardihood, scorning to complain under sufferings. Their privations and abstinence

---

[133] Jean de Brebeuf, "The Mission to the Huron (1645-37)," in Colin G. Calloway, *First Peoples* (Boston: Bedford/St. Martin's, 2012), 127.

would appear almost incredible. Originally they had no views of personal property. Further than their present subsistence. Their hospitality was only bounded by their whole possessions. To have refused a supper because it would take the family's breakfast, would have been at the price of one's reputation. Their mode of subsistence and mutual dependence would ensure such a principle and establish the habit, which would become law. All mutually dependent on the success of the chase, it became necessary to self-preservation that hunting parties … should make a common property of their good or ill success, if much was obtained they shared bountifully, if little they shared accordingly, if nothing to bear the privation with cheerfulness was the only merit.[134]

Today, Americans celebrate this generosity every Thanksgiving, but back in the day, they found fault with this remarkable trait. Quaker missionaries echoed the complaints of the first settlers that sharing left the Seneca without anything to salt away for the future. Nevertheless, the reciprocal exchange, rather than the accumulation of goods, bound families, clans, villages, and entire nations together. As well, it provided for their survival in starving times, when resources were scarce or when danger threatened. This animating spirit of self-sacrifice stemmed from their utter dependency upon the Creator or Great Spirit to whom they gave thanks at the beginning and end of all feasts, ceremonies, and councils. As Hyde explained, "As far as I have been able to discover, Indians have considered it wrong to pray unto God, or ask any favors of him. They say it implies dissatisfaction with our condition and irreverent attempt to influence the Divine being. To give thanks to God for his benefits and submit with quietness to the allotment of his providences is our duty."

Quite logically, then, Indians would see no need to improve upon their lot. In other words, they were satisfied and even grateful for what the Creator had assigned to them, in sharp contrast to what the Quakers, other missionaries, and even government officials were urging them to do. Indeed, as Hyde concluded in a remarkably modern psychological observa-

---

[134] Jabez Hyde, "A Teacher Among the Senecas," in *Publications of the Buffalo Historical Society,* 6 (1903): 241.

tion, "They will acknowledge they fare rougher, but they have less anxiety and contention, which taken into the account leaves a balance in their favor."[135] Despite Hyde's admiration for Iroquois values and virtues, missionaries and government officials worked to wean Indians away from their communal, or as Lemkin would have it, "national" patterns of living. This was especially true for the Indians' common ownership of land.

For their part, Quaker missionaries tried to impress upon the Seneca the need for individual or distinct property ownership. They were convinced that moving the Iroquois out of longhouses and into wooden homes and distributing them on individual freeholds were necessary for Indians to be assimilated, to become citizens, and to avoid extermination. The Quakers built sawmills to provide lumber for the construction of wooden houses and even built the homes themselves.

The Quakers were not alone. In 1806, Erastus Granger, the agent for Indian affairs in Buffalo, congratulated the Allegany Seneca for "their industry and attention to Raising of Grain taking care of their Cattle &c and recommended them in future to build their houses and have their farms more Detached from Each other and which would afford them a much better opportunity of persuing the Desirable object of farming and Raising Cattle—If you pass through the Country amongs the white ... you will find Each man on his farm attending to his Grain Cattle hogs &c ...."[136]

Even President Monroe weighed in on the subject. He wrote a letter to the Seneca in 1819, encouraging them to divide up their land such that "each one could say, this is mine, and he would have an inducement to put up good houses on it, and improve his land by cultivation."[137] While couched in terms of saving Seneca lands and staving off their inevitable extinction at the hands of White settlers, the counsel offered by Monroe and others that the Seneca needed to "improve" their lands was nothing

[135] Ibid., 245-6.

[136] George S. Snyderman, "Halliday Jackson's Journal of a Visit to the Indians of New York in 1806," *Proceedings of the American Philosophical Society,* 101, no. 6 (December, 1957): 587-88.

[137] Robert Berkhofer, *Salvation and the Savage* (Lexington, KY: University Press of Kentucky, 1965), 82.

more than a rehash of what John Winthrop said 200 years earlier. And like Winthrop, Monroe and the others failed to understand that dividing up into individual homesteads was actually an assault on their identity as Seneca, as Iroquois, and indeed, as Indians.

Remember, the real name of the Iroquois is *Haudenausaunee* or "people of the longhouse." Made from saplings and bark, and measuring 70 feet or more in length, these structures housed extended families headed by a clan mother through whom all property was inherited. It was in these long-houses that language, culture, traditions, customs, and survival skills were transmitted from one generation to the next. They housed large extended families, held together by matrilineal kinship or clan ties, which mission-aries in particular found so discomfiting.

Even more troubling was the fact that the house and its contents be-longed to the women. No community property here, and no need for di-vorce lawyers. The wife merely placed the husband's belongings outside, which, in the eyes of missionaries, contributed to frequent changes of spouses, a practice that, like polygamy, grated against the missionaries' moral sensibilities.

There were other, subtler motives behind the campaign to convince the Seneca to abandon their communalism or "communism," as it would be la-beled. The Quakers believed the creation of individual plots of land would limit the area available for hunting, trapping, and lumbering. Even though they fought to preserve Indian lands, they believed reducing the amount of land in Indian hands was not necessarily a bad thing. Excess land only served to perpetuate Indian dependence on extraction economies that would come to an end as soon as the game, and in the case of the Seneca, when the timber ran out.

Reducing the size of Indian holdings and dividing the remainder into individual freeholds also forced the Indians to replace hoe agriculture, which was the province of Indian women, with plow agriculture that re-quired the domestication of farm animals, the fencing of land, and more importantly, the involvement of men in planting, cultivating, and harvest-ing. The goal was to transform Indian men into independent, industrious, and hopefully, pious farmers.

At the same time, Indian women would become housewives skilled in the arts of domesticity, just as Wheelock had envisioned it. The Quakers even started a school—the Female Manual Labor School—to teach Seneca women how to sew, cook, and clean. Cleanliness was indeed next to godliness, and as we have already seen, Indians were in need of a good scrubbing. The hope was by taking up farming, the Native men would give up lazing around, drinking, and fighting. However, the private ownership of land and the adoption of plow rather than hoe agriculture, for example, not only reversed traditional male and female roles, it required families to scatter across their territories rather than congregate in villages.

The Iroquois settled into small villages along the Genesee River by the end of the 18th century. Today, if you go onto the Seneca reservations at Cattaraugus and Allegany, the names of the original Seneca settlements—Newtown, Bucktown, and Red House—are still used. The Quakers and other missionaries didn't look kindly on the Seneca's gathering in villages; it permitted the continuation of ceremonies and practices that undermined efforts to Christianize and civilize them. Better to scatter them across their territories on individual freeholds.

As a bonus, dividing up the land into individual freeholds opened up more land for White settlers, at the same time subverting the role of villages in the communal and ceremonial lives of the Seneca. Villages were essential for conducting seasonal ceremonies such as Midwinter and the Green Corn Dance. Those in the villages sent word to members in outlying areas that it was time to convene for these ceremonies or for councils, where important issues were discussed. Villages also were centers of social life through which the Iroquois entertained themselves via social dances, games, storytelling, and various other aspects of socialization, including plain-old gossiping.

Particularly annoying to the Quakers and other missionaries were the frequent "frolics" or celebrations that disrupted their efforts to civilize the savages. For example, the young Quaker missionary Henry Simmons, one of the first to reside and establish a school among the Seneca, found the frequent dances and ceremonies evidence of the Indians' intractable paganism and particularly disruptive of his efforts to educate and civilize them. As he complained in his journal, the news of an "approaching dance and frolic" put the young "scholars" into a frenzy and sent them scurrying home:

> They had been having such frolics every two or three days or nights for many weeks back. I conduct the school in one half of Cornplanter's house …. In the other half …, two large kettles, each capable of holding near or quite a barrel apiece, were being prepared with provisions for the upcoming frolic. While I was helping one of the scholars, someone informed the others about the planned frolic. This put them in such a state of agitation that I was scarcely able to teach them at any rate. Some of them left ·the school and went home to prepare for the dance. This was the second time of my being so served.[138]

While this was Simmons' second such experience, it would hardly be the last for him and other missionaries in New York and across the country over the course of the next century. Those who ministered to the Seneca and Iroquois people complained that ceremonies, visits to relatives, funerals, hunting trips, councils, and or "frolics" brought about young Indians' frequent and prolonged absences from school. Such practices and beliefs undermined missionary efforts to inoculate Native people with the republican virtues of thrift, hard work, and accumulation.

Prolonged ceremonies and dances, hunting-and-trapping expeditions, and visitations with relatives in other villages and reservations detracted from the Indians' ability to move beyond subsistence farming and other economic pursuits. Without the private ownership of property and with the persistence of such practices as gift-giving and communal sharing, there were no incentives to move beyond a subsistence economy. Indian paganism not only stood in the way of missionary efforts to Christianize the Iroquois, it prevented the Indians from adapting to the market economy that was already making their traditional ways of life untenable.

---

[138] David Swatzler, *A Friend Among the Senecas* (Mechanicsburg, PA: Stackpole Books, 2000), 42.

Little wonder, then, that ceremonies and dances were banned on reservations. Or that missionaries and government officials followed in Wheelock's footsteps and turned to boarding schools, especially off-reservation boarding schools, to isolate and insulate Indian children from their families and their pagan practices. In fact, some of the first boarding schools were started on Seneca reservations long before William Henry Pratt envisioned the Carlisle Indian Industrial School. Nevertheless, they had the same unfortunate results.

The Quakers weren't alone in their effort and failures among the Seneca. The young Presbyterian missionary Thompson Harris set up a school to "embody" or board Seneca children on the Buffalo Creek reservation in what is now downtown Buffalo, New York. As Henry Simmons bemoaned, the children often missed school for feasts, ceremonies, and harvests. To add insult to injury, parents often removed their children because they disagreed with Harris' methods for disciplining their children. Like Eleazar Wheelock, Harris found that Seneca parents "did not think it was generally the best way to correct children with the rod, but to use persuasive measures and coax them into obedience." As Harris confided in his journal, "Thus we are tried with this ignorant and inconsiderate people."[139]

But the problem was not the way Harris disciplined the children in his care anymore than it was for Wheelock; it was what he and other missionaries tried to teach them. As Seneca Chief Red Jacket complained, "Instead of producing that happy effect you so long promised, its [education] introduction so far has rendered us uncomfortable and miserable. You have taken a number of young men to your schools. You have educated them and taught them your religion. They have returned to their kindred and color neither white men nor Indians. The arts they have learned are incompatible with the chase, and ill adapted to our customs. They have been taught that which is useless to us."

Harris abandoned the reservation and his school in 1829, but at least he avoided the humiliation of the Baptist missionary on the nearby Tonawa-

---

[139] Frank H. Severance, "Narratives of Early Mission Work on the Niagara Frontier and Buffalo Creek," *Publications of the Buffalo Historical Society,* 6 (1903): 319.

nda Seneca Reservation. Opponents of this school and the missionary's methods packed up his belongings and unceremoniously carted them off their territory. The Quaker, Presbyterian, and Baptist experience among the Seneca was repeated time and time again. The results never improved.

The Seneca also resisted with equal stubbornness any suggestion of privatizing their land and turning it into a commodity. As John Marshall pointed out in *McIntosh*, the Indians lacked any idea of individual property ownership, which automatically disqualified them from citizenship. At bottom, the Seneca saw individual ownership as another ploy to steal Indian lands piece by piece, something that was already happening to them and other tribes. It also undermined the values that formed the fabric or "national pattern" of Seneca and Native culture in general.

The stubborn persistence of Iroquois traditions frustrated the work of missionary and government agents to acculturate and assimilate the Indians of New York. For these reasons, Quaker efforts among the Seneca, which were nothing more than a proxy for the federal government's plan to civilize or remove the Indians east of the Mississippi, were doomed to fail from the very beginning. Even if the Seneca bought into the idea of property ownership, they did not have access to markets or capital that would enable them to compete with White farmers or to withstand the fluctuations in the marketplace that would plague farmers for the next century. Moreover, as their lands diminished, there was less arable land available, at the very time when the average farm in America was growing. Indeed, new lands were being opened up in the West at a prodigious rate, leading to increased production that swamped smaller farms, such as those located in the shrinking Seneca territories.

Once again, Jabez Hyde provided an insightful and remarkably sensitive commentary on the dilemma of the Indians in the Buffalo area. Indians, as has been observed, bear suffering with great fortitude, but at the end of this fortitude is suffering. Suicides are frequent among the Seneca. I apprehend this despondency is the principal cause of their intemperance .... Their circumstances are peculiarly calculated to depress their spirits, especially those contiguous to white settlements. Their ancient manner of subsistence is broken up, and when they appear willing and desirous to turn their attention to agriculture, their ignorance, the inveteracy of their old habits, the disadvantages under which they labor soon discourage them; though they struggle hard little is realized to their benefit, besides the continued dread they live in of losing their possessions. If they build, they know not who will inhabit. If they make fields, they know not who will cultivate them. They know the anxiety of their white neighbors to get possession of their lands. They know that in all their transactions with white men, they have prevailed against them, and they are filled with desponding fears that it will continue to be so.[140]

Hunger can be as compelling as a soldier with a gun, and many Seneca recognized their dilemma. Land companies worked to persuade the New York Indians to sell off tribal lands, use the proceeds to feed their families, and move west. Their arguments almost worked. Bolstered by government support, land companies managed to consistently nibble away at Seneca and Iroquois lands. The Seneca retained only about 50,000 of the 4 million acres they were guaranteed in 1794. As we have seen, the Oneida and Cayuga were not so lucky; they lost all their land in New York.

Although the Seneca population stabilized, its growth lagged behind the general population and even other tribes due to higher infant and overall mortality rates. By 1900, Seneca people had an average life expectancy of 30 years, as opposed to 50 for the White population and 41 for Black people.[141] The higher mortality rates necessarily meant lower fertility rates. That the Seneca population was able to stabilize and even grow by 1900, albeit slower than the national average, was at least partially because they escaped removal across the Mississippi River. They also avoided government interference in their internal affairs, like the allotment of their lands into individually owned parcels.

Fortunately, the Seneca Nation has recovered, thanks to three casinos that take advantage of the tribe's proximity to Buffalo and Niagara Falls. Just

---

[140] Ibid., 245-6.

[141] Nancy Shoemaker, *American Indian Population Recovery in the Twentieth Century* (Albuquerque, NM: University of New Mexico Press, 1999), 40.

visit Seneca reservations at Cattaraugus and Allegany, and you'll find new housing, health-and-wellness facilities, and community centers. They've finally realized what the Quakers promised them, not by privatizing their lands, but by exercising their sovereignty. Known as *Honodadwe:ni:yo'*, it is roughly translated as, "We carry our own water."

The Quaker experiment with the Seneca was a dress rehearsal for the missionary activities and government policies of the next century. They all failed, because as the Meriam Report concluded, they were inherently wrongheaded. As if to anticipate Riley's assertions about the "magical" power of private property, the report warned that individual property ownership would do more harm than good. "When the government adopted the policy of individual ownership of land on the reservations, the expectation was that the Indians would become farmers …. It almost seems as if the government assumed that some magic in individual ownership of property would in itself prove an educational civilizing factor, but unfortunately this policy has for the most part worked in the opposite direction."[142]

Whether it was because they were forced onto marginal lands, because they lacked the capital to purchase sufficient lands and equipment to engage in commercial farming, or because cultural differences prevented them from doing so, the end result was the dramatic transfer of Indian lands into White hands. The plan to save Indians from starvation and extinction by transforming them into independent farmers did indeed work in the "opposite direction," as Indian populations and Indian lands continued to decline into the 20th century.

Those who survived became increasingly dependent on missionary and government handouts. The unremitting efforts of missionaries, government officials, and even "well-intended" reformers to persuade or coerce Indians to assimilate took many forms. Some—like boarding schools and allotment— were notorious. Others were subtler but nonetheless pernicious and far reaching. They affected nearly every aspect of Indian life, from the food they ate, to the clothes they wore, to the way they breastfed

[142] Meriam Report, 7.

their babies. However, none was more disruptive to Native families and communities than the demand that they abandon their traditional dwellings and move into single-family houses.

As we have seen, the efforts to move Indians out of their wigwams, longhouses, teepees, and hogans began almost immediately upon contact. I didn't understand just how destructive they were until I was lying in a teepee, gazing through the smoke hole while listening to the drumming and singing coming from the dance arbor at Crow Fair. It suddenly came to me that teepees provided Plains Indians with more than protection from the elements; they were essential to maintaining their identities as Indians and their ties to a way of life they were determined to preserve in the face of equally determined efforts to erase them. It was while I was lying there trying to get some sleep that I was reminded of travelers' accounts of teepees thick with smoke, and crowded and noisy with children and dogs, visitors coming and going at all hours, and oh, yes, don't forget the fleas. I could even imagine how the drumming and high-pitched singing coming from the arbor might frighten missionaries and settlers ever on guard lest the Natives go on the warpath.

The drumming was reminiscent of the rhythmic beating of tom-toms that signal the appearance of Indians in so many Westerns. As I tossed and turned, trying to tune out the din, I realized I was living that same experience. It was like a dream taking me back 200 years to a Lakota, Crow, or Pawnee camp on the Great Plains. Besides the music, there were children playing long after bedtime; babies crying; people talking, laughing, and eating; horses whinnying; and a drunk guy stumbling in looking for money or a place to crash. That was what camp life was like, and it all revolved around teepees. They represented, in Lemkin's terms, the "essential foundation of the life" for Plains Indians and symbolized their resistance to coming out of the "blanket" and embracing the modern world.

The word "teepee" or "tipi" is derived from the Lakota word *thipi,* which means "they dwell." They are certainly one of the most recognizable icons of Native American culture. Restaurants, motels, and souvenir shops across the West use teepees to attract tourists, even in areas where the local Indians didn't live in them. But teepees are more than ornaments to decorate tourist traps. They were honest-to-goodness engineering marvels.

They were designed, constructed, and perfected to withstand some of the most extreme weather conditions in the world, like the hailstorm that broke my windshield in Wyoming and peeled the paint off a restaurant I visited in Montana, and the rainstorms that shook the ground beneath my head as I tried to sleep during a thunderstorm in the Black Hills. The Great Plains are home to blinding blizzards (that's where the term was coined) and blistering heat that dries up streams and shrivels plants. In fact, North Dakota holds the world record for the disparity between the lowest and highest temperatures ever recorded in one place. The climate on the Great Plains is foreboding; just ask any farmer who has seen his wheat crop destroyed by hail or shriveled by drought, or any rancher who has lost cattle to blizzards.

While teepees sheltered Indian families from the fierceness of nature, they also were an early version of modern RVs. They could be taken down on a moment's notice, affording Indians the freedom to travel the boundless expanse of the Plains, burdened only by what their dogs or horses could carry. It's the ultimate freedom that Americans dream about as they take to the open road in—yes—their Winnebagos. Nothing to tie you down to one place; no mortgage, no taxes, no lawn to cut. If you don't like it, just pack up your teepee and leave.

I have put up and taken down a lot of teepees, in the process, gaining additional respect for Native women who were responsible for raising and then striking them on a moment's notice if the cavalry or a buffalo herd appeared. Anybody can put up teepees, but putting them up the right way is another matter. You can buy them online complete with an instructional video on how to erect them. I have known White people who have bought and used them for camping, as Boy Scout troops often do. However, putting them up to withstand conditions on the plains requires skills that have been honed for generations. It is also a process that transmits language and culture, as well as valuable skills necessary for survival.

Among the Crow, for example, the undertaking begins with a trip into the Bighorn Mountains to cut and strip lodge pole pines for new teepees or to replace broken ones. Altogether, they use 19 poles, each of which has a special name and story associated with its function, and must be placed in a prescribed order. They begin with four poles named after the seasons, followed by 10 poles that represent the number of months spent in the mother's womb. The latter explains the Crow name for a teepee: "second mother." That is, it represents a womb that embraces, protects, nourishes, and serves as the center of family life.

Each part of the teepee has a name and a story, right down to the stakes named after badger claws. It's an animal respected for its tenacity, a quality essential for securing a teepee against the unrelenting wind on the plains. The whole process is conducted with an almost scientific precision, according to a formula passed down through generations. Skipping a step or misplacing a pole courts certain disaster. I have seen teepees erected in a careless fashion blow over in one of those fierce storms that roll across the plains, and I have sat in a teepee during a howling windstorm, watching the canvas mimic a beating heart, expanding and contracting with the gusts, but never yielding. The ability to put up a teepee correctly is admired as a skill that is hard to find these days. My hosts at Crow Fair, Dewey and Wales Bull Tail, are respected for having retained those skills and are often asked by other Indians to help put up their teepees.

Not all teepees are alike, nor are they all anthropological artifacts. You can see them pitched behind houses on reservations, which has always made me wonder if they are extra bedrooms, summer homes, or symbols of wealth or status as they were in the past. Or do they just serve to remind us that Indians live there? Indeed, tribes still pride themselves on the distinctive features of their teepees, and the differences between tribes were and still are the subjects of tribal rivalries. This is especially true of the Crow and Lakota, who have a past, to say the least.

The Lakota paint their teepees, while the Crow leave theirs white. The Crow use four main poles; the Lakota use three. Even today, at festivals like Crow Fair, the self-proclaimed "Teepee Capital of the World," Indians from across the country gather to put thousands of teepees on display. The size and shape of the teepee, the length of the poles, the decorative paintings, the tautness of the canvas, the finishing touches that make a teepee authentic are sources of personal and tribal pride. The number of teepees in a camp is also a matter of pride.

In the years I've been visiting Crow Fair, the number of teepees in the Bull Tail camp has continued to grow for seemingly no reason other than a strong sense of personal and family spirit. Teepees were and still are more than shelters from the elements; they are expressions of Indian culture upon which Native people's survival depended for thousands of years. They also represent Indians' identities as Crow, Lakota, Blackfeet, etc.; indeed, their identities as Indians. Finally, they symbolize Indigenous people's stubborn refusal to assimilate, a determination that has exasperated Europeans for centuries.

It was in teepees that families gathered for celebrations and ceremonies, where babies were born, where important issues were discussed and debated, where treaties were negotiated, and where language, culture, and lessons for survival were transmitted. Traditionally, the largest teepees, with the largest number of buffalo hides, belonged to most important members of a tribe. Even today, as the oldest of the Bull Tail clan, Dewey's teepee is the biggest and stands at the center of the camp.

The 15 to 16 buffalo hides needed to build a typical teepee made them integral to the economic life of Plains Indian tribes. When they were arranged in circles, as the Lakota did, they were the center of community as well as family life. Teepees were essential to the social, cultural, religious, and political life of Indian families and communities, and to their distinctive national or tribal identities. In short, teepees were necessary for the survival of Plains Indians individually and collectively. Forcing Indians out of traditional lodging to supposedly improve their lives undermined Native families and communities, and it jeopardized their ability to survive, as their near extinction proved. Once again recalling Lemkin's words, it contributed to the "disintegration of the political and social institutions of culture, language, national feelings, religion, and the economic existence of national groups, and the personal security, liberty, health, dignity, and even the lives of the individuals belonging to the group."

These efforts did not ease. In fact, they became increasingly urgent as more Indians were concentrated on reservations. The government aided missionaries through treaties like the Fort Laramie Treaty of 1868, and policies like Grant's Peace Policy, the Indian Appropriation Act of 1871, and the Dawes Allotment Act of 1887. Working together, missionaries and government authorities were determined to force Indians to assimilate by cutting them off from their traditional economies and confining them to individual freeholds, where they would live sedentary lives as farmers, property owners, and model citizens. These policies continued into the modern era, when growing populations on reservations created a housing shortage. The government decided to solve the problem by herding Indians into housing tracts built by the Department of Housing and Urban Development and modeled after suburban developments, complete with cul-de-sacs.

The program had serious unintended consequences on the Blackfeet Reservation in northwestern Montana. Houses built on the Blackfeet Reservation during the 1970s and 1980s "were almost always built in 'row-style' developments that lacked any reference to traditional Native American family groupings, and were exclusively centered in the reservation's largest communities. Prior to the 1960s, a large percentage of the Blackfeet people lived in rural settings—small, isolated family groupings widely dispersed across the landscape. The constructions of so many housing units temporarily eased the housing shortage, but it also drew people away from long-established rural settlements, which tore at the fabric of Blackfeet society."

To make matters worse, the houses were poorly built. They had wooden foundations that eventually gave way, lacked vapor barriers to protect against black mold, and were poorly insulated with single-pane windows and hollow wooden doors. In the end, they were not built to withstand the activity of large extended families. "Under these types of crowded conditions, wear and tear causes the existing home to deteriorate rapidly. Doors and cupboards designed to be opened and closed perhaps a dozen times a day may see 1,000 uses in a single week. The major appliances, flooring, carpets, plumbing and fixtures all get worn down and worn out." In short, the houses simply fell apart as the tribe found it too costly to maintain them. The detritus is clearly visible in places like the Moccasin Flats section of Browning, which has been called a "Third World neighborhood."[143]

I saw it firsthand in the skeletons of trailers and wood-frame houses piled high on top of one another in Browning. You can also see it on Rosebud, with its sad collections of decrepit HUD houses often surrounded by barbed-wire fences and giving a new meaning to the term "gated communities." The scenes on Blackfeet and Rosebud can likewise be found on reservations throughout Indian Country. They reflect 200 years of failed government policies and programs.

Whether they were teepees, hogans, wigwams, or wikiups, it was no accident that removing Indians from their traditional housing and onto reservations coincided with the continuing decline of Native populations long after warfare, removal, and virgin-field epidemics ended. As H.M. Snee predicted, "air tight log houses" would be the end of them. The tale is in the statistics.

Indians were not included in the U.S. Census until 1860, and in truth, they were undercounted in that counting and the ones that followed. Not all tribes were confined to reservations, and many had no settled habitations. Those that had been corralled onto reservations were scattered across large and often-inaccessible tracts of land. Furthermore, they didn't trust the government. In fact, Indians are still undercounted for many of the same reasons. I have Native friends who refuse to participate in the national census. To do so would be collaborating with the enemy. Nevertheless, the trend is clear. The 1860 census counted 339,421 Indians in the United States. By 1900, after the Indian wars and the safe ensconcement of Native people on reservations under the care and watchful eyes of missionaries, governments agents, and the cavalry, the number had dwindled to a nadir of 237,000.

The Native population stabilized and rebounded, but by 1920, it had

[143] David Murray, "The crisis in our backyard: Montana's reservation housing," *Great Falls Tribune* (April 3, 2016).

grown to only 261,000 at a time when the national population grew by nearly 40% to 106 million. This decline was no accident. Instead, it was the direct result of the disruption of families and communities, and the attendant social problems that continued into the 20th—and some would argue—the 21st centuries. Indians lost their independence, self-sufficiency, and sovereignty, devolving into a debilitating dependency on government. Smallpox gave way to a sad slate of problems, including malnutrition, obesity, diabetes, heart disease, substance use disorders, violence, accidental deaths, and suicide. All of this added up to a shorter life expectancy and higher mortality rates, including infant mortality, than the general population. Pathogens gave way to pathologies that continue to take their toll on Native populations to this day.

The aforementioned Meriam Report documented in 1928 that the deplorable conditions on reservations and consequent population declines were the result of policies and practices that were, in Lemkin's term, "genocidal." It was officially titled *The Problem of Indian Administration,* a privately funded comprehensive survey of Indians on and off reservations. Directed by Lewis Meriam, the chief surveyor, it began with the sobering observation "that an overwhelming majority of the Indians are poor, even extremely poor."[144]

They were trapped in a "vicious circle" of poverty perpetuated by disease, inadequate health care, malnutrition, poor and unsanitary living conditions, and limited economic opportunities, not to mention a failed educational system exemplified by boarding schools. In fact, the Meriam Report is often credited with exposing the failings of the Indian educational system and the eventual dismantling of the boarding schools. However, the report placed the ultimate blame, as its formal title implies, on the administration of Indian affairs, including wrongheaded and destructive policies and practices, corruption and incompetence, and an insidious and even malicious culture of contempt and neglect. In a word, genocide.

The report was remarkable for its thoroughness. In 1926, the surveyors embarked on a seven-month journey during which they made a total of 404 visits to 94 sites on reservations, at Indian schools, and even urban areas

[144] Meriam Report, 3.

across 22 states. They began by compiling statistics from the office of Indian affairs to measure their accuracy against the statistics kept on several reservations. Once on the reservations, they interviewed superintendents and staff, and visited remote towns and farms, which at times forced them to travel over rugged and even dangerous terrain. They visited nearly every off-reservation boarding school, including Haskell, Rapid City, Chiloco, Sherman, and Albuquerque. They also examined on-reservation boarding schools, as well as on-reservation day schools and the public schools where most Indian children were enrolled.

They surveyed the reservations for available economic resources such as water, timber, oil, and arable land. They held councils with groups of Indians, outside the presence of government officials if the Indians requested, and they also met privately with individuals to hear their grievances and solicit information not provided by agency staff. Finally, and most importantly, the surveyors visited homes to examine residents' health and diets. However, it was the living conditions of Indian families that did more than any other factor to inform the surveyors' conclusions—and their conclusions were appalling, especially regarding housing. Although the report generally supported the policy of moving Indians out of traditional housing, it went on record with the opinion that the housing provided by the government was "characterized by poor structure, poor repair, overcrowding, [and] lack of sanitation ...." In fact, the "most primitive structures" were better ventilated than the government houses that replaced them, and "tents" (read teepees) provided better lighting.

Per the Merriam Report, government-supplied houses were generally small, usually one-room structures with leaking roofs and dirt floors. There were no fireplaces, and if there were windows, they were oftentimes not covered, giving flies "free access." Not only did they lack water and sanitation facilities, the report admitted these necessities were better when Indians were left to manage on their own, moving with their "primitive RVs" when an area became fouled, or when water or food supplies dried up.[145]

The study further concluded that most of the homes on reservations

---

[145] Ibid., 554.

were more densely crowded than city tenements that teemed with immigrant families. The overcrowding was due in part to the lack of or inadequacy of government housing, but it was also due to the size of Indian families, which were larger than those found in the general population.[146] Added to that was Indians' cultural norm or the "obligation" of individual families to the "larger group." As a result, the "two generation family was less significant" than the extended families where "several generations mingle more intimately in the households and camps, and the grandparents particularly, grandmothers, occupy a more influential positions than in white families."[147]

These large extended families tended to congregate in one home, often leaving their own single-family homes empty. The government policy of dispersing Indian families into single-family dwellings failed to take into account the gravitational pull of the "larger group" and in fact, backfired. Indians valued their social ties and familial relationships more than they feared piling into cramped and unhealthy houses.

There was yet another reason Indians tended to be in crowded and unhealthy conditions. Food supplied through what one missionary described as the "miserable ration system" was woefully inadequate. When the monthly rations were handed out, the "half-starved" Indians were forced to come together to pool their food and share it with family members and hungry visitors, as was the custom of most tribes. Unfortunately, there was never enough to go around or to last until the next disbursement, so Indians would continue to experience "starving times" as they had in the past. The shortages were so serious, Indian agents resorted to horsemeat, which the Indians claimed sickened and even killed them.[148]

To make matters worse, families had to eat from one dish, using their fingers, or communal spoons and cups. Combined with the lack of sanitation and very often the scarcity of water, which kept them from washing their meager eating utensils, the spread of infectious diseases was inevita-

[146] Ibid., 561.

[147] Ibid., 572.

[148] Ibid., 556.

ble, particularly among people "who never have enough to eat." To put it simply, bodies weakened by malnutrition were susceptible to disease.

The problem of diet and malnutrition among Indians was particularly evident at boarding schools, both on and off reservations, where the incidence of tuberculosis and trachoma were "alarming," according to the Meriam Report. While food was more available at the schools than in Indians' homes, the quality and quantity were not sufficient to ward off malnutrition, or more importantly, to deal with the large of number of malnourished children arriving at the schools.

To this end, the report cited the example of the Fort Defiance School on the Navajo Reservation in Arizona. In 1927, the school was transformed into a school for children infected with trachoma. Altogether, 450 children were transferred there from other boarding schools and from day schools on various reservations. An examination of the children revealed that 25% were on average 17 pounds under the normal weight for their age and height. Even those who appeared normal, upon closer examination, suffered from the telltale signs of malnutrition, including flaccid muscles, protruding bellies, winged scapulae, stooped shoulders, and unhealthy skin color. In general, all the students suffered from the same "faulty" diets found at all boarding schools.

The surveyors found the diets at government schools consisted largely of starchy foods and lacked eggs, milk, and vegetables.[149] The basic reason for the limited diet was the disturbingly low funding for food appropriated by the government, although school administrators claimed Indian children did not like milk, eggs, and vegetables, an argument the report rejected. Whatever the reasons, the findings at Fort Defiance demonstrated that children at Indian schools suffered from malnutrition, leading to the conclusion that, in general, the "Indian child frequently suffers from diseases influenced by a deficient diet, notably tuberculosis and trachoma." In other words, the poor health found among Indian children at boarding schools was merely a reflection of deplorable conditions back home on the reservations.

[149] Ibid., 211-2.

The prevalence of disease on reservations, most seriously tuberculosis, far exceeded national averages. For example, total deaths per capita on the combined reservations were two times higher than the national average. In Idaho, it was five times higher. Among children under 3 years old, the death rate was triple the national average. For all Indians, the frequency of death from tuberculosis was far higher than national rates as well, with Arizona coming in at 17 times the national rate.

As dismal as the picture was, it shouldn't have come as a shock. Poor sanitation, a lack of personal hygiene facilities, overcrowded living conditions, and inadequate or contaminated water supplies, made the spread of tuberculosis and other diseases on the reservations quite predictable. So dire was the situation that the report concluded conditions among Indian families on reservations were worse than in the poorest White, rural communities in the United States. In short, "… In most tribes the efforts of the government have not resulted in raising the standard of living, perceptibly reducing the amount of sickness, or increasing very much the Indians' ability to take care of themselves."[150]

The formula governing the "vicious circle of poverty" was simple. Poor housing plus malnutrition plus disease equaled poverty. "It is sometime said that the chief cause of poverty is poverty. Indians are subject to the diseases of malnutrition because they are poor; they lack energy because they are sick and undernourished; lacking energy they cannot produce the essentials of life."[151] All of this led to the awful mortality rates among Indians. It also serves to illustrate Lemkin's definition of genocide as a "coordinated plan of different actions aimed at the destruction of the essential foundation of the life of a national group."

The grinding, unremitting poverty worked to undermine Indian family structure. Indian families were "unstable," a condition that

> … is not surprising, for it has been subjected to severe strains. Indian families, like White families suffer the disintegrating effects of poverty, illness, ignorance, and inability to adjust them-

[150] Ibid., 549.

[151] Ibid., 564.

selves to an industrial world. Among the Indians these strains are peculiarly great because the race is undergoing a shift from primitive to modern life. They are further intensified by the condition of perpetual childhood in which Indians have been held, for both the system of education and the type of control exercised by the government over tribal and personal property have tended to loosen family ties.[152]

Just as Indian families were deteriorating, their communities were undergoing destructive changes almost entirely as a result of misguided, fatally flawed government policies and programs. The report concluded, "The fundamental importance of community life, like that of family life, has apparently never been recognized by the government in the treatment of Indians." Instead, as with families, government programs have only "operated to break down native forms of organization" with nothing to replace them, leaving Indians at the mercy of the government.[153]

The report provided a damning list of government failures and their disastrous consequences for Indians. "The forcible removal of whole tribes to very different physical environments resulting in the disruption of economic life, the detention of large groups as prisoners of war for long periods, the common discouragement of Indian leadership on the reservations and in the government schools, the disrespect of white employees for native customs and ceremonies, and the assumption on the part of teachers and others in the schools that all Indian ways are bad ways, have tended to breakdown native social structure."[154]

The result was, again in words anticipating Lemkin, the "disintegration of family and community life," the two institutions responsible for preserving and transmitting native culture, languages, customs and traditions, and the skills necessary to take care of themselves, like putting up a teepee. This forced Indians into a debilitating dependency on the government and paved the way for a long list of social problems, including the breakdown

[152] Ibid., 548.

[153] Ibid.

[154] Ibid.

of families and communities, drug and alcohol addiction, and behavior or personality disorders.

Why did this happen? The report had this to say: "Both the government and missionaries have often failed to study, understand, and take a sympathetic attitude toward Indian ways, Indian ethics, and Indian religion."[155] More to the point, government agents and missionaries held everything about the Indians, including the Indians themselves, in contempt. Nowhere was this lack of understanding and sympathy more evident than the health care the government provided on reservations.

The general problem was the lack of funding, and as a result, "practically every activity undertaken by the national government for the promotion of the health of the Indians is below a reasonable standard of efficiency" set for all other government health care agencies such as the Public Health Service, the Veterans Bureau, the military, and for women and children under the Maternity and Infancy Act.[156]

At bottom, however, were the racist beliefs among Indian administrators. According to the report, government officials have "seemingly given too much consideration to the fact that the economic and social conditions of the Indians are low and it has assumed, therefore, that it is unnecessary to supply them with facilities comparable with those made available by states, municipalities, and private philanthropists for the poorest white citizens of progressive communities."[157] Put another way, Indians were too poor, too unhealthy, and too backward to benefit from the health care afforded even the poorest White people. After all, Indians were a "vanishing race." All that was needed was to "treat him half way right anyhow" on his way out.

The failure to comprehend the dire conditions on the reservations was exemplified in a pamphlet issued in 1916 by Commissioner of Indian Affairs Cato Sells. Titled "Indian Babies: How to Keep Them Well," it offered advice to Indian mothers on child rearing, including a warning about

[155] Ibid., 16.

[156] Ibid., 9.

[157] Ibid., 190.

breastfeeding too long. Sells was motivated by the fact that one in three Indian babies died before the age of 3, and three out of five before they were 5. Many of the recommendations were reasonable from a medical standpoint, but they were unrealistic for most Indians.

For example, telling Indian mothers to breastfeed for no more than a year was unreasonable. The cow's or goat's milk suggested to replace breastmilk at the 12-month mark was neither readily available or attainable. When Indians were given cows, they ate them, much to the dismay of government agents, but not surprising to anyone who knows what it's like to be persistently hungry. Sells also recommended that after weaning, babies should be fed simple food such as bread and butter, baked potatoes, cereal, rice, soft-boiled eggs and fruit, none of which was supplied through that "miserable ration system."

He also suggested washing babies as well as their towels and washcloths every day, a sensible recommendation, except for people who lacked soap and clean water, or any water at all. The same was true for keeping flies away from babies; many of the houses had no glass or screens on their windows, so all manner of insects had free rein. The alternative was air-tight log or wood houses that were equally unhealthy. But the warning that exemplified what the Meriam Report labeled the "problem of Indian administration" was that Indians should avoid overcrowding. Enough said.[158]

Sells was sincerely concerned about conditions on the reservations that he and his department administered, and he believed that intervention was needed to save the Indians from the extinction he warned was imminent. Accompanying the pamphlet was a letter he penned to employees of the Indian service, in which he said, "We cannot solve the Indian problem without Indians." Keeping Indian babies alive was the first and most important step because it ensured there would be future generations of Indians. He also believed that improving the health of Indians would save them from extinction and allow them to be assimilated. Of course, Indian parents would need to "exchange indolence for industry," and "all denominations,

---

[158] Department of the Interior, "Indian Babies: How to Keep Them Well" (Washington, DC: Government Printing Office, 1916).

religious missionaries, and mission schools" would have to work together to cure their spiritual ills. Otherwise, "All our Indian schools, reservations, individual allotments, and accumulated incomes tend pathetically toward a wasted altruism if maintained and conserved for a withering decadent people."[159]

His solutions may have been uninformed and naïve, but he was correct about one thing: Indians were on the verge of extinction. On the other hand, he didn't understand that it was the "altruistic" policies administered by his agency that were killing them off. All of Sells' well-meaning actions—taking them out of teepees, wigwams, or hogans, forcing them into sedentary lives on individually owned plots of land, shipping them off to boarding schools—"operated in the opposite direction." What Sells and so many other reformers failed to grasp was that the physical and spiritual salvation they offered came at a price Indians were unwilling to pay. As a result, the reservations that were supposed to be places for Indians to live became places for them to die.

Twelve years later, the Meriam Report laid bare the government's failure to address the suffering on the reservations administered by the Department of Indian Affairs and cast blame for that failure on the agency's endemic contempt for Indians and their ways, and a calloused disregard for Indian suffering and misery. The report offered a heartrending example. "Old crippled, almost helpless Indians are required to come to the agency office in all sorts of weather to get their supplies. On several reservations the survey staff saw poorly clad old people with feet soaked by long walks through snow and slush huddled in the agency office waiting for the arrival of the superintendent or other officer who could give an order for rations to keep them from actual starvation."[160]

The insensitivity to the starving Indians shivering in their offices was the tip of the proverbial iceberg. It was behind the belief that Indians weren't worthy of adequate health care, housing, sanitation, or water. It bore the

[159] Cato Sells, "To superintendents and other employees of the United States Indian Service," January 10, 1916.

[160] Meriam Report, 487.

fruit of unwillingness to "understand and take a sympathetic attitude toward Indian ways, Indian ethics, Indian religion." It was at the root of the attitude that Indian poverty was due to the inherited inferiority of their character and culture. And finally, it fueled the "disintegration" of their families, communities, beliefs, and ways of life, and the "destruction of the essential foundation of life" and "even the lives of individuals belonging to the group."

Contempt and neglect eventually took their tolls, and they add up to genocide. Indians were the objects of scorn and neglect because authorities believed they were inherently incapable of or unwilling to make the transition from "primitive to civilized" life. Indians seemed indifferent and even hostile to the blessings of civilization, and strangely willing to remain a "withering decadent people."

Let them go as gently and as quickly as possible.

A Different Way of Seeing, Thinking, and Being

What does it mean to be an Indian? In thinking about this, I came up with a couple of half-facetious examples, like it means you don't know your shoe or clothing sizes because, in the words of Martha Moccasin, you always bought "at rummage." Or the joke that if you don't have a parole or probation officer, you're probably not an Indian. All kidding aside, this is a serious and complicated question that all tribes struggle with, not to mention politicians like Senator and would-be President Elizabeth Warren. When White people say they're part Indian, Native people respond with a wink or a jab with their elbow, and say, "Must be Cherokee," since that's the only tribe most Americans know. It inevitably gets a laugh, but it's really not funny.

In the 2010 census, more than 800,000 respondents identified themselves as Cherokee, but there are only 300,000 enrolled tribal members. Identifying tribal members is no easy feat. In order for a tribe to be recognized by the federal government, it must have existed since 1900 as a community with control over its members, including criteria for membership. That's where it gets sticky. Most tribes require members to have at least one ancestor listed as an Indian on the 1900 or 1910 census. But that was a long time ago. Since then, the percentage of Indian blood or "blood quantum" has been diluted, leaving tribes to struggle with the questions of how much is enough and what role culture should play in determining membership.

While examining this issue, I came across the case of the Lumbee of North Carolina and decided perhaps we were asking the wrong questions. Maybe the crux of it is not what makes them Indians. Rather, it's what makes them different from White people, so much so that they're willing to suffer discrimination and neglect rather than assimilate.

188

The Lumbee have lived in eastern North Carolina for around 300 years, but they can't trace their origins back to a single tribe. Instead, they are a mixture of Whites, Africans, and several Indian tribes that lived along the Lumbee River, from which the tribe finally took its name. Some believe they are descendants of Sir Walter Raleigh's Lost Colony that disappeared from Roanoke Island along the coast of North Carolina in 1586.

I once came across a Lumbee drum group at a powwow and learned from the members that they have dedicated themselves to preserving Lumbee culture. In their defense, the state of North Carolina recognized them as the Croatan in 1885, and the federal government officially declared they were Indians in 1956. However, the Lumbee are not counted among today's 573 federally recognized tribes because they are not Indian enough, according to the BIA.

Numbering around 55,000, the Lumbee make up the largest tribe east of the Mississippi River. They have lived as a distinct community, not necessarily by choice, in a racially segregated area. They have traditions, ceremonies, and a dialect. They have their own system of government, courts, schools, housing, and other services. They even have their own college, Pembroke University, which has become part of the University of North Carolina. What they don't have is a reservation. Nevertheless, they are determined to remain a culturally distinct people.

There are some questions about their authenticity as Indians since they are Christianized, and according to some Indians who oppose their recognition, too prosperous. But it is their "blood quantum" that is the real problem. They are considered a racially mixed people by virtue of the fact that they have European and African ancestry in their genes. Ironically, their mixing with Black people has been used by other Indian tribes to oppose their recognition.

Federal recognition is no small matter. It allows tribes to receive government housing, health, education, and other benefits. It gives them the ability to protect the territorial integrity of their lands and govern themselves as sovereign nations. The Lumbee have fought for recognition for more than a century, contending that racial purity is less important than going to Lumbee schools and churches, speaking the Lumbee language, and participating in the Lumbee community. On the other hand, they contend that what federal recognition offers is a distant second to the preservation of their distinct identity as Lumbee and as Indians.

As a matter of fact, that is precisely what they and the more than 800 recognized and unrecognized tribes stand to lose if the federal government imposes an arbitrary minimum blood-quantum level for tribal citizenship. It's not an idle threat; the idea of requiring a certain percentage of Indian blood for tribal citizenship goes back to the allotment period following the Dawes Act of 1887. The act granted tribal lands in 160-acre parcels to eligible tribal citizens, and it gave them U.S. citizenship when they accepted ownership of their allotments.

It was supposed to benefit Indians and solve the Indian problem by hastening their assimilation. The goal was to break up Native lands and subsequently chip away at the tribes by treating Indians as individuals and not citizens of sovereign nations. In the end, it became a massive land grab that divested tribes of millions of acres of their land and weakened tribal control over their citizens who had become landowners in exchange for their tribal membership. Furthermore, as U.S. citizens, they were subject to territorial or state laws.

The above notwithstanding, it quickly became apparent that the alienation of Indian land was not moving fast enough to satisfy land-hungry settlers, ranchers, and miners, not to mention territorial legislatures seeking statehood. To speed up the transfer of Indian lands to White settlers, the government introduced blood-quantum requirements in order to restrict the number of Indians eligible for tribal citizenship and tribal lands. Incidentally, it also reduced the number of Indians to whom the government owed trust responsibilities. Plus, there was another twist to using blood quantum to determine tribal citizenship. Indians who did not meet a minimum blood-quantum requirement were stripped of their tribal citizenship and freed from Dawes Act restrictions, which prohibited Indians from selling their lands for 25 years.

The result was a selling spree, as members of the new class of non-Indians sold their land dirt cheap. It seems foolish in retrospect, but it made perfectly good sense to the Native landowners. Often suffering from hunger and exposure, they did not have the means or desire to farm land that was very expensive to farm profitably, if in fact it was even arable. Remember the Meriam Report's observation that most of the land on reservations, particularly west of the 100th meridian, was useless for agriculture beyond a subsistence level, at least without irrigation, which was expensive and not always practical. Consequently, the report concluded that the land was so poor that even a "trained and experienced white man could scarcely wrest a reasonable living."[161]

Even with training and education, the Indians lacked the cash or credit needed to acquire "the necessary implements, livestock, and tools for a start." They were also discouraged from pursuing anything more than subsistence agriculture by the government's mendacious policy of extending credit to the Indians in the form of reimbursable loans. That is, loans that that had to be repaid.[162]

As part of treaty agreements, the federal government and missionaries like the Quakers traditionally supplied Indians with seeds and agricultural implements. They also offered training and the assistance of skilled mechanics such as blacksmiths and carpenters. After the allotment of Indian lands under the Dawes Act, the government decided to wean Indians from their dependency on the government by offering loans rather than direct assistance to improve their allotments. However, since much of the land was not arable beyond subsistence farming, it was not likely that most farmers, even White farmers, would be able to generate enough revenue to repay the loans.

Moreover, many of the allotments were eventually subdivided through inheritance until they were too small to be worked profitably. The same was true for irrigation projects, most of which did not prove viable. The end result was that Indians were unable to repay their loans, which in many

[161] Meriam Report, 5.

[162] Ibid., 495.

cases, resulted in their losing their lands and their improvements to White farmers and ranchers. Consequently, such loans were discredited among Indians. Quite cruelly and ironically, this only hardened their dependency on the government. According to the Merriam Report, "… Heavy debts that can never be repaid have a bad psychological effect. The Indian who owes such debts feels discouraged, feels that if he accumulates property, it may be taken from him, and so refuses to take an inherent interest in business or put forth an effort to improve his condition."[163]

The report's conclusions were reminiscent of what the missionary Jabez Hyde heard 100 years earlier from the Seneca who worried, "… That in all their transactions with white men, they have prevailed against them, and they are filled with desponding fears that it will continue to be so." Indeed, it did continue to be so. Despite the government's promises, there was no magic in individual property ownership, and in fact, it "operated in the opposite direction."

To add insult to injury, there was more than government incompetence and wrongheaded policies at work. Farming at the end of the 19th century was in crisis. Farmers throughout the United States were losing their land as crop prices fell due to overproduction from the influx of immigrants who clamored for 160 acres of free land under the Homestead Act of 1863. They poured into the land west of the Mississippi River, putting more acres under cultivation.

In addition, the cost and risks of farming on the Great Plains were far greater than on the more familiar and hospitable land in the East. There were droughts, hailstorms, grasshoppers, scorching summers, winter blizzards, and railroads extorting farmers for supplies and for shipping their crops. On top of that, the period was characterized by vicious economic cycles that drove thousands of farmers out of business.

So difficult was farming west of the Missouri River that the U.S. government was forced to increase the size of land grants to 320 acres for farmers and 640 acres for ranchers. One hundred and sixty acres simply was not

---

[163] Ibid., 496.

enough. There was frustration and anger among farmers as they lost their lands, their homes, and their dreams. These feelings of helplessness led to the rise of the Populist Party, which championed the free and unlimited coinage of silver. The theory was that it would save the farmers by causing inflation and driving up prices for their crops.

The protest reached a crescendo in the 1896 presidential race between William McKinley, who favored the gold standard, and William Jennings Bryan, the champion of the Silverites. The latter challenged the Gold Bugs by famously declaring, "You shall not crucify mankind on a cross of gold!" Or as the reformer Mary Elizabeth Lease bluntly put it, farmers should "raise less corn, and more hell."

The argument even received a nod in L. Frank Baum's children story and one the most famous movies of all time: *The Wizard of Oz*. Dorothy and her friends, including the Scarecrow, who represented the farmers of America, were drawn or pushed to the gold standard—aka the yellow-brick road—to the fraudulent wizard. The gist of the story is that at the very time the Dawes Act was being implemented and Indians were being encouraged to take up the plow, farmers were giving up and starting the long, slow exodus from farms to cities. It was not a good time to get into farming, especially in the areas where most Indian reservations were located. So, many homesteaders sold their land for whatever they could get before they lost it to foreclosures. By the 1920s, land that had only been settled 20 years earlier was already being abandoned.

Even today, farming is a risky business, particularly on the arid lands west of the Mississippi. I once met a crop-insurance adjuster at a restaurant in Miles City, Montana, in the center of the spring-wheat region. He was assessing the damage caused to the wheat crop by a recent hailstorm. "Hail is the biggest threat to wheat farmers," he told me. A storm can wipe out an entire crop.

I believe him, having been through a hailstorm in Wyoming that not only broke windshields but killed livestock. I heard that one hailstone from that storm was 8 inches in diameter and weighed nearly 2 pounds. Imagine being hit by that. The damage once done by a hailstorm in South Dakota was visible from space.

The long and the short of it is farming west of the Missouri was difficult even for experienced White farmers. For Indians, it was next to impossible. They lacked access to capital to buy the steel plows needed to break the tough prairie sod, to drill wells deep enough to reach the Oglala Aquifer, to purchase the newly invented barbed wire to fence their fields, and to purchase machinery to harvest their crops. Allotment was a disaster for tribes. By the time it ended in 1934, they had lost more than 100 million acres of land or about two-thirds of what they controlled in 1887.

Not only did the tribes surrender control of their lands to the government, tribal membership dwindled. At issue was just how much Indian blood was necessary to be eligible for tribal citizenship and an allotment of tribal land, or as the director of the 1870 census put it, the ratio of "superior" to "inferior" blood. I needn't tell you whose blood he considered inferior. The problem was that there were no accurate records of tribal membership, or criteria or guidelines for identifying bona fide Indians from pretenders.

Some tribes required as little as one-thirty-second of Indian blood. So, the government set up tents in Indian territories to identify and enroll tribal members on what became known as the Dawes Rolls. Without accurate records, the process was ripe for corruption. Centuries of intermarriage and the sexual colonization of Native women had produced a large population of racially mixed people with varying degrees of Native blood.

Neither were the censuses any help. When Indians were first included in the census in 1860, enumerators were instructed that "Indians not taxed were not to be enumerated." Only those who had "renounced tribal rule" were to be counted, a policy that, if strictly implemented, would have excluded most Indians at that time. The censuses were also fraught with inaccuracies, as the populations of many of the large reservations were scattered and inaccessible. Many didn't speak English, and they distrusted government motives and how the information would be used, so they hid from or refused to cooperate with the enumerators. Even today, Native

Americans are still considered a "hard-to-count" population. As a result, they are underrepresented in censuses.[164]

Blood quantum was first used in the 1880 census, becoming the primary criteria for tallying Indians after 1900. Census takers interviewed Indians and used whatever records were available to determine whether they were full bloods, had some arbitrary percentage of Indian blood, or none at all. But in the end, the determination was usually based simply on skin color. As late as 1950, census enumerators used skin color to count Native people, even relying on the highly subjective "paper-bag rule." That is, if a person's skin color was as dark or darker than an ordinary paper bag, he or she was an Indian.

The problem of identifying Indians for the census also plagued signing them up for the Dawes Rolls. It was at best a hit-or-miss proposition and worse, open to fraud. For example, unscrupulous land agents in Oklahoma approved non-Indians for allotments in exchange for bribes. The going price was supposedly $5. And since Cherokee lands were the most expansive and located in the resource-rich and more easily accessible eastern part of the territory, most $5 Indians elected to be Cherokee. Thus, it's not unreasonable for someone like Senator Elizabeth Warren, whose family has roots in territorial Oklahoma, to believe family stories told around the dinner table about a Cherokee ancestor somewhere in her past. It may also explain why there are so many Americans who claim, perhaps with some legitimacy, Cherokee heritage.[165]

There is a darker side to the use of blood quantum to identify Indians. A similar yardstick was used in Nazi Germany to identify Jews. In the American South, the "one-drop rule" was employed to classify anyone with even a single drop of African blood as "colored." By the 20th century, the rule had been adopted by most Southern states, and it was applied to Indians as well

---

[164] Jen Deerinwater, "Paper Genocide: The Erasure of Native People in Census Counts," *newswire-group.com* (December 9, 2019).

[165] Alysa Landry, "Paying to Play Indian: The Dawes Rolls and the Legacy of $5 Indians," *Indian Country Today* (September 13, 2018).

as Black people. In Virginia, the Racial Integrity Act of 1924 required all residents to register as either White or "colored." Whites were designated as those who had "no trace whatsoever of any blood other than Caucasian."

Under the new rules, Indians were reclassified as "colored" and subjected to the same segregationist restrictions that oppressed Black people. To wit: They were forbidden to marry White people, a ruling intended to prevent further dilution of White blood in the population. Although Indians were citizens after 1924, they weren't allowed to vote until the 1950s. They were also forbidden to attend White schools; Indian children were not allowed into White high schools until 1960.

The commonwealth of Virginia went so far as to change the racial identification on Indian birth certificates and other vital records to "colored" and removed their graves from White cemeteries. Ironically, the Virginia legislature added an amendment to the Racial Integrity Act called the "Pocahontas Rule," which exempted from the law anyone with less than one-sixteenth American Indian blood. The reason was that many of the oldest and wealthiest families in Virginia proudly claimed they were descendants of the original Indian princess.

The one-drop rule was eventually declared unconstitutional, but blood quantum is still required for most Native Americans to be granted tribal citizenship and receive official Certificates of Degree of Indian Blood to prove they are Indians. In the United States today, only Indians, horses and dogs are required to register their blood quantum.

The introduction of minimum blood-quantum requirements to determine tribal citizenship violated the historical understanding between tribes and the federal government, which ensured that only tribes could determine their requirements for citizenship. Setting minimum blood-quantum standards for citizenship stripped the tribes of their control over citizenship. This necessarily hastened the elimination of the tribes by reducing the number of their citizens and making it virtually impossible for them to create new generations of citizens.

Without citizens, the tribes would wither and die, thus removing the final obstacle to opening Indian lands for White settlers, ranchers, and miners. As strategies go, it was highly effective. By the 1930s, when allotment ended, the number of Indian citizens had been reduced, tribal control over their lands and people had been weakened, and 100 million acres of land had been alienated from Indian control. Blood quantum nearly succeeded where warfare, slavery, removal, and disease had failed.

Blood-quantum requirements were abolished by the Indian Reorganization Act in 1934, which also restored control over citizenship to the tribes. However, it was resurrected during the Termination Period beginning in1953, when minimum blood-quantum standards were used to end federal recognition of a number of Indian nations. The federal government finally repudiated it by the 1970s, and termination fever died down but not before more than 100 tribes had been stripped of their federal recognition, thousands of their citizens were no longer considered Indians, and millions of acres of tribal lands were lost.

The use of blood quantum was shelved under the Indian Self-Determination and Education Assistance Act. Furthermore, the Indian Child Welfare Act (ICWA) of the 1970s and various U.S. Supreme Court decisions restored tribal control over citizenship. However, blood quantum continues to rear its ugly head.

For example, it's been dusted off in court cases involving the adoption of Indian children by non-Indian parents. In the 2013 case of *Adoptive Parents v. Baby Girl*, the U.S. Supreme Court raised the question of whether a child with "close to zero" Indian blood could be considered a citizen of a tribe, in this case, the Cherokee Nation. The court didn't rule on the issue, but it opened the door to challenging the ICWA's restrictions on adopting Indian children by non-Indian parents on the grounds that children like "Baby Girl" with only 1.2% Cherokee blood were not Indian enough to be protected by the ICWA.

Attaching blood quantum requirements to the ICWA, either by Supreme Court fiat or Congressional legislation, would probably mean that even children who were tribal citizens would not be Indian enough to be protected under the ICWA. It would also amount to tribal citizens being hard-pressed to be able to produce future generations of citizens, which would effectively finish the job of eliminating tribes that was started during the allotment era. Finally, it would preclude 250 unrecognized tribes like the Lumbee from ever attaining federal recognition. If the goal is to strip tribes of their control over citizenship and undermine their sovereignty, blood quantum is the ticket.[166]

With the development of DNA technology and the availability of quickie DNA tests offered by 23andMe and a host of other DNA-testing companies, blood quantum has become an attractive alternative to tracing ancestors back to the 1910 Indian census or some other benchmark. Those methods can be messy and controversial, and they've led to what have been historical struggles between so-called full-bloods and mixed-bloods.

For example, the Choctaw, Creek, and Cherokee have struggled with what to do about their Black citizens or freedmen/freedwomen, whose ancestry dates back to the days when tribal members owned slaves. The Cherokee sought to disenroll them, claiming they could not prove they had any Indian blood. The U.S. Supreme Court ruled against the tribe on the grounds that it violated an 1866 treaty that granted Cherokee citizenship to the ex-slaves and their descendants. The issue was raised again by Choctaw freedmen seeking citizenship in that tribe. On the other hand, the Standing Rock Lakota welcomed into their tribe the NBA basketball star Kyrie Irving, whose mother is Lakota and whose father is Black.

So, what does it mean to be Indian enough? If not blood quantum, then what? Culture is even more difficult to define. Besides, in most tribes, the culture, language, and ceremonies have been lost to repression and boarding schools, and today, to television and the internet. As Duane Hollow Horn Bear, a Lakota elder and teacher on Rosebud, told me, "It's tough to compete with 'Beavis and Butt-head' when you're teaching Lakota language and culture to your children."

Just as with citizenship, there are conflicts on reservations between traditionalists, who want to restore long-standing ways, and progressives, who desire to modernize reservations through economic development like

---

[166] Abi Fain and Mary Catherine Nagle, "Close to Zero: The Reliance on Minimum Blood Quantum Requirements to Eliminate Tribal Citizenship in the Allotment Acts and Adoptive Couple Challenges to the Constitutionality of ICWA," *Mitchell Hamline Law Review*, 43, no. 4 (2017): 800-80.

casinos. Nevertheless, there is something that distinguishes them as Indians that transcends the differences and the conflicts between the 800 or so recognized and unrecognized tribes, or for that matter, within tribes. Even the Supreme Court conceded to this when it admitted in 1978 in *Santa Clara Pueblo v. Martinez* that the tribes "by government, structure, culture, and sources of sovereignty are in many ways foreign to the constitutional institutions of the federal and state governments."[167]

It's hard to put your finger on, but it's real. It permeates reservations and binds them together in the face of 500 years of assaults against their very existence. It underlies their fierce defense of their sovereignty and their resistance to assimilation. As the government recognized in the Indian Self-Determination and Education Assistance Act, "Indians will never surrender their desire to control their relationships among themselves and other entities and people."[168]

I felt this difference the first time I visited reservations, whether it was the tiny Tuscarora territory near Niagara Falls, New York, which is only a few my miles from home, or the massive Navajo Reservation in Arizona and New Mexico. I knew right away that I was entering an alternate world. Granted, I saw what everybody sees on reservations: the ramshackle trailers, yards filled with broken-down cars, and roads littered with trash. Unmistakable and even unfathomable was the contrast between the reservations I visited and my neighborhood and even the poorest sections of Buffalo, New York,

It wasn't what I initially saw but what I missed that eventually stayed with me. I learned to recognize and appreciate the beauty of people and lands impoverished by centuries of oppression and neglect. I learned to relish the loveliness of the children, with their unnaturally black hair, and in the faces of the elderly, wizened by age and hardship. I learned to view reservations not as junkyards and economic wastelands but as scenic and sacred landscapes with hidden treasures like Black Valley on Crow, the Chuska Mountains on Navajo, the Little Rockies on Fort Belknap, and the

[167] Ibid., 865.

[168] Ibid., 851.

rolling prairies in the Dakotas and Nebraska. Most of all, I learned that despite the trauma and suffering America's Native people have endured, they share a profound joy in being Indian. It's almost palpable.

It animates their dancing, drumming, and singing at powwows, ceremonies, and celebrations. It inspires the pride they take in their land, their culture, and their heritage. It motivates a kind of resilience that has allowed them to survive and resist the siren song of assimilation. But to understand this, I had to shed my cultural blinders and learn to see through Indian eyes without pretending to be Indian. In the process, I learned a great deal about myself and my cultural background. Most of all, I learned Indians simply want to be Indians.

I remember when my education began. It was at the commemoration of the Indian monument at the Little Bighorn Battlefield on the Crow Reservation. I had taken a group to the celebration, which included a number of Lakota from Rosebud. We were standing at a Northern Cheyenne ceremony honoring their tribesmen who fought and died at the battle. The ceremony itself was an educational experience. It was replete with drumming and singing, and women were doing the *leelee,* all magnified by large speakers. All of a sudden, a dust devil whirled by.

They're not uncommon in the dry, dusty high plains of Montana and the Dakotas; I had seen others. But this time, Don Moccasin, who was standing next to me, jabbed me with his elbow, and pointing to the whirlwind, told me the spirits were listening. I knew Don saw spirits behind everything, but this was the first time I was able to connect them with an actual physical phenomenon.

There is a scientific explanation for dust devils. Hot air near the ground begins to rise through cooler air above it, taking with it dust and debris. Under the right conditions, it begins to rotate. Yet, I prefer to leave it cloaked in magic and mystery. Seeing spirits in all forms of nature is what gives way to Indians' worship of mountains, rivers, and prairies, and what causes them to resist efforts to despoil sacred sites with mining, logging, or the building of pipelines and dams.

A few days later, we left the celebration and headed to the nearby Bighorn Mountains to visit the Bighorn Medicine Wheel, a circular rock formation 80 feet across with 28 spokes radiating from a central cairn or grouping of rocks. It sits on an outcropping about 10,000 feet above sea level, offering spectacular views of the Bighorns, the snow-covered peaks of Yellowstone to the west, and the Bighorn Canyon far below. Its origins and age are mysterious and controversial, although it has been estimated to be about 1,000 years old. Since no one tribe can lay claim to it, it is a sacred site for all Indians who make pilgrimages to it and leave behind hundreds of tobacco offerings draped over the iron fence that protects the wheel from desecration.

The hike to the site is about 1.5 miles uphill, which, at that altitude, can be quite strenuous. In fact, when we reached the top, a crusty old steel-worker in our group, who had not wanted to come on the excursion and had grumbled about it, was quite winded. I worried about his health and sat him down while the rest of us began to circle the monument, praying silently and leaving behind the tobacco offerings we made.

There were other visitors there besides our group, and everybody began to gather around Don Moccasin as he started to sing a song honoring a friend who passed away. Don learned about his friend's death on an earlier visit to the site, and he was reminded of it whenever he came to the Medicine Wheel. It was a mournful song, and even though the only ones who could understand it were the Lakota in our group, I noticed total strangers were sobbing.

It wasn't planned nor could it have been. Don's singing was powerful, raw, and authentic, evoking an outpouring of emotions from all who heard it. As we were getting ready to head back down the mountain, I noticed the fellow I had left sitting on the bench was crying. My first reaction was "Oh, no, he's having a heart attack! How are we going to get him down from here?" I rushed over to him, only to find he was crying tears of joy. He told me he had never experienced anything like that in his life and was so glad he came.

The spirits were certainly working among us. As we were moving down the mountain, someone pointed up to a rainbow. It wasn't cloudy or rain-ing, and it wasn't the usual kind that arches across the sky from horizon to horizon. Rather, it was more like a flag waving in the clear blue sky. Don said the Creator heard our prayers.

It wouldn't be the last time I saw a rainbow like that. At a Sun Dance one morning, as we were praying the sun out of the ground, a similar rainbow appeared, even though there was no rain and the sky was crystal clear. I assume there must be meteorological explanations for these occurrences, although I couldn't find one. Nor could I find one for what happened when I attended a memorial service for Don the year after he died.

As we gathered to honor him, the ceremony was interrupted by the piercing screech of eagles. When we looked up, there were two eagles heading straight for us. Suddenly, they clutched their talons together and plummeted toward the ground. Just as suddenly, they separated and veered off in different directions. Albert White Hat told us the eagles were Don and his wife, Maggie. Together in this life, Don was now in the spirit world, leaving Maggie behind.

I realize most people will find it difficult to believe that God or the Creator—in Lakota, *Tunkasila*—speaks and acts through the likes of animals, rocks, and trees. To Christian missionaries, anyone who believed those stories were dismissed as pagans, a pejorative term that early Christians used to describe nonbelievers or people without a religion. In fact, children admitted to the Thomas Indian School who had no religious affiliation were labeled pagans on their admission forms.

But to Don Moccasin, those beliefs were literally a matter of life and death. Indeed, he was alive because of the intervention of the spirits on his behalf. Born with a heart defect, Don was sent to Lincoln, Nebraska, for a heart valve replacement, but the operation went terribly wrong. His wife, Maggie, was told there was no hope. His heart tissue was like "cheesecloth" and couldn't be sewn back together. He was bleeding to death.

The news spread, and prayer vigils were held for him back on Rosebud and wherever Don had visited and shared his spirituality. Back in Lincoln, tobacco or prayer ties were placed over his heart. Grandma Little Elk brought two healing stones, while the hospital staff dismantled smoke detectors and opened windows so a medicine man could burn sage for smudging the room and the people gathered there. Although Don would have to undergo dialysis for kidney failure during his ordeal, he defied the doctors' prognosis. He survived. When Don regained consciousness, he said he felt Grandma Little Elk's stones breaking up and coursing through his veins. The doctors had no explanation.

I've heard other stories like that. Waycee His Holy Horse, a young medicine man on Rosebud, told me he was once summoned to Sioux Falls to pray for a young boy who had drowned and was pronounced brain dead. The doctors said there was no hope for his recovery, but the boy's grandmother asked Waycee to stay and pray with her. He did, and the boy recovered. Again, doctors had no explanations.

The same was true for a little boy who was bitten on his stomach by a raccoon. The infection had eaten away his intestines until there was only about a foot left. They did not expect him to live either. Waycee performed a ceremony, and not only did the boy survive, his intestines regenerated themselves.

There's also the story I heard from Dewey Bull Tail, who belongs to the peyote-based American Indian Church. A young woman who had several miscarriages approached him for help. He gave her two peyote buttons, one to help her recover from her most recent loss and one to prevent future miscarriages. She later conceived and carried a baby to term. Whenever I tell these stories, they're greeted with polite but obvious skepticism. I must admit, at times I secretly doubt some of the stories I hear, and I would probably still be a total skeptic if it weren't for my own strange encounter with the spirit world.

In one of my zanier moments, I invited Roy Stone—a medicine man from Rosebud—and five helpers to conduct a *yuwipi* or healing ceremony at my college. We also had one across the Niagara River in Ontario, Canada, for Native people over there. I say it was zany because I had no idea how much work would be involved in finding a place to hold the ceremony, plus housing, feeding, and transporting my guests, and hosting a reception with authentic Native food. Probably the most daunting concern was how to get the Lakota across the Canadian border and back again immediately after 911. On top of it all, I had injured my knee, and the pain was debilitating.

We finally settled on the basement of the campus chapel for the first night's ceremony, a decision that brought me a lot of criticism from devout Catholics who thought it sacrilegious to hold a pagan ceremony in a consecrated place. In the end, it was the only area we could make completely dark, a requirement for the ceremony. At the medicine man's insistence, we had to remove all florescent bulbs because they give off a faint glow even when turned off. The smoke detectors had to go because of their blinking red lights and because they would have been set off by the sage burned during the ceremony. I failed to mention that to the school's safety authorities.

The first night was open to students and the public, and it was oversubscribed. The participants were given instructions, including to use the bathroom beforehand because nobody would be allowed in or out after the ceremony began, and it would probably last into the wee hours of the morning. I was to be the doorkeeper, largely to prevent anyone from stumbling in and disrupting the ceremony. What I remember most was the pain in my knee as I paced the hallway, anxiously waiting for the ceremony to end. I was also worried that it would somehow be a flop, especially since it lasted at least four hours. I was relieved when everybody came out excited about their experience, even if exhausted. I don't know whether anyone was healed that night, but nearly 20 years later, some will still not talk about what they experienced.

The ceremony in Canada was held near Niagara Falls, where some local Natives had carved a theater out of the ground and covered it with a dome. It was my turn to participate. I crawled into the theater, knee throbbing. It was overcrowded, and the tiered seats were not deep enough for my rear end, meaning I couldn't stretch out my legs. That made my knee ache all the more. As the door closed and we were enveloped in complete darkness, all I could think of was my knee. My only relief came when I nodded off from the heat generated by the packed crowd.

In the meantime, the ceremony started. Singing and praying began in

Lakota, all to the beat of the hand drums used by the helpers. I don't know how long I dozed, but I was startled awake when bright electric blue sparks began flying about the dugout. After the initial shock, I began to think like a White man. I tried to figure out some kind of explanation for them. I had heard about things like this but never took them seriously, until I looked down and saw the bottom rims of the hand drums glowing with the same electric blue light.

Once again, I tried to come up with an explanation. The drums must have been doctored. Then I remembered they belonged to local Native people and were given to the Lakota as they entered the dugout. They had left their own drums and other material in South Dakota. After 911, they were not allowed to bring them on the plane, and they refused to check them. Still, I would not let go of my skepticism until I crawled out, stretched my legs, and realized the pain in my knee was gone. Go figure.

I've often been asked how someone becomes a medicine man. I'm sure it differs from tribe to tribe, and even within tribes not all medicine men are the same. For Waycee, it was not a matter of choice. The spirits began to speak to him when he was about 16 or 17. At first, his mother worried there was something wrong with him. He finally underwent a *yuwipi* that lasted four nights. The spirits told him he was needed to help his people, and that the spirits would guide, protect, and provide for him.

He answered their call. He heals the sick and the dying, but that's just the beginning of his life's work. As he puts it, he's a doctor, lawyer, and marriage counselor. He presides over wakes and funerals, but his most important role is keeping alive the sacred ceremonies, customs, values, and language of the Lakota. That is the only way they can survive the continuing assault on their lands and ways of life. His calling is to heal his people both physically and spiritually.

According to Waycee, the source of the problem on Rosebud and other reservations is that White people have forced Indians to be something they can't and don't want to be. They are not made to fit into the White people's system. He admits the resulting hatred of White culture has become self-destructive, noting the scourge of alcohol and drugs, and the epidemic of suicides. For him, as for so many Indians I have spoken with, the only solution is to revitalize traditional cultures, especially among the young.

For the Lakota, this means the Seven Sacred ceremonies: the sacred pipe, the sweat lodge, the vision quest, the Sun Dance, the making of relatives, the keeping of the soul, and the coming of age for women. Each of these has a distinct purpose, but together they provide participants with a common spiritual experience and a shared set of beliefs and principles that govern individual and collective behavior.

Every tribe has its own ceremonies and rituals through which values and principles are taught and passed down from generation to generation. They bind people together around a communal consensus that identifies them as Crow, Navajo, Assiniboin, or another tribe, and ensures their survival. Missionaries and Indian agents knew what they were doing when they banned ceremonies on reservations. The same goes for prohibiting Native people from speaking their languages.

As I have heard so many times, their ceremonies were created in their languages and do not have the same meaning in English. When their languages and ceremonies were taken away, the ties that bound Indian communities together frayed and eventually disintegrated. That's why it so important to revive ceremonies and languages, and why it's so heartening to see as many as 60 Sun Dances springing up on Pine Ridge alone, with another 30 on Rosebud.

Ceremonies and rituals provide spiritual, psychological, emotional, and physical healing for fractured Native communities. I've seen and participated in a number of ceremonies on various reservations, but the one that best taught me how ceremonies hold communities together was a healing ceremony on the Navajo Reservation.

I was invited by a friend at Diné College, the Navajo tribal college near Chinle, Arizona, on the reservation. It was to be conducted at night, which became the practice on many reservations as a way of concealing forbidden ceremonies from government agents. It also was to be held in a remote area somewhere near the town of Ganado. I say "somewhere" because I couldn't find it again if I tried. I received directions that led me to an unmarked dirt road indistinguishable from all the other dirt roads that turn off the highway, save for the line of cars turning onto it. I assumed they were also going to the ceremony, so I followed their taillights through a thick cloud of dust that obscured any landmarks I might have used to find my way back. Suddenly, we emerged into a clearing, where hundreds of cars and pickups were parked, and crowds of people were huddled around fires to break the October chill.

By the time I got there, the ceremony was underway. I won't go into the details, which I couldn't understand anyway, but what impressed me most was the fact that so many people had gathered to participate in a ceremony in the middle of the night. There were infants in strollers, elders in wheelchairs and leaning against walkers, and teenagers horsing around and flirting. There was a stand offering hot coffee and other refreshments. As with many of my adventures, I was the only White person there. The people were welcoming and gracious, although more than a bit curious about what I was doing there and how I ever found the place.

They explained the healing ceremony was being conducted on behalf of a man who was isolated in a house surrounded at a respectable distance by the onlookers. Every so often, "kachinas" or dancers, wearing their masks and ceremonial regalia, emerged from a nearby hut, danced to the house, conducted the ceremony inside, and then returned to their quarters.

I never learned the man's illness, and I don't know how long the ceremony lasted. I got there around 10, and it was still going strong when I left sometime in the early-morning hours. I wasn't prepared for the chilly weather, and the acrid smoke from the burning cedar finally got to me. Besides, I had a long drive back to Chinle, and I wasn't sure I would be able to retrace my route on a pitch-black night. In fact, it was so dark, I almost ran into a herd of horses standing on the highway, a common occurrence on the Navajo Reservation, where animals are allowed to roam freely.

As I drove back, I thought about what I had just witnessed. The ceremony was interesting, even though I didn't understand most of it, but more intriguing was the way entire families gathered on a chilly fall night and stayed into the wee hours of the morning to support it. It was then that I realized the ceremony was not solely for the man in the house; it was also for the community. It reassured those gathered that the community would be there for them in their time of need. The ceremony welded them together with individual and collective responsibilities to each other in times of need and times of plenty, in times of sorrow and times of joy, in times of peace and times of war.

It's not just the ceremonies themselves that hold Native communities together. Rituals performed therein express the shared beliefs and values of a people. One that I am particularly familiar with is the Iroquois Thanksgiving Address or *Ganö:nyök*. As I mentioned earlier, it is "The Words That Come Before All Else," and it is said before all social, political, and religious gatherings among the *Haudenausaunee* or Iroquois people. It is intended to clear the participants' minds of evil or negative thoughts and bring them together as one by giving thanks for the gifts of life and the natural world.

The address itself is a series of recitations or greetings to the natural world. It begins with the speaker acknowledging the people or *Ögwe´ Öweh*. "Today we have gathered, and we see that the cycles of life continue. We have been given the duty to live in balance and harmony with each other and all living things. So now, we bring our minds together as we give greetings and thanks to each other as people." The audience then responds in the call-and-response cadence, *"Da:h ne´hoh dih nëyögwa'nigo'dë:ök"* or "Now our minds are one." This is repeated as the speaker gives thanks for Mother Earth, the waters and fishes, the various kinds of plants, the animals, trees, and birds, the four winds, the thunderers, the sun, Grandmother Moon and the stars, the enlightened teachers, and finally, the Creator. To each, members of the congregation respond, "Now our minds are one" to confirm their shared reverence for the natural and supernatural that distinguished them as Iroquois, or more properly, *Haudenausaunee*, and shaped and guided their history.

The Iroquois Thanksgiving Address, along with the creation story, six sacred ceremonies, and the Great Law of Peace that served as their constitution, cemented six disparate and often warring tribes into a formidable force that held sway from New York through the Great Lakes region and the Ohio Valley. The Iroquois story reflects the power of ceremony and ritual to create a community, even across tribal lines. Unfortunately, theirs is also an all-too-familiar story, as that power waned, and they lost their lands, their language, their independence, and essentially their sovereignty.

Given the transformative power of ceremonies, small wonder that many Indians believe the only way to heal communities fractured and fragmented by the trauma of the past and the present is to revive and revitalize their ceremonies and rituals, and especially their languages. However, Waycee His Holy Horses takes it one step further: For Indians to recover what they lost, they have to reclaim their sovereignty, which he believes is a right, not a gift.

Sovereignty has become a hot issue for Indians on the one hand, and state, local, and federal governments on the other. It's at the heart of controversies over casinos, taxation, schools, policing, and pipelines, to name just a few of the hot-button issues. But at bottom, the real problem is two different definitions of sovereignty. The English definition is the ability of a nation to govern itself, but the equivalent word in Native languages means something different and deeper.

I first became aware of these variations at a meeting I attended on the Cattaraugus Seneca Reservation, where a Mohawk man explained sovereignty in Iroquoian languages. *Honöadwë:ni:yo´* in Seneca means "I carry myself" or "I carry my own water." That could refer to routine governmental affairs over which Indians now have little if any control, but the speaker offered another interpretation. To the Iroquois, it means the ability and responsibility of people, individually and collectively, to care for themselves. He pointed to the response in the Thanksgiving Address, "And now we are of one mind," as an example of that collective sovereignty.

As I was writing this, I thought back to that meeting on the Seneca Cattaraugus Reservation. As usual, I was the only White guy there, but I knew people, so I felt comfortable. There were Seneca, Cayuga, Onondaga, and I suppose others from New York and Canada. As I looked around at those who comprised the crowd, they looked like a bunch of average Americans except for their dark skin and the occasional braid. They were dressed in jeans, sneakers, and baseball hats. Judging by some of their clothing, they were Buffalo Bills fans. They all had cellphones, and there were SUVs and large pickups in the parking lot. Nevertheless, there were striking differences between them and any run-of-the-mill assembly of ordinary Americans.

For instance, their command of their respective languages and their knowledge of their heritage impressed and even surprised me. Even more striking, however, was the fact that after 200 years of public education, watching television, shopping at Walmart, and eating at McDonald's, they were fiercely determined to protect their sovereignty and maintain their identities as Iroquois and Indians. Like their ancestors, they did not want to become White men. Instead, they averred something I have heard a few times: It was the White man who wanted what Indians had, whether it was their land or their culture. It was to protect what they had that they were there on that Saturday afternoon.

They had good reason. In the 1950s, the government condemned tribal lands along the Allegheny River on the New York-Pennsylvania border, displaced hundreds of tribal members, and flooded about one-third of the reservation to build the Allegheny Reservoir. There were protests. Johnny Cash and Buffy Sainte-Marie sang about it, and Eleanor Roosevelt called it "shameful." Although the project violated the Canandaigua Treaty and the Supreme Law of the Land clause of the Constitution, both President Eisenhower and Kennedy supported it, with apologies, of course.

The Seneca lost their land, a loss they memorialize every year, but at least they fought off efforts by the federal government to terminate or disband the tribe in the 1960s. Not only did they prevail, the Seneca have jealously defended their sovereignty ever since, with the help of three casinos that make them a formidable economic and political foe. The people in the room that Saturday afternoon were there to reaffirm their identities as Seneca, as Iroquois, and as Indians, and to assert their determination to remain sovereign nations. They were there to assure themselves it would never happen again. As one Seneca put it, they don't need the government to recognize or validate them.

I've gone kayaking on that reservoir many times. It's one of my favorite spots. As I glide over the water, I can't help thinking about the heartbreak that lay below. The homes of 130 families were flooded to make way for the reservoir created by the Kinzua Dam to prevent flooding along the *Ohi:yo ´* or Allegany River on its way to Pittsburgh.

One of the houses belonged to Ralph Bowen, whom I met when I wrote my book on the Thomas Indian School. His family couldn't feed him during the Depression, so they sent him to Thomas or Salem (pronounced Sah-lam), as it was called. He eventually joined the Civilian Conservation Corps and served in the Army Air Corps during World War II, where he was an aerial gunner flying missions over Europe. He told me a funny story about how he wanted more action while he was stationed in Italy, so he volunteered for the infantry. He was finally transferred on the day the war ended. He risked his life for his country, and then he risked it time and time again as an ironworker climbing the high steel, like a lot of Seneca do.

He was one of the leaders of the fight against the dam. He recalled how his wife packed him egg salad sandwiches for his trips to Washington, D.C., to protest the project. The Seneca lost; Ralph's house was burned and his land flooded. He overcame a tough start to life, served his country in World War II, built a career for himself in a dangerous occupation, and raised a family. Then the government took everything away from him. Alone in my kayak, I realized Ralph's life was a metaphor for what has happened to Native Americans over the last 500 years.

Just a few miles away, on a tiny reservation near Niagara Falls, New York, the Tuscarora have put their determination into action, even though it has cost them dearly. Most of the wells on the reservation are contaminated with heavy metals, e-coli, lead, and/or cancer-causing hydrocarbons such as benzene. Some of the well water on the reservation smells like rotten eggs. Toxic chemicals must have leeched into the Tuscarora water supply from the factories in Niagara Falls, not unlike what happened at nearby Love Canal, where corporations dumped dangerous chemicals and covered them up. Homes were then built on top of the waste, causing serious health problems for unsuspecting families that moved into them.

So the Tuscarora persist with contaminated water, and not because there is no source of clean water near the reservation. The Niagara River runs right past it, and it sits between two of the Great Lakes: Erie and Ontario. The easy solution would be to tap into the city of Niagara Falls' public water system with the help of the federal government, but the tribe stubbornly refuses to do so, claiming that any deal with the government would impinge on Tuscarora sovereignty. Instead, tribal members rely on bottled water and water trucked in by tankers at great cost and inconvenience.

At root is the fear is that the federal government will take more of their land. More importantly, they would have to give up those rights that distinguish them as Indians and that are protected by their sovereignty. That is, their ability to govern themselves as sovereign nations as guaranteed by the aforementioned Canandaigua Treaty. If they have any right, it is the right to distrust the federal government. Like the Seneca, they have good reason to.

In the 1950s, the U.S. government took more than half of the already tiny Tuscarora Reservation to build a reservoir to feed the generators of the New York Power Authority, which produces electricity for a good part of the Northeastern United States. The tribe received $13 million, but tribal officials appealed. They wanted the land instead. As one Tuscarora told a local newspaper, if they give in, "We'd give up our sovereignty. We'd give up our rights as Native Americans."[169] For them, sovereignty means not only the right to govern their internal affairs, but a more fundamental right: freedom.

Those incidents are reminiscent of what happened to the Lakota after the Battle of Little Bighorn. To punish them, the government took the Black Hills, which were sacred to the Lakota and had been recognized as part of the Great Sioux Reservation under the Laramie treaties of 1851 and 1868. There were protests, like the one in 1970 in which Grandma Edna Little Elk participated. The Lakota went to court, and after a long, drawn-out battle, finally won.

In 1980, the U.S. Supreme Court ruled the Black Hills were wrongfully taken from the Lakota. But instead of returning the land, the court award-

[169] Lou Michel, "Tuscarora Water Woes Clouded by Sovereignty," *Buffalo News* (February 17, 2018).

ed the tribe $106 million, which it refused to accept; the Lakota people wanted their land back. That sum is worth more than $1 billion today, but the Lakota, some of the poorest people in America, and indeed, in the world, remain steadfast.

The Seneca, Tuscarora, Lakota, Northern Cheyenne, Blackfeet, and Navajo are still fiercely determined to protect at all costs their cultures, their identities, the health and well-being of their people, and above all else, their lands. A recent example is that tribes across America asserted their sovereignty by closing their reservations to outsiders to prevent the spread of COVID-19, despite threats from governors and the federal government. They've grown accustomed to being at odds with authorities. After hundreds of years of threats to either assimilate or face extermination, they remain stubbornly resistant to the siren song of assimilation and choose instead to carry their own water, as it were.

I found that in other Native languages, sovereignty has remarkably similar meanings. *Iish chiiwiillu baukucheesh* in Crow means "one who takes care of himself." In Lakota, *Wokiconze Iyecinka* translates to "we carry ourselves." In Navajo, *T´aaho´ ajit´eego* means responsibility or obligation. To those and presumably other tribes, sovereignty means not only governing themselves but caring and providing for themselves and each other. Self-government means, indeed, requires self-sufficiency. It is a principle rooted in the communalism or communitarianism that characterized Native societies and that missionaries and government agents sneeringly referred to as "communism," long before the word acquired the sinister meaning it has today. It also clashed, often violently, with the individualism unleashed in America by the seemingly unlimited abundance of land and resources just waiting to be exploited. Naomi Riley maintains that sovereignty for Indians is an illusion. On the contrary, it's the glue that has held tribes together in the face of unrelenting efforts to extinguish them. From allotment to boarding schools to the suppression of languages and ceremonies to sterilizations, adoptions, and foster care, the American government has used every trick in the book to dissolve tribal relations and erase Indians from history.

It hasn't worked. They're not going anywhere, and they're not about to apologize. Sovereignty seems like a complicated and controversial issue, but it's really very simple. Without land there can be no sovereignty. That's why unrecognized tribes like the Lumbee, the Mashpee, and others have fought so long and hard to establish reservations. It might seem curious to a non-Indian. Americans have always believed land is a commodity that can be bought and sold. In fact, Americans have most of their wealth invested in real estate, principally their homes. For Indians, land is a gift from the Creator, and more, it is the Creator itself. All life springs from it. It's the source of their material and spiritual sustenance. Their creation and other stories teach them it is their responsibility to protect and preserve it. In a sense, their cultures are organic, growing out of their diverse geographic and climatic surroundings, and giving rise to their equally diverse cultures and languages.

All of this serves to explain Indians' fierce attachment to their lands and their desire to reclaim them. Just travel around their territories with them, and you'll come to appreciate the pride and joy they feel over it. Where many would see lands that are bleak, impoverished and undeveloped, littered with trash, junk cars, and dilapidated houses and buildings, Indians see forest-covered mountains, steep canyons, rolling plains, flat-top mesas, fantastical shapes of high deserts, and islands dotting the Pacific Coast, to name but a few. As Dewey Bull Tail told me, he has everything he wants and needs on the reservation: three mountain ranges, two beautiful rivers, lots of game to hunt, and plenty of room to roam. Their land not only holds and sustains them, it draws them back when they leave.

Take, for example, the Lakota's stubborn refusal to accept money in exchange for the Black Hills, the heart and soul of their culture and the source of their material and spiritual sustenance. Shaped like a human heart, ironically enough, the hills are something of an anomaly. As you drive across the monotonously flat prairie, the Black Hills mysteriously appear almost Ozlike on the horizon, their slopes blanketed with black spruce forests from which the mountains get their name. They stand in sharp contrast to the drab plains with their clumps of buffalo grass and the occasional clusters of cottonwoods lining the dry creek beds.

The closer one gets, it's easy to see why the Lakota call the Black Hills "the center of everything that is." In the arid high plains, the Black Hills provided them with everything they needed: wood for their fires and te-pees, a variety of fish and game, and most importantly, water. The Black Hills also were the anchor of their spiritual life. It was from Wind Cave, now a tourist trap, that the *Pte Oyate*—or buffalo nation—emerged, even-tually giving rise to *Ikce Wicasa,* the human race.

According to the Lakota creation story, humans and the buffalo held a race around the Black Hills to see which one would hold dominion over the others. The humans won with the help of the magpie and came to con-trol the buffalo and other animals. In preparation for the race, the animals painted themselves, which explains their colors today. In fact, they exerted themselves so much, they left behind a trail of blood that is supposedly still visible in a reddish ring around the base of the hills.

The stories about the Black Hills are the Lakota's book of Genesis. They explain the order of things in their universe, including the importance of the many sacred sites in and around the Black Hills, like Devil's Tower in northeastern Wyoming. The Lakota see that gray monolith of volcanic rock as the actual horn of a buried buffalo skull. The other, smaller horn is nearby if you look closely from the overlooks on the road leading to the monument. It was there that Great Bear—known as *Hu Numpa*—imparted language and sacred ceremonies to the Lakota. Today it's a consecrated place where the Lakota and other Plains tribes hold their Sun Dances each summer.

The area is rife with meaning for the Lakota. *Pe' Sla* ("Bald Mountain") is the mountain meadow at the center of the Black Hills, where the morning star fell to earth and killed seven women whose souls became the seven stars in the Pleiades constellation. Lakota still gather to pray at the heart of Lakota culture. You can see *Pe' Sla* from the top of Harney Peak, the high-est point in the Black Hills, where the Lakota hold a ceremony to welcome the Thunder Beings each spring. Bear Butte or *Mato Paha* near Sturgis is a mountain in the shape of a sleeping bear. Lakota go there to fast and pray for a vision that will guide them for the rest of their lives. Supposedly,

Sitting Bull and Cray Horse visited the site. I had the honor of taking Don Moccasin up the mountain for what was his last vision quest.

The land is where they live, and it's where they worship. It's their home, and it's their cathedral. Small wonder that Mount Rushmore is considered a desecration, not unlike graffiti sprayed on a synagogue or church. The Lakota are not alone in their attachment to their lands. Spirits are alive in the landscape on the massive Navajo Reservation, which sprawls across the borders of New Mexico, Arizona, Utah, and Colorado. The sacred is everywhere and in everything.

Most Americans are familiar with the extraordinary monoliths of Monument Valley, if only through Westerns directed by John Ford. Tourists tend to stop at Monument Valley Park, now run by the Navajo Nation, to take a quick tour, snap some pictures and buy some souvenirs, hurrying past the rest of the desiccated reservation on their way to the Grand Canyon. They miss the four sacred mountains and four sacred rivers that mark the boundaries of Navajo land, known as *Dinétah* or "the land of the Diné people."

Four is a sacred number for the Navajo. There are four sacred colors, four seasons, four directions, and four clans that gave rise to the Navajo people. Tourists hurrying by on the main highways miss the beautiful Chuska Mountains that run north and south like a spine across the reservation, providing the Navajo with water, timber, and grazing land. They miss the rocky outcroppings like Shiprock, which stands all alone, 1,600 feet above the desert and looks like a clipper ship sailing on an ocean of sand. They miss the lush beauty of Canyon de Chelly, where Navajo still farm as they have for centuries in the shadow of Spider Rock, which sprouts 700 feet above the floor of the canyon. Perhaps my favorite rock formation, it marks the place where Spider Woman taught the Navajo to weave their famous rugs and blankets. Canyon de Chelly is also the site of Canyon del Muerto and Massacre Cave, where Indians believe the sounds of the Navajo women and children killed by the Spanish in 1825 can still be heard.

These and so many other places sacred to the Navajo are scattered across the desert landscape, albeit they may be invisible or seem insignificant to casual visitors. They can take the form of boulders, hills, mesas, or rocky outcroppings. They can be plant- or medicine-gathering areas, or springs like the one I discovered on the awesome but treacherous road across the Chuska Mountains from Lukachukai to Red House. (In my defense, I was told there was a place there to aid thirsty travelers crossing the mountains.) They can be ceremonial sites with special powers that are kept secret to protect their sanctity and the powers Navajo supplicants seek through prayer and offerings. They can be houses or buildings hidden from view, where clans and families gather for healing ceremonies, like the one I attended on that cold October night.

The spirits are alive in the desert, and they speak to the Navajo through stories that have informed and animated them for centuries. In fact, the spiritual attachment the Navajo have to their land explains why the largest reservation in America is adding to its land base by purchasing ranches in Colorado near Hesperus Mountain and Mount Blanca, two of the Navajo's most sacred mountains. It also explains why they can't leave, despite the depredations so many Navajo suffer. Without the spiritual sustenance and guidance of the land and its stories, they could no longer be Navajo. They would no longer be Indians.

I have found this reverence for the land on all the reservations I have visited, but nowhere deeper than on the isolated, windswept, and seemingly barren mesas of the Hopi Reservation. The Hopi people of Arizona are often called the "oldest of people" by other tribes. They have lived in the Southwest desert for thousands of years. Their stories tell them they came from the south, bringing with them the corn that would eventually spread throughout North America. They live principally on three large, arid, and dusty mesas that rise as much as 7,000 feet above sea level and tower over a severe but strangely beautiful desert landscape.

They live in settlements along Route 264 that crosses the three mesas from east to west. Their oldest town, Oraibi, is on the third and westernmost mesa and is said to be the oldest continuously inhabited settlement in North America. The Hopi are Puebloan people, related to the Zuni and the other Puebloans in eastern New Mexico. They were never conquered by the Spanish who arrived in the area around 1540 because they were interested in the more easily conquered pueblos along the Rio Grande and its tributaries. The Spanish sent missionaries, but the Hopi were never Christianized. They live an isolated life surrounded completely by the Navajo Reservation, with which the Hopi have a contentious relationship, to say the least.

The Hopi's shortest distance to the outside world is through the town of Moenkopi, which sits on the western edge of the reservation right across the road from the Navajo town of Tuba City. It was at Moenkopi that I met Wayne and Sarah Dallas, two Hopi Indians who struggle to maintain a traditional life in the White man's world.

When you cross the road from Tuba City to Moenkopi, it's like entering a different time and place. The town itself seems to slide down the slope away from the road, and it has two parts: Upper Moenkopi and Lower Moenkopi. When I was there, neither had running water, but Upper Moenkopi at least had electricity. The town has a population of about 1,000 and consists of houses or structures made of local stone and cinderblocks plastered with stucco.

The Hopi graze cattle and sheep on the mesas, but Moenkopi was established as a farming village. It lies just below the westernmost end of the Third Mesa and sits above a valley carved out by the Moenkopi Wash, a stream that dries up much of the year but provides just enough water for Navajo and Hopi farmers along its flood plain. The valley is surrounded by the bright red and white cliffs of the Moenkopi rock formation. The farmland is laid out in strips on which Wayne and the other farmers plant corn, lima beans, and additional crops. In that arid country, water is precious; it's meted out to each farmer through a system of ditches and sluices that ensure its equal distribution. It's a time-honored practice that got the Hopi in trouble with government agents and landed some of them in Alcatraz in the 1890s. Today it's more of a hobby, but it is nonetheless a central part of Hopi culture.

Water and corn dictate the rhythms of the Hopi culture and the lives of Wayne and Sarah Dallas. Both of them left the reservation when young.

Sarah was sent to the Phoenix Indian School, where she spent years behind an 8-foot fence, fearing she would never leave. She eventually graduated, went to Northern Arizona University, and after graduation, began a career as a culinary arts teacher. Wayne went to Haskell in Kansas, and then to the military and eventually the Astrogeology Science Center of the United States Geological Survey. Both had successful careers, and both were drawn back to Moenkopi by the irresistible appeal of the Hopi culture in which they were raised. They were also driven back by the discrimination they encountered off the reservation, and the aggressive and competitive nature of White society.

Doing without water in an isolated town just off the Third Mesa is a small price to pay for a return to their spiritual roots and to retain their identities as Hopi. In fact, the isolation only intensifies their faith, which is continually reinforced through a monthly cycle of ceremonies conducted in the Hopi language, as they were meant to be. Through their clans and the ceremonies, they learn how to be Hopi and live according to the prophecies of the ancestors who brought them to the mesas thousands of years ago.

The Dallases returned to Moenkopi to revitalize their lives as Hopi. I learned a lot from them, including how to make piki bread, that blue-gray flaky delicacy the women make by spreading a thin mixture of ground blue corn, juniper ashes, and water on a red-hot stone. The women then peel the sheets off the stone using only their hands, without burning their fingers in a technique of lightning-quick moves passed down from mothers to daughters. The sheets are then rolled into a tasty pastry that is served at weddings and other celebrations. I also learned how they farm using an irrigation system that apportions precious water to each farmer, but what impressed and changed me most is when I discovered that one of the reasons Wayne and Sarah came back to the Hopi Reservation was their desire to be buried there.

The Hopi have a deeply meaningful and time-honored burial tradition. They wrap their dead in a blanket, positioning the body in a sitting upright fetal position, and placing it in a grave. You can tell when you're passing a Hopi cemetery by the hollow reeds protruding from the ground, put there to free the souls of the dead. For Sarah and Wayne, being buried in the traditional way on Hopi land will be their last, almost defiant act as Hopi. Their roots are firmly dug into the thin, rocky soil of the Arizona desert, where their ancestors planted them. The land their forebearers bequeathed them may be arid, foreboding, and even hostile, unfit for much more than sagebrush, mesquite, and tumbleweed, but the Hopi nevertheless believe it is their responsibility to protect and preserve it. Without their land, they cannot be sovereign; without sovereignty, they cannot be Hopi or Indians.

That brings us back to the original question of what it means to be an Indian. It's not enough to take a DNA test and claim Indian heritage. It's not about being too poor for store-bought clothes, misusing alcohol, having a criminal record, or any of the other stereotypical Indian traits that abound. It's not about how much Indian blood one has, or the color of one's skin or hair. It's certainly not about dressing up and playing Indian. It's not about attending powwows or participating in an occasional ceremony. And it's not attainable through some mystical experience offered by a shaman.

If there is one thing the 800-plus tribes in America have in common, it's the physical, psychological, emotional, and spiritual trauma inflicted on them by White people over the past 500 years. Whether it's absorbed though raw experience or stories passed down through generations, the trauma of the past continues to haunt the present. It is tattooed on the collective psyche and even the DNA of today's Indians. It has forged a common identity that transcends tribal differences, and it unites them in their determination to retain their cultures, languages, and lands, to remain independent, sovereign nations.

Above all, it allows them to find joy in being Indian.

Toilet Paper

As mentioned earlier, the Meriam Report opened with the sobering observation that "An overwhelming majority of Indians are poor, even extremely poor ...." That was 1928, and things are not much better today. That Indians on and off reservations are the poorest people in America is hardly news, although it's only recently that the media and the public have paid them any mind.

By any measure, conditions on the 322 reservations in the lower 48 and Alaska are appalling, and life is grim. The poverty rate among Indians on all reservations is 40% as opposed to 9% for Whites, 22% for Blacks, and 20% for Hispanics, but even those statistics are misleading. They mask the deplorable conditions on the larger, more remote reservations. There, the poverty is crushing.

On Pine Ridge, a Lakota reservation in South Dakota, the poverty rate is 54% on the reservation compared to 15.6% for the nation as a whole, but by some estimates the Pine Ridge poverty rate is as high as 90%. The per capita income on the reservation is $7,773, which is meaningless until you compare it to the national average of $27,599 and the average for all Indians of $10,543. Keep in mind that the national poverty threshold is $26,200 for a family of four, which means that about 90% of families on the reservation fall below the poverty level. Pine Ridge also has the dubious distinction of having the poorest town in America in Allen, a small community where the per capita income is $2,000. Allen is also distinguished by the fact that it is the most isolated place in North America. Sadly, Allen and Pine Ridge are not alone.

The problems on Pine Ridge go beyond per capita income and poverty rates. It has the unenviable distinction of having a lowest life expectancy than any country in the Western Hemisphere other than Haiti. Life expectancy on Pine Ridge is 66.8 years compared to 78.7 years for the general population, and infant mortality on Pine Ridge is three times the national average. Of course, those figures are directly related to alcohol abuse on the reservation, where an estimated two-thirds of adults abuse alcohol, and one in four babies is born with fetal alcohol syndrome. Pine Ridge has become the poster child for poverty among Indians. Google it; you'll find any number of articles. Diane Sawyer even did a special on it for the news program "20/20."

Surprisingly, Pine Ridge is not the worst. In a shining example of a distinction without a difference, it's been displaced as the poorest place in America by Cheyenne River, one of its sister Lakota reservations in South Dakota. Reservations like Fort Peck in Montana, Standing Rock in South Dakota, San Carlos and Tohono O'odham in Arizona, and Uintah and Ouray in Utah all have poverty rates of 40% or more. The Navajo Reservation in Arizona and New Mexico, the largest of all the reservations, with a population of more than 170,000, has a poverty rate of over 40%. Again, as with Pine Ridge, these averages understate the actual conditions on these reservations. Depending on what measures are used and who's doing the counting, poverty rates can be much higher than the official numbers suggest.

Poverty strikes Indian children the hardest, if for no other reason than the Native population is so young. Until recently, the birthrate among Native Americans was substantially higher than the rest of the population. Although Indian fertility rates have declined, their families are younger and larger. The median age of Native Americans is 29 versus 37.8 for the United States as a whole. Furthermore, the size of Native families on places like the Wind River Reservation is 4.5 compared to 2.5 for the general population. In addition, the gap is widening as White birthrates and family size continue to decline, which means the rate of childhood poverty among Indians is increasing relative to the rest of the population. For young Indians, the poverty rate is 35%, but on Pine Ridge and other large reservations, it is as high as 60%. For Indian families with children, the poverty rate is four times the national rate, and Indian children are twice as likely to die before the age of 24.

At the risk of stating the obvious, there is nothing ennobling about being poor. It causes a ripple effect that can be felt for generations. In fact, it is through their poverty and the unrelenting stress of reservation life that Indian children inherit the trauma of the past and transfer it to future generations. Ronald Reagan rode into the White House in 1980 on the idea of the "misery index," the combination of unemployment and inflation. If we consider the misery index for Indians on reservations to be the combination of poverty and unemployment, things are even worse than indicated by poverty statistics alone.

Not surprisingly, the two are interdependent; poverty on reservations is the direct result of unemployment or underemployment due to the lack of jobs on or near isolated reservations that sit on marginal lands. Before the arrival of COVID-19 in America, official unemployment among Indians was about 12% compared to 3.5% for the nation at large. Indian unemployment increased with that of the rest of the nation as a result of the epidemic. However, unemployment statistics only measure those actively seeking work.

If those who have given up looking for work or those who never started a job search are included, the numbers on reservations would be markedly higher. For example, the unofficial estimate of unemployment on Pine Ridge is 90%. On Wind River in Wyoming, and Standing Rock and Rosebud in South Dakota, estimates run as high as 80%, and on Fort Peck in Montana and Hopi in Arizona, they are as high as 65%.

Part of the problem is that there are few job opportunities on isolated rural reservations and in the small border towns, which, from my observations, can be as poor as the reservations themselves. Until the 1960s, agricultural work was available for Indians like Dewey Bull Tail, who left school at the age of 12 to work for farmers to support his family. Those jobs vanished as farming declined and became increasingly mechanized. The only jobs left were with the tribal and federal governments, or the few small businesses on the reservations, such as convenience stores and gas stations.[170]

However you measure it or look at it, statistics paint a grim picture of conditions on reservations. The misery index for those places is pretty high, and that's just the start of it. I can always sense when I am approaching poor inner-city neighborhoods or reservations. There are telltale signs that poverty is at play. Billboards advertise payday and car-title loans, there are the rent-to-own stores and pawn shops, and a plethora of dollar stores and ubiquitous fast-food outlets.

From the first time I drove onto reservations like Navajo and Rosebud, or even Tuscarora in New York, I felt like I was entering a different country. There were the swayback trailers with tires on their roofs to hold them down, and yards filled with junk cars. There were also abandoned, burned-out, and boarded-up houses and buildings. There were people walking along gravel roads, from early in the morning to late at night, seemingly coming from nowhere and going nowhere. And there were half-starved dogs that had been dumped there like the trash and abandoned cars that littered the roads, or for that matter, like the Indians themselves. But it was at a powwow for Indian Day at St. Francis on Rosebud when I first realized what being poor on a reservation really means.

Indian Day on Lakota reservations is the Native people's commemoration of the killing of Custer on June 25, 1876. Everything shuts down as they celebrate with powwows or gatherings of extended families or *tiospaye*. At the St. Francis powwow, as at most powwows, ceremonies, and celebrations, families host giveaways to honor relatives and friends of the family. They also recognize anyone who may have played an important role in the life of the honoree. The long-standing and distinctly Indian giveaway tradition was so troubling to missionaries and government agents, they worked to outlaw it.

It was all for naught, however, and today as in the past, giveaways play important roles in reservation life. The premise is simple: Rather than

---

[170] The foregoing statistics are taken from a number of government, tribal, and humanitarian and philanthropic websites, including *remember.org, friendsofpineridgereservation,org, truesiouxhope. org, pewresearch.org,* and *ncai.org.*

guests giving gifts to someone being honored for, say, being graduated from high school or having a birthday, the family of the honoree gives away gifts to the guests. Hence, the term "giveaway." The Lakota have a ceremony called a *wopila,* which is a general celebration of thanksgiving that is also accompanied by a giveaway. They also have the tradition of memorializing the dead with giveaways for four years following the death of a loved one. On some reservations, when a person dies, the family might give away all the possessions of the deceased. I remember driving on Pine Ridge and listening to the tribal radio station when it was announced that someone had died near Wounded Knee. His family was giving away all his possessions. Everyone was welcome.

Most giveaways include meals or "feeds" at which everyone is invited to partake until the food runs out. I have been at giveaways where, at lunch and dinner times, people arrive with Tupperware and other containers to carry home a little takeout. I've often wondered what would happen if, at a backyard barbecue in a White neighborhood, people just showed up for a free hotdog or burger. I've also pondered how many White children would be willing to give rather than receive gifts at their birthday or graduation parties.

Hosting a giveaway is a source of pride for Indians, and it is not taken lightly. Families spend months buying and making gifts, such as the famous Lakota star quilts, and saving food and money. It is moving to see families that have so little willing if not eager to sacrifice so much to honor their relatives, to give thanks for what they have, and to share with anyone and everyone. It's a rich and ancient tradition among Native people.

I've seen plenty of examples of it. Everyone is welcome to grab a bite to eat from the Bull Tail camp at Crow Fair, for example. In that same spirit of generosity, Dewey hands out what little money he has to the children. It's delightful scene. The kids come running and shouting, "Uncle, Uncle," even though he may not be their uncle. In response, he gives each of them a little something to spend on trinkets or treats from the vendors across the road. He relishes the practice and takes it seriously; it's part of his role as patriarch of the Bull Tail family.

Sharing brings honor, a fact that's essential to grasping the spirit of give-aways, if not Indian life in general. Held at powwows, naming and coming-of-age ceremonies, celebrations of birthdays, junior high, high school, and college graduations, and the safe return of veterans from military service, they differ somewhat from one to another, but they also share common-alities.

I've been to quite a few giveaways, all of which began with the gather-ing of the honorees, plus their extended families, friends, and those who might have played an important role in their lives. A speaker, who serves as a master of ceremonies, introduces the honorees and their supporters. The person being honored may be wrapped in a prized Pendleton blanket, with its price tag showing, or in the case of the Lakota, a star quilt made for the occasion. Incidentally, my daughter was wrapped in a blanket and honored at Crow Fair for graduating from middle school, an event she'll likely never forget.

The beginning gifts, ranging from handmade jewelry, beaded pouches, and hair combs to blankets and star quilts, are spread on a blanket. Starting with the elders, everyone is welcome to come forward and select an item. For large gatherings like the St. Francis powwow, the gifts are distributed by family members carrying laundry baskets, which, become gifts when empty. They also give away horses. Real, live horses. The only problem is, you have to catch them after they've been riled up. I still remember my young son diving for the reins of one horse, only to land on barbed wire. I consoled him by reminding him that we couldn't take the horse home on the airplane anyway.

Despite beautiful, handcrafted items and the drama of the horses, most of the gifts tend to be simple and practical, including folding chairs, towels, soap, dishcloths, cleaning supplies, and toilet paper. Yes, toilet paper ... that item we all need and tend to take for granted until we don't have it. Re-member the panic over the toilet-paper shortage in 2020 when COVID-19 came ashore in the United States? Sometimes you don't appreciate what you have until it's gone—or at least in short supply.

I must confess I never considered giving toilet paper as a gift until I received some at a giveaway. At first I chuckled to myself, and then I realized that for people who lack money or ready access to stores, toilet paper is a luxury. In fact, laundry, bath, and dish soap are treats as well. There's an old saying that it doesn't cost anything to be clean, but that couldn't be further from the truth. Go to a store sometime and take note of what various personal hygiene and cleaning products cost. For people without money enough for food, cleanliness must take a back seat to hunger.

So, I took my toilet paper (it's insulting to turn down a gift), looking at it much differently from that point on. I think of that whenever I'm asked to make a donation to families or to food pantries on reservations. When the Bull Tail family on Crow took over a food pantry in the town of Lodge Grass, they asked my students and me for donations. Not knowing where to begin, I asked one of the Bull Tail sisters, Doris Gets Down, what they needed. She replied despairingly, "Everything." She later confided to me that she had lived on the reservation her entire life and had never known there were so many needy people.

We went shopping at a dollar store, and I immediately took care of the toilet paper. The students also went to work, coming up with items that, as a man, I would not necessarily have considered. For example, tampons and other feminine-hygiene products. Underwear and socks are always in demand at homeless shelters and food pantries since people will donate clothing but not their old underwear and worn-out socks. There is always a need for basic necessities such as hand soap, shampoo, toothpaste, and toothbrushes, things most Americans take for granted and many Indians do without. Cloth diapers are impractical without ready access to laundry detergent, washers, and dryers, so disposable diapers—expensive and hard to come by—are welcome gifts. I knew from volunteering at food pantries that most can only afford to hand out one per day per child. Anyone with children would cringe at the thought of being able to change a baby's diaper only once a day. Suddenly those giveaway gifts make a lot of sense.

There are government programs to help Indians make ends meet, but contrary to popular belief, they don't get anything more than other U.S. citizens. There is the common and mistaken belief that all Indians receive monthly or annual payments from the government or tribe. Some do, some don't. For example, on Crow, the tribe distributes per capita payments, or "per caps," which can amount to about $300 each month. There's also the mistaken notion that they receive as much as $100,000 when they turn 18. I don't know where this belief comes from, but it's patently untrue. So is the assumption that Indians receive lavish distributions from casino revenues.

Less than half of the more than 500 tribes in the United States have gaming, which can mean everything from bingo parlors housed in trailers and the one under the rodeo grandstand on Crow where I played bingo for the first time, to the lavish casinos of the Pequots in Connecticut, the Seneca in New York, and the Shakopee Mdewewakanton in Minnesota. While Indian gaming brings in billions in revenue, two-thirds is generated by about 10% of the casinos located near larger population centers. Those found on rural, isolated reservations in the Midwest barely make enough to pay the bills. To that point, the casino on Crow is shuttered now. Even sadder is the fact that if you visit any of those venues, you'll find that a lot of the customers are Indians, who can least afford to gamble.

It's important to exercise caution when assuming prosperous casinos are cash cows. Many have had to borrow heavily to build their gaming operations, so a good portion of their revenue goes to paying off debts and/or to the companies hired to run the casinos. Casinos are complicated operations, and most people, Indians or White, do not have the expertise to run them. Moreover, the Indian Gaming Regulatory Act of 1988, which granted tribes the right to operate gaming venues, requires gaming revenue to be channeled to the general welfare of the tribes in the form of housing or infrastructure improvements. In addition, tribes must donate to local charitable organizations. Finally, tribes are required to share their revenue with state and local governments. For example, Pennsylvania gets 55% of the slot machine take, which is the largest source of revenue for all casinos.[171]

Indian casinos also have to pay federal and state income and payroll taxes, and local and state sales taxes. What's left can be distributed to tribal

---

[171] Howard Frank, "Played out: Casino gambling revenue in Pennsylvania levels off as neighboring states ante in," *Pocono Record* (May 18, 2014).

members. Only about one-third of the tribes share their gaming revenue directly with tribal members, with payouts ranging from literal pennies to the lavish grants of a few very small tribes near big cities. The stories about Indians receiving hefty disbursements from casinos began with the Pequots in Connecticut, one of the first tribes to open a casino. They became infamous for distributing profits from their Foxwoods Resort Casino to individual tribal members, but even they have stopped the payouts.

Nor do tribal members necessarily benefit from the jobs generated by the gaming operations; about 75% of the positions at Indian casinos are held by non-Indians, although the smaller gaming operations in rural areas often employ a higher percentage of tribal members.[172] Gaming has not proven to be a silver bullet for Indian poverty and unemployment. As a matter of fact, some studies suggest that poverty and unemployment have increased since tribes jumped into the gaming business. The Pima in Arizona have a lucrative casino near Phoenix, but the town of Blackwater on their reservation is purported to be the poorest town in America with a population over 1,000.[173] As one Navajo told me, allowing gaming was the White man's way to avoid treaty and other obligations to the tribes. If they want roads, schools, or utilities, let them open casinos.

Not surprising, their reliance upon casinos has made tribes vulnerable to economic fluctuations like the one caused by COVID-19. The closing of casinos during the pandemic triggered the layoff of most employees and the loss of revenue upon which the tribes have become dependent. The casino on Wind River was transformed into a quarantine center, depriving the tribe and tribal members of much-needed revenue.[174] And it wasn't just the casinos that suffered. Tribes lost money from tourism, powwows, and the sale of arts and crafts. The lost revenue forced them to lay off tribal members, which only exacerbated the unemployment problems on reser-

---

[172] Dwanna L. Robertson, "The Myth of Indian Casino Riches," *Indian Country Today* (September 12, 2018).

[173] Chris McGreal, "A reservation town fighting alcoholism, obesity and ghosts from the past," *The Guardian* (November 22, 2015).

[174] Savannah Maher, "In Contrast to Wyoming, Wind River Tribes Counter Covid-19 With Aggressive Measures," *Wyoming Public Radio* (May 7, 2020).

vations. Ironically, the downturn also hurt states that have become dependent on casino revenues. Just ask the governor of Oklahoma. He asked for a bigger share of casino revenues to make ends meet.[175]

Casinos aren't the only sources of income on reservations. Indians are eligible for Social Security, but only if they have worked the requisite number of years (10) and earned at least $5,440 per year, as of 2019. These minimum requirements do not seem onerous, except when you consider the per capita incomes and unemployment rates among Indians. The requirements are the same for Social Security disability payments.

Indians are also eligible for unemployment compensation, but that requires them to have been employed and to have access to unemployment offices or online systems to make their claims. Even for those who qualify for and obtain benefits, there are limits to how long they can receive payments, ranging from 12 to 26 weeks. In addition, they must be actively seeking work, something that's difficult for those on rural reservations. And then there's the application process itself, which is complicated, requires employment and pay records, and may be out of reach for people on isolated reservations without transportation. If they do qualify, there are time limits and work requirements before they can receive benefits again. Nevertheless, 95% of the income on reservations comes in one way or another from tribal, state, and/or federal governments.

For example, Indians can receive Temporary Assistance for Needy Families (TANF), or welfare as it used to be called, but eligibility requires them to find work. Once again, that's something that's scarce on reservations and difficult for those without transportation and for single mothers without access to child care. If they are eligible, they often have to use the money on their electronic benefits transfer cards to pay for gasoline or utilities, without much left over for other necessities like food. Furthermore, there are dangers in turning to the welfare system for help. As we shall see later, families, especially those headed by single mothers with several children, can lose custody of their children if they seek help from the welfare system.

---

[175] Sean Murphy, "Oklahoma governor wants bigger piece of state's tribal casino revenue," *The Associated Press* (January 10, 2019).

For many social workers and county judges, welfare equals neglect, which is grounds for removal of children from their families. We'll come back to that later.

By the way, Indians pay taxes: federal income tax, Social Security and Medicare payroll taxes, and if they work off reservations, state income taxes. That assumes, of course, they have jobs. They also pay sales taxes, and they pay property taxes if they own property off the reservation. They also have to pay taxes on income from unemployment insurance or Social Security. There's no such thing as a free lunch from the government.

That does not necessarily mean that money is lacking on reservations. On a per capita basis, it doesn't amount to much, but in the aggregate, reservations generate a lot of money. There are the aforementioned transfer payments from state and federal governments, and income from tribal government jobs and from businesses, however few and small, that operate on the reservations. There's also income from the sale of arts and crafts like Louisa Tsosie's rugs or the Bull Tail's sale of deer, elk, and buffalo meat.

Then there's the money brought or sent back from those who work off the reservations or have left for greener pastures. Some also receive payments for land they lease to White farmers. And, of course, there is the income from casinos for those tribes that have them and are able to turn a profit. However, the money flows off the reservation to border towns, where Indians must buy food, clothing, and other necessities, including those used cars held together by "reservation chrome," the name Indians give to duct tape. There is little left over to support reservation businesses that can't really compete against the larger national chains off the reservations.[176]

Moreover, there are often no banks—whether on or off reservations— willing to lend money to Indians, even those with collateral. Even many businesses are reluctant to do so. For example, car dealers often won't go the extra mile to extend loans to Indians because they believe the buyers may default on the loans and disappear on the reservations, and they

---

[176] Joseph Stromberg, *Lands and the Lakota: Policy, Culture and Land Use on the Pine Ridge Reservation* (Sunnyvale, CA: Lambert Academic Publishing, 2013).

would be out both the loans and the cars. Reservations are not only food deserts; they're also financial deserts.

As a result, Indians are left to the mercy of predatory lenders and forced to take out payday loans or borrow against their car titles. When they do, they can end up paying as much as 400% interest. The same goes for buying at rent-to-own stores, where they have to pay interest at loansharking rates and are subject to a number of hidden fees that are compounded and often make it impossible to finally own the goods. Indians would be far better off using a Walmart or Target credit card, but they generally can't qualify for one. Lacking access to regular lines of credit, they all too often find themselves deeply and inescapably mired in debt and poverty.

When I first got involved on reservations, I wondered why my calls were so carefully screened. Then I realized it was to make sure I wasn't a bill collector or a process server. My Indian friends weren't being paranoid. It's not uncommon to see parking lots in border towns filled with repossessed cars and trailers. Poverty goes beyond and much deeper than toilet paper.

Hunger may not be a chronic problem for most reservation residents, but nutrition is. The federal government created a food program specifically for Indian reservations to replace food stamps, more formally known as the Supplemental Nutrition Assistance Program (SNAP). Reservation residents could not always get to government offices to apply, and they could not always use them since reservations and surrounding areas are often "food deserts," a term that for rural areas means there is no grocery store within 10 miles. For people without transportation, 10 miles might as well be a million.

People living in those areas simply do not have access to fresh, healthy, affordable food. Instead, they must rely on convenience stores or gasoline mini marts, the modern-day version of trading posts. And then there are the ever-present fast-food outlets. On many of the reservations I visited, 10 miles would be a vast improvement; there aren't grocery stores within 30 miles or even farther for some of the more isolated residents. That's why Native people on reservations often have to trade their EBT or welfare credits to pay for rides to the store. Sadly, on some of the larger, more remote reservations, it's easier to get alcohol than groceries.

I once picked up an elderly Navajo woman all decked out in a brightly colored dress and scarf, hitchhiking along a nearly deserted highway on her way to do her shopping at a combination gas station and convenience store. Those stores carry a wide selection of unhealthy food: soft drinks, chips, candy, and packaged pastries, processed and canned food, and even fried foods. They selection tends to be high in sugars, fats, salt, and calories. Granted, the food is filling, but it lacks nutritional value.

In fairness, the Navajo enjoy the luxury of Bashas', an off-reservation chain of grocery stores stocked with fresh fruit, vegetables, and meats. On reservations as expansive as the Navajo and Hopi, the lack of transportation limits access to those stores. On other reservations where grocery stores are available, they are often expensive, do not offer fresh fruits and vegetables, and as I have witnessed, often have milk and dairy products and other perishable items that are on the shelves long after their expiration dates. They often have an abundance of fried foods and processed meats such as hot dogs, lunchmeat like baloney, a reservation staple, and plenty of canned processed foods that don't need refrigeration.

In technical terms, Indians often suffer from food insecurity or the "limited or uncertain availability of nutritionally adequate and safe foods." To remedy the problem, the government scrapped food stamps for Indians on reservations, and in their stead, provides food directly through the Food Distribution Program on Indian Reservations (FDPIR), an updated version of the old commodity system. The food is of better quality and variety, but still short on fresh meats, fruits, and vegetables. The bulk of the food distributed under this program is processed or canned. Milk and eggs are powdered.

Perhaps the people formulating the program didn't realize for people without electricity, water, or cooking facilities—conditions that still exist on some reservations—preparing food is a challenge, especially when you have to cook on coal or wood fires. An estimated 30% of homes on reservations are without electricity, running water, or complete kitchens. Some have none of the three.

No less than one-third of residents on the Navajo Reservation lack running water. It's not unusual to see pickup trucks hauling 1,200-gallon water tanks for isolated communities. Others get their water from wells that are often rife with heavy metals and other contaminants.[177] The Navajo are fortunate that there are 13 Bashas' stores on their reservation, but some residents must drive 150 miles to get to them. In the end, it's simply easier to turn to McDonald's, Kentucky Fried Chicken, and other fast-food outlets in border towns or on the larger reservations.

It might seem wasteful to spend limited funds on junk food, but it's hard to beat two Whoppers or Big Macs for five bucks, or a $20 Fill Up at Kentucky Fried Chicken that could include eight pieces of chicken, a large container of coleslaw, four biscuits, and two hefty tubs of mashed potatoes with gravy. It's difficult to buy and prepare that much food for less, let alone healthy food. I once fed a large Crow family on two $20 Fill Ups. Healthy foods are expensive, take more time to prepare, and are perishable. For people who are hungry, quantity not quality is what counts, with an added emphasis on fast. Just as in the past when they experienced starving times, Indians often engage in what is known as binge eating, where they consume all the food at once, much like binge drinking. Binge eating is associated with hunger resulting from food insecurity and is recognized as a disorder that can cause severe mental and physical problems beyond obesity.[178]

Granted, FDPIR is better than the old commodity system that relied on flour, sugar, and lard—that creamy white goop my grandmother used to scoop out of tin cans for frying and baking. I've never had one, but I've heard of lard sandwiches. People no longer resort to lard sandwiches (although I have heard about spaghetti sandwiches), but the damage has already been done. Indian diets have been historically and culturally con-

[177] Frances Stead Sellers, "It's almost 2020, and 2 million Americans still don't have running water, according to new report," *The Washington Post* (December 11, 2019).

[178] Autumn Whitefield-Madrano, "Turning a Blind Eye to Eating Disorders," *Indian Country Today* (October 5, 2011).

ditioned by their removal from tribal ecologies that provided them with the necessities of life. Interned on reservations, they became dependent on government-supplied rations and commodities.

On Crow, whenever we went on an excursion into the mountains or around the reservation, and I bought healthier foods—even peanut butter and jelly—Dewey Bull Tail would be disappointed. He prefers canned foods like sardines and Vienna sausages. I always joked about it until a Seneca explained that in the days before refrigeration or for those lacking electricity, canned foods were cheap and did not spoil. Indians like Dewey were conditioned to eat canned foods as children and developed a preference for them. That may explain why SPAM is considered a delicacy by some of my Indian friends. To this day, whenever I visit the Bull Tails, I make sure to take along some of Dewey's favorite food.

As tribes were removed from their traditional ecologies and economies, and concentrated on reservations, they became hooked on what are now called "oppression foods" made from commodities. The most notorious of all is fry bread. It's not a traditional Native food; at least it doesn't date back to the days when Europeans brought wheat with them. It's nothing more than bread made from flour, sugar, and lard, and then fried in lard since they didn't have ovens. When it's being cooked, like all fried foods, it smells irresistible.

My younger son and I prefer the Lakota version known as *gabubu* bread. It's the same dough, but it's cooked on a grill over an open fire, and it's delicious. Martha Moccasin used to make it for me, and I gave her recipe to Carol Bull Tail, who made it for me at Crow Fair. Fry bread, now a staple at most Indian meals and powwows, has been blamed for the epidemic levels of obesity, diabetes, and heart disease on reservations.[179] Of course there are other contributors to those diseases, like smoking and alcohol misuse, but in general, Indians on and off the rez have lousy diets.

Most Indians today don't live on reservations; they've moved to cities or smaller towns, usually those closest to reservations, for jobs, bet-

[179] Angie Wagner, "Icon or hazard? The great debate over fry bread," *nbcnews.com* (August 21, 2005).

ter housing, and educational opportunities, or because the government moved them through the Relocation Program of the 1950s. That program was devised to speed up the assimilation process, empty the reservations, eliminate the tribes, and finally solve the Indian problem. There's also the suspicion that it was designed to blunt the propaganda from Communist countries about conditions on reservations. Agents gave Indians one-way tickets to cities far away from their reservations, promising them better jobs, better housing, and better schools. Families received $40 a week with an additional $10 a week for each child during their first month in the city. After that, they were on their own.

Unfortunately, the promises fell flat. The Indians didn't have the skills for the jobs, if the jobs were available, and they generally weren't. Landlords were reluctant to rent to Indians, so they jacked up the rents or demanded hefty deposits, detailed credit histories, and personal references, which Indians coming from reservations couldn't provide. As a result, they tended to settle in poorer neighborhoods with substandard housing and weak schools, and then were prevented from moving by such practices as redlining. The government didn't even have the decency to give them money for a return trip home. They were trapped in a world for which they weren't prepared; one that wasn't prepared to accept them.

The Relocation Program did little more than exchange rural poverty for urban poverty. Although indigence among urban Indians is generally less severe than on reservations, many Indians in cities still fall well below the poverty level. In Rapid City, which is not large but has a significant Native population, the poverty rate among Indians is 51%. In Minneapolis, it is 48%, and in Gallup, New Mexico, just off the Navajo Reservation, it is 32%. In Denver, Phoenix, and Tucson it is 30%, and 25% in Chicago, Oklahoma City, Houston, and New York.

These statistics do not take into account those who live in the smaller border towns that ring every reservation. While housing and job opportunities were supposed to be better in towns and cities, urban Indians experience many of the same health, social, and economic problems as Indians on reservations, including poor diets. To understand this, it may be useful to examine conditions among African American populations in inner-city neighborhoods.[180]

Black Americans have roughly the same poverty rates as Indians and also live in food deserts served by fast-food restaurants, convenience stores, and corner bodegas rather than full-service grocery stores. The only difference is that urban food deserts are defined as areas with no grocery stores within a one-mile radius. But lest you think it isn't a hardship to travel a mile for food, grocery stores in inner-city neighborhoods are often small and pricey, especially for fresh fruits and vegetables.

Like Native Americans, African Americans have been historically and culturally conditioned by their experiences. Slavery, and the segregation and poverty that followed them to the cities have left an indelible mark. Black Americans also gravitate to foods that are high in sugars, saturated fats, and carbohydrates, and are cheaper and easier to prepare. Lacking access to healthier foods, they suffer the highest obesity rates in the nation, and disproportionate rates of diabetes, high blood pressure, heart attacks and strokes, second only to Indians.

Fried foods, fast foods, fatty foods, food deserts and food insecurity—they all stem from poverty. It's at the root of the health problems on and off reservations. Americans in general are obese, and the problem is most acute among minorities who live in food deserts and deal with food insecurity. So, it's no surprise that 80% of Native American adults and 50% of Indian children are either overweight or obese.

The result is an epidemic of diabetes and cardiovascular diseases that were relatively rare among Indians 50 or so years ago. They are now not only the leading causes of death among Indians, they occur at rates far exceeding those of the general population. I'm not sure what happened over the past century to cause the increased incidence of these diseases, but experts suggest it was due to a change in diets and lifestyles as Indians

[180] Gloria Hilliard, "Urban American Indians Rewrite Relocation's Legacy," *npr.com* (January 7, 2012); Max Nesterak, "The 1950's plan to erase Indian Country" *apmreports.org* (November 1, 2019).

were forced onto reservations. After generations of the feast-and-famine cycles that so puzzled Europeans, Indians became genetically conditioned to store fat during times of plenty. Cut off from traditional food supplies, dependent on unhealthy government rations, and confined to sedentary lives on reservations and later in cities, their genetic heritage made them susceptible to diabetes, obesity, high cholesterol, and cardiovascular diseases.[181]

Seventy percent of Indians with diabetes are obese. To put this in perspective, diabetes runs as high as 60% in some Native communities. Diabetes among Native people was relatively rare prior to World War II, but it has been increasing rapidly since then. Dewey Bull Tail has a unique, colorful and simple explanation.

When the Crow ate a lot of buffalo, they looked like buffalo, with long hind legs, narrow hips, and broad shoulders. As the buffalo disappeared and the Crow were forced to eat more beef, they began to look like cattle. If you ever get a chance to look at a cow's rear end, you'll see what Dewey means. Just don't get too close. All joking aside, Dewey might be onto something.

On the Tohono O'odham Reservation, which straddles the Arizona-Mexico border, the tribe produced 1.6 million pounds of tepary beans a year in the 1930s. The beans were an important source of protein and other nutrients for Native diets dating back thousands of years. By 2000, only 100 pounds were produced. The corresponding change in diets led to a meteoric rise in the incidence of diabetes, from nearly none in 1960 to more than 60% today.

Changing diets, poor nutrition, and obesity have all contributed to the disproportionate rates of diabetes and heart disease among Indians, who suffer from diabetes at a rate twice that of the general population. Diabetes then contributes to the high rates of blindness, kidney failure, and lower-extremity amputations. Furthermore, it can double or even quadruple the risk of heart disease, which has been increasing among Native people

[181] Urban Indian Health Commission, Invisible Tribes: Urban Indians and Their Health in a Changing World. *nativephilanthropy.org* (2007): 15, 18.

while declining in the general population. Complicating all of this is the high rate of smoking, and of course, alcohol abuse.[182]

Interestingly enough, while the overall life expectancy in the United States has been declining, Indian life expectancy is rising, but only if they make it to 65. One study in Arizona found that for Indians between the ages of 20 and 45, the death rate is 147% higher than the national average. If Native people make it to 65, their life expectancy is greater than White Americans.[183] Perhaps it's because drinking declines in older Indians. At any rate, drugs and alcohol are behind the disparity in life expectancy.

As we have already seen, alcohol abuse among Native people is three times the national average, and drug abuse is 50% higher. Their toll is deadly. Both account for the higher number of fatal car accidents, falls, and accidental poisonings, a higher death rate for assaults and homicides, and sadly, a suicide rate that is 50% higher than the national average and disproportionately affects the young. All of this helps to explain why the death rate for Indians between 20 and 45 is so high.[184] And yet, as terrible as these statistics may be, they can't begin to describe the destructive effects of substance use disorders on reservations like Rosebud.

Even before the opioid epidemic, Rosebud was experiencing waves of methamphetamine use that have been compared to tsunamis overwhelming the reservation. Jails, which also serve as practically the only treatment centers, have been swamped with people arrested for selling and using meth and for committing related crimes such as burglary, and domestic and other violence.

I have been going to Rosebud for more than 20 years, and I have never felt threatened or worried that my students were in danger. Still, the last few times I was there, I was warned to be careful. Since then I have heard

---

[182] Jacelle Ramon-Sauberan, "Desert Rain Café serves more than food," *Indian Country Today* (June 26, 2009).

[183] Debra Utacea Krol, "Native Americans have longest life expectancy," *Arizona Capital Times* (May 4, 2007).

[184] David S. Jones, "The Persistence of American Indian Health Disparities," *American Journal of Public Health,* 96, no. 12 (December, 2006): 2122-2134; Indian Health Service, "Disparities: Fact Sheet" (October, 2019).

reports of robberies and other crimes related to meth and now opioid addiction. People, especially the elderly, understandably live in fear. Meth may not be as deadly as prescription opioids, heroin or fentanyl, but it nevertheless produces extremely irrational and violent behavior brought on by paranoia and hallucinations. Moreover, opioid and heroin addicts can kick the habit, albeit not easily, but it's nevertheless possible to get clean. Meth is more difficult to quit, relapses are more likely, symptoms can continue even after users have received treatment, and its effects on the brain can be permanent. Altogether, it's a frightening situation, especially when you consider that as many 60% of Rosebud's population may have used meth at one time or another.[185]

Drug and alcohol use during pregnancy, combined with poor nutrition and related health problems, helps to explain the high infant mortality rate among Indians. It's 60% higher than any other racial group in the country and twice that of White people. In addition, Indian women are twice as likely to die during childbirth. There are many contributing factors to those appalling statistics, but at bottom is the lack of or the inadequacy of health care.

Treaties may have obligated the federal government to provide health care on reservations in exchange for peace and land, but it wasn't until 1921 that the government finally appropriated money specifically for Indian health care. The continuing inadequacy of health services on the reservations finally led to the creation of the Indian Health Service in 1955. It provides health care to Indians on and off reservations through 26 hospitals, 59 health centers, and 32 clinics, but it has been chronically underfunded. The per capita expenditure on Indian health care in 2018 was $4,079, far below the national average of $9,726. It's even less than the $8,600 average the government spent on inmates in federal prisons in 2016, causing some wags to quip that it's healthier to be in prison than on a reservation. It would take an estimated $36 billion to bring the IHS up to national standards, but only $6 billion was appropriated in the 2020 federal budget. A

[185] Mary Ann Pember, "Meth Tsunami Overwhelms Rosebud Rez," *Indian Country Today* (May 31, 2016).

standing joke on reservations is don't get sick after June because the money to operate the hospitals and clinics usually run out by that time.[186]

Funding has increased of late, and the IHS has built impressive health care facilities on some reservations like the ones at Chinle, Arizona, and Crow Agency in Montana. Despite these improvements, the IHS is still grossly underfunded, and conditions at some of the hospitals remain at a Third-World level. A doctor from Nigeria, who worked at the hospital on Rosebud, told me he saw things he had never seen in Third-World countries. He wasn't joking.

Inspectors for Medicare and Medicaid services found conditions at four of the hospitals, including the one on Rosebud, to be so bad, they threatened to pull funding from them. For example, on Rosebud, the inspectors reported a case of a baby born in a bathroom because medical service was not available. Only one of the four was finally denied Medicare funding. If you guessed it was the one on Pine Ridge, you're right.[187] However, the lack of funding can't begin to tell the story of just how difficult it is for Indians to receive health care. Sadly, there's seemingly no end to the types of so-called deserts plaguing Indians and the reservations.

Beyond money, one of the major obstacles to the delivery of health care on reservations is difficulty in recruiting medical professionals. Reservations can be remote places, where there is limited housing and other amenities, and the nearest cities of any size may be three hours away. Health care workers often have to be flown into small local airports for two-week rotations. Not having permanent residences or other attachments to the places or people they serve, they might not develop a relationship with their patients or a commitment to their care. Perhaps they don't possess the cultural sensitivity needed to treat the poor or the poorly educated who may not speak or read English, or understand the mysteries of the health care system. In addition, Indians are distrustful of the government and by extension, IHS.

[186] Mark Walker, "Fed Up with Deaths, Native Americans Want to Run Their Own Health Care," *The New York Times* (January 3, 2021).

[187] Adrian Siddons, "The Never Ending Crisis at the Indian Health Service," *rollcall.com* (March 5, 2018).

Technically, the rural areas in which many reservations are located are designated by the government as "Health Professional Shortage Areas." Simply put, these are areas or facilities that provide health care for under-served populations, including Indian Health Service hospitals and clinics both on and off reservations, where there is a lack of medical, dental, and mental health professionals. In addition, Indians by law are automatically classified as a "Medically Underserved Population," which is based on the ratio of medical providers to population, the percentage of the population over 65, and the infant mortality rate of the population. These designations enable IHS and tribal facilities to provide government-supported incentives such as bonuses and educational loan forgiveness to attract and retain health care professionals, including primary care physicians, dentists, psychiatrists, nurse practitioners, and nurses.

I met and interviewed doctors, nurses, and a pharmacist who enlisted in these programs to work on or near reservations or in urban clinics. They told me staffing problems are just a drop in the bucket. For example, the hospitals or clinics can be too far away for people without transportation, and the border-town hospitals are often too small or too distant to fill in the gaps. Conditions are especially difficult for the elderly and disabled.

It's not uncommon for IHS hospitals to be without staff to provide emergency care and to lack modern equipment capable of detecting illnesses before it's too late. Staff members also don't have the training, and/or the hospitals don't have the facilities to treat more serious diseases. Couple that with the fact that Indians suffer disproportionately from heart disease, diabetes, cancer, and liver disease, and their only alternative is traveling to bigger cities. And those cities are often just too far away. Sometimes, they have to be airlifted out. Don Moccasin once pointed to a small plane taking off from a local airport and remarked that whenever he saw one, he was saddened because it was probably taking a seriously ill person to a hospital in Sioux Falls, Omaha, or Minneapolis.

If Native people have to be treated outside Indian Health Service, they are at a serious financial disadvantage, owing to the fact they either lack insurance, or Medicare or Medicaid will not cover all the costs of their treatment. They can submit their claims and hope for the best, but in 2016, the IHS denied as many as 500,000 requests for payment, leaving Indians with billions of dollars of medical bills they can never make good on.[188] The poorest people in America can't afford copays or deductibles, nor do they have the money to buy supplemental insurance to cover what the government plans do not. Faced with the high cost of health care, frustrated and intimidated by the paperwork and the bureaucracy, and fearful and distrustful of government agencies, they simply forego medical care. Add to that the cost of transportation, child care, and time off work, and you can understand why they just give up and tolerate illness rather than seek help.

It's a behavior that is common among Indians, whether it is out of distrust, fear, or ignorance, or simply the discrimination they face when going to the doctor. Whatever their reasons, like Carol Bull Tail, it's common to find they've waited too long. I've tried for years to get her to go to the IHS hospital in Crow Agency to see about her fainting spells, but she refuses to go. She's a good example of tolerating illness. I hope she doesn't wait too long.

The shortage of primary care physicians to serve Indians on and off reservations is acute. There are even fewer mental health professionals, especially psychiatrists. There is a lack of psychiatrists nationwide, which makes it that much more difficult to recruit them to rural or poor areas, where they would have to work for lower fees than they might get in urban, affluent areas. Unfortunately, as with physical diseases, Indians suffer disproportionately from mental health issues such as PTSD, substance use disorder, depression, attachment disorders, and suicide. The need is dire.

Most IHS facilities offer some manner of mental health treatment, but precious few have licensed psychiatrists or inpatient facilities, and most can't offer round-the-clock intervention services. They must rely on counselors, social workers, and nurses who are not licensed to prescribe medications, or they refer patients for inpatient treatment at acute-care hospitals. However—you guessed it—there is also a shortage of inpatient beds for psychiatric care in the same areas where medical staff is lacking, and

---

[188] Walker, "Fed Up with Deaths."

where many reservations are located. Regardless of the need for facilities and staff, the same barriers to treatment exist for mental health care as for primary care: distance, cost, poor roads, discrimination, and distrust, to which can be added the stigma of mental illness. The result is the same as with physical illnesses; Indians tend to wait a long time to seek help, and all too often, the delay is fatal.[189]

Most of the forgoing has been about health care for Native people living on or near reservations, but most Indians live in cities. How many there are and where they live are difficult to determine, since they travel back and forth to reservations or between cities. Also excluded are Indians from the more than 200 tribes not recognized by the government. Altogether, when it comes to statistics on Indian health care, America's Native people are invisible.

The IHS operates 51 urban health centers throughout the country. I visited one in Lockport, New York, that serves Indians in western New York. It is a state-of-the-art facility in terms of aesthetics, equipment, and services. The problem is that the IHS devotes only 1% of its budget to urban health care. Based on aggregate data gathered from those who visit IHS urban health clinics, they suffer from the same maladies as Indians on reservations: diabetes, cardiovascular and liver diseases, substance abuse, high infant mortality rates, and mental health issues, including suicide. They also suffer from the social and economic problems of poverty, unemployment, and inadequate education that are common to reservations and inner-city neighborhoods alike.

Some argue that Indians' health problems are worse in the cities. Relocation left them vulnerable to the mental and physical stresses of urban life without the family and cultural support they had back on the rez. Consider the following: Native women in urban areas are 2.5 times likelier to die in childbirth than is the general population, and urban Indians are 178% more likely to die of alcohol-related causes than the general population.[190]

[189] Daniel P. Levinson, *Access to Mental Health Services at Indian Health Services and Tribal Facilities* (Washington, DC: Department of Health and Human Services, 2011).

[190] Katy B. Kozhimanni, "Indian Maternal Health—A Crisis Demanding Attention," *JAMA Health Forum*, 1, no. 5 (May 18, 2020); Urban Indian Health Commission, *Invisible Tribes*, 5.

The latter I blame on the fact that alcohol is more readily available in cities than on reservations. Just visit any inner-city neighborhood, and you'll see what I mean. The former is simply another example of the obstacles that make health care inaccessible for Native women on or near reservations. They are without insurance, or they are not eligible for coverage under Medicaid or the IHS, they can ill afford copays and deductibles, and the costs of transportation and child care are stifling. The results are predictable; they don't seek medical care.

If life is tough on the reservations, it just may be tougher in the cities. Relocation, whether voluntary or coerced, was not and is not the answer. Either way, worn down by their struggle simply to survive, when it comes to health care, they more often than not just give up. Another case in point is that of Martha Moccasin on Rosebud, who suffered from what I call "reservation disease." That is, a deadly combination of obesity, diabetes, heart trouble, kidney failure, and needless to say, poverty. She had to travel three hours to Rapid City for dialysis. The treatment weakened her, but it was the travel that finally got to be too much. Soon after she decided to forego treatment, she passed.

I was very close to Martha. When her brother Don was dying, I promised to look after her. I did what I could, including taking her to her last Sun Dance and Indian Day powwow, but I was no match for reservation life. It finally ground her to a halt. She struggled to raise five children, and then she cared for 28 grandchildren and 66 great-grandchildren. Her house was essentially a reservation daycare center. When I first went to Rosebud, she was living in a trailer crowded with children on the bank of the Little White River, from which she had to draw her water. I was told the river was polluted by farm runoff further upstream. She never complained, even though I know she was hurting.

I was always reluctant to give her cash because she would hand it out to her family. Her spoken English was broken, but her writing was perfect, and she never failed to send cards at Thanksgiving, Christmas, and Easter. Her requests were always modest. When I went to visit her, she would ask for fresh fruit, especially grapes and "nanas." I always suspected that when she reached out to me for something larger, like a propane heater for her home, it was really for one of her children or grandchildren. One letter, written a year after her brother's death as she made quilts for his second memorial, was especially poignant.

> *Keith and Family,*
>
> *Hello. I thought I'd answer your card. The money gift came in handy just when I needed it. Our Christmas wasn't too good. I was only able to get half of the grandkids present(s). Plus I still really miss my brother Don. Sometimes I don't know what to do. They started me on depression meds but that don't help. Just whenever I can I go and sit by his graveside. I feel better. I try to keep myself sewing quilts for the memorial but I just can't do it anymore. My back is getting bad and I'm getting too old. I told my kids I don't know if I make it another year.... Well I will end here my brother. Love & prayers, Martha Moccasin.*

Being sick and poor on a reservation is hard; that it forced someone who had endured as much as Martha to give up is proof of how hard. Several years before she died, Martha was able to move into a new home with running water and propane for heating and cooking. The Rosebud tribe has invested in more housing for its members. The last time I was there, I was pleasantly surprised to see that the new housing included solar panels, a wise investment on the Great Plains, where, as the song goes, the skies are not cloudy all day.

But even if housing conditions on reservations is getting better, shortages still exist. The Native population is growing, albeit at a slower pace than before, and urban Indians appear to be moving back to their ancestral homes. As a result, poorly built reservation housing is also overcrowded. It's not uncommon for it to lack electricity, kitchen facilities, running water, indoor plumbing, and sewers, not to mention adequate food. As a Montana newspaper put it in a report on the Blackfeet Reservation, "It's not unusual to find a grandma who has fifteen people in their house. Oftentimes living hand to mouth, out of a soup pot. While at the same time trying to pay for the electricity to keep their house heated."[191] When I read that, I immediately thought about Martha Moccasin, a grandmother or *unci* in Lakota, trying to hold a large, extended family together in a tiny home on Rosebud.

Gathering so many people under one roof is, as we have seen, an old tradition that has a practical benefit. It allows people who can't afford or don't have access to housing to pool their per caps and other resources to put food on the table, pay the bills, and most importantly, put a roof over their heads at a time when homelessness can reach as high as 50% on some reservations.

Money from the federal government for housing has remained flat since 1997, although the demand has increased due to the population growth. What money the tribes do receive has to go to repair and maintain an ever-aging housing stock. The tribes also have a difficult time raising private capital for housing projects, since the land is held in trust by the government and cannot be collateralized. As a result, government housing, some of which dates to the post-World War II era, is often old, flimsy, and worn out after years of overcrowding and overuse without proper maintenance. To make matters worse, it is often infected with black mold. I have been in homes with broken doors and windows, and holes in floors. On the northern reservations, the poorly insulated homes are too expensive to heat. No wonder children often go to school just to get warm and have something to eat. In fact, overcrowding is particularly hard on young people, who are often infested with lice and bedbugs.

The Nigerian doctor on Rosebud told me he had never seen so many children with lice, even in the Third-World countries in which he had served. With too many people and too few beds to go around, the pests are spread from person to person and family to family through bed sharing and so-called couch surfing. In addition, it's often difficult or too costly to launder bedding. When there aren't enough beds or couches, mattresses

---

[191] Murray, "Montana Native American tribes struggle."

and blankets on floors must do. I've seen bathtubs and the backseats of old cars and vans serving as beds too. Some have taken to expanding their trailers by building additions out of makeshift materials, or in one ingenious case, fusing an old camper onto their trailer.

Overcrowding also has serious health consequences. Infectious diseases are spread more easily in crowded conditions without proper sanitary facilities, making Indians especially vulnerable to afflictions such as tuberculosis, which spread like wildfire through reservations and boarding schools into the 20th century. Their living conditions also made them susceptible to widespread epidemics like the Spanish flu in 1918 that killed Indians at a rate four to five times greater than the general population, due to overcrowding, lack of adequate health care, poverty, malnourishment, and pre-existing health conditions.

Nearly 100 years later, the H1N1 virus killed Native people at roughly the same rate as the Spanish flu, and for the same reasons.[192] Then in 2020 it was COVID-19's turn to infect Native populations already suffering from epidemic levels of asthma, cardiovascular disease, diabetes, and other pre-existing conditions. Epidemic on top of epidemic, all caused by the same conditions the Meriam Report found in 1928. Woefully, not much has changed since then. As one Navajo man told *The New York Times* in the midst of the COVID-19 pandemic, "The virus is really showing years and years of neglect."[193]

He knew what he was talking about. At 15 times the rate of infection of the White population, at one point, the Navajo Nation had the highest per capita infection rate in the United States. Without enough beds, staff, ventilators, and personal protective equipment to treat patients adequately, IHS hospitals on the Navajo Reservation often sent them home, where overcrowding made social distancing impossible. On top of overcrowding,

---

[192] Dana Hedgpeth, "Native American tribes were already being wiped out. Then the 1918 flu hit.," *The Washington Post* (September 12, 2020); Ariell Zionts, "Tribal nations, citizens take COVID-19 preventions seriously in South Dakota," *Rapid City Journal* (July 17, 2020).

[193] Simon Romero and Jack Healy, "Tribal Nations Face Most Severe Crisis in Decades as the Coronavirus Closes Casinos," *The New York Times* (May 13, 2020).

Navajo families suffered from a lack of hand soap, hand sanitizer, and running water, which made family outbreaks inevitable and deadly.

Such was the case with one Navajo family of 11 living in a traditional hogan and sleeping on a dirt floor with a wood stove for heat, or in an SUV when it got really cold. Eight members of the family were hospitalized, two died, and the rest were quarantined in motels along with other tribal members who were not sick enough to be hospitalized. The situation was not unusual. As Dominick Clichee, an epidemiologist on the reservation, explained, "In lots of these homes, you have up to three generations of people living under one roof, the grandparents, the children, and their children's children."[194]

Overall, the Native population in the United States has been infected with COVID-19 at a rate 3.5 times greater than the White population, according to the Centers for Disease Control and Prevention. But, as on the Navajo Reservation, the numbers are often higher. In neighboring New Mexico, Native people make up 11% of the population but 57% of the COVID-19 cases. Further north in Pennington Country, South Dakota, where Rapid City is the county seat, Indians make up 13% of the population, but they account for 46% of the COVID-19 cases.

Elsewhere on Wind River and Fort Berthold, and even in the cities, the story is always same: Overcrowding, underlying comorbidities, lack of medical care, and poverty make Indians more susceptible to the virus than other segments of the population. Add to that the fact that Indians with jobs aren't in a position to quarantine themselves. As one Lakota explained, "We can't afford to get sick."[195]

Little wonder that tribes across Indian Country began to lock down their reservations and block access by nonresidents, at the same time shutting down casinos. Their blockades drew a lot of attention and criticism as

---

[194] Matt Gutman, Lissette Rodriguez and Tenzin Shakya, "Navajo Nation: Where COVID-19 claims whole families," *abcnews.go.com* (May 21, 2020).

[195] Morgan Matzen, "Data: Native people disproportionately affected by COVID-19 in county, state," *Rapid City Journal* (July 18, 2020).

tribes exercised their sovereign rights to protect their citizens. In response to threats from South Dakota Governor Kristi Noem, the Oglala Lakota on Pine Ridge defended their highway checkpoints by declaring, "[The] tribe has adopted reasonable and necessary measures to protect the health and safety of our tribal members." One elderly woman at a tribal checkpoint put it more bluntly. "This is our land," she said.[196]

It may seem ridiculous to reduce 500 years of genocide and oppression to toilet paper, but those single-ply rolls of comfort, convenience, and cleanliness say more about conditions among American Indians than any statistics ever could. I remember being told before my first trip to Rosebud to bring my own stash. I didn't think much about it until that giveaway; now I never leave home without it.

Since then I've often wondered what it is like for children growing up without toilet paper and other necessities like toothpaste and clean underwear. Or for young mothers who go without diapers for their babies. Or for kids shivering in unheated trailers without enough to eat when school isn't in session. Or for families living without running water or electricity in cramped, overcrowded trailers.

I thought I'd finally come to terms with it until I met a little girl at Crow Fair.

---

[196] Justine Anderson, "Covid-19 checkpoints on reservations to remain," *indianz.com* (May 22, 2020).

TEEPEE CREEPIN'

AT CROW FAIR EACH August, the tribe sponsors a 5K race to raise money to fight drug addiction. It's a serious cause, but the event is a lot of fun. Every runner gets a special T-shirt, and people gather along the route to cheer, laugh, and joke. There are great prizes for the winners. In fact, over the years, two of my students have won. On the other hand, I hold the unofficial and dubious record for finishing last, year after year. One year, I managed to win and lose at the same time; I came in last, but there was no one else in my age group.

It's called the Teepee Creeper race, a name that is a fine example of reservation humor. Teepee creepin' refers to the practice of reaching under teepees and grabbing anything or anybody within reach. Like a lot of reservation humor, it's a cautionary tale warning newcomers not to sleep or place personal items too close to the edge of the teepees. As far as I can tell, it's more a joke than reality. It's always good for a laugh with newcomers.

At the start of the race one year, I noticed a little girl, maybe 5 or 6, and apparently all alone. She was trying to warm up like the big people, proudly sporting her T-shirt with a race number pinned on it. As the race began, she took off in earnest; fists clenched, legs pumping, seemingly determined not only to finish but to win the race. I lost sight of her in the crush at the starting line, but bringing up the rear as usual, I finally caught up with her.

She was all alone and no longer able to keep up with the other runners. Her little legs had stopped pumping. Falling farther and farther behind, she was on the verge of tears. Tired, alone, and lost amidst the maze of teepees, she was also overwhelmed. I offered her my hand, but she refused until she was completely exhausted. I took her hand then and walked along with her until I could turn her over to race officials, who promised to find her family. I went on my way, finishing last, as usual. I never saw her again, but I'll never forget her.

At first, I was angry with her parents for leaving her alone in a crowd of strangers. Then I realized that her experience, however frightening and painful, was merely a rehearsal for growing up on the reservation. By the time she reaches her teens, she will more than likely hit what marathon runners refer to as "the wall," at which point they are too exhausted to carry on. Indian children, especially on the large reservations out West, also seem to hit the proverbial wall, at which point they simply give up and succumb to the worst side of reservation life.

Like children everywhere, like my children, she probably began her life as she began the race, full of hope, determination, and unlimited potential. I must admit to being biased about Indian children. They are some of the most beautiful kids I've ever seen. One of my fondest reservation memories is standing on top of a building above a square in the town of Moenkopi, watching a ceremony, surrounded by children and fascinated by their beautiful, almost unnaturally black hair shining in the sun. But like so many of my reservation memories, it's tempered by the recollection of holding a little baby girl, who began to cut herself and tried to suicide as a teenager. Then there are the two young boys who grew up with my boys of the same age and who ended up in jail. Or the six young Navajo children whose mother died in a drunk-driving accident and who had to move in with their grandmother, aunt, and four cousins. Three generations and 10 kids in a reservation home. It bears repeating: Life is tough for Indians.

Why do they hit a wall? Perhaps their burdens finally wear them down. They are afflicted with unrelenting and grinding poverty and deprivation, hardships that chip away at their spirits, as they would anyone's. They live in overcrowded, mostly dilapidated housing without running water and proper sanitation facilities, and often crammed with multiple families and even strangers. They grow up surrounded by violence, drugs and alcohol, and friends and family dying untimely deaths. Even before they're born, they're affected by the toxic stress of reservation life. Compared to American women in general, Indians are less likely to receive adequate prenatal care, and they are more likely to use alcohol and drugs during pregnancy. The result is many low-weight babies with fetal alcohol syndrome.

If the science of epigenesis has anything to say about it, life won't get much easier after the babies are born. They carry the burdens of history, of defeat and removal, and of the loss of their lands, language, culture, and freedom, with every aspect of their lives controlled by a distant and unsympathetic government. Conditions such as these are obvious threats to the health, welfare, and safety of children on reservations.

There is yet another not-so-obvious but very real threat to their well-being: foster care. It's a sore subject among Indians, bringing back painful memories of Indian children being forcibly removed from their parents and families, and being sent to boarding schools. Once there, they were stripped of their language, culture, and heritage, and subjected to harsh and humiliating discipline, including physical and sexual abuse. Far too often, they never returned to their families, dying lonely deaths far from home.

Boarding schools have been singled out as one of the most destructive agents of the heavy-handed and clumsy federal policy of acculturation and assimilation, otherwise known as cultural genocide. The most infamous of these institutions was Pratt's Carlisle Indian Industrial School. While much attention has been given to federal boarding school, the policy of assimilation through education didn't begin with them. The practice of indoctrinating Indian children into a foreign culture and belief system hearkens back to the Colonial Period, when charters instructed the colonists to go forth and Christianize the heathen. It was the standard operating procedure of colonization in America and Canada, and in Australia, where it was used to educate and assimilate Aboriginal and Torre Islander children.

Those early efforts fell short in the American colonies, but the new republic saw a renewed interest in using education to solve the Indian problem. Most of the burden was initially shouldered by missionaries, with encouragement and support from the government. Then federal authorities decided to take matters into their own hands, beginning with Carlisle. Eventually there were more than 300 federal and missionary boarding schools, but the most notorious were the 25 off-reservation government schools that were modeled after early mission schools.

The schools engaged in what has been termed "education for extinction," as they worked to suppress and ultimately extinguish the children's Native identities.[197] Captain Pratt believed the children were blank pages upon which the virtues of White Anglo-Saxon Protestant civilization could be written. In his mind, all the Indians needed to do was trade their blankets for the White man's clothes, cut their hair, speak English, go to church, and become farmers and housewives. It was a simple formula dating back to the 17th century, but Pratt made it infamous when he expressed it with the unfortunate phrase, "Kill the Indian, save the man."

That motto became the operating philosophy of Indian education well into the 20th century. It required separating children from their parents and families, and placing them in what might properly be termed re-education camps. Here they were to shed their Indians ways and be prepared for assimilation. However, the children suffered far more than the loss of their language and culture. They were often torn away from their parents, sometimes at a very early age, and frequently never reunited with their families. When the children finally returned to their reservations, it was all too often to empty houses and empty lives. They found themselves alienated from their families and tribes, and unable to adjust to life back on the reservation.

Their stories are heartbreaking. The trauma of being separated from their parents and families lasted a lifetime. If you believe in the science of epigenetics, it has lasted more than a lifetime. Meanwhile, the damage to families, communities, and tribes has left its mark on generations. Schools like Carlisle contributed to what has been termed a "social death" or the destruction of the familial, social, and cultural norms that guided and sustained them for generations. Plainly stated, it was genocide.

The tragic failures of the boarding schools, and the Indian education system in general, were first exposed in the Meriam Report, which, as we

[197] David Wallace Adams, *Education for Extinction* (Lawrence, KS: University Press of Kansas, 1995).

have already seen, found near-Dickensian conditions at the schools. The students were underfed, housed in cramped and unsanitary conditions, suffering from tuberculosis and trachoma, deprived of adequate medical treatment, overworked and undereducated, and trained in vocations such as agriculture, which were either in decline or simply not viable on most reservations. In many ways, the problems on the reservations just followed them to the schools.

Particularly destructive was the half-day system that was borrowed from the missionary schools dating back to Moor's Charity School. The report concluded that the "half-day work plan" was "too much labor for children even in normal health."[198] On the other hand, even a full day of studies would not have helped, since the curricula were often outdated, and the teachers were untrained or insensitive to the needs of their charges. Furthermore, the strict regimentation and routinization, coupled with in-flexible discipline, did nothing to prepare them to live independently. Nei-ther did they provide them with the requisite skills to survive in the post-boarding-school world.

"The whole machinery of routinized boarding school and agency life works against the development of initiative and independence which should be the chief concern of Indian education in and out of school. The routin-ization characteristic of the boarding schools, with everything scheduled, left no time to be used at the child's own initiative, with every moment determined by a signal or an order, and leads just the other way."[199] Lacking the necessary skills or the individual "initiative and independence" neces-sary to survive in the world outside the school, they were often returned to the reservation, and their dependency on the government began anew. It was this dependency that ultimately led to one of the most pernicious but overlooked consequences of the boarding school experience: the disrup-tion of Indian family, community, and tribal life.

The authors of the Merriam Report made it clear from the beginning that the suffering on the reservations was not the fault of the Indians, and

---

[198] Meriam Report, 31.

[199] Ibid., 351.

contrary to popular assumptions of the times, the Indians were not content with their circumstances. The suffering from disease and poverty was too severe for the Indians to be satisfied with their condition, particularly where the illness and death of their children were concerned. If Indian families were "unstable," as the report conceded, dismal conditions on the reservations were responsible. The instability of Indian families was due to the "disintegrating effects" of poverty, disease, and other afflictions.

However, the most serious strain on Indian families was "the condition of perpetual childhood in which Indians have been held, for both the system of education and the type of control exercised by the government over tribal and personal property have tended to loosen family ties." The same was true for community life, where "Government control ... and the assumption on the part of teachers and others in the schools that all Indian ways are bad ways, tended to break down native social structure."[200] In sum, the government and the schools worked together to destroy family and community life, increase dependence on the government, and keep Indians in a perpetual state of childhood. As Marshall stated, it was a state of "pupilage," with government institutions acting as surrogate parents.

However, the report left no doubt that it was the schools that chiefly "operated against the development of wholesome family life." Especially troublesome was the "long continued policy of educating children in boarding schools far from their homes, taking them from their parents when small and keeping them away until parents and children become strangers to each other. The theory was once held that the problem of race could be solved by educating the children, not to return to the reservations, but to be absorbed one by one into the white population. The plan included the breaking of family ties .... The plan failed ... and many children have not seen their brothers and sisters for years."

To make its case, the report cited stories such as that of a Hopi boy who remembered that he and his sisters "used to have lots of fun when we were little fellows. Of course sometimes we get into fight [sic], but since then I never have seen my sisters for seven years, they both away from home like me, so I hope we will all see each other someday." Likewise, a Navajo

[200] Ibid., 548-9.

mother "hated to send this boy to school. I knew I was saying goodbye. He would come back a stranger."[201]

The saddest separations were caused by the deaths of children when they were away at school. Students at boarding schools often died lonely deaths due to the epidemics that the report attributed to overcrowding, poor diets, and inadequate medical care. In many cases, they were never reunited with their families. The deaths of parents and siblings back at home also disrupted families, as the story of one little girl revealed. "My mother died while I was away at school. Three of my other sisters died of the flue [sic] that same winter. So there was just my father and a little sister two years old and a little brother five years old, left at home. When vacation time came I went home to see the folks that remained. But I could not stand to stay at this home."[202]

Whether death or divorce separated them from their parents and siblings while they were away, the "returned students" could not go home again. As a Seneca who attended the Thomas Indian School told me, when he finally reconnected with his siblings after leaving the school, the only thing they had in common was alcohol.

The children's dependency on the schools extended to their families as well. The government did its best to ensure that parents would also remain in a perpetual "state of childhood" by depriving them of either the means or opportunity to escape their dependency on the government.[203] This reliance and the poverty it perpetuated, coupled with the loss of their children, further encouraged the dissolution of families and households. Broken homes and broken families served to worsen the economic and social problems among Indians, and it was the children who suffered the consequences. Removed from their homes, whether by coercion or necessity, the children were left without normal parental supervision and care, which served to encourage the dependency of the students on the schools and left them unprepared to raise children on their own.

[201] Ibid., 574.

[202] Ibid., 575.

[203] Ibid., 403-4.

As the report concluded, "Without this experience of the parent-child relation throughout the developmental period, Indian young people must suffer under a serious disability in their relations of their own children."[204] Removed from their families, often at an early age, they were unfamiliar with traditional Native child-rearing practices and had no idea what family life was like outside an institutional setting.

A Seneca woman who attended the Thomas Indian School told me that when she got married and had children, she had no idea where to start. So, each weekend she had her kids scrub the house from top to bottom, just like she had to do every weekend while she was at Thomas. She left the school without a compass to navigate a world that didn't have the structures and strictures that she had lived with from the time she was whisked away from her mother's graveside and sent to the school at the age of 3. Deprived of parental affection, others told me they didn't know how to hug their children or tell them they loved them. Life inside boarding schools like Thomas was hard; life afterwards was oftentimes no better.

The outside world bewildered, frightened, and rejected them, and the consequences were felt hardest by those whom the Meriam Report labeled "dependent" children. That is, orphans or children removed from their parents' care for reasons of neglect, abuse, or poverty. The report acknowledged that it was not the purpose of the boarding schools to house dependent children, but circumstances on the reservations forced them to admit children as young as 4 years old "because they have no homes." The younger children were "especially ill-fitted for the rigors of the boarding school. Even if they have brothers or sisters in the school, they are out of place among two hundred to a thousand older children."[205]

The alternative was to find those children homes with relatives or friends from their own tribes. However, locating alternative placements proved difficult, given the indigence and the general dissolution of families and communities on the reservations. Moreover, the "break down [sic] [of] native forms of organizations," that is, tribal or clan structures, undermined

[204] Ibid., 577.

[205] Ibid., 586.

the ability of traditional institutions to care for orphaned or abandoned children. Between the poverty and the destruction of family and community life, there was little likelihood of finding alternative placements for the growing number of dependent children on the reservations.

As Brenda Child explains in her book *Boarding School Seasons*, among the Ojibwe, "time honored methods of caring for the needy and parentless children proved inadequate. Disease disrupted family life and other long-standing institutions. The ranks of the poor, sick, widowed, and orphaned grew. All too often, husbands, wives, and even older siblings were left with large families to maintain after the death of a spouse or parent."[206]

Without families or communities to absorb the dependent children on the reservations, boarding schools became the only option. Even Commissioner of Indian Affairs Francis E. Leupp admitted the schools had become nothing more than "educational almshouses" by the early 1900s. Thanks to the Meriam Report, the government moved away from boarding schools in the 1930s and created the Indian Adoption Project, which operated from 1941 to 1967. Without the boarding schools, adoption really was the solution, or so they thought.

During the adoption period, the government, with the assistance of missionaries or religious groups, stole Indian children under the pretext of saving them from the poverty and social problems endemic to reservations and urban Native communities. During the 1950s, there was a shortage of White babies available for adoption, so it became popular to adopt Indian children. Authorities were often informed by Mormon, Catholic, or other Christian missionaries about children living in overcrowded conditions with extended families and without water, electricity, and sanitary facilities. In other words, the conditions that had prevailed on reservations for more than a century and had helped fill the boarding schools. In return, Mormons were allowed to take thousands of Native children in the Southwest to live in their homes and work their farms. To this day, don't ask a Navajo about the Mormons. For its part, the Catholic Church continued to

---

[206] Brenda Child, *Boarding School Seasons* (Lincoln, NE: University of Nebraska Press, 1989), 9.

put Indian children in its residential schools, from which they were to be adopted.

There were other private agencies involved, with the result that as many as 35% of Indian children were adopted away from their families during the project's operation, 85% of whom went to White families. For tribes, this was nothing more than an extension of the termination policy of the same period, which was designed to eliminate tribes altogether, in this case by robbing them of members and future generations.

Saving a poor little Indian child became a popular crusade in the '50s and '60s, as the number of White babies eligible for adoption dried up and fees charged by adoption agencies increased. Although the ostensible purpose was to rescue Indian children from the baneful influences of their families and reservation life, it actually was intended to save them from being Indian by placing as many of them as possible with White families. Children were snatched from their homes without warning for whatever reasons authorities found convenient. Sometimes parents would give up their children voluntarily on the promises that the kids would have a better life and that they would eventually be returned. To be fair, many children adopted by White families did indeed benefit from opportunities they never would have had back on the reservation or in the inner cities.

However, like the children who survived the boarding schools, many also suffered emotional and psychological trauma due to forcible estrangement from their families and cultures, the discrimination and harassment they faced in strange and hostile environments, and instances of physical and sexual abuse. They were left with the nagging feeling they didn't belong in the White world, and worse, that their problems were their fault. In other words, there was something wrong with them and something wrong with being an Indian. It was in their genes.

Their experiences left many of them with a sense of inferiority, and many suffered from depression, and drug and alcohol abuse. To be an Indian was to be a failure. To be sure, there could have been better outcomes if the federal government and states had provided the resources needed to improve living conditions, plus the services needed to repair and rebuild families and communities.[207]

The consequences of adoption by strangers into a foreign culture remain untold, and Native communities are still struggling to come to terms with them. On the other hand, foster care seemed like a reasonable alternative to adoption or boarding schools for children without parents or homes, or those suffering from poverty or abuse. And yet, it has had many of the same adverse consequences. For example, by the 1970s, as many as 90% of the Indian children in foster care were still being placed with White families.

To rectify the problems, Congress passed the Indian Child Welfare Act in 1978, which was designed to strengthen and preserve Indian families and culture by preventing what it singled out as the "alarmingly high percentage of Indian families [that] are broken up by the removal, often unwarranted, of their children from them by nontribal public and private agencies and that an alarmingly high percentage of such children are placed in non-Indian foster and adoptive homes and institutions."[208]

To this day, the ICWA governs the placement of Indian children in foster care and adoptive homes and requires that children be placed in the "least restrictive setting which most approximates a family and in which his special needs, if any, may be met." That setting should also be in "reasonable proximity to his or her home," with priority given to the child's relatives. Unfortunately, in most cases involving Indian children, foster care with Indian families is not available even though there are Indians willing to foster.

The reason is simple: most Indian families cannot meet state criteria for fostering, and the ICWA leaves it up to the states to set the standards. It's not hard to imagine White social workers, armed with the usual stereo-

---

[207] Stephanie Woodard, "Native Americans Expose the Adoption Era And Repair Its Devastation," *Indian Country Today* (September 13, 2018); Monte Whaley, "Forcibly adopted American Indians torn between two worlds," *Denver Post* (November 28, 2009); Patricia Busbee and Trace A. DeMeyer, *Two Worlds: Children of the Indian Adoption Project* (Portland, OR: Blue Hand Books, 2012).

[208] The Indian Child Welfare Act of 1978 (ICWA) (Pub. L 95-608, 92n Stat. 3069, enacted November 8, 1978, codified at 25 U.S.C.).

types about Indians, going to reservations and finding it hard to approve families for foster care. They're not likely to sign off on "Grandma's trailer" with several generations living under one roof as fit for foster children, despite the fact that "care for kin" is a tradition that predates reservation life. Besides, conditions on reservations are not necessarily conducive to the "best interests of the child," a vague and highly subjective standard that easily gives way to racial profiling and bias.

Indeed, reservations and urban Native communities, like the one in Minneapolis, lend themselves to abuses by White social workers and judges. Poverty, overcrowding, unemployment, drugs and alcohol, physical and sexual abuse, violence, and crime go a long way toward reinforcing the popular image of Indians as lazy drunks or drug addicts living off public assistance. There is also the fact that many Indian families cannot afford to take in a foster child. They may not have room or the supplies needed for another child, and they may not have or cannot afford cribs, car seats, clothing, and diapers. They also are not prepared to take in children with "special needs," that is, behavioral or developmental problems. Regardless of the obstacle, there is little room for sympathy in the social welfare system.

Whatever the reason and despite the successes under the ICWA, in states with large Native populations, more than 50% of Indian children entering foster care are still placed with non-Indian families or institutions. Even more discouraging is the fact that the number of Indian children in foster care is growing, and they, along with African American children, are disproportionately represented in the foster care population.

Studies have shown that Indian and Black children are far more likely to be victims of neglect and abuse than White children. The problem is that abuse and neglect are often conflated, and both are equated with poverty by social workers and judges who automatically assume that poor children are neglected, and neglect is a form of abuse. Poverty itself, like alcoholism, is often unfairly blamed on moral and character weakness. This is especially true for single mothers. Knowing this, Indian parents are often reluctant to approach the welfare system, worrying it will be used as an excuse to immediately and permanently remove their children.

The official definition of neglect in Minnesota, as in many states, is "a failure of a child's caregiver to: provide needed food, clothing, shelter, medical or mental health care; education or appropriate supervision; protect a child from conditions or actions that endanger the child; [or] take steps to ensure that a child is educated as required by law." It may also involve "exposing a child to certain drugs during pregnancy" and/or "causing emotional harm to a child."[209]

Poverty, overcrowding, poor housing, unsanitary/unhealthy living conditions, lack of parental supervision, inadequate diets, chronic illnesses, school absenteeism, and just about anything that social workers find unacceptable could and very often did throw Indian children into the child welfare or juvenile detention system. I've heard stories of mothers sleeping in cars rather than seeking help from the welfare system for fear of losing their children.[210] Throw in a criminal record for either parent, and almost every Indian child on reservations or in cities like Minneapolis or Rapid City could end up in the system.

As a result, America's Indian children are overrepresented in the child welfare system, which includes the foster care system, with the number of Indian children 2.7 times greater than their proportion of the general population. In states with large Native populations, like South Dakota, Indian children make up 57% of the foster care population, even though they represent only about 14% of the children in the state. In Oklahoma, they are 35% of the foster care population, although Indians make up only 9% of the state's population. Put another way, Indian children can be 10 or 11 times more likely to be placed in foster care than White children. This means that in states like Montana, with seven reservations and 11 tribes, 80% of Indian families have had at least one child in foster care, 85% of whom were placed outside their families or tribes by state welfare agencies and courts, and by private adoption agencies.

The American Civil Liberties Union found that in Pennington County, South Dakota, the home of Pine Ridge, more than 1,000 Indian children

[209] *mn.gov.*

[210] Colleen Echohawk, "For Native People the Trauma of Family Separations Is Nothing New," *The Seattle Times* (June 27, 2018).

were taken away from their families between 2010 and 2017. In neighboring Minnesota, which has more Indian children in foster care than any other state, once in the system, the children stay longer, are moved between foster homes more frequently, and are less likely to be returned to their families than are White children. When they finally age out of the system, they are more likely to be homeless, to suffer from disorders like PTSD, and to end up in jail.[211]

At bottom, the foster care system is populated by poor children—Indian, Black, and White. The bias against poor people is magnified by the bias against people of color. It's no coincidence that Native and Black children are more likely to be placed in foster care than White children and are overrepresented in the foster care system way out of proportion to their numbers in the general population. The same stereotypical assumptions about Indian families are applied to African American.

Black families are among the poorest in the nation, second only to Indians. They have high rates of single parenthood, and live in neighborhoods with substandard housing, high crime rates, and other socioeconomic ills. They are more likely to lose their children to foster care. Raising children under those conditions amounts to neglect and abuse by default. Moreover, Black and Indian families are more likely to be investigated for neglect and abuse than White families. Black children are 77% more likely to be removed and placed in foster care than White children. Evictions, the lack of child care, and relying on older children to care for younger ones can all lead to removal, and welfare authorities are less likely to find ameliorative solutions for them. Instead, they simply take their children away. As one report concluded, "Common behavior in white communities can

---

[211] National Indian Child Welfare Association, "What Is Disproportionality in Child Welfare," *nicwa.org* (2017); Debra Krol, "Inside the Native American foster care crisis tearing families apart," *Center for Health Journal* (February 21, 2018); American Civil Liberties Union, "In South Dakota, Officials Defied a Federal Judge and Took Indian Kids Away From Their Parents in Rigged Proceedings," *aclu.org* (February 22, 2017); "Disproportionate representation of Native Americans in foster care across United States," *potawatomi.org* (April 6, 2021); Brandon Stahl and Mary Jo Webster "Why does Minnesota have so many American Indian kids in foster care?," *startribune.com* (August 21, 2016).

lead to removal in minority neighborhoods, often because, police are more likely to patrol there."[212]

The ICWA outlines a process for placing an Indian child into foster care. The act requires that before any placement in foster care is made, parents must be informed at least 10 days in advance of any hearing. They also have a right to counsel and to see and challenge evidence, and there must be "clear and convincing evidence, including testimony of qualified expert witnesses, that the continued custody of the child by the parent or Indian custodian is likely to result in serious emotional or physical damage to the child."

When a decision to remove a child is made, priority must be given to placing the child with his or her extended family, and any placement must be within reasonable proximity of the child's home. Before a court can remove a child, however, it must be satisfied that "active efforts have been made to provide remedial services and rehabilitative programs designed to prevent the breakup of the Indian family and that these efforts have proved unsuccessful." The burden of proof rests with the state. Unfortunately, those provisions are usually honored in the breach. In fact, like so many other government programs, the opposite usually happens.

Just as Indian children were once removed to be placed in boarding schools or put up for adoption, today they can be seized by social workers or police officers without warning and without any effort to help remediate the family situation. Lacking telephones and sometimes permanent addresses, parents are not always notified about the hearings, or they have no way to get to them, which is often taken as *de facto* evidence of neglect. They can't afford lawyers and are not necessarily provided with counsel. Public defenders are not generally available in rural areas. Nor are parents always given the opportunity to see or challenge evidence.

Even more troubling are the strong-arm tactics used by social workers, judges, and police to convince parents to give up their children. For example, judges routinely use inducements ("your children will be re-

[212] Tanya Cooper, "Racial Bias in American Foster Care: The National Debate," *Marquette Law Review*, 97, no. 2 (Winter, 2013): 217-77; Shanta Trivedi, "Police feed the foster care-to-prison pipeline by reporting on Black parents," *nbcnews.com* (July, 2020).

turned sooner"), threats ("your children will never be returned"), and finally force (police show up at all hours to seize children). A study found that in South Dakota, hearings last about four minutes, with judges usually rubber-stamping the social workers' recommendations. This results in the emergency removal of the child for 60 days, a temporary solution that all too often becomes permanent. The initial findings of these hearings prejudice subsequent court decisions and almost always guarantee that a child will be consigned to foster care, leaving parents with little recourse. If parents waive their rights and voluntarily commit their children to the child welfare system, they find it difficult if not nearly impossible to get them out, even though they have the right to change their minds. The results are quite predictable, as the numbers demonstrate.[213]

Rates vary from state to state, and from reservation to reservation. South Dakota has the worst and most shocking record for placing Indian children in foster care. All states receive federal funds for foster care, but in South Dakota, that money makes up 50% of state revenue. Placement in foster care is almost automatic, which accounts for the fact that over 50% of Indian children are in foster care. Tearing so many children away from their families without recourse to appeal or active efforts to rehabilitate families, seems to fly in the face of the ICWA mandate to strengthen and preserve Indian families and culture.

Enforcing those requirements would deprive states like South Dakota of the revenue they receive to place children in foster care. It's a process that is often traumatic, with social workers backed by police showing up day or night and forcibly seizing the children. Resistance by parents or other adults can land them in jail, and even the children themselves can end up in juvenile detention if they resist. For this reason, Indians are often wary of strangers, especially White people, fearing they are welfare workers coming to seize their children. The foster care system is another example of the use of police powers and the judicial system to terrorize and intimidate

---

[213] Richard Wexler, "South Dakota Child Welfare: Where Kangaroo Court Is Always in Session," youthtoday.org (February 28, 2017).

Indians.[214] As a federal judge declared in the case of *Oglala Sioux Nation v. Hunnik,* South Dakota "child welfare officials were routinely removing Native children from homes and placing them in non-Native homes with little or no due process."[215]

It gets worse. For example, again in South Dakota, Indian children entering the foster care system are almost always diagnosed as "special needs" or "at risk," which allows them to be placed in group homes or psychiatric facilities and prescribed antipsychotic drugs to sedate and stabilize them. While South Dakota may be the worst, the use of such drugs is common in foster care facilities everywhere. The drugs are used to subdue and restrain children, not treat them, and are often prescribed in exaggerated doses that exceed amounts recommended for adults. The children are essentially drugged, in some cases, into a stupor.

The drugs of choice are often those reserved for the most severe mental illnesses and can trigger side effects such as seizures, hallucinations, and depression. Those symptoms are then treated with additional drugs until some children are on as many as eight or nine drugs at a time. The children become dependent upon them, which makes it difficult for them to be placed with families, or for those who age out of the system to lead normal lives without drugs.[216]

The destructive effects of the estrangement of children from their parents and families cannot be exaggerated. There are striking and instructive parallels between the historical separation of Indian children from their families and the government's program to separate the children of refugees from their parents along the border with Mexico. Started in 2017, that program was designed to deter Central American refugees from seeking asylum in the United States by threatening to take their children away from them. Thousands of children were eventually torn away without hearings

---

[214] Laura Sullivan and Amy Walters, "Native Foster Care: Lost Children, Shattered Families," Special Series, *npr.org* (October, 25, 26, and 27, 2011).

[215] *Oglala Sioux Tribe v. Van Hunnik,* 100 F. Supp. 3d 749 (D.S.D. 2015).

[216] Colleen Zickler, "Profiting off Indigenous Children in South Dakota," *sites.evergreen.edu* (Fall, 2016).

or due process, and then incarcerated in detention centers, where they were kept in what amounted to kennels. The centers were run by for-profit companies; the children were given psychotropic drugs to control their behavior.

There are other similarities as well. Parents were denied access to their children and threatened with incarceration and deportation if they resisted. Adults arrested for illegal entry into the United States lost custody of their children since they now had a criminal record and were automatically guilty of "child endangerment."

The program drew judicial rebukes, and elicited national and international outrage, particularly after the publication of *Separated* by Michael Soboroff, which chronicles the separation and eventual reunion of Juan and his son Jose. The program was terminated after only two years, and how many families were disrupted by this policy is hard to determine. However, as one report concluded, "There is no question that separation of children from parents entails significant potential for traumatic psychological injury to the child."[217]

The outrage reached hyperbolic heights. Physicians for Human Rights, a group honored with the Nobel Peace Prize, declared the "government's forcible separation of asylum seeking families constitutes cruel, inhumane, degrading treatment ... [and] meets criteria for torture."[218] Another report concluded that the "separation of parents from their children ... is so fundamentally unconscionable it defies countless international and domestic laws on child welfare, human rights, and refugees."[219] A government official warned, "Harming children means a century of suffering." He went on to accuse the government of perpetrating "the greatest human rights catastrophe of my lifetime."[220]

Hyperbole aside, the evidence suggests that ripping children as young

[217] Jacob Soboroff, *Separated: Inside an American Tragedy* (New York: Harper Collins Publishers, 2020), 317.

[218] Ibid., 367.

[219] Ibid., 124.

[220] Ibid., 358.

as toddlers away from their parents, incarcerating and isolating them in detention centers, and feeding them psychotropic drugs to control their behavior has devastating and potentially long-term effects on refugee children and their families.

All of this sounds too familiar and is reminiscent of the Minnesota Department of Human Services' warning that children placed in foster care in homes or institutions are "at great risk for experiencing psychological trauma leading to long-term emotional and psychological problems as adults." The refugee program was a failure and an abomination. It was also racist. It's no coincidence that it followed the same pattern that sent generations of Indian children to boarding schools, stole them away from their families through adoptions, and threw them into a foster care system that chews them up and spits them out with disastrous, even genocidal effects. Yet, there has been no such outrage over the separation of Indian children from their families, whether through boarding schools, forced adoption and foster care, or the destruction of Indian families as a result of wrongheaded and racially motivated policies and programs.

Statistics and studies are fine, but there is no better example of just how destructive foster care has been for Indian children than the story of Ambrose Ashley, a Navajo man from New Mexico. His father died, and his mother had a hard time caring for 11 children living in a shed in Tse' Bonito, New Mexico. As he tells it, he was 6 when strangers came in the middle of the night and took him and his brothers and sisters away. His mother wasn't home, and in his words, "We were scared, confused and crying for her." He and four of the younger brothers were placed with non-Native foster parents who kept them in a dank basement, and made him do chores and take care of his younger brothers. The children were isolated from their mother and even each other. Without any efforts at reunification, they became a family of strangers. They also lost contact with their Navajo culture, heritage, and language. The whole traumatic experience left him "feeling empty inside, invisible."

Ambrose eventually went to another foster home in Gallup and then to a mission school, where he began to drink. As he put it, "Sometimes people drink for no reason. Us Natives have all the reasons in the world." He joined the Marines and volunteered for Vietnam. When he mustered out of the service, he returned to Gallup but had no home to return to, so he lived on the streets. He continued drinking and had numerous DUIs until he found Alcoholics Anonymous. He is one of the lucky ones. Foster care and alcoholism converged in his life, but he was finally able to escape his addiction. At least he didn't end up a Popsicle.[221]

While working on this book, I came across an article in *The New York Times* about what was recently called Asperger syndrome. It was originally known as "psychopathic autism" by Hans Asperger, who worked with the Nazi regime to identify and treat children who had behavioral problems, and who were deemed a threat to or a drain on the state. The symptoms could include asocial or antisocial behavior such as a refusal to join in Nazi activities like Hitler Youth. In other words, they didn't fit in with the Nazi plan of creating a master race through the science of eugenics that sanctioned the sterilization or extermination of anyone found unfit.

Asperger eventually expanded his diagnosis to include violent, malicious acts. He created special wards throughout the Reich, where children exhibiting these traits were taken from their families and killed by administering ever stronger doses of sedatives. Asperger was never punished for his crimes. In fact, his diagnoses were adopted by the American Psychiatric Association and became part of popular culture in America.[222] Today, Asperger syndrome has been dropped by the APA as a disorder separate from autism.

It seems more than a bit far-fetched to compare the killing of autistic children in Nazi Germany to the treatment of Native children in foster care, but it seems to me that classifying children as having special needs that require special treatment in institutions where powerful drugs are administered to them amounts to the same thing. In both cases, the children were different, they didn't fit in, and they represented a threat—real

[221] Colleen Keane, "ICWA changed history, now court says it's unconstitutional," *Navajo Times* (February 28, 2019).

[222] Edith Sheffer, "The Nazi History Behind 'Asperger,'" *The New York Times* (March 31, 2018).

or imagined—to themselves or society.

Of course, Asperger's children were killed while foster children were or are eventually returned to their families, or they age out of foster care. But what kind of life do they have after being forcibly separated from their families, incarcerated in institutions, and fed drugs upon which they eventually become dependent? There isn't even a guarantee they will receive or be able to take advantage of follow-up care or receive proper medications. Officially, they're treated differently because they're deemed at risk or incorrigible, but in reality, it's because they're poor, their families don't measure up to the standards of White judges and social workers, and most of all, because they're Indian.

For parents hoping to retrieve their children from foster care, the biases against poor people and people of color must seem insurmountable. The Bureau of Indian Affairs requires that children be returned to their families as soon as the emergency ends. Unfortunately, for many Indians, the emergency never ends. Social workers are required to help repair families, but they rarely do. With poverty, unemployment, and homelessness endemic to Native communities, and with so many Indian parents having criminal records or histories of drug and alcohol abuse, it's hard to believe Indian parents could convince authorities they're capable of providing a safe and healthy environment for their children.

This is especially true for single mothers, who head up two-thirds of all Indian families. If they resort to the welfare system for help, that's a red flag that almost automatically triggers the removal of their children. Without legal counsel, the resources to challenge the welfare and judicial system, or something as simple as a telephone, parents lose custody and contact with their children.

The obstacles to retrieving children from foster care would frustrate and discourage even the most determined among us. How long they stay in foster care and how many are reunited with their families vary from state to state, but on average, Indian children remain in foster care longer than White children, and only 50% are ever reunited with their families.

To be fair, many Indian families need help, and social service agencies everywhere are underfunded, understaffed, and overwhelmed. Nevertheless, the government spends 10 times more on foster care and adoptions than it does on remedial care, and with tragic consequences. Tearing children away, isolating them from their families, and placing them in the custody of strangers for what must seem like forever, leaves the children frightened and feeling abandoned, unloved, angry, and resentful toward their families. Indian children who have been dumped into foster care, in particular those who stay longer in the system, have more than one placement or age out, leave the system believing there is something wrong them and something wrong with being Indian. They're not completely off base. In reality, they are being punished for the policies and actions that have been waged on Indian families and communities for centuries. Rather than saving Indian children, foster care destroys them. It is a sad but reliable measure of what American society thinks of its first people: They're disposable.

Terrorized by being thrown into a system they have come to fear and distrust, they feel helpless, hopeless, and powerless. They bear scars that will affect them for the rest of their lives. Some of those scars are real; one-third of all children in foster care experience abuse. The problems are even worse for children who have more than one placement and are moved around from home to home. As a result, Indian children in foster care are likely to suffer from depression and other mental illnesses, drug and alcohol addiction, and PTSD at rates higher than war veterans. However, they will likely never receive treatment for any of these issues. Of those who age out, 50% will end up homeless, and one-third of Native teenage boys in foster care will end up in jail before the age of 21, with criminal records that will dog them the rest of their lives.

Then there is the epidemic of suicide among young Indians, to which foster care is a major contributor. The victims of neglect and abuse are victimized by the very system that's designed to rescue them. While this may be true for all children placed in foster care, for Indians, the system is yet another iteration of the policy of acculturation and assimilation that brought them boarding schools and forced adoptions. The traumatic removal of Indian children from their families and their treatment in foster care compound the other trauma Indians have suffered in the past. Indelibly inscribed on their DNA, it is passed down to future generations.

There are dependent children who are eligible for adoption. However, the ICWA makes it extremely difficult for Indian children to be placed with non-Indian families. The act was passed explicitly to reverse the practices and abuses of the adoption period. The new adoption process is complicated by the fact that it requires parents to surrender their rights to their children, and tribes can and do weigh in on the adoption of Native children by White families. That, and the shortage of Indian families willing and able to adopt, result in low rates of adoption. Only 9% of Indian children waiting for adoption are placed within 24 months and only 20% within 48 months. The others wither way until they age out of the system, with the predictable results we've already discussed.

The ICWA's substantial barriers to the adoption of Indian children by White families have become controversial. Critics charge that Indian children languish in foster care even when parents relinquish their rights to their children. There are heart-rending stories in the news of Indian children treated as pawns in custody battles over their adoption by White families. Pundits have even charged that the ICWA is a racist law that contributes to the continued mistreatment of Indian children. Opponents of the ICWA have ignored studies showing that Indian children adopted by non-Indian families suffer from the same emotional, psychological, and behavioral problems as children in foster care.

For those who are fortunate enough to escape foster care and return home, life can be pretty grim. For some, school is the only refuge; they can go there to get warm and have a hot meal, sometimes the only meal they may have in a day. On weekends and school vacations, they are on their own.[223] Schools offer a refuge from the cold and overcrowded conditions at home, that is, if the children can make it there. A recent study found that roads on reservations are so bad, children aren't always able to get to

---

[223] Eleanor Goldberg, "Native Americans Who Can't Afford Heat Take Desperate Measures to Stay Warm," *huffpost.com* (January 13, 2018).

school.[224] I can attest to the quality of the roads. I have had so many cracked windshields on my rental vans, I was afraid the rental-car companies would put me on a no-rent list. Even if the children can get to school, they get shortchanged, especially if they go to one of the 183 Bureau of Indian Education schools that serve almost 50,000 children on 64 reservations.

Most Indian children go to public schools on or near reservations or in urban areas, mostly in mixed-race schools. Overall, Indian children do poorer on standardized tests than the national average. They graduate from high school at lower rates. Three out of 10 drop out before they finish, and only 17% go on to college, as opposed to the national average of nearly 70%. But these statistics, as bad as they are, don't tell the whole story about the terrible conditions at BIE schools.

At those schools, only 53% graduate from high school, with some graduation rates as low as 20%. A No Child Left Behind report in 2007-08 found that only 17% of Indian children at BIE schools attained their annual progress goals. At the Havasupai Elementary School at the bottom of the Grand Canyon, students rank in the first or lowest percentile in reading and only in the third percentile in math, which is made even worse by the fact that those are the only subjects taught at the school.

Remote schools like that have a hard time finding qualified teachers, and turnover is great, with administrators having to rely on unqualified substitutes to teach many subjects. In turn, this limits what the schools can offer. I have known Indians without any educational qualifications whatsoever who substitute at reservation schools. In addition to bad roads, schools have a hard time providing transportation for children living in isolated homes or communities, both of which contribute to Indian children's having the highest absentee rates of any group. Add to that the lack of textbooks, computers, and other supplies, and it is little wonder that scores at BIE schools are so low.

All of this takes place in facilities that even the government admits are in serious need of repair and improvement. All too often learning is some-

---

[224] Keerthi Vedantam, "Bad roads are a 'public safety and public health issue,'" *Indian Country Today* (May 16, 2018).

how supposed to take place in buildings or trailers filled with asbestos and infested with mold from leaking roofs and walls. Congress has budgeted more money for Indian education since 1994, but not enough to keep up with the rapid population growth on reservations. As a result, per capita allocations have dropped by half. Not only are superintendents, principals, and teachers hampered by inadequate funding and facilities, the Government Accounting Office has found financial mismanagement and corruption in the BIE that has robbed Indian children on reservations of educational opportunities that Indian children in public schools enjoy.

However, even in public schools, particularly those that are off reservations, Indian children have other problems. Very often a minority, they do not feel welcome, comfortable, or connected in schools that don't have Native teachers and don't offer courses or programs in Native history, culture, or language. Instead, they're forced to celebrate culturally offensive holidays like Columbus Day and Thanksgiving, and cheer racially offensive mascots. They suffer discrimination from administrators, faculty, and other students, and are the targets of racial epithets like "prairie nigger."[225]

The problems are even worse for Indian students with special needs. As with foster children, Native children entering school are more likely to be labeled as students with special needs. Sometimes it's because English is not their first language, or because their families have been shattered by poverty, or drug and alcohol abuse. Oftentimes, it's because they are more likely to suffer from disabilities like fetal alcohol syndrome, which afflicts all too many Native children. It can be because they're Indians weighed down by the stress of reservation life, or because the schools that serve Native children are simply not equipped to handle children with special needs. Sadly, these neediest of all Indian children are more likely to be expelled and more likely to be referred to law enforcement than other Native students. Consequently, Native children with special needs drop out of school at a higher rate, and once out, they stay out and end up as reserva-

[225] Lisa Ellwood, "Native American Students Face Ongoing Crisis in Education," *Indian Country Today* (September 3, 2017).

tion statistics.[226]

While there are differences between BIE schools and public schools, there is one thing they have in common: Indian children experience more suspensions and expulsions, and harsher punishments than any other ethnic group except African Americans. However, they exceed African Americans in referrals to law enforcement and subsequent arrests. More about that later. Suspensions and expulsions are handed out for many reasons: chronic truancy, disruptive or violent behavior, alcohol or drug use, and the possession of weapons. In addition, the zero-tolerance policy adopted by many schools in the wake of school shootings leaves no room for mitigating or extenuating circumstances.

Zero tolerance means just that, and for school administrators, it's a handy tool for maintaining discipline. It makes it easier to suspend or expel Native children for even minor infractions. A lawsuit against the Winner School District in South Dakota revealed that although Indian children made up only 20% of middle school students, they accounted for 60% of all suspensions, and 11% of Native students were referred to police versus only 2% of White students. It's no surprise that only 11% of Native students ever graduated, compared to 82% of White students. It's also no shock that Lakota from Rosebud are leery of venturing into Winner.[227]

The disproportionate mistreatment of Native children in public and BIE schools is no accident; it flows from the persistent stereotypes of Indians, particularly males, as ignorant savages who are prone to violence and on whom education is wasted. It's also no coincidence that Indian and African American children receive more severe punishments than other children. After all, they have much in common. Life on the reservation is not very different than life in the inner-city neighborhoods of Detroit, Chicago, and Minneapolis, which also have signification Native populations. Like the little girl lost in the race at Crow Fair, children in the cities begin life full of hope and determination, and also like that little girl, somewhere along the

---

[226] National Congress of American Indians, "Are Native Youth Being Pushed into Prison?," *ncai.org.*

[227] A Briefing Before the United State Commission on Civil Rights Held in Washington, DC, "Discrimination Against Native Americans in Border Towns," *usccr.gov* (2007).

line, they hit a wall.

Children in those inner-city neighborhoods are among the poorest in the nation, and in the same way as Indian children, they attend the weakest schools, receive the lowest-quality educations, and have the highest truancy and dropout rates. Indian children and Black children both bear the burdens of history, poverty, and discrimination, and carry with them the cumulative effects of oppression and discrimination. Powerless and hopeless in the face of overwhelming odds, they decide there is no escape and that any further effort is futile. Eventually, they simply drop out of the race. These burdens, compounded generation after generation, work to convince Black and Indian children to give up. They believe failure is their fate and their fault. It's in their DNA.

There is one more thing African American and Indian children have in common: They're more likely to be vacuumed up by what has been termed the "school-to-prison pipeline," where children who are suspended or expelled from school are referred to local or even federal law enforcement for punishment. While the practice has been applied to all children due to the fear of school violence and the zero-tolerance policy, poor children of color are more likely to be arrested for school infractions, referred to the juvenile court system, tried as adults, and incarcerated with adults.

This is especially true for children who have disabilities, are homeless, or for whom English is a second language. The criminalization of adolescent behavior that used to be handled by teachers and school authorities leaves children who are most in need of mental health or other kinds of remediation with criminal records and very often disqualifies them from returning to school. In fact, most don't go back to school, or if they do, they are behind in their studies. They grow frustrated and drop out anyway. Once they drop out, their pathologies follow the same pattern: alcohol, drugs, pregnancy, jail, and all too often, an early death by accident or suicide.

For Indian children, it means they become what a Navajo mother described as "just another reservation statistic." As another Native mother explained, "When you are a Native American, a Native American woman, you can count on having a son taken from a violent crime or suicide, or you can count on having a son taken by the penal system."[228]

Sexual abuse is yet another reason Native children fear schools. The physical and sexual abuse of Indian children is usually associated with the boarding school system, but that system has been dismantled, and most Indian children attend public schools run by local school districts or the BIE. Still, the threat remains. Dating back to at least the 1970s, there was a string of cases of non-Indian teachers sexually abusing children at BIE schools, from North Carolina to the Hopi Reservation in Arizona. One teacher on Hopi, John W. Boone, kept a record of the 142 Hopi children he sexually molested.[229]

In some of the cases, the BIE knew about the abuse and failed to act or to investigate the allegations. Or BIE officials knew about the teachers' history of abuse and hired them anyway. That notwithstanding, the most serious cases of the sexual abuse of Indian children took place at the schools and missions of the Catholic Church, and its various dioceses and religious orders continue to operate in and around reservations.

The sexual abuse scandal in the Catholic Church has received a great deal of media attention, most of it in states like Pennsylvania or cities like Boston that have large Catholic populations. Lost in the noise has been the long-standing abuse of Indian children and other vulnerable populations by Catholic clergy. Perhaps the worst cases occurred in the Oregon Province of the Society of Jesus, or Jesuits, which encompasses the Pacific Northwest and Alaska. The Jesuits had to pay $166 million to hundreds of Native children abused at the society's schools and missions, dating back to at least 1950. The province was forced into bankruptcy in 2009, but that was a small, if any, consolation to the victims. Not only did they suffer unimaginable perversions at the hands of the Jesuits, the bankruptcy denied them compensation.[230]

The Jesuits and other religious orders, and their superiors knew about

[228] Phoebe Tollefson, "'My hate button got broke;' mother of Wolf Point shooting victim wants justice, not revenge," *Billings Gazette* (December 3, 2020).

[229] William F. Rawson, "Former Reading Teacher Sentenced for Molesting Hopi Children," *apnews. com* (June 8, 1987).

[230] Janet I. Tu, "NW Jesuits to pay $166 million to abuse victims," *Seattle Times* (March 31, 2011).

these abusers and generally did nothing. Or they moved the predators to different assignments on or near reservations, where they could—and did—prey upon the most vulnerable children in America. It was the same shell game Catholic dioceses across America played with pedophile priests and nuns.

When I first heard about the Jesuit case, my mind was taken back to a conversation I had with Brother Simon, a Jesuit who ran the Red Cloud School on Pine Ridge. The school has a fine reputation and attracts students from all over Indian Country. In fact, one of my students went back there to teach. Brother Simon always dressed in a black cassock, the classic "Black Robe," and had a long beard, looking every bit the part of a monk who had exiled himself to serve one of the most distressed populations in the world.

He was a wonderful man who welcomed me and my students to the school and to the Native art show he organized each summer. One day, as he was showing me around the campus, I casually mentioned that it was probably hard to recruit Jesuits to Pine Ridge. Coming from a Jesuit college, I knew how difficult it was to find young Jesuits to teach. He simply replied, "Nobody comes out here because they want to." My first thought was that the Jesuits sent priests with drinking problems out there to dry out. But as the sexual abuse scandal broke, I realized Brother Simon's cryptic message hid a deeper, darker secret.

I shouldn't have been surprised. I once hosted a seminar on Indian boarding schools, where the principal speaker was Basil Johnston, a Canadian Ojibway, whose book *Indian School Days* inspired my own book on the Thomas Indian School. He was torn away from his family and sent to St. Peter Claver School for Boys, a Jesuit school in Spanish, Ontario. After introducing him, I stepped outside to say goodbye to some of my earlier speakers. When I returned to the room, Basil was recounting how he was sent to the school at the age of 5 or 6, and when he arrived, he was raped by one of the priests.

You could hear the proverbial pin drop. He went on to tell his story, which became part of the movement to bring to light the abuse of Indian children in Canada's residential schools. His story and those of thousands of other victims of abuse resulted in the Truth and Reconciliation Commission that exposed the abuses and paid reparations to the victims and their families. Basil's story shocked the audience. I was thinking about my conversation with Brother Simon.

Sadly, the Jesuits were not alone in dumping predatory priests on reservations. Dioceses from around the country sent clergy to New Mexico, where the Servants of the Paraclete operated the Via Coeli Monastery as a rehabilitation facility for priests "addicted to abnormal practices" that included "sins with the young." Once they completed their treatment, they were allowed to continue their ministries, often on or near reservations in New Mexico. Once there, they continued to prey upon Indian and Hispanic children made vulnerable by poverty, broken families, homelessness, neglect, and abuse.[231]

In Montana, the Diocese of Great Falls-Billings protected priests accused of molesting children by reassigning them to parishes and missions on or near remote reservations like Fort Belknap and Flathead, where Indian children were subjected to "forced fondling of breasts and genitals, anal rape, forced fellatio, digital, penile and anal penetration, vaginal penetration, sexually motivated 'washing' and 'spanking' and forced masturbation by priests, brothers and nuns."[232]

In South Dakota, the dioceses of Rapid City and Sioux Falls, along with various religious orders such as the Jesuits and Benedictines, knew sexual abuse was rampant in the schools they ran on reservations across the state. They either ignored it, shifted the clergy around, or sent them out of state, where they continued to abuse children. The sexual predations performed by priests, nuns, and lay employees at the schools and missions in South Dakota were every bit as shocking as those charged in the suits against the Jesuits in Oregon.

At the Tekawitha Orphanage on the Sisseton Dakota Reservation, which

---

[231] Kathleen Holscher, "Colonialism and the Crisis Inside the Crisis of Catholic Sexual Abuse," *rewirenewsgroup.com* (August 27, 2018).

[232] Seaborn Larson, "Montana reservations reportedly 'dumping grounds' for predatory priests," *Great Falls Tribune* (August 15, 2017).

was really a school rather than an orphanage, a student related how a priest took him into a little room behind the altar. He "sat me down, unzipped his pants, and took his penis out, and began to wipe it on my face and lips. I was terrified. I didn't know what was happening. In later sessions, sometimes behind the altar and sometimes at his house, suddenly I'd be choking and something would be running out of my mouth. He'd also turn me around and rape me, hurting me badly as he used his hands to grip my hair, neck, or shoulders." Nuns also preyed upon the children. One man recalled how, as a little boy, a nun would take him under her habit and rub his hands against her thighs. Ironically, the orphanage was named after Kateri Tekawitha, a Mohawk woman who was the first Native American recognized as a saint by the Catholic Church.[233]

The dioceses and religious orders that ran the schools in South Dakota did what others around the country did; they moved the abusers around and even sent some out of state. In the end, the national sex abuse scandal in the Catholic Church caught up with it. Hundreds of offenders have been charged and even jailed, and restitution to the tune of hundreds of millions of dollars has been paid. However, that has done little to console the survivors or mitigate the damages inflicted on reservations.

The sexual abuse of children is a problem across the United States; even the Boy Scouts of America has had to deal with it. What makes it especially gut-wrenching for Indian children is that it compounds the problems already plaguing reservations. Victims of childhood sexual abuse suffer from depression, anxiety, anger, guilt, shame, and other symptoms that result in self-destructive, risky behaviors, including drug and alcohol abuse, self-mutilation, suicide, promiscuity, and teen pregnancy.

They distrust authorities, drop out of school, and all too often end up homeless or in jail. In the case of Native women, they are vulnerable to revictimization, including rape and disappearing into the murky realm of sex trafficking. Even worse, because the children are sexualized at a young age, they develop inappropriate sexual behaviors and can become abusers of

---

[233] Stephanie Woodard, "South Dakota Boarding School Survivors Detail Sexual Abuse," *Indian Country Today* (September 13, 2018).

children themselves. Victims become victimizers, or in a phrase I've heard from social workers, "hurt children hurt." This may explain why sexual abuse of children is prevalent on reservations; the cycle never ends.

People often ask why the abused children didn't do something or say something. More often than not, they were cowed into obedience by vicious and humiliating punishments. Their parents were too far away, too poor, and likely too afraid to challenge the system and rescue their children. Or the victims had become dependent on the school for food, clothing, shelter, and sadly, affection. They weren't in a position to bite the hand that fed them, so to speak.

Indian children can't even count on doctors for help. The Indian Health Service has been found guilty of sheltering abusers like Stanley Weber, a pediatrician who was dismissed from the hospital on the Blackfeet Reservation amid allegations of inappropriate relations with children. He resurfaced at another IHS hospital on, of all places, Pine Ridge, where he continued his predations for 21 more years by offering money, alcohol, and opioids to children in exchange for sex. For children with nothing to lose, the temptations must have been hard to resist. Besides, they had nowhere to turn for help.[234]

It's not unusual for victims—adult and children alike—to remain silent. In the case of children, pedophiles are expert at selecting and grooming ideal subjects and using devious tactics to keep them quiet. When some of the abused do come forward, it is on average 25 years after the fact.

I think often of that little girl at the Teepee Creepers race at Crow Fair, and I wonder what happened to her. The odds are certainly stacked against her. She lives on one of the poorest reservations in America. In Montana, Indian children are disproportionately discriminated against in schools and in the judicial system.

Writing this brought to mind one of my favorite Motown songs, "Try a Little Tenderness" by Otis Redding. The lyrics go like this: "Oh she may be weary. Young girls they do get weary, Wearing that same old shaggy dress."

---

[234] Arielle Zionts, "Child sex abuse trial of former Pine Ridge Dr. begins next week," *Rapid City Journal* (September 16, 2019).

I hope she didn't get weary and get swept up in the school-to-prison pipeline. I hope she hasn't become another reservation statistic. I hope she's beating the odds.

Mostly, I hope she'll be able to finish the race.

HEATHENISH RITES AND CUSTOMS

THE SCHOOL-TO-PRISON PIPELINE is another example of the oppression Indians have endured for more than 500 years and without which colonialism could not have succeeded. The disproportionate punishment of Indian children is different only in degree from the disproportionate violence colonial powers used to terrorize Indigenous people around the world into submission. Just like terrorists today, colonial powers used terror to instill fear in the individual and collective consciousness of Native people, leaving them powerless and paralyzed in the face of overwhelming and unsparing brutality.

In North America, the British, Spanish, French, and Dutch operating under the Doctrine of Discovery used regular and irregular military forces to subdue, oppress, and remove Indians under the threat of extermination, a threat Indians learned early and often was only too real. Once the boundaries of the reservations had been secured, and it became clear the Indians were not going to vanish—although they came damn close—the government had to devise a system to keep order on the reservations. The result was a makeshift law enforcement and judicial system that denied Indians their rights. It also fell short in protecting them against White people who stole their land, water, and oil; kidnapped, raped, and killed Native women; and beat and killed drunken Native men.

In the early republic, President George Washington tried to follow the British model of not interfering in the internal affairs of tribes. The preferred way to modify Indian behavior was to dispatch missionaries to convert and educate them. After the bloody wars along the frontier in the late 18th and early 19th centuries, missionary activities were intensified with financial support provided by the Civilization Act of 1819, and the creation of the Bureau of Indian Affairs in 1824.

As John Marshall declared in *Worcester v. Georgia* in 1832, Indians were considered "domestic dependent nations" whose relationship to the federal government was that of a "ward to a guardian." The BIA was charged with the responsibility of protecting and supporting its wards. Unfortunately, neither the BIA nor Chief Justice Marshall could prevent the passage of the Indian Removal Act of 1830 that effectively cleared the way for nearly every tribe east of the Mississippi River to be removed from its traditional territories and concentrated on reservations in the supposedly empty lands of the West.

The most infamous, of course, was the relocation of the Cherokee along the Trail of Tears in the 1830s, when thousands died during a poorly planned and poorly executed march from Tennessee to Oklahoma. The Cherokee, along with their Choctaw, Chickasaw, Creek, and Seminole brethren in the Southeast, and other Eastern Indians, were among the more than 100,000 Indigenous people removed from the eastern United States and incarcerated on reservations under the watchful and menacing eyes of the military.

Using the military to remove and police Indian nations become standard operating procedure. Over the next half century, the military orchestrated other trails of tears with the same tragic results. There was the Long Walk of the Navajo in 1864, when 10,000 Navajo were marched 450 miles from Arizona to Fort Sumner in southeastern New Mexico. Once there, they were concentrated on a 40-square-mile patch of uninhabitable land known as Bosque Redondo. More than 2,000 died before they were allowed to return to their ancestral lands.

Then there were the Ponca and the Paiute trails of tears in 1877 and 1879, not to mention the bloody battles to return the Northern Cheyenne and Nez Perce to their respective reservations. In reality, almost every tribe, especially those east of the Mississippi River, suffered their own removals, often at the point of a gun. However, once the tribes were safely ensconced on reservations, the Army proved too clumsy to police and enforce the regulations and restrictions that the government imposed on the tribes.

As more and more tribes were removed to reservations, the BIA found it necessary to develop a judicial system to replace the military's role in law enforcement, but not before they intersected dramatically and tragically in the Dakota War of 1862.

The Dakota War is infamous for the execution of 38 Dakota Sioux in the largest mass hanging in American history. They came in the aftermath of an uprising in Minnesota that resulted in the deaths of anywhere from 400 to 800 civilians and soldiers. The war ended with the surrender of the Dakota, most of whom fled Minnesota. Of those who remained, 498 men were tried on charges of murder and rape, as might be expected of libidinous savages. The men went on trial without lawyers, with as many as 42 tried in one day. The verdicts came in quickly; 303 were found guilty and sentenced to death for murder and rape, the old bugaboo of Indians ravishing White women, although only two were found guilty of violating women.

As is well known, President Abraham Lincoln reviewed the verdicts and commuted the death sentences of all but the 38 who were hanged. Because they were not pardoned, the rest remained in prison, where one-third of them died. Lincoln spared most of the Dakota, but still, the hanging of 38 of their number stands in sharp contrast to the fact that only one Confederate official, the commandant of the notorious Andersonville prison, was executed after a war that took the lives of more than 600,000 Americans. Confederate soldiers, officers, and government officials went unpunished and were allowed to return home, while Jefferson Davis, president of the Confederacy, served only two years in prison.[235]

The Dakota War was the first time the government charged Indians with crimes committed during a military conflict. Although the trials were highly irregular, they validated the force taken against the Dakota and the subsequent imprisonments, trials, and hangings, plus the massacre of Dakota at Whitestone Hill the next year by General Sully. These actions sent a message to Indians that they would not receive justice at the hands of White

---

[235] Scott W. Berg, *Lincoln, Little Crow, and the Beginning of the Frontier's End* (New York: Vintage Books, 2013).

Americans. It was a lesson the 73 Cheyenne, Comanche, Arapaho, Kiowa, and Caddo learned from their imprisonment at Fort Marion in Florida, where they served as guinea pigs for Pratt's educational experiment at Carlisle. It was a lesson 502 Apache and Geronimo learned as a result of their imprisonment, also at Fort Marion, in 1886 before being sent to Alabama and then to Fort Sill in Oklahoma, where they stayed along with Geronimo as prisoners of war until 1914. Finally, it was a lesson repeated often as the BIA imposed an ever-greater number of restrictions on the behavior and movement of Indians on reservations.

Already by 1851, Indians were prohibited from leaving their reservations without permission, a restriction that was enforced by the U.S. Army in bloody battles with the Nez Perce in 1877, the next year with the Northern Cheyenne, and at Wounded Knee in 1890. With most Indians interned on reservations by the 1870s, the BIA turned to more restrictive assimilationist policies and practices. The one that has received the most attention is the creation of Indian schools, beginning with Carlisle. However, there were more pervasive and insidious restrictions enforced through a makeshift reservation judicial system. As a result, reservations became laboratories for large-scale experiments in behavior modification, long before the world ever heard of B.F. Skinner.

For example, in 1882, Secretary of the Interior Henry Moore Teller wrote a letter to Commissioner of Indian Affairs Hiram Price, calling for the discontinuance of dances and feasts such as the Sun Dance and scalp dance that served only to "stimulate the warlike passions of the young warriors," as the dancers recounted their deeds of murder and rape. He went on to suggest that plural marriages and the easy dissolution of those marriages be discontinued. He wanted men to be compelled to stay in those relationships under punishment "by confinement in the guardhouse or agency prison, or by a reduction of his rations." Teller also targeted giveaways, especially at the time of a person's death. He argued that this practice discouraged the accumulation of property, since a person's possessions would be distributed to the community rather than retained in the family and passed down to future generations. Like so many before and after him,

Teller believed that property ownership was essential for civilizing and assimilating the Indians. However, he saved his greatest disgust for the medicine men, whom he labeled "imposters."

Teller blamed them for using "various artifices to keep the people under their control, and are especially active in preventing the attendance of the children at the public schools, using their conjurers' arts to prevent the people from abandoning their heathenish rites and customs." In his view, the medicine men were "anti-progressive," a curious and telling term, and kept their people shackled to the past. He recommended that Indians be compelled to renounce and abandon these practices "which are not only without benefit to the Indians but positively injurious to them."

Teller admitted it would be difficult to force Indians to give up these practices, and he never explained how they could be compelled to do so. He left it up to Price, who appended Teller's letter to a set of directives entitled "Rules Governing the Courts of Indian Offenses" that was sent to Indian agents across the country in 1883. To meet Teller's concerns, Price ordered the creation of Courts of Indian Offenses, consisting of three judges selected from tribal police forces or other tribal members, and approved and paid by the local Indian agents. The courts were needed to enforce Price's Code of Indian Offenses that was intended to regulate and modify Indian behavior and finally wean them from their "heathenish rites and customs."[236]

The Code of Indian Offenses was not a criminal code. The crimes it covered were not the kinds of misdemeanors—theft, assault, and drunkenness, for instance—usually addressed in tribal courts. Instead, they were directly and deliberately aimed at suppressing Native culture. Price incorporated Teller's concerns into his code, and he specified the punishments that could be meted out for violating its provisions. For example, the code outlawed Sun Dances, scalp dances, and war dances, and violators could be denied government rations or imprisoned for up to 30 days. Similar punishments could be imposed for polygamy or taking gifts from giveaways,

[236] Hiram Price, *Rules Governing The Court of Indian Offenses* (Washington, DC: Department of the Interior, Office of Indian Affairs, 1883).

but medicine men were singled out for more serious punishment.

Any Indian who "resorts to any artifice or device to keep Indians under his influence" and "operates as a hindrance to the civilization of a tribe" or performs any act of an "anti-progressive nature" could be imprisoned for no less than 10 days or until he can prove to the court and the Indian agent that he will "forever abandon" those practices. Price added to the list the tradition of giving gifts in exchange for offering a daughter in marriage, which could be punished by up to 60 days in jail. The harshest penalty was reserved for the use, sale, or introduction of alcohol on reservations, an offense punishable by up to 90 days in jail or the withholding of rations for a period determined by the court or the agent.

The list of crimes was expanded as time went on, and enforcement tactics were strengthened. Indians could be punished for wearing face paint and Native clothing, and for refusing to send their children to school. After 1902, at President Teddy Roosevelt's behest, Native men could be compelled to cut their long hair. For violating these restrictions and other regulations, they could be denied rations or imprisoned, like the 19 Hopi men who were incarcerated on Alcatraz in 1895 for refusing to send their children to boarding schools.

The most egregious example of the enforcement of these codes is the case of Sitting Bull, who was killed in 1890 during his arrest by tribal police for supposedly supporting the Ghost Dance. Sitting Bull's murder set off a chain of events that ended with the massacre at Wounded Knee on Pine Ridge. Alarmed by his murder, Spotted Elk, aka Big Foot, fled his Cheyenne River Reservation for what he believed was the safer confines of Pine Ridge. He never returned home. While Wounded Knee is most often associated with the Ghost Dance, Big Foot's actual offense was leaving his reservation without permission, in violation of the Indian Appropriation Act of 1851. He and his people were about to be transported by train back to Cheyenne River when the shooting started.

Wounded Knee is just another example of how far the government was willing to go to restrict Indian movement. By 1890, Indians were concentrated on reservations under threat of force to prevent them from going off the reservation and onto the warpath, so to speak. Keeping them stationary also forced them to give up the hunt, especially the Plains Indians, who were the most truculent and troublesome. Once grounded, they had no choice but to become entirely dependent on the government for survival. After that, they could be manipulated by simply withholding their rations.

At the same time, Sitting Bull's murder proved the government was deadly serious about enforcing the Code of Indian Offenses, under which the promotion and practice of heathenish rites and customs like the Ghost Dance was forbidden. It comes as a surprise to many that those so-called heathenish rites and customs normally protected by the First Amendment were not legalized until 1978. With the adoption of the Major Crimes Act of 1885, which placed murder, rape, arson, manslaughter, assault, larceny, and burglary under federal jurisdiction, the government finally replaced traditional tribal justice systems with a colonial judicial system that punished minor and major crimes, and also criminalized traditional Native religious and cultural practices. This limited tribal courts to misdemeanors committed on reservations and severely restricted tribal sovereignty.

Many of the offenses addressed in the code were lifted in 1936 by John Collier, the reform-minded commissioner of the Indian bureau, but the lessons learned from 400 years of oppression lived on. It's easy to say, and I have certainly heard it said far too many times, that the Indians need to get over the past. If they don't, they'll never be able to make any progress, nor will they be able to escape the poverty and deplorable conditions on the reservations. That's what Commissioner Price meant when he called medicine men and other traditionalists "anti-progressives." That was also the philosophy behind boarding schools. Killing the Indian to save the man meant tearing Indians away, literally and figuratively, from the past.

The problem was then, as it is now, the lessons of the past are not so easily forgotten. As we have seen, they can be burned into DNA and affect the lives of generations far removed from the traumatic episodes of the past. In other words, Indians' DNA carries the lessons or genetic memories of trauma that they have experienced in the past—genocide, slavery, removal, epidemics. These can be transported across generations, accumulated over time, and condition individual responses to the trauma and toxic stresses of everyday reservation life. The memories are then reinforced on a daily basis through fresh encounters with the police and courts, foster care and social welfare agencies, and schools.

For Indians, it's pretty simple. After being beaten on the head for so many years, they've come to expect the worst. So, they give up, isolate themselves, and take refuge in alcohol and drugs, or worse. Whether the lessons of the past are inherited or learned the hard way, Indians know to keep their heads down, be good little Indians, and not challenge authority—or else. The approach has served them well on the reservations and when they venture into border towns, where they're subjected to the same racial profiling experienced by Black people. It's not only police who harass them; storekeepers follow Indians around and make them feel unwelcome, and townies hurl epithets and even eggs at them, taunting them with war whoops, calling them drunks, and telling them to go back to the rez.

Or they might be doused with beer like the Lakota schoolchildren who were at a hockey game in Rapid City.[237] The kids were from the American Horse School in Allen on Pine Ridge, the poorest town in America. They were on a well-deserved trip for successfully completing their lessons, when a group of drunken adults began to call them "prairie niggers" and tell them to get back on the rez. The Rapid City police dragged their feet in investigating the incident until one of the perpetrators was finally charged with a misdemeanor, but even that minor charge was dropped by the judge for lack of evidence. What should have been a happy, celebratory field trip turned into a dismal teaching moment. The children learned the same lesson their ancestors had repeatedly been taught: For Indians, there is no justice in the justice system.

Many believe, and again, I've heard it said often, that Indians' problems are of their own making, a belief that is based on the racial stereotype of the drunken, ignorant, lazy, and violent Indian, which dates back to Europeans' first contact with America's Native people. These stereotypes are

---

[237] Seth Tupper, "Native students racially harassed, sprayed with beer at Rush game," *Rapid City Journal* (January 27, 2015).

at the bottom of the discrimination and even violence against Indians, especially in the town bordering reservations. I've heard the same stories on Navajo, Northern Cheyenne, and Wind River reservations. Small wonder that Indians everywhere hate to go into border towns like Havre, Montana, where, according to two women I talked to on Rocky Boy Reservation, they were forced to step off the sidewalk to let White people pass, not unlike how Black people were treated in the segregated South.

It's better today, but reservation residents nevertheless prefer to travel 100 miles to Great Falls rather than 30 miles to Havre to do their shopping. The same is true for nearby Fort Belknap, where the *Nakoda* (Assiniboine) and *Aaniiih* (Gros Ventre) willingly travel 200 miles to Billings, rather than frequent the border town of Harlem, just off the reservation. Or the Crow Indians, who travel all the way to Sheridan, Wyoming, to shop rather than to nearby Hardin.

My friend Don Moccasin wouldn't go into Winner, South Dakota, and felt uncomfortable in Sioux Falls, where he had to go for medical treatment. Wayne Dallas, a Hopi, left a successful career with NASA to move back to the reservation, in part because of the discrimination he experienced in Flagstaff. It doesn't just happen in border towns either. Sadly, it can happen on college campuses, as it did at Colorado State, when a White mother on a campus tour reported two young Indians walking around the college because they didn't "belong."[238] Unfortunately, she wasn't wrong. Indians are reminded they don't belong whenever they step off their reservations.

I've experienced the racial hatred that plagues Indians in border towns. One summer, I stopped at a combination gas station, general store, and bar in Interior, South Dakota, which is near the Rosebud and Pine Ridge reservations. What began as a friendly conversation about where I was from and why I was there quickly turned ugly. When I told the manager I had brought a group of students to Rosebud, his sneering mispronunciation of "Lakota" expressed his contempt for me and my Indian hosts. We glared at each other for a few seconds, but discretion overcame valor. I retreated,

---

[238] Sam Levin, "'They don't belong:' police called on Native American teens on college tour," *theguardian.com* (May 4, 2018).

since the bar was full of cowboy-hatted men who didn't look very sympathetic toward me.

I had a similar encounter with a store manager in Hardin. I mentioned we were visiting Crow Fair and had been visiting various sites, like the Medicine Wheel in the Bighorns. He insisted the Indians couldn't have built it; instead, it was constructed by a bunch of Boy Scouts. He didn't like my response. Fortunately, a rather large Crow woman, whom I had brought with me, separated us and backed me out of the store. We laughed about it when we got back to the reservation and told our story, except for one older Indian, who quietly but pointedly said, "I just walk away." That's what Indians have learned to do.

If the harassment is intended to keep Native people on the reservations and out of the border towns, it's working. If they fight back, they receive the same disproportionate punishments as children sucked into the school-to-prison pipeline. Worn down, Indians very often voluntarily withdraw to the safety of reservations. Despite my own experiences and the stories I've heard, I couldn't understand just how this historical trauma worked and how deeply ingrained are Indians' fear and distrust of authority until I was in the middle of an incident on the Crow Reservation during Crow Fair.

Each summer, my students and I participated in a sweat lodge ceremony. Per usual, all the men who were going to sweat headed down from Crow Agency to the town of Lodge Grass, where the ceremony was being held in Wales Bull Tail's backyard. We prepared the lodge, started the fire to heat the rocks used in the sweat, filled the drums of water for rinsing afterward, cut chokecherry branches for the switches used during the ceremony, and waited for the fire to burn down. We were sitting under trees preparing the students for what was to come, while telling jokes and swapping stories. Out of the blue, came a group of armed White guys.

Judging by the weapons at their sides, we knew they had to be from a law enforcement agency, even though they didn't wear uniforms or badges, and did not identify themselves. The one who appeared to be the leader offered some clumsy attempts at folksy humor, much like Sam Gerrard, the character played by Tommy Lee Jones in the movies *The Fugitive* and

U.S. Marshals. It didn't work; it was clear they wanted to intimidate us. They didn't offer an explanation or a warrant. Their weapons provided all the authority they needed to intrude on our privacy, not to mention the sanctity of the sweat lodge ceremony. Their tactic worked. What had been a garrulous gathering went stonily silent. They scrutinized and questioned us, and just as suddenly as they appeared, they left without an explanation, let alone an apology. It was only later that we learned they were federal marshals looking for a White fugitive from the law said to be hiding out on the reservation.

When they questioned me, I bristled, more at the tone than the nature of the questions. I didn't want to get into a confrontation in front of my students, and I especially did not want to get my hosts in trouble, so I was compliant. Nevertheless, I was angry. Angry at the unwarranted invasion of our privacy and at myself for not having said something … anything. Most of all, I felt powerless. I suddenly understood how my Indian friends must feel when confronted by police or other authorities.

I was embarrassed for them. The descendants of the proud warriors who had once ruled the high plains had been cowed into silence. Indeed, they had been humiliated, and like me, they must have felt powerless. I could see it in their faces and hear it in their silence. And little wonder. They had been forced onto reservations and became dependent on the government for their food, clothing, and shelter. They knew better than to challenge authority; their survival depended on keeping quiet. As I have said many times, hunger can be just as compelling as a soldier with a gun. They learned long ago that resistance was futile, and as we have seen, would be met with a disproportionate response. The powerlessness that we shared for that brief moment had been internalized, and their reticence was merely a silent recitation of the lessons of the past. They have an inherent and even inherited distrust and fear of police and the legal system that has been tattooed on their DNA.

As we began the sweat, my anger abated. But as I sat in the darkness and solitude of the lodge, I couldn't help wondering what would happen if the police barged into a family gathering at my house. I would challenge their purpose and their authority, but that would hardly be necessary. I am White and live in a fairly affluent neighborhood. They would know that if they did anything untoward, I would resort to that greatest of all American traditions: I'd sue. Instead, they probably would politely introduce themselves, explain the reason for their visit, and even apologize for the intrusion. Unfortunately, those courtesies were not extended to my Indian friends; the officers did not feel they needed to. My friends didn't have the wherewithal to challenge their authority, and they knew better than to try. Five hundred years of oppression has taught them to be wary of authority, leaving them paralyzed and powerless. Actually, they probably learned it directly from their own personal experiences with law enforcement and the judicial system.

I know for certain that some of the Indians there that day and many more I have met over the years have criminal records, mostly for alcohol-related offenses. I can tell by their jailhouse tattoos. Most arrests in and around reservations involve alcohol. I also know now that at least one of the young men who was there that day ended up in jail; I had to bail him out.

It doesn't come as a shock. Overall, Native Americans are 38% more likely to be arrested than the national average, and Native men are four times more likely to be incarcerated, while Native women are six times more likely. Nationally, there are about 23,000 Natives in state and federal jails with another 10,000 in local jails. Lost in the uproar over the deaths of Michael Brown, Eric Garner, George Floyd, and other Black men is the fact that Indians are killed by police with greater frequency than any other ethnic group, and they are three times more likely than White people to die in police custody. No wonder they keep quiet.[239]

Again, the young pay a heavy price. We have already seen how Indian children are discriminated against in the school-to-prison pipeline. They are expelled from school, arrested, and jailed far more than any other group. They are three times more likely than White children to be incar-

---

[239] Roxanne Daniel, "Since you asked: What data exists about Native Americans in the criminal Justice system?," *prisonpolicy.org* (April 22, 2020); Jake Flanagan, "Reservation to Prison Pipeline: Native Americans are the unseen victims of a broken US justice system," *qz.com* (April 27, 2015).

cerated, and to make matters worse, they often end up in the federal criminal justice system. In fact, Indians make up 70% of the juveniles in federal prisons. As a result, the median age of Native people in federal prisons in America is 20 compared to the overall median age of 24. That's because the federal courts have jurisdiction over more serious crimes involving Indians.

In addition to the infractions that fall under the Major Crimes Act, if the victim, perpetrator, or both are Indians, and the crimes are committed on the reservation, both federal and tribal courts have jurisdiction. However, the cases almost always end up in federal courts because tribal courts have limited sentencing powers. Since there are mandatory sentencing requirements under federal law, young Indians are more likely to receive longer sentences than if they were tried in tribal or state courts. They also tend to receive harsher penalties than non-Indians would receive in state courts for the same crimes.

Unfortunately, Indian youth don't fare much better in state and local courts. Here's how the system works in South Dakota. Indian children in that state are 3.5 times more likely to be arrested than White children. In Rapid City, for example, Indians make up 12% of the population but 40% of juvenile arrests. When they're arrested, they are 30% more likely to be referred to court than to have their charges dropped, and twice as likely to be detained after their court appearances. Finally, they are six times more likely to be incarcerated. As a result, Indians make up 31% of juvenile prisoners in South Dakota even though they make up only 8% of the population. Those children leave the criminal justice system with a criminal record and are more likely to end up back in jail.[240]

South Dakota is not alone. In North Dakota, Indians are seven times more likely than White people to be incarcerated.[241] In Montana, where Indians are also overrepresented in prison, when they leave jail on probation or parole, their problems are just beginning. Probation and parole are sup-

---

[240] Adie C. Rolnick, "Native Youth & Juvenile Injustice in South Dakota," *South Dakota Law Review,* 62 (2017): 705-27.

[241] Daniel, "Since you asked."

posed to prevent recidivism by helping people return to their communities and lead productive lives, but in Montana, they are traps. In the first place, the programs are not free. There are court costs and fines, and fees for the drug and alcohol tests people must take as a condition of their release, not to mention the prohibitive costs of treatment for their addictions or mental health issues.

They start off in a hole. They are very often homeless, penniless, and without a job or the prospects of getting one. Finding a job, if there are any, is difficult with a criminal record or a history of drug or alcohol abuse. Treatment is generally not available on reservations, and they very often have to travel long distances to get regular drug and alcohol testing or counseling, or to make regular meetings with their parole or probation officers. Failure to complete any of the conditions of their release means going back to jail.

Most of the Indians in Montana correction facilities are there for parole or probation violations. According to a report by the American Civil Liberties Union, they seem to take their incarceration with a sense of resignation. For Natives, "… Their incarceration felt inevitable given blatant discrimination against Indigenous people in the criminal justice system. Given the way that Montana's parole system seems to punish them rather than serving as a rehabilitative tool, it's easy to see why they would feel the system is set up to entrap them."[242]

Why? The answer is complicated. At bottom, as with so much about Indians, is poverty. When Indians are arrested, they can't afford representation, so they are assigned to public defenders, who are too few in many rural areas or small border towns to handle their cases. The result is that most Indians are forced to settle for plea deals. In fact, many automatically plead guilty, believing they don't stand a chance against White juries, judges, and prosecutors. White public defenders are short staffed and too busy to represent them properly, or they're too biased to care.

Indians often aren't released on bail since they don't have cash or col-

---

[242] Sarah Mehta and S.K. Rossi, "Why Are So Many Indigenous People in Montana Incarcerated?," *aclu.org* (September 11, 2018).

lateral, and in some cases, bail bonds are not accepted. When they go to court, they are less likely than White people to have their charges dropped or reduced, and more likely to be sentenced to jail. Once in jail, they are less likely to be paroled and more likely to serve longer terms. And they are more likely to end up with criminal records, which disqualifies them from a good many jobs when they get out. If they are ever charged with even minor offenses in the future, their cases are prejudiced by their prior records. Admittedly, this is a shorthand version of very complicated legal issues, but it helps to explain why Indians distrust and fear police and the judicial system. However you look at it, the cards are stacked against them, and they know it.

Poverty also affects their encounters with law enforcement in ways that are not so obvious. On reservations, traffic laws are not strictly or ever enforced. I remember my first time on the Crow Reservation, following Dewey Bull Tail's beat-up pickup with its lone working taillight dangling by its wires, not to mention the passenger side door didn't open. I couldn't help wondering how it ever passed inspection. The answer was, of course, it didn't. Then there was the time Thomas Bull Tail offered to teach my daughter how to drive one of those oversized pickup trucks. The only problem was, they were both in eighth grade.

Speeding and driving underage, without a license, or in cars or trucks that are not registered, insured, or could never pass inspection are not rarities on reservations. On the big settlements out West, cars are a necessity. There's no public transportation, no taxis, no Uber to get to border towns for shopping or to get medical care in places like Rapid City, Billings, and Flagstaff. Without a vehicle, there's no way to get to ceremonies and visit relatives. Most Indians can't afford insurance or the cost to repair cars that are held together with duct tape—aka reservation chrome—to pass inspections. Hence, my experience of driving on a Pine Ridge highway and dodging the hood that came flying off the car in front of me.

I don't recall ever seeing a repair shop on any reservation, except for a tire repair shop run by an enterprising young Navajo in Chinle, Arizona. Besides, it's no secret that car repairs are expensive. This explains why there are so many junked cars in reservation yards and abandoned on highways. Indians buy them used and cheap, and just leave them when they break down. AAA doesn't respond on reservations. I know; I've tried. Indians also do not have ready access to state departments of motor vehicles to register their cars or get drivers' licenses. In states like South Dakota and Montana, the few DMV offices are out of reach for many Indians, not that they have the money to pay the registration fees, insurance, inspections, and fines anyway. The things that most Americans take for granted are simply not available to them.

To get these and other services, Indians must venture off their reservations, where local police often establish speed traps and checkpoints to stop them for drunk driving and drugs, as well as lesser traffic violations. Once again, I know because I got caught in one of those speed traps. Nebraska state police were waiting just across the state line outside Rosebud while I was on my way to Valentine, Nebraska. There is no doubt that local and state police in states with heavy Indian populations use racial profiling to stop Indians. To borrow a phrase, they're pulled over for driving while Indian.

It's more than just another way of hassling Indians to keep them on the reservations. Such stops can have serious legal consequences. In towns like Rapid City, police profile Indians, who make up 12% of the population but account for 59% of arrests.[243] Officers wait outside bars that cater to Native people, probably hoping to make arrests, but not outside bars frequented by White people.[244] While most arrests are alcohol related, many are for traffic violations that are overlooked on reservations. Those infractions may not bring jail time, but if the drivers have criminal records, outstanding warrants or tickets, are on parole or probation, or are under the influence of alcohol or drugs, minor offenses quickly become major ones, and they end up behind bars. As in Montana, a large share of Indian arrests are for parole and probation violations. Granted, many of these charges are

---

[243] Brandon Ecoffey, "New data proves Natives arrested at a higher rate in Rapid," *Lakota Country Times* (October 9, 2015).

[244] Tim Giago, "In Rapid City, South Dakota, there are many ways to put a knee on Oyate's neck," *The South Dakota Standard* (June 11, 2020).

not trivial, and most Americans would never consider driving without a license, proper registration, or safety inspections, but like so many other encounters with police and the judicial system, they amount to criminalizing poverty.

Charges about the mistreatment of Indians by law enforcement, and state and federal courts were investigated by the South Dakota Advisory Committee to the U.S. Commission on Civil Rights. The committee issued a report in 2000, appropriately titled "Native Americans in South Dakota: An Erosion of Confidence in the Justice System." Today it's a bit dated, but still relevant is the disturbing evidence of abuses Indians have endured in the South Dakota criminal justice system, including pervasive racism, racial profiling by police, police brutality, unreasonable bail, all-White juries, judges, and prosecutors, and overworked public defenders, all of which led to more arrests and more Indians serving longer sentences in jail.

There was even evidence that the old and long-since-abandoned practice of convict leasing was still used in South Dakota. Native prisoners were leased to farmers and ranchers to work off unreasonable fines. The committee also heard testimony about incidents of Indians being harassed and denied service that its own staff witnessed in Rapid City, where the hearings were held. There is too much damning evidence in the report to include here, but the cases of Justin Reddy, Melanie Seaboy, and Robert Many Horses stand out.

The Reddy and Seaboy cases involved young Indians in drunk-driving homicides. In the Reddy case, Justin, an Indian, was intoxicated and walking on a highway when he was struck and killed by a car driven by a Mark Appel, a White 17-year-old, who also was intoxicated. The driver was indicted for vehicular manslaughter, but the charges were dropped. He pled guilty to DUI and violating probation and was sentenced to three years in jail, but only because he violated probation. In explaining the charges, the local prosecutor made it clear that part of the blame was Reddy's, since he was drunk and had a record of drunken behavior, a classic case of blaming the victim.

In the other case, Melanie Seaboy, an Indian, was driving while intoxicated when she struck a truck and killed the driver, a White man. Within a month, she was convinced to plead guilty to vehicular manslaughter and was sentenced to 14 years in jail, three times more severe than the average sentence for the same crime in that jurisdiction. When her sentence was appealed to the judge who sentenced her, he refused to hear the case. The local prosecutor explained the difference in sentencing by saying that Appel could not be tried as an adult because he was 17, while Melanie, who was only 18, had taken "her medicine like an adult." In other words, Melanie had been a good little Indian, but in reality, she realized the futility of fighting a system that was stacked against her.

The disparity in sentencing is obvious and appalling. The report concluded, "That Native Americans are arrested and sentenced to prison disproportionately to their numbers is indisputable ...." Neither is the abuse limited to South Dakota. The report cited the statistic that the number of Indians in the criminal justice system was 2.4 times the national average. However, the commission hedged its conclusions by saying the causes of this disparity are "unclear." In the cases of Melanie Seaboy and Justin Reddy, the causes were very clear. Mark Appel received a far lesser sentence than Melanie Seaboy because Justin Reddy was drunk and had a record, while Appel was a local White boy who could afford better legal representation and favorable treatment by the police and courts.

If there is any question that race entered into these cases, that racism was widespread in South Dakota, or that Indians were treated like Blacks in the Jim Crow South as alleged by several speakers at the hearings, consider the following. In Roberts County, where these incidents took place, 75 to 85% of the inmates in the county's jails were Indians. Or better, consider the case of Robert Many Horses, who was drinking with four White teenagers who roughed him up in a ditch, and after he passed out, stuffed him in a garbage can, leaving him to die. The coroner ruled that Many Horses succumbed to alcohol poisoning and dismissed the possibility that he died because he was stuffed in a garbage can. The four boys were not charged.

I was struck by the sentence and the horrific nature of the crime, as are most who read this, but it was the testimony of the chief of police from Rapid City that explained everything. He confessed that when he joined the police force 30 years earlier, it was common practice to stuff drunken Indians in garbage cans to sober them up. What those four boys did to Robert Many Horses was not some foolish, if deadly spur-of-the-moment prank, but a socially acceptable way of humiliating and degrading Indians in South Dakota.

The intoxication of the victims of violent crime is used to justify and excuse the failure to investigate the assault and murder of Indians in South Dakota and elsewhere in Indian Country. For example, in 1998-99, eight homeless Native men in Rapid City were found dead in Rapid Creek. The cases were never investigated because they were ruled accidental drownings due to intoxication. Consequently, nobody really knows how many Indians have been stuffed into garbage cans, have frozen to death in ditches outside Gallup or on the road from White Clay to Pine Ridge, or have been murdered like Ronnie Ross in Albuquerque, who was shot 12 times just for fun. Equally if not more heartbreaking is the case of a developmentally disabled Navajo who was kidnapped by White supremacists and branded with a swastika. Add to those the thousands of Native women who have disappeared over the years and whose bodies have never been found.

The report ends with a revealing and damning conclusion that found discrimination against Indians to be "systemic" long before that word became part of the popular lexicon in 2020:

> The expressed feelings of hopelessness and helplessness in Indian Country cannot be overemphasized. There is a long-standing and pervasive belief among many Native Americans that racial discrimination permeates all aspects of life in South Dakota and that prejudice and bigotry play out on many levels, including schools, business, and public accommodations. Ample research exists to establish disparities in almost all indicators of social well-being including, income, health, education, employment, and housing. While some overcome the obstacles and achieved great success, most American Indians have been left behind. For the most part, Native Americans are very much separate and unequal members of society. Thus, it is not surprising that they are underrepresented in terms of economic status and overrepresented in the population of the State's jails, juvenile facilities, and

prisons. Systemic, institutionalized, and historic discrimination disadvantage Native Americans in many ways and therefore the problems they encounter when caught up in the criminal justice system are wholly consistent with other forms of discrimination.

It should be noted, that while the focus of the report is South Dakota, it extended its findings to include "most American Indians" in "Indian Country." Helpless, hopeless, and without legal or political representation, Indians are powerless to challenge a system that is stacked against them, which explains why my friends stayed silent when confronted by the federal marshals that August afternoon

It's bad enough that Indians are victimized by the criminal justice system, but that same system also falls far short in protecting them. There are plenty of examples of how the government has failed to protect Indian lives and property, with one of the most serious cases involving the Osage of Oklahoma in the 1920s.

Oil was discovered on their land in the 1890s, and the rise of the automobile drove up demand and prices, and with them, the value of their individual allotments assigned under the Dawes Act. The Osage became fabulously wealthy and were proclaimed by the popular press to be the richest people in the world. Probably prompted by Oklahomans who had their eyes on Osage holdings, Congress passed a law in 1921 that required Osage lands and finances to be managed by "guardians," aka White people, on the pretext that Indians were not competent to manage their own affairs. Needless to say, this opened the door for unscrupulous lawyers and judges to swindle the Osage out of tens of millions of dollars. Not satisfied with stealing their money and lands, some resorted to murder. The numbers are not precise, since many of the killings were not reported, investigated, or prosecuted, but approximately 60 Indians were murdered in just a few years, and their lands and oil taken by hook or by crook.[245]

Until recently, the Osage murders were unknown, although the 1959 movie *The FBI Story,* starring Jimmy Stewart, did contain a segment on

[245] David Grann, *Killers of the Flower Moon* (New York: Vintage Books, 2017).

them, with Stewart's character responsible for bringing some of the culprits to justice. Also unknown until just recently was another case, also in Oklahoma, where two Seminole boys were burned alive in 1899 by a mob, with the knowledge and participation of the local deputy U.S. marshal. As in the Spicer case in North Dakota, the boys were accused of killing a White woman, Mrs. Leard, in front of her children on a farm on Seminole land.

A posse scoured the countryside "taking into custody nearly every Indian who came across its path." The suspects were brought before the oldest Leard child, who could not identify any of them. According to a report by the U.S. marshal in charge of the area, the Indians were hanged and "tortured in an effort to make them confess that they were the ones, or had something to do with the crime." Finally, "... A confession of guilt was extorted from Palmer Sampson, an ignorant full-blooded Seminole Indian, who also implicated Lincoln McGeisy." The two were held and tortured for several days, and then under orders of the deputy marshal, they were chained together by their necks and taken to Oklahoma, out of reach of tribal jurisdiction. There, they were fastened to a tree and set afire while, according to one report, "... A howling mob, maddened with liquor, danced around them." Perhaps the most sickening part of the lynching came when a minister, who had knelt before the boys and prayed with them, rose to his feet and "set fire to the brush that was heaped around them."[246]

The story made national headlines. The outrage forced authorities to take action against the more than 100 participants in the lynching. Not surprisingly, the roundup of the suspects was temporarily interrupted by a false report of Seminole killing 25 White men, women, and children in revenge for the murder of the two boys. The report had been sent out by a local railroad telegraph operator "to shield the members of the mob ...." It is an old tactic: Blame the Indians to distract from the real crimes. It's not an unreasonable strategy, since everyone expected Indians to murder, rape, and pillage. Eventually, more than 50 of the mob were tried, and some were

---

[246] Daniel F. Littlefield, Jr., *Seminole Burning: A Story of Racial Vengeance* (Oxford, MS: University Press of Mississippi, 2017); Seminole Nation, Indian Territory, "The Seminole Burnings," *seminolenation-indianterritory.org* (May 23, 2021).

convicted. The families of the two boys were given reparations, but it was never determined if the two boys were guilty. If they were innocent, who killed Mrs. Leard?

The sordid affair is another example of how Indians were presumed guilty because, well, they were Indians. It's also an illustration of how law enforcement authorities, in this case a federal marshal, not only failed to protect Indians but actively participated in their murder. That the Osage murders and the lynching of the two Seminole boys have only recently been brought to light is not surprising, since crimes against Indians are still underreported. They aren't newsworthy, despite the fact that seven out of 10 Indians are victims of violent crime, twice the national average. The real crime is that 85% of those acts are committed by White people, but few are investigated or prosecuted.

Federal authorities admit that 75% of serious crimes on reservations are not prosecuted. If a non-Indian commits a crime on Indian territory, the tribe has no authority over the case, per the law of the land. The U.S. Supreme Court ruled in *Oliphant v. Suquamish* in 1978 that tribal courts cannot prosecute non-Indians for crimes committed on reservations. The most tribal police can do to non-Indians on Indian land is issue traffic tickets.

State and local police can investigate crimes committed by non-Indians against other non-Indians on reservations, but police departments in rural areas are generally understaffed and underfunded, or they simply choose not to get involved on reservations. This leaves the FBI, which has jurisdiction on reservations, but they're busy, and their offices too far away to investigate crimes on reservations, where the general perception is that there is no law anyway. This gives non-Indians a free hand to commit crimes on reservations, which attracts criminals and criminal activities.

Drug cartels often set up operations on reservations to produce and distribute drugs that invariably spill over into the Native community and overrun some reservations. Rosebud is a perfect example of that. The problem of drugs and alcohol on reservations is well known, but perhaps even more disturbing and despicable is the sexual exploitation of Native women. In contrast to the activities of drug cartels, the plight of these women comes as a surprise to most people.

To that point, we don't know exactly how many Native women have been kidnapped, sexually exploited, and murdered. There are more than 5,000 reports of missing Native women across the country, but that's an understatement. Four out of five Native women experience some kind of violence in their lifetime, and half experience sexual violence. We also know that 80% of sexual assaults against Native women are carried out by non-Indians. Violence against women is an all-too-common occurrence in America, but what makes the rape of Native women different is that it is mostly interracial. Most sexual assault in America is committed by members of the same race; among Indian women, 85% of it is committed by non-Indians.

In the end, it doesn't matter, since sexual assault of Indian women is not investigated, prosecuted, or even reported. Like other crimes against Indians, many of the missing-person reports about Native women are not investigated by local or state police, and therefore, not counted. When they are reported and investigated, the ethnic identity of the victims is often logged as "other" or not reported at all. As mentioned earlier, federal authorities fail to prosecute 75% of violent crimes on reservations, including sexual assault. The reasons vary, from lack of manpower and funding, to lack of concern about Native women. Many of the young women raped or missing are not deemed worthy of investigation because they have criminal records for drugs and prostitution, or they were the homeless products of foster care or the school-to-prison pipeline. In fact, in one study, 75% of the missing women were in foster care when they disappeared.[247]

Indian women, especially teenagers, are particularly vulnerable to sexual exploitation and human trafficking. Many of the young women forced into prostitution are those thrown-away kids who are products of the child welfare system. They may have aged out of foster care, only to be left home-

[247] Erik Ortiz, "Lack of Awareness, Data Hinders Cases of Missing and Murdered Native American Women," *nbcnews.com* (July 30, 2020); Jack Healy, "In Indian Country. A Crisis of Missing Women. And a New One When They're Found," *The New York Times* (December 25, 2019).

less and penniless, been expelled from school, run away, or become addicted to drugs and alcohol. More likely, they're simply poor, broke, and hungry, willing to turn to anyone who promises them a hot meal and a roof over their heads.

Their rescuers can turn out to be sex traffickers who supply women for so-called man camps like the infamous ones for pipeline workers near Fort Berthold, North Dakota. More recently, pipeline workers along the Enbridge Line 3 in northern Minnesota were accused of sexually assaulting and harassing women, and two workers were arrested in a sex- and human-trafficking sting.[248] Women invited to parties on ships in ports on the Great Lakes are raped and may simply disappear. Or they can just be lured into prostitution at truck stops by pimps who prey upon young, vulnerable girls.

Just as in the past, hunger can be used to exploit Indians, and it's the case for these young women who are raped, kidnapped, trapped into prostitution, and end up missing and probably dead. When they are found and identified, the crimes against them are covered up or deliberately misrepresented, like the women in Washington whose bodies were tossed on train tracks and their deaths recorded as "railroad accidents." Or maybe they just end up stuffed in a garbage can like Rhonda Jones, a Lumbee in North Carolina. Sound familiar?[249]

Murder is the third leading cause of death among young Native women, and Native women experience violence at 10 times the rate of women in the general population. One study found that of the more than 2,000 missing women it traced, 31% were under 18, and 60% were murdered. While the problem is severe on and around reservations, it's worse in cities. Surprisingly, Seattle has the highest number of cases of missing and murdered Indigenous women, followed by Albuquerque, Anchorage, Tucson, Billings, and Gallup. New Mexico is the state with the highest number of

---

[248] Brooks Johnson, "Pipeline workers arrested in northern Minnesota sex trafficking sting," *startribune.com* (June 28, 2021).

[249] Reuben Jones, "'There's a Sickness in Robeson': Families of Slain Native Americans in N.C. Want Justice," *spectrumlocalnews.com* (March 11, 2021); Stephanie Woodard, "The Police Killings No One Is Talking About," *inthesetimes.com* (October 17, 2016).

cases. This is in keeping with the fact that most Indians have gravitated to urban areas.

These cases tend to fly under the radar. They are not thoroughly investigated by police because they are usually attributed to drugs, alcohol, prostitution, gangs, and other criminal activity in which the victim may have been engaged. The media more often than not ignores them or gives them brief and passing coverage for the same reasons police fail to investigate them thoroughly. Nobody's interested in the deaths of hookers, junkies, drunks, and homeless Indians. Blaming the victim based on racial stereotypes is nothing new. Nor is the sexual exploitation of Indian women by White men. Almost 100 years ago, the Meriam Report warned about men from border towns preying upon Indian women.[250]

More often than not, crimes against Indian men and women aren't reported to authorities. Supposedly, only 5% are reported. Based on 500 years of experience, Native people have learned not to trust the White man's law. They simply don't believe law enforcement officials will take them seriously, they fear retaliation, or they may have outstanding warrants, which would place them in jeopardy if they go to the police. Crimes against Indians go unreported to authorities, and therefore, are not investigated or prosecuted. Neither are they are reported in the news. With the recent exception of the Dakota Access Pipeline protests, news from reservations rarely makes headlines. Evidently, the fact that seven out of 10 Indians are victims of violent crimes, most of which are committed by White people, is not of interest.

Nor is the fact that thousands of Native women are missing, and countless, nameless others are raped by non-Native men. Native people are arrested and jailed at rates far greater than White people, and Indians are more likely than any other ethnic or racial group to be killed by police or die in police custody, but who would know? And while Americans fall all over themselves to condemn the use of the "N-word," and rightly so, it's evidently no big deal when the slurs "prairie nigger" and "timber nigger"

---

[250] Urban Indian Health Institute, Missing and Murdered Indigenous Women and Girls, *uihi.org* (2018); Sara Jean Green, "'They feel no one cares': Washington State Patrol report outlines misssteps in reporting, tracking missing Native women," *The Seattle Times* (June 2, 2019).

are hurled at Indian children. These incidents are not newsworthy because Indians are not deemed worthy of interest by the police, the FBI, the media, and most Americans. They are the silent victims of racism. Hate crimes committed against them are pretty much ignored.

Contrast this with of the coverage of African American protests over police brutality. As fate would have it, I returned to the Crow Reservation when the troubles in Ferguson, Missouri, erupted over the murder of a young unarmed Black man named Michael Brown. As I listened to the news reports and read newspaper accounts, it occurred to me the fear and distrust of the police and the judicial system in the African American community in Ferguson is the same as what I had witnessed a year earlier at the sweat lodge on Crow.

Like Indians, African Americans are incarcerated more often and serve longer sentences than White people do for the same crimes, and Black people are more likely to be killed by police. In Ferguson, police arrested Black people, and the courts levied unreasonable fines for heinous crimes like walking in a roadway or not mowing lawns, but experience taught the defendants the futility of challenging the police or the legal system until incidents like the murder of Michael Brown outraged the nation and forced them to react.

As events unfolded in Ferguson, I was taken back to that incident on Crow a year earlier. I remembered the eerie silence that descended over our group as my Indian companions froze when confronted by the federal marshals, and I remembered how powerless I also felt at that moment. It was then that I realized, like my friends on Crow, African Americans must feel the same way that I felt, only magnified many times over by centuries of oppression and exploitation. The encounter with federal marshals on the Crow Reservation was an allegory for the collective and cumulative injustices experienced by Black and Indian people alike, which brings me back to Kadoka.

It's been more than 60 years ago since my family stopped at that saloon and saw the "No Indians Allowed" sign. Since then, a great deal has been done to combat racism in America, even if a great deal more needs to be done. Yet, Indians continue to be left out of the public discourse about race in America. Even the coverage of Standing Rock protests focused on the so-called water protectors, most of whom were White, and ignored the historical mistreatment of the Lakota and the deplorable conditions on Standing Rock itself, one of the poorest places in America. The poverty, the discrimination, the harassment, the injustices, the violence are all ignored or are justified by the Indians' intractable inferiority.

After 500 years, not much has changed.

WHITE PEOPLE ARE CRAZY

IN ONE FORM OR another over the years, I've heard Indians say, "White people are crazy." Sadly, it's probably been said about me. It's usually said jokingly, but not always. Indians have a wonderful sense of humor and love to laugh, and White people are easy targets, especially if they try too hard to be Indians.

I remember a time at Crow Fair when a busload of French tourists rolled into camp. Two men, dressed in what they thought was traditional Indian garb, strode into the dance circle and began to dance all by themselves without any accompanying drumming or singing. It led the emcee of the powwow to quip, "Why is it that the only people dancing are White guys?" That was good for more than a few laughs in the crowd that had gathered to watch, but he raised a good question.

Why indeed? Why are so many White people trying to be like Indians after they tried for so long to erase them from America, American history, and American consciousness? Or, as one Indian asked, "Why do more White people want to become Indian than Indians want to become White? The answer may depend less on what Indigenous people have to offer than on what is missing in the lives of many non-Indians.

You can find them everywhere in Indian country. They're at powwows, ceremonies, Indian arts-and-crafts shows, and even protests like the one against the Dakota Access Pipeline. They're easy to spot, with their turquoise jewelry, headbands, fringed buckskin bags and leggings, beaded moccasins, bone chokers, Native-themed tattoos, and dreamcatchers hanging from their rearview mirrors. They come from all over the United States, and from all over the world. A lot come from Canada, and from more distant places as well. In fact, I've encountered them from Australia,

Europe, Latin America, Japan, China, and even Africa.

I've taken people from China, England, Hungary, and South Sudan on my reservation trips. Most are tourists on family vacations or bus tours that stop at reservations on their way to Mount Rushmore, Yellowstone, the Grand Canyon, and other national parks and monuments. They stop out of curiosity to take pictures with real, live Indians at powwows, buy jewelry and bead work, and eat fry bread and Indian tacos. Some take pilgrimages to sacred sites like Chaco Canyon, while others are willing to pay for what is advertised as an "authentic" Indian experience, only to be ripped off by White people posing as Indians.

Once, while camping at Bear Butte, we watched a White man with a long braid and a deep tan passing himself off as an Indian and trying to teach some tourists how to put up a teepee, even though he had no idea how to do it. We all laughed when my teenage son went over and showed them how it's done. There's no end to scam artists who prey on people's desire to experience a genuine aspect of Indian culture, such as a sweat lodge. I even heard of one that offers the opportunity to take part in a genuine Sun Dance.

Sweat lodges are not to be taken lightly; they are not saunas. I've seen skin blister like a bad sunburn. The ones that are offered, even by Indians who, as a Crow man put it, "do not have the way" to conduct one, can be fraudulent and dangerous. I need only point to the Spiritual Warrior retreat in Arizona, where two people died in a non-traditional sweat. The people who get taken by these scams are not simply naïve. Rather, they're sincerely searching for something missing in their lives.

Over the years, I've met all kinds and heard all manner of stories. Some are sad and even pathetic. Like the guy who showed up on Rosebud looking for a job on a reservation, where unemployment is near universal, and the few jobs there generally go to Indians. He hooked up with our group and tagged along with us. We fed him, and I even bought him a tank of gas and gave him a few bucks after he tried to bum money from the students. He claimed to be a journalist looking for a job on the *Todd County Tribune*, a small newspaper serving Rosebud.

I thought to myself that he must have passed a lot of other newspapers on his way to Rosebud, and then I realized he was not looking for a job. Not surprisingly, he didn't find one. He departed in the middle of the night just as suddenly as he appeared. He left for me a plastic grocery bag filled with some newspaper clippings of articles he had written and a few personal items; I couldn't help thinking they were the sum total of his life. As I thought about that, I wondered how far he could get, since he had no money and just the tank of gas I bought him. I immediately checked my teepee to see if my wallet was missing. I felt bad about that soon after. He wasn't dishonest; he was just a lost soul like many more I would encounter on reservations, all of them trying to escape empty, failed, or troubled lives.

Not all of the stories I heard were as sad. Some were really comical. For instance, a woman from Italy came to Rosebud to have an Indian baby. While I'm sure there were any number of Lakota men willing to oblige her, she left disappointed. She returned a few years later, proclaiming she had an Aztec baby back in Italy. A woman from New York wanted almost the same thing, save for the baby. She came to Crow Fair hoping to take an Indian back home with her and seized upon one of my Crow friends. She offered him money, and evidently, more, as I discovered when they sneaked off into the woods close to where we were preparing a sweat lodge. That's when I learned there is a Crow word for "quickie."

And then there was Marcel from Geneva, Switzerland, who didn't know a word of English and showed up at Crow Fair all by himself. My daughter found him wandering around and brought him back to our camp. We had two Canadian students in our group who spoke fluent French, so we were able to communicate with Marcel. As a matter of fact, he was a delightful addition to our group. He was ecstatic over the buffalo hunt and the sweat lodge, but what I remember most was his standing alongside the rail line that runs through the reservation and watching a coal train whiz by. When it passed, he turned and triumphantly cried out, "113!" He had never seen a train that long and decided to count the cars. If you ever get the chance, try it. It's a dizzying experience. I attempted it a few times and always lost count until I finally bore down, concentrated, and counted 124 cars and four engines!

Of all the people I've met on reservations, the most intriguing are the Germans. The first time I met them on a reservation was at a ceremony on Rosebud to honor the cottonwood tree that was selected to be the center pole for a Sun Dance the next summer. It was down in the valley of what I believe was the Little White River. I knew a few of the Indians but none of the White people, and I really didn't know what was going on, since the ceremony was conducted entirely in Lakota.

As the singing began, I listened intently to some White guys who were singing in what sounded like perfect Lakota but with a curious accent. It turned out they had come from Germany for this ceremony and were hoping to return the next summer for the Sun Dance for which we were preparing. I learned from my Lakota friends that several Germans and other Europeans attended that particular Sun Dance, although I never really found out exactly how any of them ended up on Rosebud of all places. Like most Americans, I didn't know that Germans have a long-standing cultural connection and fascination with Native Americans and the American West that date back to the 1890s.

It all started with the prolific German author Karl May, who wrote about many things but is most famous for his stories chronicling the adventures of a fictional Indian character named Winnetou, a wise Apache chief, and his faithful White companion, Old Shatterhand. Kind of like the Lone Ranger in reverse. The two travel around the Southwest battling corrupt, greedy, land-grabbing White people, and hostile Native tribes, always exhibiting traits and characteristics that generations of Germans and many Europeans have found—and continue to find—attractive: honesty, generosity, bravery, and most of all, selfless devotion to family, friends, and the group. There is nothing more noble than the willingness to sacrifice for the greater good, even in the face of torture and certain death.

May endowed Winnetou and his father, Inchu Chunna, with these qualities that he clearly considered superior to the greed, injustices, and cant of contemporary European society. May was particularly contemptuous of Christian hypocrisy. As Winnetou's father points out to a railroad engineer seeking access to Apache lands, White people speak often of "their holy book, which is the law of love. But is it love when you want to destroy us? Your law has two faces: it allows everything to you, and nothing to us."[251]

Old Shatterhand represents the transformative power of contact with the primitive world of the Indians. He is a German who has emigrated from Germany to America and worked for a railroad surveying team before quitting on moral grounds. He didn't believe White men had a right to drive Indians off the land to build railroads. He eventually joins up with Winnetou, embraces the primitive ways of the Indians, and sheds the conventions of Western civilization. Together, Winnetou and Shatterhand risk their lives to fight evildoers wherever they find them, just like the Lone Ranger and Tonto.

May sold more books—200 million copies—than any other German author, and his fans included Einstein and Hitler. His writings spawned Indian-themed clubs, such as the Cowboy Club of Munich, which was founded in 1913. Today there are more than 400 such clubs active in Germany alone, and many more in other European countries. May gave detailed descriptions of Indians, even though his only encounter with them came during a brief visit to the United States, where he met some Iroquois people near Buffalo, New York, long after he had written his Winnetou trilogy.

He conflated all Indians into a stereotypical horse-riding Plains Indian like Inchu Chunna, who "tied his black hair to a helmet-like shape. A huge eagle feather stood out of it. It was the symbol of the office of the chief. His fringed leggings, moccasins, and coat were simple, but finely produced. There was a knife in his belt. Many bags, with the necessities he needed in the forest, hung from his belt. His medicine bag and his peace pipe, whose head was made of the sacred clay, hung from his neck."[252] May eventually confessed that he made everything up. Nevertheless, his depictions of Indians and their ways of life provide the details for the outfits of the Indian hobbyists in Germany and elsewhere, including those Frenchmen who danced at Crow Fair.

The clubs May inspired hold encampments, where members adopt In-

[251] Karl May, *Winnetou, The Chief of the Apache* (Liverpool, UK: CTPDC Publishing, Ltd., 2014), 55.

[252] Ibid., 48-9.

dian names, don black wigs, live in teepees, and wear clothes made from animal skins they have tanned and sewn together with animal sinew. They cook over open fires, make Indian jewelry and other artifacts, drum, dance, and sing like Indians, learn to shoot bows and arrows, and even study Native languages. A British hobbyist who tagged along on one of my trips taught himself Lakota as he commuted to work in London. The clubs also hold powwows and reenactments of famous battles, complete with the Plains Indian tradition of stealing the enemy's horses. There are trading cards, theme parks, German-made Westerns, and for those willing and able, a requisite trip to America for an authentic Wild West experience.

This fascination with Indians and the American West is not limited to Germany. In the 1960s, May's stories became popular in Russian satellite countries of Eastern Europe, where they represented a rebellion against oppression and were an expression of the freedom those countries lost, and that they associated with life on the American frontier. The longing for freedom from oppression may be gone with the collapse of the Soviet Union, but not so the interest in things Indian in those former Soviet bloc countries.

An Onondaga storyteller I know was invited recently to tell traditional Iroquois stories in Croatia and Serbia. Hobbyists throughout Europe have chosen to live imaginary lives, even if only for a weekend or a few weeks at a time, based on May's descriptions of Indian values, beliefs, and primitive ways of life. Just as Winnetou and Old Shatterhand symbolize freedom from the greed, hypocrisy, dishonesty, and injustices of European culture at the end of the 19th century, hobbyism or Indianism offers an antidote to the materialism of the modern world, from which many Europeans have become alienated.[253] For an occasional weekend, or a week or two, the hobbyists are transformed into Indians, much like Shatterhand in May's stories. Shunning the comforts and technology of the modern world allows them to practice a kind of primitivism or paganism that connects them to nature in a very real and immediate way, offering a spiritual, almost cult-

---

[253] Red Haircrow, "Germany's obsession with American Indians is touching—and occasionally surreal." *Indian Country Today,* (September 13, 2018).

like alternative to traditional religions.

Indeed, for some it is not merely a weekend or summer vacation lark. They argue they are the only authentic Indians left, the ones in America having fallen away from the virtues of their ancestors. Some even believe they are the reincarnation of Indian warriors of the past. As Inchu Chunna says, "The palefaces are strange people."[254] While May's influence never extended to America, except for a few Westerns in the 1960s, I found things Native hold the same romantic, almost strange attraction for many Americans as they do for the European hobbyists. However, I didn't fully appreciate or understand that until a friend suggested I read Ian Frazier's *On the Rez.* I had read his work *Great Plains* and even used it in a class. I found the new book fascinating but for reasons he would not necessarily appreciate.

The book revolves around Frazier's relationship over the course of several years with an Oglala Lakota named Le War Lance—or Lee—from Pine Ridge. More to the point, the story revolves around Lee's alcohol-soaked adventures, some of them true, others too fanciful to be authentic, and others pure fabrications. Frazier ignores or seems dismissive of Native ceremonies and even more dismissive of wannabes.

To his credit, he doesn't want to play Indian by participating in sweat lodges, dancing at powwows, or dressing like Indians, and he never explores the relationship between Lee's self-destructive behavior and the woes engulfing the Lakota people of Pine Ridge. In fact, you might not know the story is about Indians if it weren't for the drinking and the frequent trips to Whiteclay, Nebraska, or some other border town to buy beer. Instead, the story is less about Indians and more about Frazier, who finds Lee's reckless behavior strangely liberating.

Lee has what is missing in Frazier's life: freedom. He lives a wandering, rootless life, on and off the reservation, free from the burdens and responsibilities of mortgages, paying bills, and holding a job. He is always broke and bums money from Frazier and others, including celebrities who believe his stories and feel sorry for him, or just wanted to rub elbows with a real, live Indian. Lee thumbs his nose, or better, gives the finger to social

---

[254] May, *Winnetou,* 50.

conventions. In many ways a stereotypical Indian, to Frazier, he is a hero.

Indeed, Lee is a resistor in the tradition of Tecumseh, Geronimo, Sitting Bull, and especially Crazy Horse, Frazier's favorite dead Indian. Frazier longs for the freedom Crazy Horse enjoyed as he rode unfettered and unbounded across the prairies, refusing to sell out and become an agency Indian, or what the Indians used to call "hangers around the fort." His willingness to die rather than surrender his freedom made him heroic, a trait Frazier admires and finds lacking in Americans and in himself. He believes his countrymen, unlike Crazy Horse, have forfeited the individual freedoms Indians bequeathed them, choosing instead to pursue the material comforts, and corresponding responsibilities and restrictions of the modern world.

According to Frazier, Indians taught Americans the spirit of individual freedom and self-reliance that gave birth to an egalitarian democracy and a revolution that turned upside down European ideas about the proper order of society. That same spirit thrived in the rough-and-tumble, every-man-for-himself crucible of the frontier, where, as the historian Frederick Jackson Turner argued, the American character was forged. Unfortunately, that spirit also unleashed the relentless and ruthless expansion that subdued the interior of the continent and the people living there in a naked and destructive burst of colonialism.

It gave settlers license to fell the dense, dark, and foreboding forests east of the Mississippi River, string barbed wire across the wide, open prairies where Crazy Horse and the buffalo roamed, drill for oil, and dig deeply into the earth to mine gold, coal, and copper. By 1900, the wild was taken out of the wilderness and the Wild West, and Americans had squandered their inheritance. The frontier conditions that gave rise to and nurtured the characteristics associated with America and Americans were gone. They became disconnected from their past and began to take their freedoms for granted. As a result, they were in danger of losing them.

Frazier complains that America has become overcrowded, paved over with asphalt, and choked with traffic jams. To regain those freedoms, Americans have to relearn them from Indians. He believes he has rediscovered them on Pine Ridge, where, as Peter Matthiessen said, the spirit of Crazy Horse was resurrected in 1973 at the second Wounded Knee. He claims he found the real America on Pine Ridge, where "there are fewer curbs, fewer sidewalks, and almost no street signs, mailboxes, or leashed dogs. The earth here is just the earth, unadorned, and the places people walk are made by feet not machinery. Those smooth acres of asphalt marked with lines that tell you where to park and drive which cover so much of America are harder to find on the reservations. The Oglala Sioux reservation, actively or otherwise, continues to resist the modern American paving machine. Walking on Pine Ridge, I feel I am in the actual America, the original version that was here before and will still be here after we're gone."[255]

Frazier longs for the freedom of the Wild West that Indians, gangsters, and bikers possess. Yes, gangsters and bikers, because they break all the rules, and like Lee, they refuse to sell out. Lee is certainly unfettered, unburdened, and unbounded as he roams on and off the reservation and across the country without ties to any person, place, or thing. He possesses all the heroic qualities Frazier admires in Crazy Horse and the AIMsters who took over Wounded Knee; the same brand of people lacking in his own life.

Frazier confesses he wants to be a hero like Crazy Horse. He wants to do something heroic like rescuing people from a fire or other catastrophe. He longs to do something nobler and higher than most of his contemporaries, who want to do nothing more heroic than become millionaires. Given that Frazier protests the idea that he is a wannabe, he probably would not like to admit he has a lot in common with European hobbyists.

Both are alienated from the materialism of the modern world and are seeking something that is missing in their lives. They fill that void by taking refuge in the past, in the real heroic actions and values of Crazy Horse, and the imagined ones of Winnetou and Shatterhand. To them, the modern world is a spiritual desert, and they are looking to be heroic, to sacrifice in the name of something larger than themselves. To be like the Indians of

---

[255] Ian Frazier, *On the Rez* (New York: Picador, 2000), 15.

old, for whom sacrifice for family, friends, and tribe was more important than the accumulation of worldly goods or power.

Borrowing from Indians, otherwise known as cultural appropriation, is a long-standing tradition in America. Like hobbyists in Europe, Americans have always mimicked Native outfits, rituals, and customs, even as they expressed disgust and contempt for Indians. They have been "playing Indian," as Philip J. Deloria calls it, ever since Bostonians dressed as Native people to dump English tea into the harbor.[256] It has taken many different forms over the years, the most familiar being Halloween costumes, dressing kids up like Indians for elementary school Thanksgiving plays, and the notorious team names, mascots, and insignias.

There have also been fraternal organizations like the Improved Order of Red Men; evidently the original red men needed improvement. There were also the Tammany Societies, named after Delaware Chief Tamanend and associated with Tammany Hall, the corrupt political machine in New York, which was also known as the Great Wigwam.

However, of all the groups, the Boy Scouts has been the worst offender of appropriating elements of Native culture. Members of the Order of the Arrow dress in faux Indian regalia, paint their faces red, and mimic dances and ceremonies, while the Tribe of Mic-O-Say gives titles such as Fire Builder, Tom-Tom Beater, Keeper of the Scared Bundle, Shaman, Sachem, and Medicine Man to those who have devoted their lives to scouting. At summer camps like Kia Kima in Arkansas, a name supposedly borrowed from the Zuni in New Mexico, scouts learn traditional Native skills, crafts, games, ceremonies, and culture.

Playing Indian allows White people to become Indian without becoming Indian. Like the blackface in minstrel shows, it is something you can put on and take off without having to suffer the trauma and indignities Indians experience. I've heard Indians say that White people want what they have, but I never understood what they wanted until I visited a Sun Dance on a reservation in South Dakota. It was only then that the pieces began to fall into place.

---

[256] Philip J. Deloria, *Playing Indian* (New Haven, CT: Yale University Pres, 1999).

I had been to Sun Dances before but only for brief visits, usually to give my students a taste of the experience. As I was preparing to write this book, I decided it was time to take up past invitations to visit a Sun Dance in its entirety. I chose one on a Lakota reservation, where I had a lot of friends and wouldn't feel out of place. I was surprised to find that there seemed to be more White people than Indians at the ceremony. I knew spiritual leaders from a number of tribes had spoken against the practice, and some have prohibited non-Indians from sacred ceremonies, including and especially the Sun Dance, so I took my invitation as a kind of special privilege.

I must admit that my ego took quite a hit when I realized that more than half of the 70 or so dancers, and far more than half of the larger number of supporters and other random attendees were White. Even worse, I was treated as an outsider by some of them. I also hate to admit that it was probably the snubbing I received that shifted my interest away from learning more about the ceremony itself to explaining why so many non-Indians would be willing to spend their time and money to vacation on a reservation that, for so many of them, is far, far from home, and foreign to their cultural and religious backgrounds.

Since I had already been to Sun Dances and knew something about them, I became more interested in people watching. At any rate, I can't and won't divulge the details of the ceremony itself; that's not my story to tell. Besides, there's a great deal written about Sun Dances already. There's even a depiction of the dance in the movie *A Man Called Horse*. Suffice it to say they generally involve four days of preparation and purification followed by four days of dancing. If you're really interested, just Google them. I'll focus instead on the people I met and their reasons for being there.

The other Sun Dances I visited were small, intimate, almost family affairs, so I was stunned when I came upon an expansive compound crammed with tents, campers, RVs, lean-tos, teepees, and the igloo-shaped domes of sweat lodges. Although crowded, it was very well organized. People at the entrance were giving directions, others were tending fires for the almost round-the-clock sweat lodges, and still others were preparing food. Some were cleaning up the grounds, cutting the grass inside the dance circle, chopping wood, and covering the arbor around the dance circle with cottonwood boughs. Many were returning from previous years and were welcoming each other back. There was a sense of anticipation, excitement, and almost giddiness in the air.

The first four days are spent in preparation for the ceremony, so I had a chance to walk around, talk to people, help stack wood for the fires, set up tents and teepees, and take in a sweat or two. I learned quite a bit from roaming around the area. License plates told me there were people from all over the United States, and their SUVs, RVs, and campers suggested to me they were relatively well off. As I suspected, there was a contingent of foreigners; I met an Italian, a Columbian, and a Dane.

I tried not to be too intrusive or obvious, but when I had the chance to ask why they were there, I seized the moment, receiving the same answer each time. Over and over again, I heard them say they finally felt centered, anchored, grounded, connected. They seemed to be adrift or rudderless in a world they could not navigate, and the Sun Dance gave them a place to belong and be connected to something larger than themselves. Above all else, it offered them a place to heal. I heard sickening stories of childhood physical, mental, and sexual abuse, and the destructive consequences of drug and alcohol addiction. For others, their own religions had failed them.

I met a young man from Colombia who was disillusioned with the Catholic Church at home and came to the ceremony at the invitation of a friend to learn what the Indians had to offer. There was an Italian who told me the Catholic Church of his youth had changed, so he traveled all the way to South Dakota in search of an alternative. Then there was a Protestant minister from Colorado, who left the church in which he had been ordained to become a street minister to the homeless and addicted. I listened as he broke down in tears and lamented the fact that the traditional, orthodox Christianity he had preached and practiced all his life no longer seemed adequate for the problems he encountered in his work. So, they came seeking answers at a Sun Dance on a remote reservation far removed from the world they left behind.

It's not all that surprising that so many people are turning to spiritual alternatives like a Sun Dance. Although most Americans still believe in God or some higher power, church attendance and membership have been dwindling for years, especially among mainline Christian denominations. People without any religious affiliation, labeled "nones," are the largest and fastest growing religious group in America. Not surprisingly, church attendance is also declining, with less than 20% of Americans frequenting their churches on a weekly basis. Where have they all gone? They've turned to individuals, groups, and programs that offer spiritual guidance and healing for their mental and physical maladies.

Yoga, for example, has become a multi-billion-dollar industry. There are also meditation, mindfulness, self-help gurus, 12-step programs, and spiritual retreats. The latest craze has been the use of ayahausca, a hallucinogen favored by Amazonian Natives. It's become popular in Silicon Valley, New York City, and everywhere in between. It's made its way to rural Kentucky, where a convicted bank robber, Shaman Steve, and his partner, Shamanista Teri, offer ayahausca retreats out of a trailer that houses their Native American church. They even have their own television show. Incidentally, neither is a Native, and ayahausca has no place among American Indians. Put "Native American" in a tagline, and people will come or buy.

That so many Americans are turning away from mainline churches and seeking spiritual enlightenment elsewhere help to explain why so many White people were willing to travel to a Sun Dance on a hot, dusty reservation that, to most Americans, is foreign and foreboding. If someone is seeking an alternative, a Sun Dance is certainly the place to find it. There is nothing remotely like it in the Judeo-Christian tradition, which may explain why it was banned.

To missionaries in charge of saving Indians' souls, Native ceremonies were proof of their unrepentant heathenism, and none more so than the Sun Dance. It was the most important and most powerful ritual for Plains Indians, and it represented a pagan resistance to Christianity. Moreover, it symbolized a rejection of European civilization, and by extension, assimilation. A raw, exotic, primal, almost vestigial experience, it hearkened back to a time long before Europeans rudely intruded and ruined everything by taming the wilderness and putting clothes on those naked savages.

Today, Sun Dances have been resurrected on reservations across the Great Plains. For Indians, they offer healing to those suffering the inherited trauma of the past and its residual effects on the Native population today. For non-Indians, their very presence is an indictment of the materialism and spiritual vacuity of Western civilization and the modern world. That's what makes them so attractive.

Sun Dances are spiritual experiences. I've been told many times that Indians do not have a religion. Rather, they have a way of life governed by practices such as ceremonies, dances, prayers, songs, and stories. For most, if not all Natives, the concept of god is not some distant transcendent being external to the natural world. Rather, I've often thought of their Creator as a power or force, much like the force in *Star Wars*. It permeates, shapes, and sustains the natural world, and is often associated with sacred sites scattered throughout the United States and throughout the Western Hemisphere.

The Creator imbues everything in nature, animate and inanimate, with a soul or spirit that can be worshipped and summoned through the appropriate rituals or observances, of which the Sun Dance is probably known the best. All of them stem from their creation stories.

For the Lakota, in the beginning there was Inyan, a massive power that gave its blood to create everything in the universe. Inyan's blood eventually was depleted, became brittle, and was scattered across the earth in the form of rocks and stones. The belief that everything was created out of Inyan's blood is expressed in the fundamental and often misunderstood philosophy of Lakota life: *Mitakuye Oyas'in*. It is generally translated as "all my relatives" or "all my relations," and it expresses the interconnectedness of all things animate and inanimate. That we are all connected through Inyan's blood may be a uniquely Lakota belief, but it is nonetheless attractive to disaffected White people and finds expression in the popular meme that Indians are one with nature. It also brings people from all over the world to ceremonies like the Sun Dance I visited in South Dakota.

Contrary to popular assumptions, Sun Dances have nothing to do with the summer solstice. They were generally held around that time because that was when Plains Indians gathered for the summer buffalo hunts. The Lakota name for the ceremony, *Wi wanyang wacipi,* means "sun gazing" and has been generalized even though other tribes have names for the ceremony that do not refer to the sun. The format varies from tribe to tribe and even within tribes. I won't and really can't divulge the details. So guarded are Indians about the ceremony, notebooks and cameras are forbidden. They'll be confiscated and the violators forcibly expelled from the dance grounds.

In general, the participants endure a grueling ordeal of dancing to the beat of drums from sunup to sundown without food or water for four days. They dance to secure the blessings of the Creator and spirits for their family, friends, and tribe. Their supporters—again family, friends, or visitors like me—join in the singing and prayers, and dance along with them under the arbor that surrounds the dance ground. It is not just men who dance and sacrifice; women also dance, although they are not allowed to take part in certain aspects of the ceremony. As mentioned earlier, some dances do not allow women in the dance circle at all. In the Sun Dance I attended, there were about 40 women dancers, the majority of whom were White.

While the male and female dancers make the most extreme sacrifices dancing all day under the scorching sun, it is nevertheless a community enterprise. Friends and families begin planning, preparing, and gathering supplies a year in advance. They are responsible for sustaining the ceremony and making it a success. During a break in the dancing, when the dancers are resting and secluded, a speaker gives the supporters a pep talk. One told them they could be sitting in a pew in an air-conditioned church right now, but instead they chose to sacrifice themselves on behalf of the dancers, sacrifice being the common unifying theme of Sun Dances. Dancers even sacrificed their blood like Inyan did in creating the world.

There certainly were no pews; everyone stood and padded their bare feet as the drums beat out a pulsating rhythm. And there certainly was no air conditioning; the arbor provided precious little relief from the 105-degree heat. Their selfless devotion and sacrifice gave them a direct and immediate spiritual connection to something larger and more important than themselves.

This was not a show for picture-taking tourists, anthropologists studying primitive folkways, or historians like me chronicling the revival of banned ceremonies. This was serious business, and perhaps no one was more solemn than the White attendees. You could see just how serious they were in the way they went about their chores. You could feel it in the sweat lodges as they sang ceremonial songs in perfect Lakota. You could see it in the way they listened with rapt attention to the speakers, and the way they danced and raised their hands in unison at the appropriate times in the ceremony.

I remember one young woman whose exaggerated movements seemed as if she had been seized by the rapture, and the Italian who danced from morning until night, sweat pouring off his body as he performed a combination of the Mashed Potato, the Twist, and the Boogaloo. You could see it in the way helpers scurried around, carrying pots of smoldering sage for smudging like acolytes or altar servers at a Catholic Mass. It was obvious in their almost cultlike enforcement of the rules.

I'll never forget the young man with long curly blond hair wrapped in a red bandana who patrolled the grounds and admonished people for wearing shoes under the arbor, or in my case, wearing short pants during the opening ceremony. Maybe it wasn't a church, but it surely resembled an old-fashioned revival or camp meeting where members of the congregation get so caught up in the ecstasy, they roll around on the ground and are born again—hence, the term "holy rollers." After all, the Sun Dance is a ceremony of spiritual rebirth and revitalization.

I came to understand how their sacrifices welded them together into a community of believers and set them on a path toward the spirituality that was lacking in their lives. Their spiritual hunger brought them together like Catholics gathered for Holy Communion to share in Christ's suffering and sacrifice. They'd finally found what the hobbyists and Frazier hungered for: a place where they belonged, where they felt connected, anchored, centered, grounded. When it was over, they packed up their SUVs, RVs, and campers, said their goodbyes and promised to return next year. They left exhausted but feeling good about themselves.

What troubled me was they took what they needed and left behind the despair and desperation that characterize life on a reservation. Never once did I hear anyone express concern over the poverty and myriad other problems right outside the dance grounds. Indeed, they had been sheltered in the hermetically sealed world of the Sun Dance. My first thought was to cry "cultural appropriation!" Then I remembered an article in *Indian Country Today* entitled "Everybody wants to be Indian, but nobody wants to be an Indian." It seemed to be more fitting for what I found at the Sun Dance than to decry cultural appropriation. As the author of that article pointed out, more White people than ever want to "play Indian," to borrow Philip Deloria's apt phrase, but nobody really wants to live like one. Everybody wants to share in Indian spirituality, but nobody wants to experience the poverty, disease, and violence that wrack reservations. They pick and choose what they want or need, and they ignore the messy, inconvenient parts of Indian life.

It's easier to deal with the dead Indians of the past like Crazy Horse than live Indians of today like Le War Lance. That's the reason many non-Indians leave the reservations disappointed; live Indians don't measure up to their expectations of Rousseau's noble savage. I found the same ignorance about conditions on reservations when I visited Standing Rock during the Dakota Access Pipeline protest in November 2016.

I was taking a cross-country trip to Montana for a Thanksgiving dinner with the Bull Tail family on the Crow Reservation (yes, they do celebrate Thanksgiving), and had stopped in to visit friends and do a few interviews on Rosebud. The protest had been in the news for weeks, with the "water protectors," as they billed themselves, vowing to stop the completion of the pipeline that was to carry oil from Canada across North Dakota and under the Missouri River. There were two issues. First, the pipeline was being built across land claimed by the Standing Rock Lakota under the Fort Laramie Treaties of 1851 and 1868. The land had been taken away from them after their embarrassing victory at Little Bighorn. It also—and more importantly—contained burial and sacred sites.

The second was that it posed an environmental threat to the water supply of Standing Rock and downstream reservations and communities, hence the name "water protectors." It had become an international cause *celebre*, with entertainers and other celebrities offering their voices and money in support of the protestors. The journalist Amy Goodman and actress Shailene Woodley were arrested at the protest a month earlier, and there were acts of violence against protestors by militarized police using attack dogs, pepper spray, and riot gear. These incidents were broadcast around the world and eventually attracted thousands of supporters to descend on the isolated reservation on the border between North and South Dakota.

By the time I got there, the pipeline had already reached the Missouri River just above its confluence with the Cannonball River, and crews were readying equipment to drill under the river. At night, the lights of their camps were visible behind the hills that rose above the rivers. The water protectors had gathered along the Cannonball to protest and hopefully stop the construction of the pipeline that needed only the segment under the Missouri River to be completed.

I decided to take a detour and head up there to see what all the hype was about. I had been to Standing Rock before, and as I drove across the reservation skirting Lake Oahe, which was created by damming the Missouri and flooding Lakota lands, I saw nothing out of the ordinary. That is, until I reached the cusp of the hill overlooking the Cannonball basin. As I drove down the hill, I saw two large camps along the riverbanks. When I reached the gates, I was greeted by guards who were checking for alcohol, drugs and other contrabands, and spies. Yes, spies supposedly sent by the pipeline company and police to infiltrate the camp. I should have known right then and there what I was going to find; the guards seemed to take themselves a little too seriously. In retrospect, their paranoia may not have been so far-fetched, as we now know the police and pipeline company employed a number of dirty tricks against the protestors.

After I parked my car, I walked along the Blackwater Bridge over the Cannonball to the barricade that separated the protestors from the police. I may have heard the term "militarized police" before that day, but I certainly didn't expect what I saw across the river. The police and security guards, and their equipment were arrayed along the banks as if they were expecting an attack from the German Wehrmacht. They even had called in reinforcements from out of state. I should have guessed something serious was about to happen, but for the moment, all was peaceful.

The camps themselves were quite impressive. They were much larger than I expected and very well organized. The activity reminded me of the Sun Dance. Everywhere people were busying themselves cooking meals, chopping wood, preparing teepee poles, and erecting tents and more permanent shelters. There were multiple canteens serving food to the hungry, huts supplying coats and sleeping bags to those who came unprepared for what was already a frigidly cold North Dakota winter. There was even medical care available. As I walked around the camps, I was fascinated by the sheer diversity of the protestors who had come from all corners of the country, from many different backgrounds, and for many different reasons.

There were curiosity seekers who were there for a few days or weekends, or for Thanksgiving break, and then there were those who were determined to hunker down against the bitterly cold Dakota winter. There were clergy from various denominations lending moral support for the cause, and lots of photographers, amateur and professional, hoping to chronicle a historic event or capture the shot of a lifetime. There were reporters and writers working on stories, anthropology students looking for a research topic, and lots of veterans, Native and non-Native. I met a med student from California who was skipping classes, a self-professed "bum" who was just "bumming around," and a woman who claimed to be a professional organizer of protests. There were two recent college graduates and a couple of budding photojournalists traveling across country, all of whom took a detour to be where the action was.

And then there were those who had traveled thousands of miles from countries around the world to lend a hand and support to the protest. Judging by the number of BMWs and other luxury cars in the parking areas, many were substantially well off. And posted everywhere were the signs proclaiming *Mni Wiconi* or "water is life" to remind the protestors why they were there.

Of course, there were a lot of Indians there from Standing Rock and its sister Lakota and Dakota reservations, and based on the tribal flags posted around the camp, there were representatives from hundreds of other reservations from across America and Canada. The protest was started by La Donna Brave Bull from Standing Rock as an act of peaceful, spiritual resistance to the pipeline. She believed, as did others, that the pipeline represented the "blacksnake" that, as traditional Lakota teachings prophesied, would devastate Earth, and destroy sacred sites and burial grounds. The pipeline carrying the heavy, toxic black crude oil from Canadian tar sands was already cutting its way through Lakota lands, literally and figuratively, and was threatening to pollute them as well.

She established the Sacred Stone camp on a bluff above the river to serve as a center of prayer and ceremony, and provide the spiritual foundation of the protest. Spiritual leaders from all over the world and from different faiths came to the camp to pray and participate in or lead ceremonies, and their spirituality had great influence on the protestors. I saw at least one instance where "elders," as the protestors called them, stepped in to disperse a crowd itching for a fight. And itching for a fight, they certainly were.

It began purely as a movement by Indigenous people, but as news of the protest and police abuses spread and people flocked to the reservation, the two additional camps were established in the river bottom closer to the pipeline's right-of-way. The new camps adopted the name *Oceti Sakowin,* the Lakota name for the Seven Fires of the Great Sioux Nation. Eventually there were 3,000 to 4,000 protestors in the camps, the majority of whom were not Indians. Faith Spotted Eagle, a Dakota from the Yankton Reservation and one of the leaders of the protest, estimated that as many as 80 to 90% of the protestors were non-Native. By my estimation, that seems accurate.[257]

They would have stood out if they were not in the majority. They wore the usual outfits of White people trying to be Indian, but they were not very convincing. I chuckled at the sight of White women wearing traditional long skirts with expensive UGG boots sticking out beneath them.

[257] Tracy Rector, "Faith Sotted Eagle on the Settler-Colonial Mind-Set," *Indian Country Today* (January 17, 2017).

They may have come from different places and backgrounds, but they were searching for the same thing. They proclaimed themselves water protectors, but they really wanted to be Indians by living like Indians, dressing like Indians, and rubbing elbows with real, live Indians.

As environmentalists, they identified with the Native reverence for nature, and they hoped to tap into Native spirituality. The DAPL protest gave them the chance to connect with the Native community by sacrificing their time, money, and potentially even their lives to heroically demonstrate against the "blacksnake" and the "militarized police," even if it was only for a weekend or for Thanksgiving vacation. Standing Rock gave them a place to belong.

Faith Spotted Eagle summed them up perfectly. "We have non-Native people who come here, bless their hearts, who are looking for their spirits …. Now they're looking to try to be Indians." She worried aloud that the influx of so many non-Natives would subvert the movement that she and LaDonna Brave Bull and other Natives started. She said they were taking up space and making independent decisions at the *Oceti Sakowin* camps, which she considered just another form of "settler colonialism" that threatened to overwhelm, obscure, and call attention away from the Indigenous origins and foundations of the movement. They wanted to become Indians without becoming Indians.

While I heard a lot of talk of killing the blacksnake through prayer and meditation, it was also clear that the protestors had their own agendas. I remember one young woman pulling into the camp, sticking her head out of the car window, and excitedly asking whether there was going to be an "action" that day, the term used for the protests on the Blackwater Bridge. I was present for several actions that welled up during the day.

The groups assembled carrying placards, shouting slogans, carrying garbage-can lids as shields, and wearing bandanas across their faces to protect against tear gas and to shield their identities. They marched to the barricade erected to prevent them from traveling up the road toward the pipeline about a mile away. At the barricade, they chanted, swore, and threw things at police, who watched from a safe distance across the bridge. So much for spirituality.

Some protestors tried to swim across the river, only to be met on the other side by police officers. They were an excitable lot. One budding young novelist who was looking for a story, remarked to me that the protestors acted as if it was some kind of a game. Eventually, the actions broke up and everyone return to the camps. Except for the night of November 22, when the game turned deadly serious.

It was so cold that night, my cellphone stopped working. I was trying to reach some people from Rosebud for a place to sleep, and there was poor service in the camps (attributed by some to jamming by the police), so I went back up the hill to thaw out my phone and my body, and to get phone service. As I was driving around and warming up, looking for what I later learned was LaDonna Brave Bull's camp, police car after police car came screaming by, headed for the Oceti Sakowin camps. I tried to return to the camps, but the road was blocked. I got out of my car to find out what was going on. I could hear police sirens and what I took to be gunshots and some kind of explosions. I finally gave up and left to find someplace warm to sleep. I wasn't able to return to the camps until the next morning.

What happened that night is well known. It was on the national and international news. The peaceful confrontation between the water protectors and militarized police across the Blackwater Bridge became violent. When I finally got back to the camps the next morning, I saw the debris from the battle and talked to people who had been there. I helped scour the riverbank for rubber bullets and evidence that the police used concussion grenades against the protestors. I didn't know what I was looking for, and I didn't find anything anyway. The camps were rife with talk about police brutality and conspiracy theories like one I heard about police using electronic devices to jam cell phones, and spraying the camps with chemicals to sedate the protestors.

I don't know exactly what prompted the police to act that night, but having seen other actions, I can't believe it was necessary for them to use water cannons, rubber bullets, or force of any kind against the protestors. It was all too reminiscent of the disproportionate force White people historically used against Indians. On the other hand, I had become skeptical about the motives of the water protectors. Their single-minded cultlike devotion to their cause blinded them to the realities of reservation life. I do not doubt their sincerity. They were serious about protecting Standing Rock's water supply, a legitimate issue, but when I asked them about Standing Rock itself, they knew very little about the land on which they were squatting or the people whose water they were protecting.

For all their talk about Native spirituality and reverence for nature, the protestors to whom I spoke were tone deaf when it came to the conditions on Standing Rock, the other Lakota reservations, and reservations across America, for that matter. When I spoke with a group of college students who were visiting on Thanksgiving break, I was struck by their lack of knowledge about conditions on Standing Rock and among Native people in general. No one I talked to had spent any time on the reservation except to drive through it on the way to the protest or to visit a nearby convenience store or the tribal casino, or to use the bathrooms. Port-a-potties can be very cold in North Dakota in November.

They didn't know Standing Rock is one of the five poorest reservations and one of the poorest places in America, with a poverty rate three times the national average and an unemployment rate of 79%. And while the water protectors championed environmental justice, Indians like the young woman I interviewed on Standing Rock live in fear of the injustices Natives have experienced at the hands of the North Dakota judicial system. It is a legitimate fear, dating back to the massacres of the 19th century and the Spicer lynching in nearby Williamsport in the 1890s. Those fears were again realized. Although more than 800 protestors were arrested on state charges, very few resulted in convictions. The stiffest penalties were reserved for the five Native protestors who were convicted in federal court and received lengthy prison sentences. I shouldn't have been surprised.

I remember how exhilarating it was marching against the Vietnam War when I was in college in Ohio and bravely facing off against National Guard troops after the Kent State shootings. For people caught up in the excitement and idealism of the moment and full of themselves for confronting militarized police, it probably would have been deflating to admit the problems on Standing Rock were more serious than the threat to their water supply. On the other hand, it may just have been that, like most Americans, they didn't know any better. It wasn't until I viewed a video posted online by a young man at the protest that I understood why the protestors seemed so unaware of the conditions on Standing Rock.

As he streamed the video of activities at the camps and the battleground at the bridge, he offered a running soliloquy in which he opined that the police were not all bad and didn't really want to be there. They were simply acting out of fear of losing their jobs and paychecks. He went on to invite the police to join the protestors in prayer and meditation and not be afraid of living in poverty or doing without. That was easy for him to say as he proudly sported his new iPhone. Perhaps he should have asked the Indians from Standing Rock and other reservations whether they view poverty as a good deal.

As I viewed the video, I thought of the interview I had with the Native woman who ran the convenience store at the top of the hill overlooking the camps. The place was very busy with protestors buying supplies. When I suggested to her that business must be very good, she replied that it was, but she wished customers would be nicer. I asked her what she meant, and she gave me the example of someone just that morning who had berated her for being a capitalist and making a profit off the protest.

The protest took on a life of its own separate from and even in conflict with the people of Standing Rock, whose water supply the protestors were vowing to protect and on whose land they were squatting. The actions of the water protectors and the violent reactions of the police overshadowed the peaceful and spiritual intentions of the movement's founders. I could try to explain this, but Faith Spotted Eagle said it best. "A lot of White people who came to the protest put themselves at the center rather than our culture first." In other words, they appropriated what they needed to cloak themselves and their movement in the authority of Native spirituality without regard for their effect on the Natives themselves.

Eventually the protest sucked resources from the community. The roads were blocked, so businesses were suffering. When the community said, "It's time to go home now," most of the tribal people of other communities re-

335 White People are Crazy

spected that decision and left, but a lot of non-Native people stayed. In fact, some stayed despite tribal requests for them to leave. Finally, they had to be forcibly removed in the dead of winter in February 2017, leaving behind an environmental mess for the tribe to clean up at a cost of at least $1 million.

I wasn't surprised when I heard about the eviction and arrest of the remaining squatters from the *Oceti Sakowin* camps. Their search had ended, and they had sacrificed too much to leave peacefully. They finally found a place where they belonged. It was a place where they felt centered, anchored, and connected; they were part of a community, like the people I met at the Sun Dance. It was a place where they could cast off the conventions, constraints, comforts, conveniences, and even the clothes of modern society, sacrificing themselves in the process in the name of something higher and nobler. It was a place where they could practice a kind of paganism or primitivism that brought them closer to nature, like the hobbyists in Europe. It was a place where they could enjoy the kind of freedoms that Frazier found on Pine Ridge; there were no sidewalks, no curbs, no acres of asphalt, and none of the responsibilities of modern life. It was a place where they could do something heroic as they faced off against the militarized police arrayed across the Cannonball, like Frazier's Crazy Horse at Little Bighorn or the Indians who occupied Wounded Knee. Above all, it was a place where they could cloak themselves in Native spirituality and culture, and play Indian without having to become Indian. Bless their hearts.

Before I left, I traveled around the reservation, talking to people to gauge their opinions about the protest. When I asked a Native woman at a local bar what she expected to come of the protest, she predicted nothing would change. I returned a year later and asked her whether the situation had improved. She told me no. In fact, things might have gotten worse. The tribe had lost millions of dollars in casino revenue. There was also suspicion and resentment caused by the apparent disappearance of millions of dollars raised online, money that never found its way to the people of Standing Rock. The protest may also have set back relations with neighboring White communities, which were not very good in the first place. If there was any consolation, it cost the state $22 million to police the protest.

As I was leaving, I stopped at a diner near the protest area, where I overheard a conversation among some locals. They referred to the protestors as "those dumb sons of bitches" down on the rez who tried to burn down a concrete bridge, likely not knowing most of those "dumb sons of bitches" were White people.

The protest wasn't a complete failure. It called the nation's attention to issues like treaty rights and tribal sovereignty. It brought tribes from around the country together in support of a common cause, something they have never been particularly good at. It ignited Native activism and emboldened tribes to more vigorously defend their sovereignty. It raised the nation's consciousness to the environmental threat posed by pipelines. In fact, President Joe Biden canceled the Keystone XL pipeline that would have provided a shortcut for Canadian tar sands oil to get to market.

However, the protest did little to raise the nation's consciousness to the plight of the Native people on America's reservations. I went back and Googled media accounts of the protests, and I couldn't find one that even mentioned it in passing. Just as at the Sun Dance, when most of the protestors packed up their RVs, SUVs, and campers, they pipeline protesters probably left feeling good about themselves. They could take with them stories to tell their children and grandchildren about the sacrifices they made in the battle for Standing Rock. Sadly, things haven't changed for the Indians they left behind to suffer the burdens of the past on their own.

As Inchu Chunna observed, "The palefaces are strange people."

They Tried to Bury Us; They Forgot We Were Seeds

THE STORY OF THE American Indian has historically been couched in terms of a technologically advanced, morally superior, and more numerous civilization overwhelming a scattered, primitive, and feral population that ferociously, albeit heroically, resisted the benefits and beneficence of well-meaning Europeans.

The only question has been whether it was virgin-field epidemics that wiped out 95% of the Indigenous people of North America, or whether their demise was the result of an intentional and genocidal campaign of extermination. While it's true epidemics took a terrible toll on the Native people of North America, just as they did in Europe, they didn't bring about the sudden demographic collapse of the Native population.

The decline was gradual over the course of 500 years. It was the result of disease and warfare, slavery, removal, starvation, and exposure, combined with malignant hatred, contempt, and neglect. Americans might console themselves with the excuses that what happened to the Indigenous people of North America was the result of diseases, was in retaliation for the atrocities committed by the Indians, or was the inexorable replacement of an inferior, primitive culture by a morally, physically, and intellectually superior civilization. But a more appropriate word for it is genocide.

At this point, it's worth recalling the words of David Standard, who concluded, "The colonists were driven by a racist zeal to eliminate the Indians," a racist fervor the Europeans brought with them and eventually exported around the world. From the very first contact, Europeans found the dark-skinned Native people who inhabited the "wildernoes" along the Atlantic coast to be less than human, perhaps even a separate and degraded species. Their fierce resistance to the European invasion proved they were beasts,

337

brutes, vermin, savages, and heathens who deserved only to be purged or exterminated to make way for the agriculturalists who would improve the fallow land and its resources, and who could not live safely in the same neighborhood as the Indians.

These sentiments were repeated continually by settlers, missionaries, government officials, newspaper editors, the Declaration of Independence, U.S. Supreme Court justices, and even presidents. They were behind the slave raids, and the enslavement and exportation of Native women and children that began the slow and inexorable decline in Native fertility. They fueled the hundreds, if not thousands, of murderous assaults in a 500-year campaign of total warfare that disrupted Native communities, destroyed villages and food supplies, and spared nothing and nobody, including "squaws" and their "whelps." After all, "lice have nits." They were behind the deportation of tribes from their traditional lands and their concentration on isolated and often barren reservations as Native populations were replaced, in Lemkin's words, with the population of the colonizer.

Once there, they were incarcerated without adequate food, water, sanitation, housing, and medical care, and deprived of their freedom to roam, worship, speak their own languages, and simply be Indians. Even government officials admitted Indians were sent to the reservations not to live, but to die. The idea that Indians were a vanishing race and were too primitive, too vicious, and too depraved to need, deserve, or appreciate the benefits of civilization was directly responsible for the deplorable and deadly conditions on reservations that contributed to the population decline long after the Indian wars ended. Spurred on by their virulent and violent racial antipathy toward Indians, the American people supported, cheered on, and even participated in the murderous and genocidal onslaught.

We can protest there was no intent to exterminate the Native people, a key element in the crime of genocide, but our public statements, not to mention our actions, say otherwise. What happened to America's Indians was the will of the people. As Abraham Lincoln once said, "In this age, in this country, public sentiment is everything." Even those who never saw an Indian or lifted a finger against one is guilty; to be complicit in genocide you only need to lack empathy and compassion for its victims.

The disdain for Indians and the indifference to their suffering didn't die when their resistance ended. Government neglect, incompetence, and corruption institutionalized the poverty and despair on the reservations. Assimilationist policies and programs like boarding schools, forced adoptions, and foster care made matters worse. Almost 100 years after the Meriam Report, too many Native people still lack the necessities of life and suffer from higher rates of disease, addiction, and death than everyone else in America.

When they step foot off reservations and travel to border towns to shop, live, or work, they do so at their own peril. They face discrimination, harassment, beatings, arrests, and murder. If they relocate to cities, the problems follow them. They have to deal with the same food and housing insecurity, inadequate health care, and other social problems that plague reservations. While Americans have become more sensitive to the issue of systemic racism and have sought to remedy the situation with reparations, police reform, and hate-crime legislation, Indians have been left out of the conversation. The underlying belief is that since Natives resisted assimilation from the very beginning, their problems are of their own making. If that's the case, then the solutions also must be of their own making.

Everywhere I go around Indian Country, I see signs that Native people are taking matters into their own hands. Meet Matt Hill, a Seneca, an operating engineer, and a friend of mine who got caught speeding in the Cattaraugus Seneca territory. It was a routine traffic stop, and Matt admitted he was speeding. The only problem was that he was stopped by police from the town of Brant, which borders the reservation. Police from neighboring communities often operate on the reservation on the pretext that their jurisdiction extends onto Seneca lands under the authority of United States Codes 232 and 233, which grants "The State of New York jurisdiction over offenses committed by or against Indians on Indian land within the State of New York ...."

Matt was willing to take his punishment, but not from the officials of Brant. He went to court armed with documents, including the minutes of a 1947 tribal council meeting that showed the tribe had never agreed to allow the state to extend its jurisdiction over Seneca lands. The case was dismissed to avoid setting a precedent. It was a small victory for Seneca sovereignty. It didn't make the evening news or the local newspapers, but it is nevertheless an example of what I find everywhere in Indian Country: Tribes and individuals are fighting to regain control over their lands and their lives.

For their part, the courts have upheld Indian rights. In the 2016 case of *Dollar General v. Mississippi Band of Choctaw*, the U.S. Supreme Court affirmed a lower-court decision that the tribal courts had jurisdiction over civil cases involving non-Indians on tribal lands. In 2019, the court ruled that a group of Crow Indians, including a friend of mine, had the right to hunt on federal lands in the Bighorn Mountains—in violation of Wyoming laws—under the Fort Laramie Treaty of 1868. In 2018, the Supreme Court ordered the state of Washington to redesign roads in order to protect the salmon-fishing rights of Native people.

A lower court ordered the Dakota Access Pipeline to cease operation, something the water protectors couldn't do, while an Oklahoma court ordered Enable Midstream Partners to dismantle its pipeline on lands owned by Kiowa, Apache, and Comanche tribal members. But perhaps the most significant decision was in the *McGirt* case in 2020, in which the Supreme Court, citing treaties that established reservations in Oklahoma, effectively placed much of the eastern part of the state under jurisdiction of the Muskogee or Creek tribe. By extension, that meant much of the rest of the state would fall under the jurisdiction of the Choctaw, Chickasaw, Seminole, and Cherokee tribes, who, like the Creek, had been exiled to Oklahoma in the 1820s and '30s. In these and other cases, Native people have weaponized their treaties to regain and protect their rights as sovereign nations.

Discussions about Indian sovereignty almost always revolve around economic development driven by casino revenue. There certainly has been a great deal of that already. The Pequot and Mohegan have built impressive gaming and entertainment complexes in Connecticut, which inspired other tribes to pursue gaming as a source of employment and revenue for impoverished reservations across the country. The Seneca have three casinos in and around Buffalo and Niagara Falls, New York, that have allowed them to build community centers, health-and-wellness clinics, and housing for tribal members. Their success also has enabled them to flex their economic muscles in legal battles with the state of New York over taxes, casino revenues, and the state's portion of the interstate highway that passes through Seneca territory.

In Minnesota, the casino of the Shakopee Mdewankanto Sioux tribe generates an estimated $1 billion a year, the profits from which the tribe distributes among its 500 members, making them the richest Indians and some of the wealthiest people in America. The money generated by Indian casinos has led to almost apocryphal stories about Indian children buying candy bars with $100 bills, or worse, buying drugs with their windfalls. It's also led non-Indians to assume that gaming is the solution to what has long been termed the "Indian problem."

But not every tribe has casinos. Among those that do, not all of them are profitable, and tribes have to share their take with state and local governments, plus the operators of their casinos. Moreover, gaming is a risky business. There is increasing competition from other casinos and online gambling as well. When the COVID-19 pandemic forced gaming-and-entertainment venues to close, revenue dried up, and everyone learned the brutal lesson that nothing is a sure thing.

Concerned over substituting a dependency on the government with a dependency on gaming, tribes have begun to diversify their business development efforts. The Choctaw Band of Mississippi is an example of such. The tribe is a model for economic development in Indian Country, attracting businesses to their reservation long before there was an Indian Gaming Act. From American Greeting Corporation to an Israeli defense company to an enterprise that produces plastic cutlery for McDonald's, the tribe opened its territory to investment, and then used the revenue to invest in tribal businesses, such as a forestry management company, a laundry service for local hotels and restaurants, and facilities for manufacturing auto parts. In turn, the tribe reinvested its profits in housing, a shopping center, and other conveniences for tribal members, not to mention generating employment opportunities for tribal members and Mississippians. As a result, the Chocktaw Band has become an economic and political force in one of the poorest states in the country. Moreover, it's inspiring other tribes to follow suit.

For example, the Southern Ute in New Mexico have a casino, and they have created a growth fund that has invested in real estate, oil, gas, and clean energy. The tribe has become the largest employer in the Four Corners Region. And, as the young lady I met at the tribal museum reminded me, all without government money.

There are a lot of other success stories about tribes diversifying in business ventures on and off reservations. The Potawatomi of Wisconsin have bought a stake in Commerce State Bank, while their brethren in Michigan bought an office building in downtown Grand Rapids. Others, like the Red Lake Band of Ojibway in Minnesota, and Lakota on Pine Ridge and Cheyenne River in South Dakota, are investing in solar- and wind-power projects. Likewise, the Mountain Ute have built a solar-power array on their massive reservation around Mesa Verde National Park and the Four Corners states, which will not only make them energy independent, but reduce their greenhouse emissions and enable them to sell electricity to the surrounding area.

The 32 tribes in the state of Washington are investing hundreds of millions of dollars in infrastructure and environmental projects that are making them less dependent on government transfer payments and gaming, and more reliant on revenue from their investments.

There are plenty of other examples. On the surface, it looks like Indians have become capitalists and maybe even have drunk Naomi Schaefer Riley's magic potion of private property. However, behind all this economic development is the determination to strengthen their sovereignty and protect their ways of life. As a report on tribal economies in Washington state explained,

> Prior to what is widely referred to as the Self-Determination Era, Federal and state governments proved themselves unwilling to incapable of addressing Indian social and economic challenges. Privatization of Indian land under the Dawes Act did not work. Disbanding tribes in the Termination Era did not work. And Great Society anti-poverty programs were not designed,

sustained, or funded adequately. Contemporary strengthening of Indian communities' capacities to govern themselves—powers long under assault or neglect— explain the resurgence of tribal economies. Tribal sovereignty is not just the law, it is a good idea.[258]

Without land, sovereignty is meaningless, as the more than 200 unrecognized tribes will tell you. But even recognized tribes across the country are fighting to regain lands that were stolen from them through force, deceit, or desperation. The several Lakota tribes have purchased and placed into federal trust *Pe' Sla,* a centrally located high mountain prairie known as Bald Mountain and thought to be "the center of everything that is" in Lakota spiritual life. The tribes rescued the land from being auctioned to a gold-mining company, which is certainly divine retribution, since it was the discovery of gold that set off the wars that ended with Little Bighorn and led to the loss of the Black Hills.

Similarly, the Snoqualmie of Washington purchased the Salish Lodge and Spa east of Seattle for an investment and also to save from development the property's towering waterfall that is considered sacred by the Salish Coastal tribes. The Northern and Southern Cheyenne, and the Arapaho spent $2.3 million for land near Bear Butte in the Black Hills, a site considered sacred by many Plains Indians. Other tribes have followed suit. The Oneida in Wisconsin, Seneca in New York, Osage in Oklahoma, Ho-Chunk or Winnebago of Nebraska, Blackfeet in Montana, Shakopee in Minnesota, Nez Perce in Idaho, and the Kumeyaay near San Diego, just to name a few, have all purchased lands near their reservations.

For some it's an investment, for others it's room for a growing population, and for others it's reclaiming traditional lands containing sacred sites and burial grounds. For all, it's re-establishing their relationship with the land that defines them as Indians and members of their respective tribes. Land is not only a gift from the Creator, it is the Creator. All life springs from it; it's the source of material and spiritual sustenance. Creation and

---

[258] Jonathan B. Taylor, "The Economic and Community Benefits of Tribes in Washington," *washingtonindiangaming.com* (2019): 5.

other stories teach Indians it is their responsibility to protect and preserve the land. In a sense, their cultures are organic, growing out of their diverse geographic and climatic surroundings, and giving rise to their equally diverse cultures and languages.

That explains their fierce attachment to their lands and their desire to reclaim them. Just travel with them around their territories, and you'll come to appreciate the pride they take in their land and the joy it brings them. Most Americans would see spaces that are bleak, impoverished, and undeveloped, littered with trash, junk cars, and emaciated dogs. Indians, on the other hand, see the beauty in the forest-covered mountains, the steep canyons, the rolling plains, the flat-top mesas, the fantastical shapes of the high deserts, and the islands dotting the coast that make up their lands. More than where they live, it's where they worship. More than their home, it's their cathedral.

Economic development and the reclamation of traditional lands are big news in Indian Country, but the little things are equally important, for they touch Native lives directly and immediately. There's the Rolling Red Bus of the Lakota Federal Credit Union. It brings banking services to the sprawling Pine Ridge Reservation, which otherwise is a financial desert. The Tuba City, Arizona, hospital on the Navajo Reservation has started relying on midwives and inviting families into the delivery room to assist with deliveries, which has reduced Cesarean sections, even as they continue to increase in the general population.

The Iroquois in New York have returned to planting traditional white corn. Along with beans and squash, it was a staple of their diet until their crops and stores were destroyed during the American Revolution, and missionaries introduced them to yellow corn soon after. White corn is smaller than yellow corn, and it has to be harvested, husked, hulled, and ground by hand. It is used to make corn soup and cornbread, offering an entirely different texture and taste than the cornbread made with yellow corn. The White Corn Project has been instrumental in bringing back white corn, with the help of the Onondaga Seed Keepers, an organization that has preserved heirloom seeds and distributed them to tribes across the country.

In Minneapolis, the "Sioux Chef" (pun intended), Sean Sherman from Rosebud, has opened an Indigenous food lab to teach Native communities how to replace so-called oppression foods made with wheat flower, butter, sugar, and beef or pork, with fish, wild rice, onions, turnips, nuts, sunflower seeds, berries, and wild game like deer, turkey, and rabbit. Food sovereignty is important for Indians, particularly the elderly. Lacking food security, they rely heavily on fast and processed food, and suffer with high levels of diabetes, heart disease, and other maladies as a result.

Of all the cases of economic resurgence I found in Indian Country, I was most intrigued by the Rosebud Economic Development Corporation. REDCO, as it's called, is under the leadership of Wizipan Little Elk, the grandson of Edna Little Elk. A graduate of Yale and the University of Arizona Law School, he returned to Rosebud after serving under President Barack Obama. I might also add he is a Sun Dancer. While Wizipan is trying to move the Sicangu Lakota people of Rosebud into the future, he has one foot firmly planted in the past. The belief that the Lakota people can only move forward by reverencing their history is clearly set out in REDCO's mission statement. It outlines a Lakota-style plan to revitalize and sustain the Sicangu via "Lakota values and ideas."

The plan includes food sovereignty, health care, housing, and a Lakota education. It's already showing results, with housing projects sporting solar panels; community gardens and farmland; language-immersion programs; a grocery store selling fresh fruit, vegetables, and food that hasn't expired; and construction and propane companies owned by the Lakota. Probably the most ambitious project is the establishment of the largest tribally owned buffalo herd.

The goal is to use Indigenous solutions to create a better world for the next seven generations or 175 years; or better, for their "great-grandchildren's great-grandchildren." Either way, it's a long time, but that's just fine. They aren't planning on going anywhere. They have chosen to remain, and most of all, they have chosen to remain Indian.

BIBLIOGRAPHY

BOOKS

Adams, David Wallace. *Education for Extinction* (Lawrence, KS: University Press of Kansas, 1995).

Bailyn, Bernard. *The Barbarous Years* (New York: Alfred A. Knopf, 2012).

Beidler, Peter G. *Murdering Indians* (Jefferson, NC: McFarland and Co., 2013).

Berg, Scott W. *Lincoln, Little Crow, and the Beginning of the Frontier's End* (New York: Vintage Books, 2013).

Berkhofer, Robert. *Salvation and the Savage* (Lexington, KY: University Press of Kentucky, 1965).

Bryant, William Cullen. "The Prairies" in *The Poetical Works of William Cullen Bryant*. Parke Goodwin, ed., Vol. 1 (New York: Russell & Russell, 1967).

Burich, Keith R. *The Thomas Indian School and the "Irredeemable" Indian Children of New York* (Syracuse, NY: Syracuse University Press, 2016).

Busbee, Patricia and DeMeyer, Trace A. *Two Worlds: Children of the Indian Adoption Project* (Portland, OR: Blue Hand Books, 2012).

Butt, John, ed. *The Poems of Alexander Pope*, Vol. 2. (New Haven, CT: Yale University Press, 1963).

Child, Brenda. *Boarding School Seasons* (Lincoln, NE: University of Nebraska Press, 1989).

Colden, Cadwallader. *The History of the Five Nations of Canada* (London: T. Osborne, 1747).

Cooke, Frederick. *Journals of the Military Expedition of Major General John Sullivan Against the Six Nations of Indians in 1779* (New York: Knopf, Peck & Thomson, 1887).

Cronon, William. *Changes in the Land* (New York: Hill and Wang, 2003).

Deloria, Philip J. *Playing Indian* (New Haven, CT: Yale University Press, 1999).

Edmonds, Walter D. *Drums Along the Mohawk* (Boston: Little Brown, 1936).

Franklin, Benjamin. *The Autobiography of Benjamin Franklin* (New Haven, CT: Yale University Press, 1964).

Frazier, Ian. *On the Rez* (New York: Picador, 2000).

Gibson, Carrie. *El Norte* (New York: Atlantic Monthly Press, 2019).

Gibson, Jon L. *Ancient Mounds of Poverty Point* (Gainesville, FL: University of Florida Press, 2001).

Grann, David. *Killers of the Flower Moon* (New York: Vintage Books, 2017).

Greeley, Horace. "Lo! The Poor Indian" in *An Overland Journey from New York to San Francisco in the Summer of 1859* (New York: C.M. Saxton, Baker and Co., 1860).

Gwynne, S.C. *Empire of the Summer Moon* (New York: Charles Scribner's Sons, 2011).

Harden, Kathryn Paige. *The Genetic Lottery: Why DNA Matters for Social Equality* (Princeton, NJ: Princeton University Press, 2012).

Hauptman, Laurence M. *Conspiracy of Interests: Iroquois Dispossession and the Rise of New York State* (Syracuse, NY: Syracuse University Press, 1999).

Hemingway, Ernest. "Ten Indians" in *The Complete Short Stories of Ernest Hemingway* (New York: Charles Scribner's Sons, 1987).

Holmes, Oliver Wendell, Sr. "The Pilgrims of Plymouth" (Oration, December 22, 1855) in Cephas Brainer and Eveline Brainerd, eds., *The New England Society Orations*, Vol. 2 (New York: The Century Co., 1901).

Institute for Government Research, *The Problem of Indian Administration* (Baltimore, MD: Johns Hopkins University Press, 1928).

Jefferson, Thomas. *Notes on the State of Virginia* (Boston: Lilly and Wait, 1785).

_____. "Letter to Handsome Lake, November 3, 1802" in *Thomas Jefferson: Writings*, 555-7 (New York: Library of America, 1984).

Jordan, Winthrop. *White Over Black* (Chapel Hill, NC: University of North Carolina Press, 1968).

King, Thomas. *The Inconvenient Indian* (Toronto: Anchor Canada, 2013).

LeBlanc, Laurence. *The United States and the Genocide Convention* (Durham, NC: Duke University Press, 1991).

Lemkin, Raphael. *Axis Rule in Occupied Europe* (Washington, DC: Carnegie Endowment for International Peace, 1943).

Lindqvist, Sven. *Exterminate All the Brutes* (London: Granta Publications, 1990).

Lindsay, Brendan C. *Murder State* (Lincoln, NE: University of Nebraska Press, 2012).

Littlefield, Daniel F., Jr. *Seminole Burning: A Story of Racial Vengeance* (Oxford, MS: University Press of Mississippi, 2017).

MacLeitch, Gail D. *Imperial Entanglements: Iroquois Change and Resistance on the Frontiers of Empire* (Philadelphia: University of Pennsylvania Press, 2011).

Madley, Benjamin. *American Genocide* (New Haven, CT: Yale University Press, 2017).

Magnuson, Stew. *The Death of Raymond Yellow Thunder* (Lubbock, TX: Texas Tech University Press, 1998).

Mann, Charles. *1491* (New York: Charles A. Knopf, 2005).

May, Karl. *Winnetou, The Chief of the Apache* (Liverpool, UK: CTPDC Publishing, Ltd., 2014).

Parker, Arthur C. *The Code of Handsome Lake* (Albany, NY: Univ. of New York, 1913).

Resendez, Andres. *The Other Slavery* (Boston: Mariner Books, 2017).

Richter, Daniel K. *The Ordeal of the Longhouse* (Chapel Hill, NC: University of North Carolina Press, 1992).

Riley, Naomi Schaefer. *A New Trail of Tears* (New York: Encounter Books, 2016).

Roosevelt, Theodore. *The Winning of the West,* Vol. 4 (New York: The Current Literature Publishing Co., 1905).

Schultz, Eric B. and Tougias, Michael J. *King Philip's War* (Woodstock, VT: Countryman Press, 2017).

Seaver, James E. *A Narrative of the Life of Mary Jemison Who Was Taken by the Indians in 1755* (Syracuse, NY: Syracuse Univ. Press, 1990).

Shoemaker, Nancy. *American Indian Population Recovery in the Twentieth Century* (Albuquerque, NM: University of New Mexico Press, 1999).

Smith, Andrea, *Conquest* (Cambridge, MA: South End Press, 2005).

Soboroff, Jacob. *Separated: Inside an American Tragedy* (New York: Harper Collins Publishers, 2020).

Stannard, David E. *American Holocaust* (New York: Oxford University Press, 1992).

Orin Starn. *Ishi's Brain* (New York: W.W. Norton & Co., 2004).

Stromberg, Joseph. *Lands and the Lakota: Policy, Culture and Land Use on the Pine Ridge Reservation* (Sunnyvale, CA: Lambert Academic Publishing, 2013).

Swatzler, David. *A Friend Among the Senecas* (Mechanicsburg, PA: Stackpole Books, 2000).

Woolford, Andrew, Benvenuto, Jeff, and Hinton, Alexander Laban, eds. *Colonial Genocide in Indigenous North America* (Durham, NC: Duke University Press, 2014).

Wylie, Paul R. *Blood on the Marias: The Baker Massacre* (Norman, OK: University of Oklahoma Press, 2017).

ARTICLES

Anderson, Justine. "Covid-19 checkpoints on reservations to remain," *indianz.com* (May 22, 2020).

Andrews, Evan. "9 Things You May Not Know About the Oregon Trail," *history.com* (October 28, 2018).

Athearn, Robert G. "The Fort Buford 'Massacre,'" *The Mississippi Valley Historical Review,* 41, no. 4 (March, 1955).

Archibald, Robert. "Indian Labor at the California Missions: Slavery or Salvation," *The Journal of San Diego History,* 24, no. 2 (Spring, 1978).

Berry, Carol. "When Genocide Lost a Debate," in *Indian Country Today* (April 22, 2012).

Boetel, Ryan. "Teenage attacker to Homeless victim: 'Eat Mud.'" *Albuquerque Journal* (July 25, 2014).

Braine, Theresa. "The Real Bowling Green Massacre," *Indian Country Today* (February 4, 2017).

Bryan, Susan Montoya and Fonseca, Felicia. "Finland agrees to return Native American remains to tribes," *Denver Post* (October 3, 2019).

Clawson, Roger. "Death by Drink: The Sad Battle of America's Indians," *APF Reporter* (1989).

Colville, Chip. "'As Native Americans, We Are in a Constant State of Mourning,'" *The New York Times* (April 4, 2019).

Cooper, Tanya. "Racial Bias in American Foster Care: The National Debate," *Marquette Law Review*, 97, no. 2 (Winter, 2013).

Cutter, Barbara "The Gruesome Story of Hannah Duston Whose Slaying of Indians Made Her an American Folk Hero," *smithsonianmag.com* (April 9, 2018).

Daniel, Roxanne. "Since you asked: What data exists about Native Americans in the criminal Justice system?," *prisonpolicy.org* (April 22, 2020).

de Brebeuf, Jean. "The Mission to the Huron (1645-37)," in Colin G. Calloway, *First Peoples* (Boston: Bedford/St. Martin's, 2012).

de Bruxelles, Simon. "Calls for the redesign of royal honour over 'offensive' image," *The Guardian* (June 22, 2020).

Deerinwater, Jen. "Paper Genocide: The Erasure of Native People in Census Counts," *newswiregroup.com* (December 9, 2019).

Dunbar-Ortiz, Roxanne and Gilio-Whitaker, Dina. "What's Behind the Myth of Native American Alcoholism," *Pacific Standard* (October 10, 2016).

Ecoffey, Brandon. "New data proves Natives arrested at a higher rate in Rapid," *Lakota Country Times* (October 9, 2015).

Echohawk, Colleen. "For Native People the Trauma of Family Separations Is Nothing New," *The Seattle Times* (June 27, 2018).

Ellwood, Lisa. "Native American Students Face Ongoing Crisis in Education," *Indian Country Today* (September 3, 2017).

Etheridge, Robbie. "Global Capital, Violence, and the Making of a Colonial Shatter Zone," in *Colonial Genocide in Indigenous North America*.

Fain, Abi, and Nagle, Mary Catherine. "Close to Zero: The Reliance on Minimum Blood Quantum Requirements to Eliminate Tribal Citizenship in the Allotment Acts and Adoptive Couple Challenges to the Constitutionality of ICWA," *Mitchell Hamline Law Review*, 43, no. 4 (2017).

Fixico, Donald L. "When Native Americans Were Slaughtered in the Name of 'Civilization,'" *history.com* (March 2, 2018).

Flanagan, Jake. "Reservation to Prison Pipeline: Native Americans are the unseen victims of a broken US justice system," *qz.com* (April 27, 2015).

Frank, Howard. "Played out: Casino gambling revenue in Pennsylvania levels off as neighboring states ante in," *Pocono Record* (May 18, 2014).

Giago, Tim. "In Rapid City, South Dakota, there are many ways to put a knee on Oyate's neck," *The South Dakota Standard* (June 11, 2020).

Goldberg, Eleanor. "Native Americans Who Can't Afford Heat Take Desperate Measures to Stay Warm," *huffpost.com* (January 13, 2018).

Green, Sara Jean. "'They feel no one cares': Washington State Patrol report outlines missteps in reporting, tracking missing Native women," *The Seattle Times* (June 2, 2019).

Gutman, Matt, Lissette Rodriguez, and Tenzin Shakya. "Navajo Nation: Where COVID-19 claims whole families," *abcnews.go.com* (May 21, 2020).

Haircrow, Red. "Germany's obsession with American Indians is touching—and occasionally surreal." *Indian Country Today* (September 13, 2018).

Healy, Jack. "In Indian Country, A Crisis of Missing Women. And a New One When They're Found.," *The New York Times* (December 25, 2019).

Hedgpeth, Dana. "Native American tribes were already being wiped out. Then the 1918 flu hit.," *The Washington Post* (September 12, 2020).

Holscher, Kathleen. "Colonialism and the Crisis Inside the Crisis of Catholic Sexual Abuse," *rewirenewsgroup.com* (August 27, 2018).

Hurley, Dan. "Grandma's Experiences Leave a Mark on Your Genes," *Discover* (June 24, 2015).

Hyde, Jabez. "A Teacher Among the Senecas," *Publications of the Buffalo Historical Society*, 6 (1903).

Jensen, Mari N. "Unexpected wood source for Chaco Canyon Great Houses," *news.arizona.edu* (December 7, 2015).

Johnson, Brooks. "Pipeline workers arrested in northern Minnesota sex trafficking sting," *startribune.com* (June 28, 2021).

Jones, David S. "The Persistence of American Indian Health Disparities," *American Journal of Public Health,* 96, no. 12 (December, 2006).

Jones, Reuben. "'There's a Sickness in Robeson': Families of Slain Native Americans in N.C. Want Justice," *spectrumlocalnews.com* (March 11, 2021).

Keane, Colleen. "ICWA changed history, now court says it's unconstitutional," *Navajo Times* (February 28, 2019).

Keenan, Jerry. "The Battle of Whitestone Hill," *Wild West,* 21, no. 1 (June, 2008).

Kozhimanni, Katy B. "Indian Maternal Health—A Crisis Demanding Attention," *JAMA Health Forum,* 1, no. 5 (May 18, 2020).

Krol, Debra. "Inside the Native American foster care crisis tearing families apart," *Center for Health Journal* (February 21, 2018).

_____. "Native Americans have longest life expectancy," *Arizona Capital Times* (May 4, 2007).

Landry, Alysa. "Paying to Play Indian: The Dawes Rolls and the Legacy of $5 Indians," *Indian Country Today* (September 13, 2018).

Larson, Seaborn. "Montana reservations reportedly 'dumping grounds' for predatory priests," *Great Falls Tribune* (August 15, 2017).

Lewey, Guenter. "Were American Indians the Victims of Genocide?," *Commentary* (2004).

Lee, Tanya. "Study Says the 'Drunken Indian' Is A Myth," *Indian Country Today* (February 24, 2016).

Levin, Sam. "'They don't belong:' police called on Native American teens on college tour," *theguardian.com* (May 4, 2018).

Levinson, Daniel P. "Access to Mental Health Services at Indian Health Services and Tribal Facilities" (Washington, DC: Department of Health and Human Services, 2011).

MacDonald, David B. "Genocide in the Indian Residential Schools," in *Colonial Genocide in Indigenous North America.*

Madley, Benjamin. "'Unholy Traffic in Human Blood and Souls:' Systems of California Indian Servitude Under U.S. Rule," *Pacific Historical Review*, 83, no. 4 (November, 2014).

Matzen, Morgan. "Data: Native people disproportionately affected by COVID-19 in county, state," *Rapid City Journal* (July 18, 2020).

McCleary, Carrie. "Of Horses and Men: Superintendent Asbury's Deadly Assault on the Crow," *Tribal College*, 14, no. 3 (February 15, 2003).

McGreal, Chris. "America's poorest white town: abandoned by coal, swallowed by drugs," *The Guardian* (November 12, 2015).

_____. "A reservation town fighting alcoholism, obesity and ghosts from the past," *The Guardian* (November 22, 2015).

McNally, Robert Aquinas. "Four More Heads for the Indian Trophy Room," *Indian Country Today* (June 15, 2016).

Mehta, Sarah and Rossi, S.K. "Why Are So Many Indigenous People in Montana Incarcerated?," *aclu.org* (September 11, 2018).

Michel, Lou. "Tuscarora Water Woes Clouded by Sovereignty," *Buffalo News* (February 17, 2018).

Murphy, Sean. "Oklahoma governor wants bigger piece of state's tribal casino revenue," *The Associated Press* (January 10, 2019).

Murray, David. "The crisis in our backyard: Montana's reservation housing," *Great Falls Tribune* (April 3, 2016).

Nabokov, Peter. "Indians, Slaves, and Mass Murder: The Hidden History," *The New York Review of Books* (January 24, 2016).

Nesterak, Max. "The 1950's plan to erase Indian Country," *apmreports. org* (November 1, 2019).

Newsom, Linda A. "The Demographic Collapse of Native Peoples of the Americas, 1492-1650," *Proceedings of the British Academy*, 81 (1994).

Ortiz, Erik. "Lack of Awareness, Data Hinders Cases of Missing and Murdered Native American Women," *nbcnews.com* (July 30, 2020).

Ostler, Jeff. "Genocide and American Indian History," in *Oxford Research Encyclopedia of American History, oxfordre.com* (March, 2015).

Parry, Darren. "Voice from the Dust: A Shoshone Perspective on the Bear River Massacre." Lecture, Brigham Young University, Charles Redd Center for Western Studies, Provo, UT (November 8, 2018).

Pember, Mary Ann. "Meth Tsunami Overwhelms Rosebud Rez," *Indian Country Today* (May 31, 2016).

Pierpont, Mary. "Was Frank Baum a racist or just the creator of Oz," *Indian Country Today* (October 25, 2000).

Raffles, Hugh. "Jews, Lice, and History," *Public Culture*, 19, no. 3 (September 1, 2007).

Ramon-Sauberan, Jacelle. "Desert Rain Café serves more than food," *Indian Country Today* (June 26, 2009).

Rawson, William F. "Former Reading Teacher Sentenced for Molesting Hopi Children," *apnews.com* (June 8, 1987).

Rector, Tracy. "Faith Sotted Eagle on the Settler-Colonial Mind-Set," *Indian Country Today* (January 17, 2017).

Redman, Samuel. "When Museums Rushed to Fill Their Rooms With Bones," *smithsonianmag.com* (March 15, 2016).

Robertson, Dwanna L. "The Myth of Indian Casino Riches," *Indian Country Today* (September 12, 2018).

Rolnick, Adie C. "Native Youth & Juvenile Injustice in South Dakota," *South Dakota Law Review,* 62 (2017).

Romero, Simon, and Healy, Jack. "Tribal Nations Face Most Severe Crisis in Decades as the Coronavirus Closes Casinos," *The New York Times* (May 13, 2020).

Rose, Christina. "Native History: Alcohol and Murder Result in Theft of Fifty Million Acres," *Indian Country Today* (April 6, 2014).

Rosenberg, Eli. "'I believe in white supremacy': John Wayne's notorious 1971 Playboy interview goes viral on Twitter." *The Washington Post* (Feb. 20, 2019).

Sellers, Frances Stead. "It's almost 2020, and 2 million Americans still don't have running water, according to new report," *The Washington Post* (December 11, 2019).

Seminole Nation, Indian Territory. "The Seminole Burnings," *seminolenation-indianterritory.org* (May 23, 2021).

Severance, Frank H. "Narratives of Early Mission Work on the Niagara

Frontier and Buffalo Creek" in *Publications of the Buffalo Historical Society,* 6 (1903).

Sheffer, Edith. "The Nazi History Behind 'Asperger,'" *The New York Times* (March 31, 2018).

Sidder, Aaron. "Earliest Evidence of Indigo Dye Found at Ancient Peruvian Burial Site," *smithsonianmag.com* (September 15, 2016).

Siddons, Adrian. "The Never-Ending Crisis at the Indian Health Service," *rollcall.com* (March 5, 2018).

Snyderman, George S. "Halliday Jackson's Journal of a Visit to the Indians of New York in 1806," *Proceedings of the American Philosophical Society,* 101, no. 6 (December, 1957).

Stahl, Brandon, and Webster, Mary Jo. "Why does Minnesota have so many American Indian kids in foster care?," *startribune.com* (August 21, 2016).

Szalavitz, Maia. "No, Native Americans Aren't Genetically More Susceptible to Alcoholism," *The Verge* (October 2, 2015).

Taylor, Jonathan B. "The Economic and Community Benefits of Tribes in Washington," *washingtonindiangaming.com* (2019).

Tollefson, Phoebe. "'My hate button got broke;' mother of Wolf Point shooting victim wants justice, not revenge," *Billings Gazette* (December 3, 2020).

Tory, Sarah. "Fatal shooting in Wyoming raises questions about racism," *High Country Times* (August 11, 2015).

Trivedi, Shanta. "Police feed the foster care-to-prison pipeline by reporting on Black parents," nbcnews.com (July, 2020).

Tu, Janet I. "NW Jesuits to pay $166 million to abuse victims," *Seattle Times* (March 31, 2011).

Tupper, Seth. "Native students racially harassed, sprayed with beer at Rush game," Rapid City Journal (January 27, 2015).

Vedantam, Keerthi. "Bad roads are a 'public safety and public health issue," *Indian Country Today* (May 16, 2018).

Wade, Lizzie. "New Mexico's American Indian population crushed 100 years after Europeans arrived," *Sciencemag.org* (January 25, 2016).

Wagner, Angie. "Icon or hazard? The great debate over fry bread," *nbc-news.com* (August 21, 2005).

Walker, Mark. "Fed Up with Deaths, Native Americans Want to Run Their Own Health Care," *The New York Times* (January 3, 2021).

Wexler, Richard. "South Dakota Child Welfare: Where Kangaroo Court Is Always in Session," *youthtoday.org* (February 28, 2017).

Whaley, Monte. "Forcibly adopted American Indians torn between two worlds," *Denver Post* (November 28, 2009).

Whitefield-Madrano, Autumn. "Turning a Blind Eye to Eating Disorders," *Indian Country Today* (October 5, 2011).

Woodard, Stephanie "Native Americans Expose the Adoption Era and Repair Its Devastation," *Indian Country Today* (September 13, 2018).

_____. "South Dakota Boarding School Survivors Detail Sexual Abuse," *Indian Country Today* (September 13, 2018).

_____. "The Police Killings No One Is Talking About," *inthese-times.com* (October 17, 2016).

Wright, Bobby. "The Broken Covenant: American Indian Missions in the Colonial Colleges," *Tribal College*, 7, no. 1 (Summer, 1995).

Zickler, Colleen. "Profiting off Indigenous Children in South Dakota," *sites.evergreen.edu* (Fall, 2016).

Zionts, Ariell. "Child sex abuse trial of former Pine Ridge Dr. begins next week," *Rapid City Journal* (September 16, 2019).

_____. "Tribal nations, citizens take COVID-19 preventions seriously in South Dakota," *Rapid City Journal* (July 17, 2020).

ACTS, REPORTS, PROCEEDINGS

A Briefing Before the United State Commission on Civil Rights Held in Washington, DC, "Discrimination Against Native Americans in Border Towns," *usccr.gov* (2007).

American Civil Liberties Union, "In South Dakota, Officials Defied a Federal Judge and Took Indian Kids Away From Their Parents in Rigged Proceedings," *aclu.org* (February 22, 2017).

Cato Sells. "To superintendents and other employees of the United States Indian Service," January 10, 1916.

"Constitution of the Cherokee Nation," *Cherokee Phoenix* (February 21, 1928).

Department of the Interior, Indian Babies: How to Keep Them Well (Washington, DC: Government Printing Office, 1916).

"Disproportionate representation of Native Americans in foster care across United States," potawatomi.org (April 6, 2021).

Indian Child Welfare Act of 1978 (ICWA) (Pub. L 95-608, 92n Stat. 3069, enacted November 8, 1978, codified at 5 U.S.C.).

Indian Health Service, Disparities: Fact Sheet (October, 2019).

National Congress of American Indians, "Are Native Youth Being Pushed into Prison?," *ncai.org*.

National Indian Child Welfare Association, "What Is Disproportionality in Child Welfare," *nicwa.org* (2017).

Report of the Advisory Committee to the U.S. Commission on Civil Rights, Native Americans in South Dakota: An Erosion of Confidence in the Justice System (Washington, DC, 2000).

Rules Governing The Court of Indian Offenses (Washington, DC: Department of the Interior, Office of Indian Affairs,1883).

Urban Indian Health Commission, Invisible Tribes: Urban Indians and Their Health in a Changing World. *nativephilanthropy.org* (2007).

Urban Indian Health Institute, Missing and Murdered Indigenous Women and Girls, *uihi.org* (2018).

MISCELLANEOUS LETTERS

Eleazar Wheelock to George Whitefield, July 4, 1761, MSS, Dartmouth College History.

Eleazar Wheelock to Governor John Wentworth, September 12, 1762, MSS, Dartmouth College History.

Sarah Bingham to David McClure, August 1, 1787, MSS, Dartmouth College History.

Miscellaneous Newspaper Articles

"Family of Six Murdered: Drunken Indians Supposed to Have Committed the Crime," *The New York Times* (February 19, 1897).

"Foully Murdered," *Bismarck Daily Tribune* (February 19, 1897). "Horrible Details," *Bismarck Daily Tribune* (February 21, 1897). "Horrible Details," *Jamestown Weekly Alert* (February 25, 1897). "Horrible Murder," *Bismarck Daily Tribune* (February 20, 1897). "Indians and Skunks," *The New York Times,* (February 18, 1881).

"Indians Murder Family of Six," *The Chicago Daily Tribune* (February 19, 1897).

"Not one of our people," *Bismarck Daily Tribune* (February 21, 1897).

Court Cases

City of Sherrill v. Oneida Indian Nation, 544 U.S. 197 (2005).
Johnson & Graham's Lessee v. McIntosh, 21 U.S. 543 (1923).
Oglala Sioux Tribe v. Van Hunnik, 100 F. Supp. 3d 749 (D.S.D. 2015).
U.S. ex Rel. Standing Bear v. Crook, 25 F. Cas. 695 (D. Neb. 1879).

Movies

Kit Carson. George B. Seitz, director. 1950. United Artists Corp.
The Searchers. John Ford, director. 1956. Warner Bros. Pictures.

Television, Radio Programs

Hilliard, Gloria. "Urban American Indians Rewrite Relocation's Legacy," *npr.com* (January 7, 2012).

Goodyear, Sheena. "FBI finds thousands of Indigenous bones in raid on elderly missionary's home," "As It Happens," *Canadian Broadcasting Corporation* (February 27, 2019).

Limbaugh, Rush. "Limbaugh on 'holocaust' of 'Indians': 'They have all the casinos—what's to complain about?,'" The Rush Limbaugh Show on Premier Radio Networks (September 25, 2009).

Maher, Savannah. "In Contrast to Wyoming, Wind River Tribes Counter Covid-19 With Aggressive Measures," *Wyoming Public Radio* (May 7, 2020).

Sullivan, Laura, and Walters, Amy. "Native Foster Care: Lost Children, Shattered Families," *npr.org* (October, 25, 26, and 27, 2011).